The Double Message

THE DOUBLE MESSAGE

Patterns of Gender in Luke-Acts

TURID KARLSEN SEIM

ABINGDON PRESS
NASHVILLE

Contents

Acknowledgements

The frail beginning of this book goes back many years to a seminar some students encouraged me to do in the early eighties on 'Women in the Gospels'. Since then the project has come a long way, and the original Norwegian version on which this English version is based, was completed in 1990 as a doctoral thesis at the University of Oslo. Hopefully it still reflects how my scholarly identity is based in a positive affirmation of womanhood, a commitment to equal partnership between women and men, a keen theological interest – and faithfulness to the exegetical skill I once was taught.

Since 1991 I have been the Dean of the Faculty of Theology at the University of Oslo during a period of significant changes in the life of the faculty. I would have wanted to revise the text further and especially to up-date it. I regret that the constant administrative demands have made this impossible so that literature appearing during the very last years is not included.

A book remains the responsibility of its author. But the working process by which it has come into being still is a project where many have contributed knowingly or unknowingly. I have been nurtured by the active and cross-disciplinary community of women at the university while at the same time savouring the wisdom, knowledge and encouragement of my native 'fathers' and fellows in the New Testament, of whom I would like to mention Prof. Nils A. Dahl, Prof. Jacob Jervell, Prof. Edvin Larsson and Prof. Halvor Moxnes. My Danish friend and colleague, lecturer Bente Bagger Larsen, another member of 'the Lukan community', has never ceased to encourage me, and I make her the representative of all those here not named to whom I am greatly indebted.

The work involved would not have been possible without the financial support granted partly by my own faculty and partly by what used to be the Norwegian Research Council for Science and the Humanities. The Research Council also funded the translation of the original Norwegian version into English. This translation was energetically undertaken by Dr Brian McNeil. The indices I owe to the diligent accuracy of cand. philol. Vemund Blomkvist who did them at very short notice. Finally, I am indeed grateful to Prof. John Riches for including my contribution in this series.

For their patience with an absent-minded mother who at times appears to live in the past rather than in the present, and for their unyielding and obstinate faith in the future, this book is dedicated to my two daughters, Ingrid and Runhild Seim.

Oslo, Summer 1994
Turid Karlsen Seim

Chapter One

Prolegomena: Luke and Women

Are Luke's writings friendly or hostile to women? Can Luke be said to represent 'a vigorous feminism'?[1] Is he the only New Testament writer who reflects, ideologically and theologically, an equality that women are presupposed to have had in early Christian communities, so that the distance or even the contradiction between praxis and paraenesis that characterises the epistles, is abolished in his writings?[2] Or does Luke represent a programmatic androcentrism which consciously is silent about women and makes them invisible?[3] Does he plead, by means of a narrative influenced by Jewish patterns, for the subordination of women in an indirect and more subtle manner than the open admonitions in this regard of the authors of the New Testament epistles?[4]

---

[1] Swidler, *Biblical Affirmations*, 280.

[2] Schottroff, 'Frauen', 121ff. Cf. also Kopas, 'Jesus and Women', 192ff., 202.

[3] Schüssler Fiorenza continually maintains in her works that the Lukan construction has been an essential contribution to the process of making women invisible at the earliest period, cf. 'The Apostleship of Women', 138ff.; 'Beitrag der Frau', 68–72; *In Memory*, 49f., 161, 167; 'Biblische Grundlegung', 32, 35–8. She calls this 'the Lukan silence' and maintains that it is an androcentrism that consciously excludes women, i.e. something more than an unconscious androcentrism that is taken for granted and a vocabulary that says and writes 'men' when women are included too, as is supposed by Schottroff, 'Maria Magdalena', 4. Cf. also Tetlow, *Women and Ministry*, 101–9.

[4] According to Jervell, 'Töchter Abrahams', 77–93, the women are presented as Jewesses who live up to all the traditional expectations of withdrawn submission. Cf. also Drury's somewhat speculative, but interesting theory in *Tradition and Design*, 51f., that Luke's interest in women is not due to his 'courteous interest in ladies', but that he follows Old Testament (Deuteronomist) models in emphasising the prominent role of women in the events of salvation history. At the same time, 'a prime benefit of her capable activities is the glory which they reflect upon her husband whose superiority is not challenged. This continued subordination gives the theological force to God's action in raising up women in his cause'. On the question about Deuteronomist influence on Luke's writings more generally, cf. Wall's overview, 'Martha and Mary', 20f., 30f.

1

If we take a representative choice of the scholars who have dealt with this subject recently, we find opinions ranged very sharply against one another. It is, besides this, usual practice for exegetes to state in relatively general terms that Luke shows a particular interest in women. Most relate this to his broader concern for the poor and various other marginalised groups, and possibly see in this also an expression of his universalism.[5] Moreover, the presence of women in Luke can be given as an example of his emphasis on the success the Christian proclamation had in noble and well-off circles, since many of the women appear, in various ways, to be relatively wealthy.[6] But instead of a treatment of this theme in depth, the result is often a discussion of the individual texts without relating their contents to one another to any great extent.

There are virtually no comprehensive presentations of this theme in monographs.[7] As the bibliography shows, most of the discussion is scattered in articles and as elements in work dealing more generally either with women in Jesus' life and/or in early Christianity, or in various ways with Luke-Acts. Synthesising presentations of the question occur, showing the variations in the material, but these are usually both brief and insufficiently analytical.[8] The gulf between the general programmatic declarations and the fragmentary analysis means that the alleged impression of a totality is in fact without a foundation. Commentaries too, as a natural consequence of their literary genre, will often be content with a treatment *en passant*, with a few short observations, of the presence of women in the individual pericopes – often on the level of a footnote.

---

[5]   For further examples from the commentary literature, cf. Jervell, 'Töchter Abrahams', 77f. Cf. also Bernhard, 'Women's Ministry', 662; Brock/Harvey Ashbrook, *Holy Women*, 25f.; Horn, *Glaube*, 202; Karriss; *Luke*, 34; O'Toole, *Unity*.

[6]   Malherbe, 'Not in a Corner', 196; Richardson, 'From apostles to virgins', 247.

[7]   An exception here is Augsten, *Stellung des lukanischen Christus*, from 1970, but apart from a few observations (Luke is critical of marriage and children, and according to Augsten, thereby also critical of women), this work is a compilation of texts and it has never been published as a book.

[8]   Talbert, *Reading Luke*, 90–3, is typical: after briefly mentioning various roles women play in Luke-Acts, he says: 'Their ministries varied just as their roles in society did, but each of them had a ministry within the context of her particular role', 92. Cf. also Tannehill, *Narrative Unity*, 132–9, who devotes a special section to women in the chapter on 'Jesus' Ministry to the Oppressed and Excluded'. His analysis goes somewhat deeper.

It is a statistical fact that, compared with the other New Testament writings, the gospel of Luke contains more material about women. As many as forty-two passages in Luke are concerned with women or with female motifs.[9] Most of these come in the specifically Lukan material.[10] Three of the examples are common to all the evangelists, nine to the three synoptics, five to Matthew and Luke, and two to Luke and Mark. This means that twenty-three are specifically Lukan, and most of these occur in a context peculiar to Luke. Within the material peculiar to Luke, three-eighths of the total number of persons mentioned are women, while they comprise two-fifths of all named persons.[11]

Since the material peculiar to Luke is so rich in traditions about women, it is all the more striking that the proportion of material in Acts relating to women is much smaller than in the gospel. Relatively fewer examples of women occur, and those who are mentioned, are given little space and attention. In Acts, women seem to play a withdrawn role on a stage dominated by the missionary activity and leadership of the 'great' men.[12] The difference between the gospel and Acts in the treatment of women can also, to some extent, explain the divergences among scholars: the profile in their interpretation is clearly the result of which document has been their primary starting-point or the object of their main interest. While work on the gospel texts seems to draw the interpretation in a direction friendly to women, the silence and the restrictions in Acts seem to provide a basis for the opposite conclusion.[13]

[9] Swidler, *Biblical Affirmations*, 255, 261. The point of the number is not to make a comparison between the total number of 'passages dealing with women' and, whatever is taken to be the total number of passages in Luke's gospel. The point is to make a comparison with the other gospels, and the numbers show that Luke has more passages dealing with women than any other, even when taking into account the total length of the various gospels. I do not find it necessary here to enter into the detailed and complicated discussion about what constitutes 'femaleness' or 'femininity', even though I am well aware that gender definition is a major theoretical problem within women's studies for the moment, cf. Friis Plum, 'Kvindehermeneutik', 36–41; Ingebrigtsen, 'Kjønn og ulikhet'.

[10] Cf. Harnack, *Mission*, 593 n. 1: 'Ein bedeutender Teil des Sondergutes ist weiblich bestimmt'.

[11] Munro, 'Women Disciples', 226.

[12] Jervell, 'Töchter Abrahams', 78 n. 7, registers as an indication of this that 'in den Registern zu den Acta-arbeiten, Kommentaren und Darstellungen der Theologie das

3

It is indeed true that many men too are made invisible in Acts, reduced to extras *vis-à-vis* the main roles which are played by the apostles and Paul,[14] but it has nevertheless been maintained that this quantitative difference between the gospel and Acts is connected with an intensification of Luke's redactional tendency against women.[15]

Is it fruitful at all to ask which of the two documents is 'most Lukan'? To say that 'since Luke wrote not only the Gospel but also Acts, he is able to interpret the reports on women in the Gospel by his form of presentation in Acts',[16] is to express an understanding of the relationship between the two writings in which it is Acts rather than the gospel that reveals the author's own position. The status of the gospel as a composition remains more unclear: is it to be counted primarily as tradition? This question suggests at any rate a

Stichwort "Frau" meistens fehlt'. Like most others, I presuppose in this study that the gospel and Acts are written by the same author, and I do not discuss the radical possibility that the tensions between the two 'volumes' could be due to their having been written by different persons – as suggested most recently by Dawsey, 'Literary Unity', although finally even he backs away from such a conclusion, 56 and 60.

[13] E.g. Jervell and Schüssler Fiorenza deal primarily with Acts, while Schottroff almost exclusively deals with gospel texts.

[14] Cf. Weiser, 'Rolle der Frau', 175 n. 46, 177 n. 56.

[15] Apart from Schüssler Fiorenza, cf. Collins, 'Ministry of Women', 161, who, like Jervell, 'Töchter Abrahams', 78, 93, sees this as an expression of Jewish influence or a Jewish orientation in Luke. Augsten too, *Stellung des lukanischen Christus*, 16, attributes to the author Luke a tendency to be critical of women and children which is opposed to 'the loving treatment' of women in the tradition of the material peculiar to Luke. She deduces this, *inter alia*, from his criticism of marriage; i.e., uncritically and almost automatically she makes a positive connection between women and marriage, and does not see that asceticism could have the effect of liberating women. Also Richardson, 'From apostles to virgins', 247, is interested in isolating the various sources and traces interest in women to 'Proto-Luke' whom he hypothetically reconstructs. Harnack, Mission, 590f., 595f., for his part 'absolves' Luke and maintains that Acts came into the hands of a redactor early in the second century who, in keeping with that period's 'anti-feminist current', tried to limit the significance of women by means of simple changes in the text. Witherington, *Women in the Earliest Churches*, 129f., 143, solves the problem first by establishing different roles and then by presenting the various narratives about women in Acts as vignettes of these roles: 'their choice, position and content reveal a deliberate attempt on the author's part to indicate to his audience how things ought to be'. By virtue of the role system he has established extraneous to the text, they take on exemplary value, with the result that the small quantity of references does not cause him many difficulties. But he must all the same admit that in general Acts' silence is problematic, 143.

[16] Jervell, 'Töchter Abrahams', 93.

4

traditional redaction-critical application of methodology in which the interpreter looks for redactional 'key comments' that clearly show what the author really meant about all the traditional material he more or less unwillingly had to include. Redaction is understood as a struggle with tradition, and is evident in a particular 'top level' stratum in the text which therefore constitutes the basis for the redaction-critical interpretation.

It is not my intention here to reject the idea that concern for traditions and perhaps for sources, must play a role in the interpretation of Luke-Acts. But it is at least difficult to reduce the problem to a question about the boundaries of the source material – in other words to maintain that Luke did not know anything better about the activity of women in the earliest church because he had limited access to information. The letters of Paul, for example, give at least glimpses of a much more complex picture of the early Christian mission and leadership of the communities. And even if the Lukan ambiguity is to be explained to some extent by his relationship to the tradition, so that we could say the available traditions about Jesus had a stronger profile in favour of women than Luke himself approved of,[17] this may possibly give a historical explanation, but it does not represent a satisfactory literary solution.

The exegetical thrust in the work presented here is also based upon redaction criticism of a sort. The author of Luke-Acts is understood as an organising and creative will in the text itself. But over against a 'divide and conquer' treatment of the text, this work will distance itself from a form-critical fragmentation of the total picture given in the text. Inspired by recent work within biblical scholarship on literary models, it assumes that the text as we have it, constitutes a unit of literary

---

[17] Leipoldt's classical explanation, *Jesus*, 105ff., is that while the gospel reflects Jesus' activity in the villages, Acts bears the mark of the early communities' lives in the cities, where women had to submit to a stricter regime. The insight we have today into women's lives both inside and outside the early church makes such an explanation no longer acceptable – quite apart from the fact that it leaves the author of the gospel without any great part in the presentation. Nevertheless, it still crops up in revised versions that clearly reveal their underlying christological interest. For example, this is expressed in such judgments as that all traditions and texts that are friendly to women echo Jesus' exceptionally radical attitude – cf. Swidler, *Biblical Affirmations*, 280, and also Witherington's approach in both his books, especially the first, *Women in the Ministry of Jesus*.

composition creating a consistent meaning – within certain limits. Nor is the personality of the author behind the text (or antecedent to the text) regarded as interesting in itself. In other words, the questions relating to who Luke was, and what he really wished to say, are less interesting than what the text communicates in its present form. In what follows, the author's intention is relevant to the extent to which it comes to expression as the coordinating subject of the text which is called Luke. But the meaning of the text is not exhausted in the author's intention. Within more precisely defined boundaries, which the exegete must draw in relation to the concrete text, it has a richer potential meaning.

As this presentation will show, I have found it fruitful only to a very limited extent, to enter into the tradition-critical considerations concerning individual pericopes. In other words, the analysis is internal to the work itself. It is not, however, an ahistorical literary analysis, but works by consciously relating text and historical situation. The text operates with an implicit knowledge about its own period which the interpreter must reactivate in order to avoid anachronisms and to be able to give an adequately informed interpretation. This does not necessarily involve particular hypotheses about the historical and geographical location of the author; such a locating of Luke must be based on a more comprehensive analysis of the author's whole work.[18] But I hope that the following analysis of gender organisation in Luke-Acts can contribute to the continuing work that seeks to identify the particular place of Luke's composition within the history of the early church.

Both in terms of methodology and of content, this presentation has also profited from work with early patristic literature, both texts and interpretations. The use made of this material does not presume a genetic connection (although a documentation of this could be an interesting and large-scale project of its own); rather, it is an attempt to

---

[18] Cf. Johnson, 'Finding the Lukan Community', 92f., who argues that it is very important to pay heed to the totality. In respect of conclusions about the Sitz im Leben, he shows how a simple theory of reflection, when applied to individual motifs and passages in Luke, leads to sheer guesswork with minimal methodological safeguards in many presentations. Johnson also shows how the complete Sitz im Leben of Luke's writings presupposed when all the various pieces are assembled, makes a chaos that is historically impossible.

try out the relevance of perspectives gained from the analysis of one material on another material which, evaluated in broad terms, belongs to the same tradition.

The lines in the picture which are to be drawn in what follows, take their starting-point in the gospel part of Luke's work. The simple justification for this, is that it is the gospel that offers the most substantial quantity of material with which to work. But at the same time it is a goal to integrate texts from Acts to see if it is possible to identify threads in Luke's texture which can explain the tension between the two writings in this aspect. Luke's presentation is not a systematic treatise, but a narrative. This means that it tells a story, a series of developments, a sequence of events, in which the individual narratives are pieces that are given their place at a particular stage in the larger and over-arching narrative. This has methodological consequences for the analysis of the Lukan construction.[19] Events and persons receive their significance from their location and function in the sequence of the narrative. The order is therefore not arbitrary, and the location at various stages in a narrative sequence can itself be an effective means of dealing with tensions and contradictions in materials or situations. In terms of the interpretation, this means that pieces cannot be plucked out from any place in the work and brought together to form a stable and unambiguous theological system that reveals Luke's constant opinion on various themes, his firm polemical or paraenetical profile. The narrative cannot be frozen at an individual scene: rather, what we have is a complex movement, a process – a path. The narrative form invites polyphony in a special way, it allows several and even contradicting voices to be heard in the course of the narrative. This means that the message of the narrative is not necessarily the same as the outcome of the course of events; a hearer/reader can also choose to give ear to the voices *en route*.

Since, methodologically, the work is redaction/composition-critical in the sense which has been set out above, the analysis is concerned primarily with documenting and understanding the Lukan composition. This means that it is only indirectly a contribution to a feminist programme of reconstruction. The more general hermeneutical ques-

---

[19] Cf. on this, Gaventa, 'Toward a Theology of Acts', 150–7.

tions about subjectivity and objectivity or intersubjectivity which are decisively important, precisely in relation to the hermeneutical project of reconstruction,[20] need not therefore be touched on here. At the same time, it could be interesting in a longer perspective to discuss the results of this study in the light of such questions. In this connection, it is only necessary to state specifically that the intention of this work is not to establish whether Luke is a friend or foe of positions which I may happen to take. In this sense, I am not carrying out an apologetic task, and I see no reason to confuse an attempt at exegetical description and analysis with presumed claims to theological normativity. And even the admission that all research is biased does not give license to employ anachronistic characteristics and methodology. As much as possible Luke must be allowed to remain in his own time.

All the same, this work has come into being from a desire to contribute to women's studies in a way that can demonstrate its potential. In order to combat the massive process that has rendered women invisible, it is an essential task to make them visible again in text and history, whether they appear as heroic role models, as is the emphasis of what is called 'dignity studies', or as oppressed victims, as 'misery studies' documents, or as both of these.[21] But it is not just a question of making women the object of special thematic interest or of making them visible and thereby supplementing other research in an area that has been neglected but is not very central. This would be to accept the presup-

---

[20] This is the main concern of Schüssler Fiorenza, cf. the methodological section of *In Memory*, 3–95, and her insistence that this difficult section must come first. The methodological introduction, together with the articles published in *Bread not Stone*, make it clear that she is not concerned with a historical reconstruction – i.e., with arriving at 'wie es eigentlich gewesen ist' even if her own reconstruction has often been read in this way, cf. Friis Plum, 'Kvindehermeneutik', 30ff. Schüssler Fiorenza purposely gives a version aimed at the liberation of women – a feminist reading of the 'story'. Put simply, the question of verification has thereby become a question of what interests the research wishes to serve. For a feminist adaption of the category of 'Vorverständnis' and further adjustment of the critical hermeneutic's understanding of subjectivity as over against a positivist position, cf. also Tolbert, 'Defining the Problem'.

[21] On the shifting character of women's research as 'dignity studies' and 'misery studies', cf. the brief but informative and accurate presentation in Friis Plum, 'Kvindehermeneutik', 20f. She is correct to maintain that both moods are often found in the work of the same scholar. In my opinion, this is also a methodological necessity over against an ideologically determined simplification.

position that women are peripheral additional phenomena, secondary variants and obligatory objects, 'the others'. Ironically enough, some women's studies, seeking to dispose of the myth about 'otherness', end up by strengthening the myth through exclusive alternative feminist variants of interpretation.

A simplistic and popular expression of this is to be found in the many edifying presentations of women that seek to enlist biblical support for commitment and work for women's equality in today's church and society.[22] It is true that material dealing with women is brought out energetically in such presentations, and examples of women are listed tirelessly in the service of making them visible. They are often extreme examples of 'dignity studies'; but they tend to compile more than to analyse, and they have the effect of fragmenting and isolating, in spite of all their compilations of examples. The picture thus painted easily becomes a distortion. The individual examples listed, are set only to a limited degree in relation to one another and to the larger and smaller contexts from which they are drawn; and not the least problem is that, lacking a 'hermeneutic of suspicion',[23] they pretend that the pieces they take out of the existing construction can serve as an immediate reconstruction. In other words, they lack both the necessary insight into the construction of the biblical authors and a conscious hermeneutical path to reconstruction.

The desire of 'dignity studies' to bring forward positive models of identification from the past has, however, both its justification and its function. When women are made visible as subjects, not as objects, this is in itself to set up a model of dignity. But it is difficult to avoid facing

---

[22] Despite its attempt to classify the material, Swidler's *Biblical Affirmations* is, in my opinion, a typical example of this, with its extensive and anachronistic characterisation. Blank, 'Frauen', and Shelkle, *Braut und Gesit*, both come close; the same is true of Augsten, *Stellung des lukanischen Christus*, and Heister, *Frauen in der biblischen Glaubensgeschichte.* McNamara, *New Song,* takes the text's word at face value and, in spite of her apparently historical approach, she totally lacks a historical-critical reading of the gospel material. The same charge must be levelled all the more strongly at a number of popular presentations which were common especially a few years ago, e.g. Nunnally-Cox, *Foremothers*; Pape, *God & Women*; Stagg, *Women in the World of Jesus.*

[23] On 'the hermeneutic of suspicion' as a fundamental first move in a critical hermeneutic of reconstruction, cf. Schüssler Fiorenza, *Bread not Stone*, 15–20, and Knutsen's review in *Religious Studies Review* 12 (1986), 199f.

the fact that history is to a great extent a history of oppression, of women as victims. 'Dignity studies' must be balanced by insight into mechanisms and structures of oppression and silencing. This balancing duality, full of tension, means that an analysis of the construction of Luke's text will have to be an insight into conflict and debate and into movement, in which women act as subjects and are treated as objects in the account of the story.

Instead of supplementing existing 'knowledge' with further quantities of information, in this case about women, women's studies involve a fundamentally critical approach that unveils the androcentrically determined gender-blindness in traditional research. Positively, it represents a renewed understanding, not only of 'everything that has to do with women and their world', but of the wholeness with significance for all – both women and men. This means that my project is not to describe Luke's view of women or to see 'women' as one theme among other themes in the Lukan texture, but rather to trace some of the warping threads through which the shuttle is pulled. The original question about making women visible has thus had the further effect of mobilising *gender as an analytic category* which itself questions gender systems.[24] Gender as a constant has a biological basis. It is, however, articulated in forms of extreme variety in terms of culture, social history and geography, and the significance attached to sexuality in determining the relationship of the sexes may vary. But gender relationship will always have all-embracing structural significance. In a widened perspective, therefore, it is necessary to investigate how mutual dependence, interplay and power structures between women and men are conceived. What follows is an attempt to make this type of investigation into Luke's account – but in such a way that special attention is paid to the role of women.

[24] On this, cf. Scott 'Gender'.

Chapter Two
Men As Well As Women

Luke has a tendency in his composition to generate doublets and parallels. This 'Zweiheitsgesetz'[1] can be seen on the levels of words, sentences and pericopae in the text, and is found both in direct speech-material (mainly words of Jesus) and in epic descriptive material. This pattern is not necessarily original to Luke; approximations can be found in the other synoptic gospels,[2] and it may be explained as an expression of a literary convention.[3] Lists of two and three are also well-known devices in the art of oral storytelling. Luke, however, develops this pattern to serve certain stylistic, pedagogical and substantial goals, and much of the specifically Lukan material is arranged in view of this.[4] It is important not to confuse this tendency to create doublets with an inclination to repeat oneself. For Luke also seems on some occasions to wish to avoid sheer repetitions, economising his presentation in such a way that he omits doublets of identical narratives, cf., for example, the narrative of the multiplication of the loaves which is doubled in Matthew, but which Luke has only once.[5] But this is not a rule without

---

[1] Morgenthaler documented the phenomenon in his *Lukanische Geschichtsschreibung*, and both his observation and his explanation of it have found wide acceptance. Cf. Bode, *First Easter Morning*, 60; Egelkraut, *Jesus' Mission*, 70f.; Flender, *Heil*, 15; Navone, *Themes*, 228; Parvey, 'Theology and Leadership', 139f.; Tannehill, *Narrative Unity*, 132f. Sometimes, the doublets are located within longer catenae, and there are some who wish to identify a liking in Luke for triadic lists, cf. Freed, 'Judge and Widow', 40; Käser, 'Exegetische und theologische Erwägungen', 244.

[2] McEachern, 'Dual Witness', 270.

[3] Talbert, *Literary Patterns*, 80f.

[4] Flender, *Heil*, 15; McEachern, 'Dual Witness', 271.

[5] Schürmann, 'Dubletten', 272–8, and 'Dublettenvermeidungen', 279–89, argues that Luke avoids doublets. He has been followed by Schaller, 'Sprüche', 86. However, Egelkraut, *Jesus' Mission*, 71, is basically correct to point out that Schürmann does not

11

exceptions. Important events such as the women finding the empty tomb, the stories of Cornelius' and Paul's conversion, are first narrated and then repeated once more in direct speech – in the case of Paul's conversion, repeated even twice.[6] These repeated narratives are beyond doubt different from the doublets of which we shall speak in what follows, and which can more appropriately be characterised as coupled parallels.

Even the Lukan construction of a two-volume composition can itself be interpreted as an expression of such a principle of duality,[7] and a great deal of comparison between the gospel and Acts has been carried out with the intention of establishing parallel patterns. The emerging parallelism is often expounded as an imitatio model in which the life in the early church and the activity of the apostles and of Paul repeats the history of Jesus, which thereby takes on the character of a principal example.[8] More generally and commonly, the principle of duality in Luke has been interpreted on the basis of Israelite-Jewish regulations about witnesses and has been characterised as the formal expression in the composition of the reliability of the tradition and the message.[9] Some scholars speak of the 'dual witness' motif almost as if this were a shorthand expression.[10]

One of the claims continually made in scholarship is that part of this parallel material in Luke should be classified in terms of pairs of men and women so that a complementary gender pattern is established.[11]

---

define what he means by a doublet. Dawsey, 'Literary Unity', 61f., whose one-sided aim is to emphasise the stylistic and linguistic differences between the gospel and Acts, holds that while Luke in the gospel removes repetitions in the sources, Acts shows a tendency to doubling and to repetition. However, he has to admit that we also find doublets 'in description' in the gospel, cf. also n. 22 below.

[6] Cf. p. 156 n. 181.

[7] Cf. Gasque, 'Fruitful Field', 122; McEachran, 'Dual Witness', 271.

[8] Talbert, *Literary Patterns*, 98f. Cf. also Radl, *Paulus und Jesus*, 44, 60.

[9] Morgenthaler, *Lukanische Geschichtsschreibung*, II 8, followed by most of those already mentioned in n. 1 above.

[10] Karriss, *Luke*, 112; Navone, *Themes*, 226f.; McEachern, 'Dual Witness', 271. Cf. also Gerhardsson, *Memory*, 226.

[11] Morgenthaler, *Lukanische Geschichtsschreibung*, I 104, and not least Flender, *Heil*, 15, who briefly but effectively develops the motif by making a list of presumed gender doublets. This point in Flender has been frequently referred to since then: cf. Kopas, 'Jesus and Women', 192; Parvey, 'Theology and Leadership', 139f.; Swidler, *Biblical*

But even if the phenomenon has been referred to repeatedly, these 'gender pairs' have in fact never been investigated or explained properly. For example, since women were normally unacceptable as witnesses, the 'witness explanation' cannot be applicable without further qualification to these cases. Yet even so, it is often used summarily as an explanation.[12] Besides this, the 'gender pairs' are explained as an expression of the so-called universalism of Luke, overcoming divisions and resulting in inclusiveness and equality between woman and man.[13] Some explain it as a pedagogical devise oriented to the audience: by means of the 'gender pairs', the same point is presented in a way that communicates respectively to female and to male hearers or readers.[14] This, however, reduces the insistent pattern in the composition primarily to a reflection of a Sitz im Leben where women play a considerable role alongside the men. The literary aspects integral to the work remain without investigation, and the historical conclusion bears the stamp of a mere supposition which is not based on any more detailed analysis of the text itself.

Another problem, of course, is how the duality and/or parallelism is to be determined, above all at the level of the pericope. When do two narratives correspond so closely that it is meaningful to call them a pair? Often it seems that the identification of 'gender pairs' and of other parallels is based on a more or less fortuitous understanding that there exists a 'similarity' between two examples or episodes with regard to contents, language, form, structure or quite simply the theme.[15] It must

Affirmations, 164; Tannehill, *Literary Unity*, 133; Witherington, *Women in the Earliest Churches*, 128–9.

[12] First already by Morgenthaler, *Lukanische Geschichtsschreibung*, II 13. On the question of the validity of women's evidence, cf. p. 156f. and p. 156f. n. 186.

[13] Flender, *Heil*, 16; Karriss, *Luke*, 113; Kopas, 'Jesus and Women', 192; Tannehill, *Narrative Unity*, 132f.; Talbert, *Reading Luke*, 92. Navone, *Themes*, 224, 226f., combines this closely with the motif of witnessing, but without discussing it in greater detail.

[14] Parvey, 'Theology and Leadership', 139f., repeated by Kopas, 'Jesus and Women', 192; Swidler, *Biblical Affirmations*, 164f., who also wishes by a very simple manoeuvre to trace such a form of presentation back to Jesus' own excellent ability to communicate both with women and with men.

[15] Praeder, 'Jesus-Paul', 29, has investigated twelve different presentations with regard to this, and shows the arbitrary and approximate character of the choice and use of – usually implicit – criteria. It is also clear that 'the interpretative schemes' established by

be maintained that, normally, parallelisation which has an exclusively thematic character does not permit us to speak of doublets or pairs. It is not enough for two narratives to touch on the same theme; there must be formal similarities as well, whether these are verbally identical formulations and/or a common and clear location of two or more instances in the same list of examples or narrative sequence. Naturally, this implies that some statements or narratives can be doublets of several others in different ways and at different levels. Nor need the pairs function only as positive parallelisations; elements of contrast can also be included. In the very phenomenon of the 'man-woman pair' we find not only a juxtaposition of the two, but also clear elements of distance and tension, of complementarity and of differentiation.

A more rigorous use of criteria will lead to a considerable reduction in the number of examples found in the available lists of Lukan 'gender pairs'.[16] In my opinion, there is insufficient reason to consider the following examples as pairs:

The possessed man	Peter's mother-in-law	Lk 4.31–39
Officer at Capernaum	Widow at Nain	Lk 7.1–10/11–17
Good Samaritan	Martha and Mary	Lk 10.25–36/38–42
Tax-collector	Widow	Lk 18.9–14/1–8
Importunate friend	Widow	Lk 11.5–8/18.1–8
Jailer	Lydia	Acts 16.13–34
Emmaus disciples	Women at tomb	Lk 24.13–35/1–11[17]

Further examples, formally so different from the rest that it is confusing to have them on the same list, may be added:

Simon and Pharisee	The sinful woman	Lk 7.36–50
Ananias	Sapphira	Acts 5.1–11
Dionysius	Damaris	Acts 17.34

the interpreters themselves make their own significant contribution to the discovery or creation of parallels. Cf. also Egelkraut's criticism of Schürmann, mentioned in n. 5 above.

[16] . This is in reference to Flender's list, *Heil*, 15, which broadly speaking has simply been repeated by others without being discussed by them.

[17] This is added by Navone, *Themes*, 224, when compared to Flender's list.

When these examples are rejected, it is because they cannot be said to satisfy formal criteria for 'similarity'. Given the lack of convincing argument in favour of this choice, the list has convinced a remarkably large number of scholars. Some of the examples are adduced presumably because they can be said, more or less, to deal with the same theme, for example, prayer. But, as can be seen from the references, most of them are simply juxtaposed in the text, and the similarity can consist, for example, in the simple fact that they are both healing stories. It should not be denied that such combinations of material in the course of composition can contribute to a general impression of an inclusiveness in which the genders are complementary to one another. But this does not create a formal basis for us to operate with the concept of pairs.

There remain, however, sufficient man-woman parallels for it to be meaningful still to claim that they constitute a striking and repeated trait in Luke's presentation. They are not distributed in such a way that they can be attributed or explained as due to a particular source:

Zechariah	Mary	Lk 1.11–20/26–38; 46–55/67–79
Simeon	Anna	Lk 2.25–35/36–8
Naaman	Widow in Zarephath	Lk 4.27/25–6
Jairus' daughter	Widow's son	Lk 8.40–56/7.11–17
Jairus	Woman with issue of blood	Lk 8.40–1, 49–56/43–48
Men of Nineveh	Queen of the South	Lk 11.32/31
Man healed on sabbath	Woman healed on sabbath	Lk 14.1–6/13.10–17
Abraham's son	Abraham's daughter	Lk 19.9/13.16
Man sowed a seed	Woman hid yeast	Lk 13.18–19/20–1
Shepherd with sheep	Woman with coins	Lk 15.3–7/8–10
Men sleeping	Women grinding	Lk 17.34/35
Peter at tomb	Women at tomb	Lk 24.12/1–11
Aeneas	Tabitha	Acts 9.32–5/36–42

Of these examples, Zechariah and Mary, Simeon and Anna, and Peter and the women take their places in narrative sequences that make the parallelism clear. Two of these especially, Simeon and Anna and Peter and the women at the tomb, will be discussed in greater detail in later sections.[18] Naaman and the widow in Zarephath, the men from Nineveh and the queen of the South, and the men sleeping and women grinding are all found in discourse material and function as parallel concretisations in sequences of exemplificatory lists. A further gender-determined contrast is also built into the example of the queen of the South when it is specified that she will rise at the judgment μετὰ τῶν ἀνδρῶν τῆς γενεᾶς ταύτης. Not only do the two pairs of parables mentioned here occur side by side, but there is a further parallelisation through the identical introduction, form and/or the concluding observation.[19] All of these examples ought to be indisputable. The last two groups especially are marked by a verbal repetition that makes the parallelism formally convincing. In terms of their substantial meaning, similarly, the examples of parables especially show little variation, as we see for example in the virtually identical concluding observations at Lk 15.7 and 10. With support in the plot of both parables, they are interpreted as an expression of the undeniable joy that one who was lost, has been found. That on the level of the images, the two narratives are totally different is due to the gender specification, and to the fact that the plot, which is similar in its basic structure, is played out in a different setting, one determined by the gender of the protagonists. Thus the different places in which men and women live are made visible, as well as the distance between them.

In the case of the healing stories that are included here, it can be doubted whether the two healings on the sabbath truly deserve their inclusion. But the two narratives have in fact more in common than the theme of healing and the temporal setting on the sabbath.[20] The man and the woman are introduced in the same way, with ἰδοὺ (13.11, 14.2); when he defends his act of healing, Jesus argues in both cases –

---

[18] Cf. p. 176f. and p. 157f. The parallel between Zechariah and Mary is justified in detail, e.g. by Brown, *Birth*, 297f.; Laurentin, *Truth of Christmas*, 152ff.

[19] In my article, 'Gudsrikets overraskelse', 1–17, I argue for the consistent unity between form and content in the different variants, and carry out a parallel interpretation of the parables in Lk 13.18–21 emphasising the aspect of surprise in the story.

[20] Cf. Tannehill, *Narrative Unity*, 135.

though not in identical words – on the basis of an inference *a minore* from the treatment of an ox on the sabbath day (13.5 and 14.5). The fact that the two versions by means of tradition criticism may be traced back to one logion of Jesus that defended healings on the sabbath, is no objection in this case. It is rather a point in favour of the hypothesis that we here have a pair of narratives.

Likewise, the two narratives about Jesus' raising of a widow's son and of a man's daughter have more in common than the fact that both are healing stories. Not only are both specifically resurrection narratives, but in both cases it is also significant that the raising reflects a family situation. This is also expressed in a couple of emphatic verbal agreements. It is said of the widow's son in 7.12 that he was μονογενὴς υἱός. The same point is made as a Lukan addition in the description of Jairus' daughter in 8.42. She is θυγάτηρ μονογενὴς. This implies that, even as a daughter, she has great value because she is her parents' only child. In both cases too, Jesus' words to the mourning relatives are identical: μὴ κλαῖε in 7.13 and μὴ κλαίετε in 8.52. In this case, the gender 'doublet' is itself double: a relation between father and daughter (only child) on the one hand corresponds to a relation between mother and son (only child). The parallelisation between Jairus, the leader of the synagogue, and the widow is further characterised by the social contrast. This is true also of the placing of Jairus alongside the woman made unclean by her flow of blood. Here, two narratives were already welded together into one account in Mark's version, in which the woman delays Jesus *en route* and prevents him from arriving in time to heal the daughter of the synagogue leader.[21]

In Acts, the volume of this kind of epic material in pairs is much less – indeed, one might say that it is non-existent, since even the example that is included in the list given above is doubtful. It is true that Peter's healing of Aeneas and his raising of Tabitha belong together in one narrative sequence. But neither the structure nor the observations at the beginning and close linking the two together, give any indication of parallelisation. The central word of healing, however, is identical in the two narratives: Peter says ἀνάστηθι to both the sick man and to the

---

[21] Both of these parallels are discussed in greater detail on p. 55f.

17

dead woman (9.34 and 40). In addition, both are addressed by their names.

This stricter delimitation of narrative pairs does not mean that the narratives which are defined here as lying outside this category, are irrelevant for the understanding of the complementarity between women and men in Luke. Rather, it means that not all of Luke's material dealing with women can be subsumed under a pattern of gender parallelisation. But the rest of the material does contribute as a whole to give a greater weight to the women's side in the setting-up of gender pairs. It is also clear that this additional material is important in providing a sounding-board for Luke's particular mode of expression in pairs.

The parallelisation in pairs which can be observed both in discourse and in parts of the epic material corresponds to a repeated gender specification in a number of editorial-like notices. And while the narrative pairs are virtually non-existent in Acts, there is wide evidence for coupled group-descriptions. Indeed, this is almost more clearly marked in Acts than in the gospel.[22] An intermediary type is found in Lk 12.53, which describes the quarrel Jesus causes in the family. The conflict is between the generations, but in such a way that while son quarrels with father, the women in the family too, are against one another, daughter against mother and mother-in-law.[23]

A further type would be the married couples or sibling pairs who appear: Priscilla and Aquila in Acts 18.2, 18, 26; Felix and Drusilla in Acts 24.25; Agrippa and Berenice in Acts 25.13, 23. More important is the repeated emphasis that those who followed Jesus were both men and women (Lk 8.1–3; 23.49; 24.9–11) and correspondingly in Acts, the groups of those who believe in Jesus and who are converted (Acts 1.14; 17.4, 12; (21.5). In many places in Acts we have also an almost

---

[22] Dawsey, 'Literary Unity', 62ff., makes this almost a linguistic distinguishing feature of Acts as opposed to the gospel. However, his emphasis on the difference makes him overlook the fact that some material is found in the gospel too, although he does admit that the gospel contains individual doublets 'in description'. Because of his exclusively linguistic interest, however, he does not see the connection between the various types.

[23] Cf. p. 38 and p. 38 n. 41.

formulaic description of the community in gender-specific terms, ἄνδρες τε καὶ γυναῖκες (cf. Acts 5.14; 8.3, 12; 9.2, 36ff.).[24]

Whatever the term οἱ ἅγιοι καὶ αἱ χῆραι in Acts 9.41 may mean, the combination is once again an example of a gender-specific image of the community. And the doublet of Dionysius and Damaris in Acts 17.34 fits better here than in the list of narrative doublets; in the same way as in Lk 8.1–3; 24.9–11 and Acts 1.14, some persons in the larger group are mentioned especially by name.[25] In this case, the woman Damaris suddenly makes us see that the masculine terms elsewhere in this verse conceal the presence of women.[26] A special case is Lk 23.27, where those who follow Jesus on the way to the cross are described as πολὺ πλῆθος τοῦ λαοῦ καὶ γυναικῶν αἳ ἐκόπτοντο καὶ ἐθρήνουν αὐτόν.

The examples show that it is not a matter of firmly-established groups, *viz.* one group of women and one group of men.[27] The varying groups, names and circumstances permit us rather to speak of a set pattern. It cannot be reduced to a stylistic quirk or a literary convention in Luke, expressing itself in various sorts of material according to a principle of duality. Even so, stylistic means of expression and literary conventions themselves create substance. The distinction between men and women in collective notices like these has in most of the cases the effect of rendering the women especially visible. It is made quite clear that the women belong to the community, even in the cases where a masculine terminology otherwise dominates. At the same time, the gender specification also serves to identify the group of men and the group of women as clearly distinct from one another.[28] The corollary of women becoming visible seems to be an inclusiveness still tasting of segregation.

---

[24] Dawsey, 'Literary Unity', 63, shows that τε καὶ is a linguistic recurrence in combinations of pairs in Acts.

[25] Cf. p. 31.

[26] On this, cf. p. 134ff.

[27] Karriss' attempt, *Luke*, 112, to identify οἱ γνωστοί in Lk 23.49 with the apostles (that is to have the same two groups as in 8.1–3) seems, for example, to have no other justification than his desire to have the apostles present at the cross in order to strengthen their position as witnesses.

[28] This is very clear in Lk 24.1–11, cf. p. 157f.

19

When compared with the earlier version in Mark, Luke's treatment of the crucifixion (Lk 23.49) adds not the women, but the group of men, οἱ γνωστοί. This does not involve any mimimalising of the women's importance;[29] it is rather the expression of a more general pattern of gender complementarity which has the effect in other passages of emphasising and making visible the group of women (cf. Lk 8.1–3). It is a matter of discussion whether the linking καί in Lk 23.27 and 49 is to be understood merely as carrying juxtaposing significance, or whether it has a more emphatic meaning, such as 'especially', or somewhat more weakly, 'also',[30] – which would explain why in both places γυναικῶν/γυναῖκες lacks the definite article. Such an interpretation of καί means that the group of women in these cases is not mentioned in addition to 'the people' or 'all his acquaintances', but is given a prominent position as especially representative of the greater group which is mentioned first. In 23.49, the masculine plural form οἱ γνωστοί would then have to be read inclusively, and the weeping women in 23.27 as a part of τοῦ λαοῦ. This strengthens the claim of inclusiveness in examples like these, and not only is the special visibility given to the group of women made extra clear, the women are also given a representative function. The context further underlines this: in Lk 23.28, it is precisely the women whom Jesus addresses,[31] and the mention of the women from Galilee in 23.49 prepares the role they will play throughout the subsequent narratives of the cross and tomb.[32]

The pattern which is demonstrated here, and the coupled group-descriptions which sometimes emphasise women, indicate that the women are not added on summarily merely to strengthen the significance or magnitude of what occurs – as for example, when Matthew in the context of the multiplication of the loaves, adds on 'women and children' in 14.21 to render the miracle even more spectacular.[33] While

---

[29] As is claimed by Tetlow, *Women and Ministry*, 105 – cf. also p. 147f. and p. 148 n. 152.

[30] This is claimed by Giblin, *Destruction of Jerusalem*, 98. However, a juxtaposing significance of καί need not mean such a contrasting of the groups as he seems to presuppose.

[31] Cf. p. 205ff. for a more detailed discussion of Lk 23.27–31.

[32] For greater detail, cf. p. 147ff.

[33] Friis Plum, *Tilslørede Frihed*, 15. She has no hesitation about attributing the same to Luke. Cf. also Schottroff, 'Maria Magdalena', 4.

it is true that Acts 8.3 and 9.2 emphasise Saul's zeal as a persecutor, this is not specially linked to the fact that women too are subject to his persecution. If the women are mentioned in the context of persecution, this is only a natural consequence of the reality that many women have come to the faith (Acts 5.14) and that women as well as men have been baptised (Acts 8.12). In this context, further, we are told that the persecutor Saul in his zeal invades the domestic world, the private sphere, and drags out those whom he finds there.[34] It is only in this indirect manner that the fact that women are mentioned, is a special proof of Saul's extreme thoroughness as persecutor.

A passage which breaks with the usual pattern however, is Acts 21.5 which relates that, when Paul took farewell of the disciples in Tyre, these had with them 'women/wives and children'.[35] It is significant that the combination ἄνδρες τε καὶ γυναῖκες is not used here, but the conventional pairing of 'women and children', σὺν γυναιξὶ καὶ τέκνοις. This combination has the connotation of minority and signal that women and children are additional persons who do not really belong to 'all'. At the same time, the very fact that women and children are even present, nevertheless contributes to giving greater numerical significance to the event. In comparison with the corresponding fare-well at Miletus with the elders from Ephesus (Acts 20.36–8), where they too fall on their knees and pray before Paul goes on board ship, it is precisely the addition of family members in Acts 21.5 that implies something of the same 'growth effect' as in Mt 14.21. The grouping of 'women and children' in Acts 21.5,[36] and the employment of this as a

---

[34] On women and the relationship between the private and the public sphere, cf. the subchapter IV.3 'Domestic Women'.

[35] It may be worthwhile to note that 21.5, unlike the other texts, belongs to the itinerary source. But this does not mean that this source in general deals with women as an appendage: on the contrary, this source's interest in hospitality and hosts leads to many references to women in chs. 16 and 18, and 21.9; cf. Cassidy, *Society*, 185 n. 11. His presentation is, however, too uncritically positive in regard to Luke's portrait of women – in Acts as well.

[36] Few commentators deal with this point at all. Haenchen, for example, and Munck have nothing to say, while Schneider, *Apg.*, II 303, sees no difference at this text from other texts and asserts in a general manner that 'Lukas nennt neben Männern häufig auch Frauen', giving a whole series of texts to support this. Schille, *Apg.*, 408, is an exception.

medium to strengthen the report of the event, is therefore an exception that breaks with the common pattern.

The manuscript D has a variant of Acts 1.14 which makes it clear that, in the more common text Luke's inclusion of women is not immediately to be understood in an enhancing way. After σὺν γυναιξί D adds καὶ τέκνοις and the combination 'women and children' weakens the implicit reference to the women from Galilee and the women as a group by themselves. They are simply enrolled as the family of the apostles. According to D's version, therefore, the first group of those who believed in Jesus in Jerusalem consisted of the apostles with their wives and children, in addition to Jesus' family of his mother and his siblings. D's text of Acts betrays in other places too 'anti-feminist' features.[37] A manoeuvre corresponding to the one in Acts 1.14 can be seen in 17.4 and 12 as well, where the many noble women are turned into wives of the many noble men, γυναῖκες τῶν πρώτων οὐκ ὀλίγαι. In 17.34, the woman Damaris is omitted completely, so that, according to D, only men are converted at Athens. These variants in D are not predominant in the textual tradition, but they, nevertheless, suggest that the Lukan majority text does not warrant a complete subordination of women to men. Women are not simply an addition to the men, nor their accompaniment, but a group of their own.

As a rule, therefore, the group of those who believe in Jesus is summed up as ἄνδρες τε καὶ γυναῖκες. The complementarity in this short formula is reflected also in the more detailed description in the résumés, that a group of men and a group of women together make up Jesus' followers and later constitute the community of those who believed in Jesus. Both men and women come to faith and are baptised, and a corresponding gender-specific duality can be perceived, though not frequently, in the description of the group of adherents. The differentiated combination emphasises inclusiveness, but implies at the same time distance and difference. The parallelisation in pairs both in discourse and narrative material, especially in the gospel, functions as an epic correspondence to the description of the group.

[37] Cf. Schüssler Fiorenza, *In Memory*, 52; Witherington, 'Anti-Feminist Tendencies', 82–4.

The constantly-repeated theory of an all-pervading principle of 'dual witness' offers no satisfactory explanation of the man-woman parallelism in Luke. It is not possible to presuppose in general terms that all the Lukan doublets relate to Jewish demands about the calling of witnesses and that this dominating principle of composition strengthens the credibility of the account while at the same time serving to give women a place similar to that of men in the spirit of egalitarian universalism. For one thing it has to be argued specifically that a Jewish perspective of witness can be relevant, when an essential part of the force of the testimony is to be borne by women who had at best a limited acceptability as witnesses. A further point is that the epic pairs especially qualify in any case only indirectly, to have formal value as testimonials.[38]

This is not to exclude the possibility that the aspect of witnessing and multiple affirmation play a role in Luke. For example, Luke understands the twelve apostles above all as 'witnesses', but their position is a chosen and exclusive one. It becomes clear, however, in connection with the election of a new apostle in Acts 1 and the introduction of a criteria of maleness, that Luke's dealing with the credibility of women's testimony is ambivalent in a way that consequently excludes women from public witnessing.[39] Women are described as credible, but at the same time they are rejected as useful witnesses, because their voice would not be able to make itself heard in a man's world. In keeping with this, messengers in Luke-Acts are often characterised explicitly as men, whether they be heavenly or earthly. Moreover, these men often appear in groups of at least two: for example there are two men at the transfiguration (Lk 9.30f.); in the empty tomb (Lk 24.4); and at the ascension (Acts 1.10). When Tabitha dies, the community at Joppa sends two men to Peter (Acts 9.38), and the delegation from Cornelius (Acts 10.19f.) is likewise composed only of men. In the same way, only

---

[38] For Morgenthaler, *Lukanische Geschichtsschreibung*, II 8, the principle of 'Doppelzeugnisse' is a 'Fundamentalsatz', *viz.* almost a *sine qua non* for *all* early Christian exposition, and this holds true of all kinds of material. He does however betray a certain uncertainty *vis-à-vis* the epic doublets when he says, II 17, that they 'gehören ebenfalls in das Gebiet dieser nur noch *ganz indirekt* erkennbaren Doppelzeugnisse' (my emphasis).

[39] This is argued in greater detail on p. 162f.

men are chosen as the deputation from the apostles' meeting (Acts 15.22). In all these cases, the men's mission has the desired effect. On the few occasions on which women come with a message, however, they are not believed (cf. Lk 24.10f. and Acts 12.14f.),[40] at least not by the group as a whole.

It is, in other words, not possible to explain the gender pairs in Luke-Acts simply as expressing a motif of 'dual witness'. But even if this motif must be rejected in the traditional understanding of establishing a total and credible attestation, it may still have something to be said in its favour as a duplication. The overview of the various sets of parallelisation in pairs indicates that it is a gender-determined completeness or complementarity that is to be confirmed rather than a formalistic consideration demanding that everything must be attested twice in order to claim credibility. Luke has integrated the narratives about men and women known to him into one coherent text, and in the same text a portrait is being drawn of a reference group both of men and of women. At the same time, he conveys a picture of a world divided by gender, of a culture and a mediation of tradition in which men and women, within the same community, nevertheless keep each to their own sphere of life. As an anonymous Attic aphorism says,[41] Ἄλλος γυναικὸς κόσμος, ἄλλος ἀρσένων.[42] Even within the community, they have their primary membership within a group of women or of men. An essential challenge in what follows is to explore the implications of this in greater detail.

---

[40] On the similarity between these two passages, cf. Nuttall, *Moment of Recognition*, 4; Portefaix, *Sisters Rejoice*, 168.

[41] Burrus, *Chastity*, 68–75, adduces some folkloristic material which attests that a gender-divided mediation of tradition is not only customary in most cultures, but is also marked by characteristic and broadly-found cross-cultural traits. Burrus makes use of this in an analysis of the narratives about women in the Apocryphal Acts while attempting to trace traditions mediated by women. Even if the limited Lukan material does not allow a similar analysis, it is, however, interesting to note that the pair of parables in Lk 15.3–10 also gives evidence of a gender-divided mediation, cf. further p. 128.

[42] Cf. Meeks, 'Image of Androgyne', 180 (though with a typographical error).

Chapter Three

Do You See This Woman?

III.1   *The women from Galilee.*

In Mk 15.40–1, some women suddenly appear as witnesses – at a distance – to Jesus' crucifixion and death. Three of them are mentioned by name, but it is emphasised that the group of women is larger than these three.[1] We are told that they[2] had followed Jesus already in Galilee, ἠκολούθουν αὐτῷ, and had served him, διηκόνουν αὐτῷ. Now they had come up to Jerusalem together with him, αἱ συναναβᾶσαι αὐτῷ εἰς Ἱεροσόλυμα. Both the scene that is set[3] and the terms of expression, ἀκολουθέω, διακονέω, συναναβαίνω, serve to associate the description of the women in 15.40f. with the terminology used elsewhere in the gospel to characterise discipleship.[4]

---

[1]   This is true of most of the 'lists of women'. The phenomenon is discussed in greater detail on p. 31f.

[2]   I prescind from the question whether this is true of the whole group of women, or only of the three among them who are mentioned by name. The Greek can be read in both ways.

[3]   Cf. Munro, 'Women Disciples': 'Marcan redaction is at pains to include both the crowd and the disciples in the story... . In 15.40f. the scenario is similar except that the following is entirely female... . This pattern rather than the fact that they "followed him" taken in isolation, identifies them as disciples ...', 230f., cf. also 234.

[4]   There is indeed a certain lack of unanimity on this point. In my opinion, the interpretation presented here, alongside Munro's argumentation as referred to above, is convincingly justified by Schüssler Fiorenza, *In Memory*, 320f.; Malbon, 'Fallible Followers', 41f., and Schottroff, 'Maria Magdalena', who also notes that Lukan texts cannot immediately be drawn on for the interpretation of Mark. This implies that she believes the same not to be true of Luke. The criticism proposed by Schweizer, 'Scheidungsrecht', takes too little account of the fact that the discussion is not based only on διακονέω, but on the close juxtaposition of ἀκολουθέω, διακονέω, and συναναβαίνω. His objections demonstrate, however, that individual verses cannot be used as a short cut to establish women's status as disciples. Cf. also Gill, 'Women Ministers', 18, who tackles a corresponding criticism by Kingsbury concerning the Matthean parallel, Mt 27.55f. Anderson,

The women therefore represent in Mark the presence of the disciples at Jesus' cross.[5] The imperfect form of the verbs and the reference to Galilee show that their presence is not an acute emergency measure, 'a newly constituted following in the absence of the men who have fled'.[6] The rest of the disciples have reacted to Jesus' arrest by flight, 14.50ff., and by denying him, 14.66–72. But the women following him from Galilee hold out still, even if at a great distance.[7] Mark's gospel ends with the women fleeing too – from the tomb in terror and silence, 16.8, so that Jesus' words in 14.27, πάντες σκανδαλισθήσεσθε, are thereby fulfilled.[8]

Thus the presentation in Mk 15.40f. gives the retrospective impression that this group of women had been among those already following Jesus in the Galilee period. But they become visible in the gospel narrative, only at the cross.[9] As this remark stands in Mark, it intro-

---

'Matthew', 20, emphasises that the women's presence at the cross shows their fidelity to Jesus, but in positive contrast to the 'disciples'. She finds that the women in Matthew's gospel appear as a serving support-group who can appropriately fit into the disciple's place. But 'gender seems to prevent their identification as disciples'.

[5] Schottroff, 'Maria Magdalena', 13, who, however, uses this to weaken the gender aspect: 'Es geht um die Kreuzesnachfolge; dass hier nur *Frauen* stehen, ist eine Tatsache, die er nicht auswertet'.

[6] Munro, 'Women Disciples', 231.

[7] Cf. Heine, *Frauen der frühen Christenheit*, 86f., and Schottroff, 'Maria Magdalena', 5f., who emphasise the danger to which the women expose themselves by the very fact of their presence. The military guard means that they must keep a certain distance. The women's distance may also be a premonition of their later fear and flight, (16.8), as the same is said about Peter when he follows Jesus before betraying him: ἀπὸ μακρόθεν (14.54).

[8] Cf. Hengel, 'Maria Magdalena', 253; Schottroff, 'Maria Magdalena', 20ff. I find the interpretation convincing, also because it is in keeping with the explanation of the women's distance from the cross referred to in the previous note. It is insufficient, at this final stage in the gospel narrative, to explain the women's fear primarily or exclusively as a characteristic of epiphanies, as does Malbon, 'Fallible Followers', 44f., with support in Catchpole, 'Fearful Silence'. I also consider Munro's theory, 'Women Disciples', 237ff., that Mark in this way brings the 'Jerusalem circle' (to which it is presumed that the women as well as the core group of the named disciples belong) finally to silence, inconvincible. Schüssler Fiorenza's attempt, *In Memory*, 322, at an interpretation favourable to Mark which avoids reproaching the women for disobedience and silence, seems somewhat forced. It is, of course, a positive point that the women do not flee from the angels, from the message of the resurrection or (for that matter) from Jesus himself, but from the empty tomb where in any case they are instructed not to remain. But their flight and silence are still the last word, and there is no reason for supposing, as Schüssler

duces the role the women play throughout the narrative sequence of the cross, burial and the empty tomb.[10]

Much of this is different in the gospel of Luke. The continuous presence of the women at the cross and grave is still emphasised.[11] But there is no previous flight of the disciples, and at the cross of Jesus – although at the same distance as in Mark – there stand all(!) those who knew him (23.49). Even so,[12] the women are mentioned specially with an amplification telling who they are, καὶ γυναῖκες αἱ συνακολουθοῦσαι αὐτῷ ἀπὸ τῆς Γαλιλαίας.

Despite this amplification in Lk 23.49, Luke's account is much more concise than Mark's at this point. No names are mentioned, and nothing is said about the women's function. The essential point is to iden-

Fiorenza does, that the women told the disciples and Peter while they maintained silence *vis-à-vis* the rest. This means that she must understand οὐδενι in 16.8 artificially as 'anyone else'. A more detailed discussion here about the abrupt conclusion of Mark's gospel would, however, take us too far afield.

9   There may be various reasons for this, both from the history of tradition and on the redactional level. It can be noted critically that the women become visible only when there are no men available. Positively, it can be claimed that 'the Markan narrator delays explicit reference to the women disciples or followers until that moment when the true meaning of discipleship ... can be understood ...', Malbon, 'Fallible Followers', 42. I am critical of a retroactive use of 15.40ff. in the reading of the previous story of the gospel of Mark; – cf. Munro, 'Fallible Followers', 231, who in this way wishes to break the gospel's silence before explaining it. Schottroff too, 'Maria Magdalena', 4f., is tempted to read women into the various contexts, cf. my analysis of her position in 'Fattig og likestilt'.

10   Hengel, 'Maria Magdalena', 246: 'Die drei Frauenperikopen bei Markus gehen ... wohl auf einen vormarkinischen Traditionszusammenhang der Leidens – und Grabesgeschichte zurück, ja, man darf sie als verbindendes Glied derselben betrachten. Der 1 Kor 15 sichtbare, auf die früheste Urgemeinde zurückgehende und durch die γράφαι bezeugte Dreiklang "gestorben, begraben ... auferweckt", wird hier ergänzt durch die dreifache Zeugenschaft der Frauen ...'. It is important to be aware that this does not necessarily imply a statement on the question about historicity. It is possible that the Markan tradition or the Markan text may represent a combination of two different streams of tradition: one characterised more by formulae and confessional statements with a triadic pattern, which did not know (or refused to acknowledge) the tradition about the empty tomb and/or the role of women witnesses, and another narrative tradition in which the story of the empty tomb and the women's function as witnesses was central.

11   This means that the two-source theory is presupposed, to the extent that it claims that the author of Luke's gospel knew and made use of Mark's gospel, perhaps in a somewhat shorter version.

12   The duality in this description of the audience, was discussed on p. 19 above.

tify the women as those who have followed Jesus all the way from Galilee to Jerusalem. The possible reasons why this identification is so important in the crucifixion scene, will be dealt with later. Here, we shall simply note that the description may be abridged at this point, partly because these women and their service have already been presented to Luke's readers. The retrospective perspective in Mark is activated in Luke and developed also on the basis of material of his own. The women are made visible in the course of the gospel in a quite different way than in Mark, and they are thus given a continuous narrative role to a greater degree than in either Mark or Matthew.

The passage in Luke's gospel which most clearly preludes 23.49 (par. Mk 15.40f.), is 8.1–3. It is probable that Mk 15.40f. in Luke's text has been distributed over both 23.49b and 8.2f. Some of the elements which are lacking in 23.49b in comparison with the parallel text in Mark are therefore covered instead by 8.2f. At the same time, both texts clearly bear the imprint of Lukan specialities and their present form is a redactional combination of Markan material and peculiarly Lukan material.[13] The special Lukan element is particularly extensive in 8.1–3, which already, because of its positioning in the gospel, is less of a parallel text. To what extent this is due exclusively to redactional activity, or whether it also reflects pre-Lukan units of tradition, has been the subject of some discussion. The discussion deals both with the fact that the presence of women is explicitly emphasised during the time in Galilee itself and with the reason why this emphasis comes precisely at this point in the progress of the narrative. It deals also with the information about the women which is new to Luke when compared to Mark. Luke gives other names, and all the women are said to have been healed by Jesus. There is general agreement, as far as the names are concerned, that these are based on particular Lukan tradition.[14] More controversial is the suggestion that something similar to 8.2f., in a previous source, served as a general concluding remark to a series of narratives about women. The narratives were presumably those now found in Lk 7.11–17 (the widow at Nain) and 7.36–50 (the sinful

---

[13] Blank, 'Frauen', 50f.; Guillaume, *Luc*, 45f.; Lohfink, *Sammlung Israels*, 67; Munro, 'Women Disciples', 233; Witherington, 'On the Road', 243–8.

[14] Cf. Jeremias, *Sprache*, 174–8.

woman who is forgiven).[15] Such a source theory is, however, of only limited help in interpreting the present context – even less so, in that the arguments in favour of it are very slender, apart from the point that the pericopae in question are all specifically Lukan material in which women play an important role, and that they occur in close order. The three pericopae are very different, and do not presuppose one another. It is, for example, not the case that the two preceding narratives can explain the insertion about healing in 8.2f., since in both these cases we have a 'healing' of women only in an indirect or transferred sense.

Lk 8.1–3 is very similar to the summaries, that is to say this pericope does not deal with one particular episode, but gives a dense description covering the general situation.[16] This renders typical character to the contents, and makes it representative of the stage in the narrative at which it is inserted. Jesus goes on through cities and villages, proclaiming the good news. Together with him are the twelve and a number of women. In 8.1–3, therefore, as has been shown earlier, a distinction is made between a group of men and a group of women among those who follow Jesus. The complete group of followers is to be understood corporately.

The mention of οἱ δώδεκα in 8.1 refers back to 6.13–16, where the list of the names of the twelve is introduced briefly by an account of Jesus' choice of them from among the disciples and of his bestowal of the name apostle on them, οὓς καὶ ἀποστόλους ὠνόμασεν. Luke speaks of a choice and of a naming, so that the term apostle is linked specifically to the twelve, as distinct from the wider group of 'disciples', οἱ μαθηταί. The apostles, however, are given no commission at this

---

[15] Cf. Marshall, *Luke*, 315, and Schürmann, *Lukas*, 448. The latter goes so far as to claim that 'Der "Sitz" im Gemeindeleben dieser kleinen Komposition wird die Frauenfrage gewesen sein: Jesus hat einer armen Witwe geholfen, eine Sünderin angenommen und besessene Frauen geheilt ... in seine Gemeinschaft aufgenommen und sich von ihnen bedienen lassen'. This source theory is completely rejected by Blank, 'Frauen', 51. Fitzmyer also sees 8.1–3 in its totality as a Lukan composition. Hengel, 'Maria Magdalena', 245, describes the placing of 8.1–3 as 'unvermittelt', i.e. not determined by sources, and sees in Lk 8.2f. and Mk 15.40 two older pieces of tradition with totally different origins. This is, however, determined primarily by the fact that the lists of names are so different.

[16] Blank, 'Frauen', 39. Fitzmyer, *Luke* 696, compares with 'the use of frequent summaries in Acts'.

early stage: this takes place only in 9.1f.[17] In 8.1, the twelve are still serving their apprenticeship, and it is not to be assumed that they join Jesus in preaching. On the whole, the apostles play a remarkably passive role while Jesus is still with them. Apart from the commission in 9.1ff. and in the multiplication of loaves taking place immediately afterwards, they participate almost only as 'onlookers' and 'persons also present'.[18] This is expressed clearly in 8.1ff. Nothing more is said about them than that they were with Jesus while *he* (according to the singular form of the verbs) travelled round preaching. The formulation thus informs us that neither the twelve nor the women preached, but only Jesus himself.[19]

When compared to the summary description of the twelve, the women in 8.1–3 are given more attention, so that the picture of them is filled out in greater detail. The grammatical construction connects the statement about the women in 8.3–4 to what is said in 8.1 about Jesus and the twelve. This does not however make 8.1 the 'Akzent der Perikope' in the sense that the author is concerned mainly with 'Jesus and the twelve'.[20] Such an interpretation is determined by certain theological presuppositions regarding ministry, and overlooks the fact that grammatically the connection is made by means of a paratactic juxtaposition of the women and the twelve.[21] Moreover, in terms of quantity, the information given about the women, takes up the largest part. In the summary account as a whole, attention is concentrated first on Jesus'

---

[17] In our present context, it is irrelevant that the sending of the twelve in 9.1ff. does not give them tasks which are exclusively reserved to the twelve, as is clear from the later doublet in the sending of the seventy (two) in 10.1ff. Cf. Jervell, *Luke*, 87, who appositely emphasises that: 'According to Luke the Twelve are chosen neither to follow Jesus nor to be sent out as preachers during Jesus' activity on earth. Their primary task lies in the future'. Luke's understanding of the concept 'apostle' will be discussed in greater detail on p. 161ff.

[18] Jervell, *Luke*, 78.

[19] Against Heine, *Frauen der frühen Christenheit*, 70, who claims that 'Der Zusammenhang von Nachfolge und Verkündigung ist bereits in diesem ersten Satz für Männer und Frauen gleicherweise hergestellt'.

[20] Kirchschläger, *Jesu exorzistisches Wirken*, 237, claims so – not to give prominence to Jesus, but to the twelve.

[21] Cf. Grundmann, *Lukas*, 174, and Marshall, *Luke*, 316: 'they appear on the same level as the men'. This means that Jervell's argument, 'Töchter Abrahams', 84, that the women are characterised as 'Gemeinde', is untenable.

own activity, and then on the women who follow him.[22] The fact that they are mentioned as a group by themselves is connected with the Lukan principle of pairs, and they come last due to the function they fulfil in relation, not only to Jesus himself, but to the whole group of followers (cf. the plural form αὐτοῖς in 8.4).

Some of the women are identified in 8.3–4; we are told how all the women have come into contact with Jesus, and the task they have undertaken. While it is not yet clear what role the twelve are to play, the women are already active. The information variously given about the women in 8.2–3 stands in close interconnection, and following the sequence of the text, we must first ask who some of the women are claimed to be, and how their relationship to Jesus is said to have been established.

Like Mark in 15.40f., Luke mentions three of the women by name. In most of the 'lists of women', some of the women are named specifically whether two of them (Mk 15.47; Mt 27.61; 28.1) or three (Mk 15.40; 16.1; Mt 27.51; Lk 8.2f.; 24.10; Jn 19.25). In Jn 20.1, Mary Magdalene is mentioned alone. The mentioning of names does not exclude their representative character.[23] It means on the contrary that they represent a larger group. Such a presentation of an 'inner circle' within a larger group is a common phenomenon. The selection of three recalls corresponding selections of three male disciples elsewhere in the gospels (Mk 5.37; 9.2; 14.33; Lk 8.51). Some names, often three, are given special prominence among the list of names of the twelve, and these constitute a kind of core group.[24]

The examples of men and especially the examples of women show variations in the number of names, but even so variants in the names that are mentioned, and the names mentioned within this limited 'quorum' can vary even within each gospel. A good example of this is Lk 24.10, where the list does not simply summarise the 'names from the

---

[22] Evidence in Kirchschläger, *Jesu exorzistisches Wirken*, 237 n. 3, shows that this is the usual understanding in the commentaries. Lohfink, *Sammlung Israels*, 67, also points to an element of surprise which contributes to focus the women: 'an der Stelle, wo man eine Erwähnung der übrigen Jünger erwartet, einige Frauen …'.

[23] As is claimed by Jervell, 'Töchter Abrahams', 90, – although with reference to Acts.

[24] On the evidence and the evaluation of this, cf. Hengel, 'Maria Magdalena', 248ff.

31

Lukan material', as we know these from 8.2f., in addition to the 'names from Mark' that is to say, five names in all, but combines them so that the result is a total of three names. Mary from Magdala is the one name common to both lists. Luke also retains the second name from 8.3, Joanna, but the last name, Susanna, is replaced by Mark's Μαρία ἡ Ἰακώβου, who comes second in the Markan list 6.1 – before Salome. In Luke, she is given the third place, while Salome is omitted. These redactional maneouvres indicate that the sequence of the names is also significant. In Lk 24.10 priority is given to the two women named first in 8.3 while the third names on both lists are left out. This means that the list in 24.10 includes the two most important names from each of the traditions available.

Mary of Magdala is the only woman whose name is included in all the lists of women as we know them in the gospels. With the exception of Jn 19.25, she also heads the lists.[25] Her prominent position probably reflects that she enjoyed the greatest prestige in many early communities and had an authority equalling Peter's on the male side.[26] In other words, her first place among the women listed was a univocal point in the tradition. In the Lukan text her priority is further justified by an

---

[25] Including the narrative in Jn 20, where she is the only woman together with two male disciples. The Johannine narrative ensures a special and remarkable distribution of priorities among the various actors in the story. None of them is consistently the first, but each of them is first in some aspect. The testimony is complete only when their various contributions are gathered together, cf. Seim, 'Roles of Women', 67. In Jn 19.25 Mary of Magdala is mentioned last after the mother of Jesus and her sister. Hengel, 'Maria Magdalena', 250f., has convincingly shown that the principle at work in the structuring of this list is a blood relationship to Jesus, something that shifts Mary of Magdala downwards on the list. Her prominent position is nevertheless obvious in that she is still counted among those present and mentioned in the circle of close female relations. In my article, 'Roles of Women', 60–5. I have developed a theory of why kinship plays such an important role in the crucifixion scene in John.

[26] This is connected primarily with her role in the resurrection tradition; cf. Hengel, 'Maria Magdalena', 248-56; Brown, 'Roles of Women', 692f.; Schneider's, 'Women', 43f.; Schürmann, *Lukas*, 446; and Schottroff, 'Maria Magdalena', 10, who shares the same primary point of view, but is unwilling, apparently for ideological reasons, to assume that it also reflects concerns about ranking among the women. The role played by Mary of Magdala and the conflict with Peter in some of the gnostic material is interesting, but falls outside our scope here. On this theme, cf. Bovon, 'Privilege Pascal', 50–60; Pàgels, *Gnostic Gospels*, 64ff.; Schüssler Fiorenza, 'Word, Spirit and Power', 51–7.

explicit association with the preceding characteristic of the women: they have been healed by Jesus. Her case is exemplified as an extreme one: ἀφ' ἧς δαιμόνια ἑπτὰ ἐξεληλύθει. Seven demons meant a particularly powerful possession, cf. Lk 11.26 par.[27]

As has been mentioned above, the list of women's names in Lk 8.2–3 represents a tradition peculiar to Luke, and, with the exception of Mary of Magdala, it differs from the list in Mk 15.40. Even if Mary of Magdala is prominent in both lists, her name is given in different forms.[28] In Mk 15.40 (and Mk 15.47; 16.1), she is called Μαρία ἡ Μαγδαληνή and is thereby distinguished from the other Mary in the same list, who in turn is identified more closely as Μαρία ἡ Ἰακώβου τοῦ μικροῦ καὶ Ἰωσῆτος μήτηρ.[29] It was customary for women to

---

[27] Such a possession does not in itself characterise Mary of Magdala as a 'sinner', and there is nothing in the Lukan text which makes it probable that she is to be identified with 'the sinful woman' in Lk 7.36–50. This also means that problems of interpretation in 7.36–50 cannot be solved on the basis of 8.2f., as evidence of a prior meeting and perhaps a healing between Jesus and the woman. References to a reputation which the town Magdala is said to have possessed for being especially immoral, should perhaps be seen in the light of this, cf. Grundmann, *Lukas*, 174, and Schürmann, *Lukas*, 446 n. 13, both with reference to Strack-Billerbeck, which cannot be said to bring convincing evidence in the case.

There is today broad agreement in rejecting the earlier legendary and well-known iconographic merger of Mary Magdalene first with Mary of Bethany because of the similar name, and then with the prostitute who anoints Jesus in Lk 7.36–50 – like Mary of Bethany according to John. Brown, *John*, I 452, gives a good overview in an excursus of how the combinations could arise. Friis Plum, *Tilslørede Frihed*, 98, emphasises the fact that Mary of Magdala, since she did not belong to any man, could easily acquire the reputation of being available to all, and that this permitted the growth of ideas about her immorality. But there are still scholars like Munro, 'Women Disciples', 240, who maintain, for the lack of alternative suggestions – that 'in terms of renown no one qualifies better than Mary Magdalene', that is, for the role as a previously sinful woman. In patristic literature, 'the converted whore' is a repeated hagiographic motif, cf. Ward, *Harlots*, who examines the relevant material.

[28] On the forms of names in the lists, and etymological explanations, cf. Marshall, *Luke*, 316f.

[29] In Mk 15.47 she is called Μαρία ἡ Ἰωσῆτος and in 16.1 Μαρία ἡ (τοῦ) Ἰακώβου. Mk 15.40 seems to combine these two. The two different male names are thus explained by means of μήτηρ, i.e. they are sons and not husbands, as the designation would normally have implied, cf. Schottroff, 'Maria Magdalena', 8. But consequently, I disagree with Schottroff when she claims in the same passage that the list in Mk 15.40, with support in Vaticanus, must be read as four female names: Mary Magdalene, Mary the wife (or mother) of James the lesser; Mary, the mother of Joses, and Salome.

be identified and named by their relationship to men – as daughter, wife or mother.[30] In these lists, however, it is clear that the man's name does not serve as an actual component of the woman's full name, but rather as a means of distinguishing from one another, various women with the same first name. This is especially true of the many Marys. The purpose is, therefore, not so much to gain a footing for the women in the audience group by emphasising their link to men who may have been better known to the community/addressees. It is rather a practical device for distinguishing them from each other.

Even if no other Mary occurs in the list in 8.2–3, it is still necessary to name her more fully in order to separate her from the various other Marys in the gospel. She is, however, identified by a wider description Μαρία ἡ καλουμένη Μαγδαληνή, ἀφ' ἧς ... . The formulation sounds more like a way of identifying her, than a regular name given to her. In 24.10 we find a further variation, when the adjective Μαγδαληνὴ is prefixed to the name, which is thus chiastically contrasted with Μαρία ἡ Ἰακώβου. This means that her name did not have a fully fixed form, and therefore the example shows even more clearly the need to clarify in each case, which Mary is being spoken of. At the same time, the example is unique, because her identity is established, not through her relationship to a man, but by a geographically-determined surname indicating that she came from Magdala, a small town on the western shore of the Lake of Genesareth, just north of Tiberias.[31]

It remains an open question how this is to be explained. A woman might be identified by her first name only, without any further determination, as with 'Susanna' in the list in 8.3. But it is overwhelmingly the case that, when further information is needed, the women are distinguished by means of reference to various men, independently of whether the addressees of the text knew these men or not.[32] This male-orientated identity was not, it seems, a point to be made in

---

[30] Irvin, 'Ministry of Women', 77.

[31] Schottroff, 'Maria Magdalena', 9, points out that 'Diese Herkunftsbezeichnung ist in der Fremde entstanden, setzt also voraus, dass Maria Magdalena nicht mehr in Magdala lebt'.

[32] The assumption that this Mary is identified by means of the place from which she came because she did not have any male relations of whom the Christian community was aware (cf. Schottroff, 'Maria Magdalena', 9) is thus unsatisfactory.

its own right, and it was clearly neither desirable nor possible in the case of Mary from Magdala. She presumably had neither husband nor son by whom she was named. At any rate, she appeared on her own account within the group of those who followed Jesus. What is characteristic of her is her home town and her story. Is this true only of her, or is this a more typical trait for the group of women to which she is supposed to belong? Did they live without the traditional bonds that created identity, and/or did this not play any particularly positive role? These are central questions to which we shall have to return later.

The two others mentioned by name is 8.2–3, Joanna the wife of Chuza and Susanna, are otherwise unknown. Susanna is mentioned only here, while Joanna is also included in the list of names in 24.10. Susanna comes last, and apart from her name we learn nothing about her but that which is generally said to be true of all the women. She contributes to make up the number of three, and as the last in the list, she can most easily be replaced in 24.10 by a name from Mark's list.

Joanna is characterised in the apparently conventional manner through her belonging by marriage. She is the wife of Chuza (a Nabataean name). In this case, the man's name does not have the function of distinguishing her from others, since there is no other Joanna with whom she could be confused. Does this then simply mean that she is the only married woman among the three, and so she is named in accordance with the conventions?[33] Or were there other special reasons for the husband to be named? Chuza is not known elsewhere in our material, and nothing warrants the supposition that he was better known than Joanna to those addressed by Luke (or by the Lukan tradition), so that his name could serve to provide credentials. It is noteworthy that when Joanna is mentioned for the second time in 24.10, the identifying addition is missing. This may, of course, be due to the fact that as she has already been introduced, she no longer needs legitimation. Or perhaps there are other and particular reasons in 8.3 to mention her husband. Unlike the identifications by men which otherwise occur in connection with women's names (cf. Mk 15.40 par; Lk 2.36; 16.10;

---

[33]   This is Fitzmyer's solution, *Luke*, 696.

Acts 12.12), Chuza himself is further characterised by means of his position: he is ἐπίτροπος at the court of Herod Antipas, presumably a high position, possibly meaning that he was in charge of the king's property.[34] He himself plays no independent role in the text, and everything said about him is consistently presented in the genitive form as part of an extended identification of Joanna. The added information serves to make clear and emphasise the economic and social level of his wife.[35] This may be the reason why he is omitted in 24.10, while attention is paid to him in 8.3, since it is presupposed immediately after this latter reference that the women have access to means of sustenance, διηκόνουν αὐτοῖς ἐκ τῶν ὑπαρχόντων αὐταῖς.

Although this can be a bonus point, no independent significance should be attached to the fact that Luke combines a possible interest in Herod's house with his interest in highly placed and well-off sympathisers, when providing this information about Chuza.[36] A different though related question is whether association to Herod gave a positive or a negative social signal. It has been claimed that, rather than bestowing social status on a person, a position at the court of the client king Herod would have engendered social suspicion and even contempt in the contemporary Jewish context, in other words a kind of dubious 'tax-collector' status. Understood in this way, the presence of Joanna would not serve to enhance the social legitimacy of the group around Jesus; instead, she fits in nicely with the other marginalised persons who join Jesus and/or support him.[37]

[34] Cf. Fitzmyer, Luke, 698.

[35] Cf. Gardner, Women, 67f., who gives evidence, especially by reference to eastern provinces, that a married woman received the social status of her husband.

[36] Hengel, 'Maria Magdalena', 246. This is an element mentioned by many commentators – as a typical example, Fitzmyer, Luke, 698. Hastings devotes a whole chapter in his book to Joanna, Prophet and Witness, 38–49. But his interest is nevertheless in the portrait of Herod, and the mention of Joanna in 8.3 serves in his opinion primarily to refer special Lukan tradition about Herod to a trustworthy source, Joanna. This theory is extremely speculative, and it does not make any exegetical contribution to the understanding of Lk 8.1–3.

[37] Cf. Theissen, 'Legitimation und Lebensunterhalt', 198f.; Dillon, Eye-Witnesses, 10 n. 27. In his more popular book, Shadow of Galilean, 119–26, Theissen gives a relatively romantic and, in my opinion, anachronistic portrait of Joanna and her husband Chuza: the anachronism is in terms of mentality. He also places them without further discussion among 'the upper class'.

This shows first of all that wealth and position did not necessarily confer enhanced social status,[38] but it does not alter the fact that they were persons with resources at their disposal. In the context of 8.3, the material resources are more essential than social legitimation – all the more so, given that other traits in the text itself create a picture of social uncertainty and exposure: first illness and then, after the healing, a life on the road with Jesus breaking with the expectation of a seemly pattern of living.[39]

This means that none of the women who are mentioned receives her identity by her family relationship to a man. Even in the case of Joanna, the prominence given to the information that she was the wife of Chuza, the steward of Herod Antipas, serves primarily to establish the women's function in the group who followed Jesus. To the extent that their identities are determined by relationships, this is now by reference to Jesus and the twelve.

Since many interpreters find it totally inconceivable that married women could have left home and family in this way in Palestine at that period, various suggestions have been made about what kind of women really are involved here. The women are supposed to have been the wives of disciples, travelling together with their husbands, or they are named as widows, divorced women or women rejected by their husbands.[40] One can, of course, ask whether the majority of the women in the Jesus-movement originally were less well integrated into family structures than the male disciples who must be called directly to break with their families. This would make the following of Jesus by these women less controversial and more natural – even if what is difficult to accept is not necessarily impossible. This would also help to explain

---

[38] Countryman, *Rich Christian*, 24, 42 n. 54. For Palestinian Judaism, the example of tax-collectors shows precisely that there was no automatic coincidence between wealth and status.

[39] This point is seldom noticed. It is usual to regard Joanna as an example of the way in which the Christian communities referred to rich and prominent persons to establish social legitimation. Marshall, *Luke*, 317, is typical. The lack of proportion between material prosperity and social status is rarely discussed – apart from the obvious case of the tax-collectors.

[40] Augsten, *Stellung des lukanischen Christus*, 9; Leipoldt, *Jesus*, 29; McNamara, *New Song*, 8ff., – a book that is on the whole disfigured by a lack of critical evaluation of the literary sources.

37

why the list of the costs of discipleship in Lk 14.26 and 18.29f. includes leaving a wife, but does not mention leaving a husband. Nevertheless, sayings like Lk 12.53 reckon also with the possibility that women
who believe in Jesus, come into conflict, if not actually with their
husbands, at least with others in the family – mother against daughter
and daughter against mother, mother-in-law against daughter-in-law
and daughter-in-law against mother-in-law.[41]

Others dismiss this kind of speculation, and solve the problem exclusively in terms of tradition history, seeing the description of the women
at 8.2f. primarily as a retrojection into Jesus' life of later situations from
outside Palestine as we see them displayed in Acts. Thus, the historical
subtext is the well-off female benefactors (patronae) in the Greco-
Roman world.[42] It is quite clear that Luke's portrait in Lk 8.2-3 has
been coloured by a later situation, so that the women in 8.2f. must be
related to female figures appearing elsewhere in Luke-Acts who show
similar traits. But rather than begin by asking how (un)realistic, (un)usual
or (un)thinkable it can have been for women to leave home in this way
and/or to have the disposal of their own means, the information as it is
provided by the text itself, must be sorted out more properly. What is
said explicitly, and what does the text pass over in silence, and why?
The individual pieces of the jigsaw puzzle must be set in their place in
the larger picture. The location within the narrative sequence in Luke-
Acts must also be defined before it can be really profitable to ask about
the historical situation. In what follows, this is precisely the aim: to
shed light from the larger Lukan context and the progress of the story
on what is said in 8.1-3 about the women, about their healing and
about the service they carry out.

---

[41] The conflict is between the younger and the older generation, and it follows a
gender-divided pattern, with fathers against sons and daughters against mothers and
mothers-in-law. The detailed way in which it is expressed, is due to the allusion to Mic
7.6.

[42] Horn, *Glaube*, 321 n. 138, with reference to Conzelmann and Schürmann; Thraede,
'Ärger', 96, Friis Plum, *Tilslørede Frihed*, 42. Schottroff, 'Frauen', 102, considers Lk 8.2f.
as a seam of discrepancy between the historical tradition about the poor, expelled women
in the Palestinian Jesus-movement, and a Lukan redactional retrojection of the prominent, rich women who supported the communities in the Greco-Roman cities and whom
we also meet in Acts. In relation to otherwise simplistic theories of projection, she
thereby catches the ambiguous tension in the presentation.

III.2. *'Abraham's daughters' – healed by Jesus.*

Luke gives no clear signals in 8.1–3 that the presence of the women should represent anything unusual or controversial.[43] It belonged to the tradition, and perhaps also corresponded to the situation which he was addressing in his own day. But the description of the women does carry a particular presupposition for their presence among the followers of Jesus: they have all been healed by him. The women are almost ambiguously presented, located as they are within a tension between social integration and social marginalisation, between the relative wealth which is emphasised by Joanna's family background and their exposed situation which is underlined by the fact that they all have been sick and possessed.

The tradition about the women's sickness and healing is material peculiar to Luke. He tells that as many as seven demons have been cast out of Mary of Magdala.[44] This means that more precise traditions were available in her case, even if there is no specific account of this particular exorcism in the gospel. As has been shown earlier, the information in Luke about Mary of Magdala can serve to justify her prominent position as first in the list of names.

Nor do we know of any healing narratives linked to the other women named in 8.3. This means that their stories are never specified, while Luke mentions summarily that the healing experience applies to many more than to the three whose names are given, καὶ ἕτεραι πολλαί, (8.3). We are told in 8.2 more generally about the group as a whole that they were women αἳ ἦσαν τεθεραπευμέναι ἀπὸ πνευμάτων πονηρῶν καὶ ἀσθενειῶν. Such generalisations tend to be a characteristic of the summary accounts. The summaries in 4.40f., 6.17–19 and 7.21 also give the impression of a large-scale healing activity on the part of Jesus. It is therefore not difficult to understand the lack of individual narratives that can refer to these particular cases. The question must

---

[43] To this extent, Jervell is correct when he claims, 'Töchter Abrahams', 79, that Luke does not reflect any surprise at the fact that Jesus had women among his followers. It does not attract any special attention as unusual or shocking, as commentaries often assert without further discussion.

[44] The verb ἐξέρχομαι can be used in koine to express the passive of ἐκβάλλω, cf. Marshall, *Luke*, 316.

rather be why the text emphasises that the *whole* group of women had been led to follow Jesus by experiences of healing.

We can reject without further discussion the theory that the women had to remain near Jesus out of fear that their illness might recur.[45] Much more convincing is the argument that 8.2–3 represents a typically Lukan connection between miracles and the disciple relationship.[46] Jesus' miraculous power is demonstrated in Luke (4.31–41) before he calls any disciples at all, and the story of the call of Simon (5.1–11) is also in itself a miracle narrative. Those who have experienced his power are called to follow him. After having caught the largest number of fish in their lives, they give up everything and follow him. The miracle changes their lives totally, and they become disciples of Jesus.[47] The portrait of the women in 8.2–3 includes the same components: the wondrous experience and the consequent departure to follow Jesus.

We also find a number of miracle narratives in Luke's gospel where Jesus heals particular women and renews their lives. Half of these narratives are based on Markan material, while half are peculiar to Luke; taken together, there are more in Luke than in any other gospel:[48]

– Peter's mother-in-law (4.38–9).
– The widow at Nain (7.1–11 – her son is raised up, not out of concern for him, but out of concern for her, because she needs him. It is her misery Jesus pities and remedies).[49]

[45] Vividly suggested by Leipoldt, *Jesus*, 29.

[46] On this and what follows, cf. Achtemeier, 'Lucan Perspective', 160ff. He also mentions Lk 8.2f. briefly in his article: 'The fact that they (the women) are identified both as followers and as recipients of wondrous acts from Jesus, adds further evidence that Luke understood discipleship intimately connected to Jesus' ability to perform mighty acts'. Cf. also Dunn, *Baptism*, 168ff. who is very critical of Luke on this point. Moreover, this implies that Tetlow's claim, *Women and Ministry*, 103, that the reference to the women's healing is the expression of 'a Lukan device' always to include a negative aspect in women's characters, is untenable.

[47] Busse, *Wunder*, 194, takes this point too far when he claims, with allusion to 8.38ff., 17.12ff. and 18.43, that 'Die Rettung, die jemand von Gott erfahren hat, verlangt nach Verkündigung'.

[48] It may be significant in this connection to note that later rabbinic miracle narratives are seldom concerned with women who are being cured. Cf. some examples in Leipoldt, *Jesus*, 17.

[49] Cf. Busse, *Wunder*, 165, 171, 173; Vogels, 'Semiotic Study', 285f., 292.

- The woman with the unstoppable haemorrhage (8.43–8); woven into the narrative about
- Jairus' daughter (8.40–56).
- The woman possessed by Satan and bent double (13.10–17).

Perhaps also
- the sinful woman in the Pharisee's house (7.36–50) can be included in this list, since this story has some similarity with the miracle narratives.

None of these more fully related healings of women ends clearly in a departure to follow Jesus, that is to the kind of itinerant service with Jesus that is supposed in the summary account. It is not, however, the case that the group of disciples in Luke is limited to those who follow him on his journey. It is not only a direct call to follow Jesus that is constitutive of discipleship, but the positive response to Jesus and openness for the word of the Lord.[50] Moreover, many of these healing narratives also have concluding formulations which emphasise that women are now included in the community of God from which they had been excluded or to which they had been granted only a very peripheral membership. This is especially true of the two women whose suffering rendered them constantly unclean so that they were subject to social restrictions even stricter than those which normally applied to women:[51] the woman with the unstoppable haemorrhage and the woman who was bound by Satan and bent double. In the latter case, the sickness's character of possession gives the healing the meaning of exorcism and liberation. It is typical for Luke that the narratives of healing take on a mark of exorcism.[52] This is seen also in the parallelising mode of expression in 8.2, ἀπὸ πνευμάτων πονηρῶν καὶ ἀσθενειῶν. In 13.11, we have indeed the combination πνεῦμα ἀσθενείας. Some

---

[50] Cf. Seccombe, *Possessions*, 104f.

[51] Cf. Schottroff, 'Frauen', 106.

[52] Cf. Kirchschläger, *Jesu exorzistisches Wirken*. Busse, *Wunder*, 302, shows that Luke several times equates a demon of illness with Satan. Hamm, 'Freeing of Bent Woman', 32, interprets this phenomenon to mean that 'for him (Luke) the category of the demonic has more to do with eschatology than diagnosis'.

textual variants to 8.2 give evidence of the close linking to concepts of impurity, when instead of reading ἀπὸ πνευμάτων πονηρῶν they have ἀπὸ πνευμάτων ἀκαθαρτῶν – impure spirits. This means that the actions of healing become Jesus' involvement with what is impure, in order to create purity: the healing marks a transition from impurity to purity.[53] The tendency towards exorcism also gives the healings more emphatically the character of a liberating act and of an eschatological experience.

The story of Jesus' healing of the woman bent double at 13.10–17 is material peculiar to Luke, and it is heavily coloured by Lukan redaction.[54] This is one of the three narratives in Luke's Gospel about healings on the sabbath. Both the localisation in time (sabbath) and place (synagogue) are typically Lukan, and these are found frequently both in the gospel and in Acts. This means that something exclusively Jewish is emphasised both temporally and locally. Within Luke's text, this localisation in time and place has an interpretative point of reference to Jesus' introductory programmatic address in the synagogue at Nazareth on a sabbath day (4.16–30) about the liberation proper to the Jubilee year, which he had come to realise.[55] The actions which Jesus performs on a sabbath 4.38ff.; 6.1ff., 6ff.; 13.10ff.; 14.1ff.; sometimes also in the synagogue, 6.6ff.; 13.10ff. – are thus to be understood as the realisation of the message about liberation which he proclaimed in the synagogue at Nazareth. Through his good deeds, Jesus fulfils the reading in the sabbath worship from the prophets about the ultimate liberation of Israel.

The narrative in 13.10–17 not only presupposes that Jesus carried out functions in the synagogue worship, but it also takes for granted

---

[53] In connection with the healing of the woman with haemorrhages, Friis Plum *Tilslørede Frihed*, 46, emphasises that this healing does not differ from that of one who is leprous or blind. It does not imply a confrontation with the tabooisation of women because of their biology and hence their regular monthly period of impurity. Friis Plum claims that the Jesus-movement did not question the ritual demands of purity and the prescriptions for purification. This is a surprising claim, in view of the many sharp confrontations in the gospels with the Pharisaic rules of purity.

[54] Cf. Busse, *Wunder*, 302; Hamm, 'Freeing of Bent Woman', 23; Moloney, *Woman*, 62.

[55] Cf. Ringe, *Jesus*, 33–44.

that women were present. No particular reason is given for this.[56] What is emphasised is the woman's sickness and possession, something that would normally have brought cultic impurity with it. The scene is therefore not primarily a realistic one, but confers a particular significance on the action, and gives the occasion for an ensuing conflict with the leadership of the synagogue. As well as what has been mentioned already, some terminological traits, especially the use of λύω/ἀπολύω,[57] play on Old Testament associations with creation and liberation. The converging point is that Jesus' wondrous act fulfils the liberating intention of the sabbath in that the woman is set free precisely on this day (13.16)[58] as is becoming according to God's will (ἔδει). Jesus refers to the woman in this connection as a 'daughter of Abraham', ταύτην δὲ θυγατέρα 'Αβραάμ οὖσαν. Although this expression is emphasised by being placed grammatically and emphatically at the beginning of the sentence,[59] it has seldom received any deeper explanation, even though many commentators note it.[60]

The only New Testament evidence for the term 'daughter of Abraham' is in Luke. The same is true, strictly speaking, also for the term 'Abraham's son' (cf. Lk 19.9, καὶ αὐτὸς υἱὸς 'Αβραάμ (ἐστιν)),

---

[56] This is probably in agreement with the actual situation at the time, cf. Brooten, *Women Leaders*, 139ff. She argues convincingly that women regularly took part in the synagogue worship. She also attempts to prove, on the basis of epigraphic material, that women could have leading positions in the synagogue administration, at least in the Diaspora. She is supported by Kraemer, 'New Inscription', 431ff. Hamm, 'Freeing of Bent Woman', 25, 41 n. 9, makes use of this to establish the scene presupposed in Lk 13.10–17.

[57] Hamm, 'Freeing of Bent Woman, 28, also wishes to emphasise the use of ἔνδοξος as a noun in 13.17, in order to bring in exodus-traditions which connect creation and liberation even more closely.

[58] Cf. Schüssler Fiorenza, *In Memory*, 126; Hamm, 'Freeing of Bent Woman', 28.

[59] Cf. Reiling/Schwellengrebel, *Translator's Luke*, 508.

[60] Jervell, 'Töchter Abrahams', 81 n. 18, gives evidence for this. Jervell himself takes up the designation as a 'slogan' for his own interpretation of women in Luke-Acts, well adjusted to his main perspectives on Luke: 'Der Einfluss der Judenchristentums macht sich geltend. Das lukanische Interesse für die Frauen ... ist ... ein Interesse ... für die Judinnen in der Kirche, die Töchter Abrahams ... . Sie sind ein Teil des Volkes Israels in der Endzeit, also der Kirche. Als solche treten sie auch als fromme Judinnen hervor. Lukas weiss nicht von einer Gleichberechtigung der Frau in der Kirche, obwohl er die Berechtigung gar nicht anzweifelt, 93. For criticism of Jervell's understanding of the term, cf. below n. 85.

and perhaps also Acts 13.26. But while 'Abraham's son' is a traditional Jewish designation, it has been claimed that 'Abraham's daughter' may be a Lukan innovation, because there is no evidence of the term 'Abraham's daughter' being used in earlier and contemporary Jewish literature.[61]

When one examines the question more closely, however, it does not appear that this claim to originality can be upheld without further qualification. Abrahamic categories applied to a woman are found in many passages in 4 Maccabees:[62] 14.20; 15.28; 17.6; 18.20. All of these passages speak of one and the same person: an exemplary strong and God-fearing martyr, the mother of the seven young men. First she sees her sons undergo a cruel death at the tyrant's hands, before she herself seeks death courageously and unafraid. One of the references especially, 15.28, is linguistically very close to the Lukan expression, although in a somewhat longer and ambiguous form. This is also one of many more examples of a terminological affinity between Luke's writings and 4 Maccabees which may indicate a common background.[63]

These passages must be seen in the context of the use of Abrahamic categories elsewhere in 4 Maccabees. In his speech in 6.16–22, the aged Eleazar employs the term Ἀβραὰμ παῖδες, as an honorific designation of the Jews. The implicit appeal of the designation is that they must live up to it without compromise, even if this should cost them their life. In 9.21, one of the young brothers is described as Ἀβραμιαῖος νεανίας precisely when he sustains bravely under the heaviest torture and thus demonstrates reason's (λογισμός) victory over passion. 13.12 contains a clear allusion to Abraham's sacrifice of Isaac,[64] where the

---

[61] Jervell, 'Töchter Abrahams', 81. According to Jervell, the aim is to show 'was es mit den Frauen in den Gemeinden auf sich hat'. Cf. also Tannehill, *Narrative Unity*, 136 n. 50.

[62] Written in the Hellenistic Diaspora (Alexandria or Antioch) in Greek some time in the first century before the year 70, cf. Schwankl, *Sadduzäerfrage*, 259f.

[63] Cf. Dahl, 'Story of Abraham', 141f., 155. Like Fitzmyer, *Luke*, 1013, Dahl mentions in a footnote 4 Macc 15.28 as a possible parallel to Lk 13.16, but without really examining it.

[64] In the Jewish traditions about Abraham, this was a key story, the most extreme expression of Abraham's obedient faith, cf. Baird, 'Abraham', 368.

young men are to remember Abraham (who is mentioned only indirectly in this verse, but where identity is made more broadly explicit when the point is repeated in 16.20), but they are to take as their model Isaac, who endured the prospect of being slaughtered for religion's sake. This identification of the sons with Isaac permits the mother to be compared in 14.20 with Abraham himself. She is τὴν ᾿Αβραὰμ ὁμόψυχον ... μητέρα because she does not waver or give way out of compassion for her children. She too lets reason prevail over her natural feelings as a mother, which the author takes considerable space to justify and depict in his panegyric style. In the hour of trial, she stands fast, and, because of her faith in God, she is a strong witness to the cruel death of her beloved sons. A variation of this is given at 17.6 and also implies that her sons should be compared with Isaac: ἦν γὰρ ἡ παιδοποιία σου ἀπὸ ᾿Αβραὰμ τοῦ πατρός.[65] It is presupposed, therefore, that her children are to be understood as true sons of Abraham, while her own position is less determined in titular terms. If she is to be compared with anyone on this basis, it ought to be with Abraham himself, as in 14.20, or for that matter with Sarah, even if she plays no role in the story about the sacrifice of Isaac.

In 15.28, the motif of her sharing in Abraham's steadfast strength is retained, but here the term θυγάτερ is suddenly introduced: ἀλλὰ τῆς θεοσεβοῦς ᾿Αβραὰμ καρτερίας ἡ θυγάτηρ ἐμνήσθη. As the genitive link is constructed, τῆς καρτερίας is qualified by the θεοσεβοῦς ᾿Αβραὰμ which lies within it.[66] The double genitive construction has an ambiguous function in the sentence. It can be the object of ἐμνήσθη while can also be read, in keeping with 14.20, as giving a more precise designation of ἡ θυγάτηρ. Grammatically speaking, the object designation is the clearer. But it is not necessary to choose between the two options, since the ambiguity itself gives a good meaning. As the 'daughter of the God-fearing Abraham's steadfast strength', she also recalls his strength. It is in any case misleading when translators of 4 Maccabees tend to link ἡ θυγάτηρ in various ways specially to θεοσεβοῦς

---

[65] With SinVen reading πατρός instead of παιδός.

[66] I prescind from Sinaiticus' original reading, θεοσεβίας, which directly links the fear of God to steadfastness.

'Αβραάμ, while τῆς καρτερίας is linked to the verb.[67] In this way, they create the false impression that this text is evidence of the simple designation 'daughter of Abraham'.[68]

Thus, the mother of the martyrs is not directly called 'Abraham's daughter' in 15.28, but more precisely 'the daughter of the God-fearing Abraham's steadfast strength', or perhaps 'the daughter' who 'recalled the God-fearing Abraham's strength'. The formulation thus moves clearly within the typological framework from 13.12; 14.20 and 16.19f., which bases the association with Abraham explicitly on a similarity to the actions and attitudes expressed in Abraham's obedient willingness to sacrifice Isaac. The emphasis is laid on particular, explicitly 'Abrahamic qualities' in the woman. Up to this point, the mother of the martyrs has featured on a different level from that of her sons in the typological comparison. While they have Isaac (or a mixture of Isaac and Abraham) as their model, she has primarily been like Abraham. The term 'daughter' in 15.28 changes this. It is however, improbable that the term bears particular connotations of its own in the context. The close connection in the verse emphasises that she remembers, and what she remembers, and this is what characterises her as a daughter. But it is inescapably the case that, in the context, ἡ θυγάτηρ represents a typological discontinuity. Both the designation itself and the form with the article come surprisingly and abruptly, and it is not repeated again.

In 18.20, the expression, ἡ 'Αβραμιτις 'the Abrahamic woman', is used, and this is often misleadingly translated as 'Abraham's daughter'.[69] The variant 'Αβραμιτις expresses a close link to Abraham and has a titular quality (cf. the corresponding term for the sons in 18.23 and the moralistic exploitation over against the addressees of the writing at 18.1). The expression can, however, be understood very well on the basis of the writing's own position on the mother's similarity to

---

[67] The Revised Standard Version of *The New Oxford Annotated Bible with the Apocrypha*: '... but as the daughter of the God-fearing Abraham she remembered his fortitude'. Deissmann's translation in Kautzsch's edition of *Die Apokryphen und Pseudepigraphen des Alten Testaments*: '... sondern der Standhaftigkeit des gottesfürchtigen Abraham bedachte seine Tochter'. Riessler's German translation of 1927 is similar, as is Townshend's translation in Charles' *The Apocrypha and Pseudepigrapha of the Old Testament*.

[68] As is presupposed by Dahl and Fitzmyer.

[69] Cf. the translations mentioned in n. 67 – but with the exception of Deissmann.

Abraham. This means that the daughter-term at 15.28 remains an isolated instance. Precisely because it breaks with the rest of the pattern, it is possible that it is due to influence from a terminology that was known to the author, but for which we have no further evidence. It is therefore important to emphasise that the form of expression in 4 Macc 15.28, as has been shown, is different from the simple form in Lk 13.16. A dominant trait in 4 Maccabees' use of Abrahamic categories is, moreover, that the persons in question, both men and women, are extreme examples of piety, and it is developed within the framework of a typological pattern. Their rigorous religious zeal with its willingness to accept sacrifice show that they are Abraham's children.

There is some scattered evidence in later Jewish sources of the use of the expression 'Abraham's daughter'. In the Talmud, the designation is concretely used twice (bKeth 72b; Git 89a) in identical statements: 'then you do not allow any daughter of our father Abraham to remain with her husband'. Both texts discuss what – in various circumstances – is required for a man to divorce his wife. This was subject to discussion, and the quoted statement functions as an argument that the rules must not be unreasonably strict against women, lest too many be affected by them. The designation 'Abraham's daughter' is therefore presumably used to speak of 'respectable' women: excessively rigorous regulations would lead to a situation in which even many of these would have to be dismissed. But the designation is used concretely of Jewish women, and it is used in a natural manner that possibly reflects the fact that it was not a totally unusual expression. But here too, the expression has the value of a positive moral qualification. A similar expression, 'daughter of Abraham, Isaac and Jacob', is attested in the third century (Sukka 49b) and also in the fourth century (Pesiq 110b), but in both these cases it is used symbolically of Israel as God's chosen people.

The examination of the Jewish material has shown that when a woman in Lk 13.16 is specifically and emphatically called 'Abraham's daughter', this constitutes an original, though not a unique, use of language. But more important than the question of whether this is a linguistic neologism is the question about its employment and meaning – also in comparison with the signs of a corresponding terminology to be traced in contemporary Judaism. The material reviewed so far has also shown that the designation involves a particular qualification, and is not in simple technical terms a circumlocution for 'Jewess'. In other words, it is necessary to examine more closely the use of θυγάτηρ Ἀβραάμ in 13.16 in relation to other Lukan references to Abraham, Abraham's progeny and Abraham's children. Further, we must ask what resonance this contributes to the use of θυγάτηρ in other Lukan passages.

The formulation of the text in 13.16 is an observation of fact, not the emphatic bestowal of a designation. The woman *is* Abraham's daughter; she does not become one. It is one of the premisses of the healing, not a consequence of it. It is not, however, a statement about a great piety on the woman's part. It sounds like a self-contradiction when it is said of her:

ταύτην δὲ θυγατέρα Ἀβραὰμ οὖσαν,
ἣν ἔδησεν ὁ Σατανᾶς ἰδοὺ δέκα καὶ ὀκτὼ ἔτη.

In relation to the examples discussed above, the surprising element is not primarily the fact that a Jewish woman is called Abraham's daughter. Abraham normally had sons, but daughters could exist too. The surprising element is rather that the woman about whom this is said, is not a paragon of piety, but a woman who has been possessed for a great part of her life. She is not given any attributes that might legitimate a special likeness or relationship to Abraham. Abraham thus plays no role as model or typological prototype. A possessed woman is quite simply confirmed as Abraham's daughter. She is included without conditions in Abraham's family. But this also conditions the change as it is described in the same verse, in a correspondence which chiastically reflects the opening situation:

λυθῆναι ἀπὸ τοῦ δεσμοῦ τούτου
τῇ ἡμέρᾳ τοῦ σαββάτου.

She is set free as a daughter of Abraham – appositely enough on a sabbath day, the day of rest which was an essential sign of the covenant. Her healing is linked to her status as daughter such that the healing realises her status as daughter. As a daughter of Abraham, she shares in the blessing that is promised to Abraham's progeny, and this has a liberating effect on her life. It has already been mentioned that terminological peculiarities in this narrative, together with the emphatic mention of the sabbath day, play on Old Testament traditions of liberation. All these elements converge in 13.16 where the relationship to Abraham is a key factor. It is a consistent trait in Luke-Acts that the motif of liberation is central in the traditions about Abraham: 1.52–3; 1.73–5; Acts 7.6–7.[70]

References to Abraham play an important role in many Lukan passages.[71] The total of fifteen passages is a considerable number, when compared with the other synoptic gospels. The references which have the greatest interest in our present context speak of Abraham's progeny or children and of the divine promise to him and to his descendants: Lk 1.55; 1.72f.; 3.8; 19.9; Acts (2.39); 3.25f.; 7.2–8, 17; 13.26, (32f.; 26.6). As these passages show, the motif tends primarily to appear in typically interpretative passages dealing with salvation history, that is to say the prophetic hymns in the infancy narratives and the speeches in Acts. To a large extent, this is Jewish material which Luke transmits with an accent of his own, but without radical changes.[72]

For Luke, Abraham is primarily the original receiver of God's election and of the promise to the fathers. This is developed further in the history of God with his people in a relationship alternating between fulfilment and renewed promise until the fulfilment in Jesus' life, death and especially his resurrection. The typology too is subordinated to this recurring pattern of promise and fulfilment.[73] Abraham remains a 'historical' person in the past,[74] and his contemporary relevance lies in the fact that Luke's Jewish contemporaries are to be understood as his

---

[70] Moxnes, *Theology in Conflict*, 176.

[71] On the description of this, cf. Dahl's important article, 'Story of Abraham'; and Moxnes, *Theology in Conflict*, 169–79.

[72] Baird, 'Abraham', 368f.; Moxnes, *Theology in Conflict*, 171, 176. It is also remarkable that Luke never alludes to Abraham's sacrifice of Isaac.

[73] Dahl, 'Story of Abraham', 147.

[74] He is indeed also an eschatological figure in some passages in Luke (13.28 and 16.22–31), but his eschatological role in these texts seems to be determined by his historical role. Lk 20.37f. expresses how the association is established between the historical and the eschatological Abraham.

progeny. He is 'father Abraham'. The promise holds good for Abraham's progeny, and to be Abraham's child becomes both a privilege and an obligation. This is why 'Abraham's progeny', 'Abraham's children', 'Abraham's sons' and similar expressions can appear both as verbal variants of 'Jews', 'Israelites' and similar terms, and be used for religious and paraenetic purposes as for example in 4 Maccabees. This naturally also raises the question of defining who is truly to be counted among 'Abraham's children'. Is this a dominant problem for Luke too?[75]

In Acts 7.8, Luke refers to the covenant of circumcision, without any attempt at avoiding this or weakening it.[76] Membership of Abraham's progeny and thereby of the people of the covenantal promise is confirmed by means of the circumcision which is carried out on generation after generation of sons. This is a traditional Jewish idea, and Luke's use of it has been correctly understood as an emphasis on the exclusively Jewish element.[77] This interpretation does, however, overlook the gender aspect and the androcentric point in the intimate connection between membership in the covenant and circumcision – understood in a literal sense and carried out ritually. Only men can possibly carry this mark of membership in covenant, the sign of Abraham, on their bodies and thus physically prove that they are Abraham's sons who beget new sons for him. This is impossible for women; in their very biological shape, they are at best secondary, at worst excluded. Circumcision as the sign of the covenant expresses a male preference which corresponds to the dominance of masculine terms expressing relationships to Abraham. 'Son' becomes the primary category. This makes it all the more necessary to ask how a possessed daughter of Abraham can appear in the Lukan story.

Unlike Paul, Luke neither engages in polemic against circumcision nor spiritualises it. It seems, however, that circumcision no longer plays a decisive role in the definition of membership among Abraham's children. Despite the apparent intact preservation of Jewish tradition, the

[75] This is the opinion both of Karriss, *Luke*, 34, and of Moxnes, *Theology in Conflict*, 174, 176f., 216. According to Moxnes, this was 'a burning issue' among Christian Jews even before Paul.

[76] Moxnes, *Theology in Conflict*, 175.

[77] Dahl, 'The Story of Abraham', 144.

wider context in Luke shows that the social situation which it interprets is special and controversial. Already in the initial phase of the gospel, in the concluding lines of Mary's hymn of praise at 1.54f., reference is made to Old Testament phrases about God's promise τῷ Ἀβραὰμ καὶ τῷ σπέρματι αὐτοῦ and God's fidelity to this promise. The hymn makes it clear that the promise is fulfilled by means of a total social transformation. Through her hymn of praise, the pregnant Mary gives a prophetic interpretation of Jesus' significance, and predicts that the covenantal promise will be fulfilled radically in Jesus' life for the existing progeny of Abraham. When Abraham is mentioned later on, this tends precisely to be in connection with drastic and surprising reversals of fortune, as in 3.8; 13.28; 16.22–31 (and 13.16; 19.9). The individual examples take on the character of a concretisation of salvation history. They show how God's promise to Abraham is fulfilled through Jesus' activity, and the individuals affected thereby are confirmed as the children of Abraham.

With one exception, Luke uses terms inclusive of both women and men, such as σπέρμα and τέκνα, when speaking of Abraham's progeny. Of these terms, σπέρμα has male connotations, but they apply to the figure of Abraham himself. The one exception is found in Acts 13.26, in a direct address to a gathering of male Jews (cf. also 13.16).[78] In other contexts, it is emphasised that the re-established people of God includes men as well as women, ἄνδρες τε καὶ γυναῖκες, (Acts 5.14; 8.3, 12; 9.2, 36ff.; cf. also 1.13f. and 12.12), and sons and daughters, υἱοὶ ... καὶ ... θυγατέρες, (Acts 2.17). In Acts 2.15–21, the outpouring of the Spirit is interpreted on the basis of Joel 3.1–5. Through a repeated gender differentiation, the quotation from Joel is evidence that when God pours out his Spirit in the last days, it will be without respect to age certainly, but also without respect to gender. Only this common share in the Spirit renders eschatological legitimation.[79]

It is especially important in this context, that Peter's Pentecost speech proceeds by making it clear that this gift of the Spirit represents the fulfilment of the promise which God had given earlier (Acts 2.33,

---

[78] The androcentric rhetoric which characterises the speeches in Acts, is, of course, in itself a phenomenon that demands a closer examination, cf. p. 134ff.

[79] This is discussed in greater detail on p. 170ff.

38f.).[80] The Spirit begins to break down divisions, and will not become accommodated to the established structures of authority: Jesus whom they killed has been raised up by God, who has made him Lord and Messiah. He now pours out the Holy Spirit on despised Galileans, and also on the women among them. In the light of this, it is perfectly possible that the quotation from Joel in Acts 2.17 with the promise that 'your daughters' too shall prophesy, represents yet another reference-point for the term 'daughter' in Luke – with a certain, though not explicit, reference to the Abraham tradition. And it provides a basis for the supposition that when Jesus addresses the woman with a haemorrhage in Lk 8.48 with a dismissal formula echoing the liturgy, θυγάτηρ, ἡ πίστις σου σέσωκέν σε: πορεύου εἰς εἰρήνην, he expresses more than a personal and intimate form of address.[81] The terms εἰρήνη and σωτηρία mark the woman's share in salvation and her membership in God's people,[82] and the 'daughter' is thereby given a share in the promise to Abraham's progeny. This case too has the character of a reversal and change, of a surprising overcoming of distance.

Thus it is noteworthy that the two women who are called (Abraham's) daughters, are both sick, socially stigmatised and impure. Impure persons were normally regarded as a threat to the collective purity of the people. Impurity is attached to impure persons and things as an infective and contagious power. This was why the question of pure and impure was a matter of fundamental social and religious allocation. It is characteristic that the only man in the gospel to be called Abraham's son is the tax-collector Zacchaeus (19.9).[83] In 19.1, he is presented as a

---

[80] Cf. Moxnes, *Theology in Conflict*, 216, who holds that this is in keeping with Paul's interpretation as well.

[81] As is claimed by Blank, 'Frauen', 15, with support in Pesch and Gnilka.

[82] Ἑιρήνη is the keynote of the community of God. Cf. Moxnes, *Patrons*, 157, with reference to Lk 1.79; 2.14; 10.5f.; 19.44. On the relationship between εἰρήνη and σωτηρία in Luke, cf. Swartley, 'Politics and Peace', 34f.

[83] Karris, *Luke*, 34; Leipoldt, *Jesus*, 123 n. 127, who interprets this as a previous stage to Paul's discussion in Rom 4.11. Witherington, *Women in the Ministry of Jesus*, 70, has no hesitation in seeing here 'Jesus' use of the term'. Tannehill, *Narrative Unity*, 125f., 136, has given an apposite analysis of the use of the term in the story about Zacchaeus, son of Abraham; cf. also Kariamadam, *Zacchaeus-story*, 41f. On the impurity of tax-collectors because of their contact with impure superiors and with impure money, cf. Jeremias, 'Zöllner', 294.

superintendent of taxes and very rich, and we are told plainly in 19.7 that general opinion held him to be a sinful man with whom there should be no social contact. This is the one of whom Jesus says, καὶ αὐτὸς υἱὸς 'Αβραάμ ἐστιν, and the form of expression has the same quality of just stating a fact as was seen in the case of the possessed woman in 13.16. The statement justifies (καθότι) the coming of salvation to Zacchaeus' house through Jesus' presence and the consequent change of life. Jesus reaffirms that the tax-collector Zacchaeus is a son of Abraham and thereby heir to the promise of salvation. Thus he reinstates Zacchaeus also as a true Jew, in opposition to the initial evaluation which defined him as an alienated sinner.[84] This set of designations is used in Luke only to speak of women and men who were considered in Jewish society to be impure and excluded, and who are then rehabilitated through Jesus' intervention.[85] They are indeed far removed from the pious heroic portrait of 4 Maccabees.

God is now raising up children for Abraham whom no one had expected, – the warning word here should be noted of John the Baptist in 3.8, καὶ μὴ ἄρξησθε λέγειν ἐν ἑαυτοῖς Πατέρα ἔχομεν τὸν 'Αβραάμ λέγω γὰρ ὑμῖν ὅτι δύναται ὁ θεὸς ἐκ τῶν λίθων τούτων ἐγεῖραι τέκνα τῷ 'Αβραάμ. The question about who is to be counted as Abraham's children (note the gender-inclusive term)[86] and thus share in God's fulfilment of the promise, as foretold in 1.55f. and 1.74f., is raised here with full weight and with critical sharpness. There is no use in appealing to Abraham as their father, unless they bear the fruit of repentance. Also regarding Abraham's children, God is

[84] Tannehill, *Narrative Unity*, 124f., sees this as the main point of the whole story and underlines, 125 n. 34, in a critical commentary to the use made of Zacchaeus by Schottroff, Stegemann and Pilgrim as a paradigm for rich Christians in Luke's situation: 'While we need not deny that Zacchaeus has relevance for rich Christians, this interpretation ignores the fact that the story speaks first of all to the problem of alienation within Judaism'. Cf. also Moxnes, *Theology in Conflict*, 176.

[85] Jervell does not pick up this aspect in his article about Abraham's daughters. It is an aspect that the designation does not explicitly convey in a linguistic sense, but it is in keeping with the use of Abraham traditions elsewhere in Luke, and becomes very clear through the concrete instances to which the designation is applied.

[86] Another example of the use of τέκνα because this can cover both sons and daughters, can be found in Acts 2.38 cf. Acts 2.17. Mt 3.9 indicates that the saying of John (from Q) was known to Luke in this suitable form.

sovereign with regard to creation and election. These words of John are part of the theological programme carried out by Jesus in the gospel narrative: God raises up children to Abraham from the stones. There is also an emphasis on the critical and controversial aspect of this miracle of God. These children replace others who claim their rights as the children of Abraham,[87] and the legitimation of these new children creates conflict with the established Jewish leadership.[88]

This social expansion does not, however, necessarily imply a general universalism,[89] even if it betrays a universalist potential. Israel's boundaries are stretched, but they are not broken through. The discussion in Acts 15 of the status of the Gentile Christians and of whether the demands of the law of Moses apply to them, is not directly relevant here, since in Luke non-Jews are never called Abraham's children (as they are in Paul). Luke's exclusive concern is with Jewish women and men, in other words the designation is employed exclusively within a Jewish framework: Israel is still the chosen people of God, Abraham's progeny,[90] even if this Israel looks surprisingly different. The suggestion that the verb ἀνορθόω in 13.13 is to be associated with the use of the same verb in Acts 15.16, demands that the healing of the woman bent double is taken as a symbolic expression for the reconstruction of Israel in the group of those who believe in Jesus. The designation 'Abraham's daughter' would then have the same corporative symbolic meaning as in some rabbinic texts.[91] Quite apart from the fact that the connection between the two passages is extremely slender, this interpretation completely overlooks the value of the narrative in Lk 13.10–17 as a concretisation. At the same time, it is correct in pointing to its exemplary significance.

The daughters of Abraham whom God raises up through the activity

---

[87] Cf. Moxnes, *Patrons*, 149: 'Luke portrays the Pharisees as slaves of mammon, not of God, and in the parable in 16.19–31, it becomes obvious that the rich, the slaves of mammon, cannot be sons of Abraham'. Moxnes has published an abridged version, *Economy*, but my references are to the previous and longer manuscript, *Patrons*.

[88] Cf. for 13.10–17, Egelkraut, *Jesus' Mission*, 214; Kariamadam, *Zacchaeus-story*, 42.

[89] As is supposed by some, for example Fitzmyer, *Luke*, 1012.

[90] Dahl, 'Story of Abraham', 151: 'Luke does not claim that the church has replaced Israel as the people of God, nor does he call the Gentile believers Abraham's children'. This point is taken up emphatically by Jervell.

[91] Hamm, 'Freeing of Bent Woman', 34f.

of Jesus do not attribute this status to themselves. They neither lay claim, nor do they fight their way to any right. It is Jesus who sovereignly acknowledges that they have such a status, and this acknowledgment is accompanied by a dramatic, healing alteration in their lives. Salvation has come to them.[92] In this way, it is characteristic that in the narrative about Zacchaeus too, the decisive initiative comes from Jesus himself. This is similar to the healing narratives in which women are helped. An exception is the 'sinful woman' who anoints Jesus in Lk 7.36–50 in sovereign disdain of all norms for respectable conduct. But otherwise, the women do not come openly and courageously to Jesus with their request for help. Their appeals are indirect: others ask for help on their behalf (Lk 4.48), or they hide themselves in the crowd (Lk 8.43). For the most part, they are in the same place as Jesus, and he sees them and acts; thus a certain respect is retained for rules of decency which made it improper for women to address an unknown man.

This becomes especially clear when comparing narratives about men and women which can be said, for various reasons, to be parallel. Already the contrasting parallelisation between Zechariah and Mary exemplifies such a difference. Zechariah is told that his prayer has been heard (Lk 1.13), while Mary surprisingly becomes the one who re-ceives; she is κεχαριτωμένη (Lk 1.28).[93] The contrast fits into the gender-determined pattern, but it is also understandable on the basis of their different ages and life situations. It would be incredible that the young virgin Mary had already besought God for a child.

The distinguished Jairus appeals very humbly but still directly to Jesus and begs him to come to his home (Lk 8.41). The woman with haemorrhages does indeed reach out to get help for herself,[94] but she

---

[92] Seen in this way, it makes sense that the story about the healing of the bent woman is followed by two parables about the wonderful growth of the kingdom of God, 13.18–21. Cf. Busse, *Wunder*, 303. For the miraculous element in Luke's version of these two parables, cf. Seim, 'Gudsrikets overraskelse'.

[93] Laurentin, *Truth of Christmas*, 20, 151.

[94] Tannehill, *Narrative Unity*, 136, lays extreme emphasis on this when he claims: 'The primary issue is not whether the woman will be healed ... – but how Jesus will respond to an unclean woman who violates religious taboos by touching him without permission'. This is to overlook the role which the history of the illness, the healing and, not least, the public proclamation play in the story.

comes under the cover of the crowd of people, hidden and approaching Jesus from behind, fearful and afraid. The dramatic interweaving of the two narratives[95] thus plays on a set of contrasts between the synagogue president Jairus and the impoverished and impure woman. They are also played off against one another when the woman with haemorrhages is the cause, in the combined narrative, of Jesus' delay on the way to Jairus' dying daughter.

A similar parallelising contrast is found between Jairus and the widow in Nain.[96] Both have an only daughter (θυγάτηρ μονογενὴς 8.42)[97] or son (μονογενὴς υἱός 7.12) called back to life. Jesus raises up Jairus' twelve-year-old daughter, who is of marriageable age,[98] and the widow's son who provides for her. But while Jairus himself takes the initiative for this to happen and comes to fetch Jesus with his request, the woman is quite simply seen by Jesus and awakens his compassion, καὶ ἰδὼν αὐτὴν ὁ κύριος ἐσπλαγχνίσθη ἐπ'αὐτῇ 7.13.

There may be several reasons for the omission in Luke of the narrative about the Canaanite woman in Mk 7.24–30. But provided that Luke did know the story from Mark, it is not impossible that the woman's quick-witted insistence has been seen as 'out of order'.[99] As she is described in Mark, she is a capable, argumentative variant of Jairus, and she would be an excellent parallel to the Gentile officer at Capernaum (Lk. 7.1–10). Instead, the latter is placed next to the widow

---

[95] It remains an open question, at what stage of the tradition this interweaving took place, but in any case, it is clear that Luke has known it in this form from Mark.

[96] Cf. Fitzmyer, *Luke*, 744.

[97] The expression indicates that she is the only child, not merely the only daughter, cf. Fitzmyer, *Luke*, 745.

[98] Twelve years was probably the marriageable age for girls, cf. Jeremias, *Jerusalem*, 363ff.; Gardner, *Women*, 38ff. In the Jewish context, the father had full rights over daughters until they reached the age of twelve and a half: in other words, they were usually married off before they had any right to speak for themselves. The number twelve constitutes a connecting link between the two interwoven stories: Jairus' daughter is twelve years old and the sick woman has suffered haemorrhages for twelve years. Cf. Schüssler Fiorenza: 'The girl gets up and walks, she rises to womanhood ... . The young woman who begins to menstruate like the old woman who experiences menstruation as a pathological condition are both given a new life'.

[99] Jervell, 'Töchter Abrahams', 81, indicates that she is omitted because she is not a Jewess, but he makes the reservation in n. 21: 'wir haben ja hier mit der grossen Lücke zu tun, Mk 6, 45–8, 26'.

of Nain, who needs her son to be alive and is the passive object of Jesus' compassion. The coupling of these two narratives also corresponds to the parallel examples of Elijah and Elisha to which Jesus refers in his speech in Nazareth at Lk 4.24–7 (cf. 1 Kg 17 and 2 Kg 5).[100]

On the whole a respectable reserve is maintained on the part of the women who appear in Luke's healing narratives. They do not fight their way, and when a woman does once reach out to take help for herself (8.44), she attempts to remain hidden and must make the greatest efforts to overcome herself when she does step forward (8.47). The women are helped by Jesus to achieve a vital transformation in their lives – and by crossing the boundaries created by concepts of impurity and by social marginalisation, the women are rehabilitated as Abraham's daughters with a right to share in the community of the people of God and salvation. But in the healing narratives thus far, they have been portrayed primarily as recipients.

III.3. *Women – healed to serve the family of God.*

Healed by Jesus, the women actively carry out a function. as is evident from the summary narrative in 8.1–3, the women serve Jesus and the twelve. The miracle narratives contribute to the Lukan description of Jesus as a benefactor, εὐεργέτης,[101] also in relation to women. His benefaction consequently makes them benefactors.[102] This happens in a

---

[100] This means that Jesus is to be understood as the great prophet, also seen in relation to John the Baptist, cf. Brodie, 'Luke 7.36–50', 465f.; Johnson, *Literary Function*, 97–100; Muhlack, *Parallellen*, 58f.

[101] Danker, *Luke*, 6–17, argues that the fundamental christological model in Luke is Jesus as benefactor. This is an important feature in the contemporary ideal of the ruler. Cf. also Danker's more detailed exposition in *Benefactor*.

[102] It would have fitted well if Witherington, 'On the Road', 245, had been correct in saying that 'Luke's fondness for parallelism may be seen in his use of κηρύσσω and εὐαγγελίζω, θεραπεύω and διακονέω, and πνεῦμα and δαιμόνιον'. In support of this, he argues that θεραπεύω in 'secular' Greek can mean to serve, and thus has the same meaning as διακονέω. But he himself mentions the fundamental objection that θεραπεύω in the New Testament is never used 'with only the sense of serve' (with the possible exception of Acts 17.25).

Cf. also Danker's designation, *Luke*, 15f., of the apostles as 'delegate benefactors'. This involves a certain democratisation of the ideal of the ruler.

way that breaks with an ideal of total reciprocity in which the one service is worth the other.

Jesus' second miracle in Luke's gospel is his healing of Simon's mother-in-law (4.38–9). Luke's relocation of this narrative, when compared to Mark's, means that Simon (Peter) is mentioned here for the first time in this gospel. Thus the reason for the healing is not Simon's status as a disciple: rather, the healing prepares the way for the narrative of Simon's calling in 5.1–11. The woman is sick with a high fever, and Jesus threatens (ἐπιτιμάω)[103] the fever so that it leaves her. The conclusion of the story relates that, when the fever has left her, παραχρῆμα δὲ ἀναστᾶσα διηκόνει αὐτοῖς. Just as the fever was serious, so the demonstration of her recovered health is immediate. At once, she rises and serves them. Some textual witnesses alter the plural αὐτοῖς to a singular αὐτῷ. This is the case both in Mark and in Luke, but not for the same textual witnesses. Ἀυτῷ is, however, a harmonising reading under the influence of the parallel passage in Matthew (Mt 8.15) and possibly also of Mk 15.40. For Matthew's text the endeavours at harmonising have gone in the opposite direction. The singular form would give a christological emphasis, and also enhance the impression that the woman's service would be the repayment she makes according to a customary pattern of reciprocity.[104] The plural form tones this down. Jesus becomes the benefactor who, rather than ensuring repayments in kind for himself, creates benefactors for the larger group. It is therefore of less interest to establish more precisely which persons receive the woman's service.

The verb διακονέω occurs for the first time in Luke in 4.39. In normal Greek usage, the verb has the meaning 'to serve' with a strong connotation of waiting on someone.[105] This can have a more general reference, but it tends to be linked to meals and food. The social associations were in the main negative: such service was a task of lowly status. But in the Jewish context, this was ambiguous. If the person one served was worthy of honour, the service itself was also a matter of honour. It is,

---

[103] This is a further example of how Luke describes healing in exorcistic categories.
[104] This is how Moxnes interprets it in 'Meals', 162f.
[105] Bauer, 'διακονέω', 83.

however, striking that the LXX never uses the verb διακονέω in its translation of equivalent Hebrew terms like 'abad' and 'sheret', and that the nouns διακονία and διάκονος occur only very seldom.[106] Other contemporary Jewish sources like Philo and Josephus employ διακονέω – Philo in the ordinary Greek sense, and Josephus also as an expression for obedience and for the priestly service, that is in a more metaphorical sense.[107] While dignity is linked to the metaphorical significance of the word, its concrete meaning retains the note of social debasement. The concrete usage is also by far the more common.

Luke uses διακον-terms with a clear preference for the verb. A table of the frequency compared with other New Testament writings gives an interesting picture:[108]

	Lk	Acts	Mt	Mk	Jn	Paul	NT–rest
Διακονέω	8	2	5	4	3	5	7
Διακονία	1	8	0	0	0	16	4
Διάκονος	0	0	3	2	3	11	10

The overview shows that Luke is the New Testament author who most often employs the verb διακονέω, ten times in all if we take Luke and Acts together. The substantive διακονία which he employs nine times, even if here, Paul has far more occurrences than Luke. On the other hand, Luke is the only writer who does not employ διάκονος. He avoids this substantive completely, even in cases where the already-existing Markan text uses it. It is also interesting to look at the internal distribution of the various terms in Luke. While διακονέω dominates in the gospel, διακονία has a corresponding sovereignty

---

[106] For a more general analysis of the concept and use, cf., apart from Beyer, 'διακονέω' in *Theologisches Wörterbuch*, also Hennessey, 'Diakonia', and Cranfield, 'Diakonia', on which Hennessey is based to a very great extent.

[107] The verb 'abad' is variously translated by δουλεύω, λατρεύω and even ἐργάζομαι, and the noun 'æbæd' by παῖς or δοῦλος. 'Sheret' is usually translated by λειτουργέω, which takes care of the cultic usage. Cf. Hennessey, 'Diakonia', 62f.

[108] The statistical information is taken from Via, 'Women', 37. This overview does not count Colossians and Ephesians as Pauline, nor is the list assigned to different categories in terms of variants of meaning.

in Acts. This reflects to some extent the picture common to most writings in the New Testament: while there is traditional broad attestation for διακονέω (also in the gospel material), it is clear that διακονία is a term strongly linked to Pauline contexts. Nonetheless, this difference between the gospel and Acts is a challenge to the interpretation of Luke's two-volume work at this point. The same is true of the relationship between the various spheres in which διακονέω is used in the gospel. It is used (1) in the narrative description of women (4.39; 8.3; 10.40); (2) in parables, that is in a narrative, but on a metaphorical level about the servant, δοῦλος, who waits on his master (17.8) or vice versa (12.37). This prepares for the transition to (3) a christologically based usage (22.26–7).[109] At the outset, however, it is important to establish that the various spheres of use need not imply that the meaning of the word changes accordingly. It can nevertheless retain its connotation of concrete service, waiting on others and caring for them.

As far as Peter's mother-in-law in 4.39 is concerned, it is best in the immediate context to understand διηκόνει αὐτοῖς to mean that the woman, thanks to Jesus' healing, was immediately able to fulfil the obligations of hospitality in seeing that Jesus and his party were served.[110] The preparation and serving of food were traditionally the women's responsibility and task, unless slaves took care of it. The extent to which the women of the house also served at table when the family (the male members) had guests varied according to religious norms, ideals of propriety, and cultural and social location. Often, while women had the responsibility for the preparation of the food, they did not always

---

[109] Via, 'Women', 38, makes things too simple when she claims that the examples of διακονέω in Luke fall into two clearly-distinguished categories: διακονέω as the role of women or as a model of discipleship.

[110] Since this statement closes the story, Kirchschläger, *Jesu exorzistisches Wirken*, 58, wishes to give it a 'deeper meaning' and 'einen bekenntnishaften Inhalt' in line with other closing statements in healing narratives. It is a question not only of 'äussere Bedienung, sondern um die echte Gesinnung des Dienens als zu – und Unterordnung zu Jesus'. However, a convincing exegetical argument is lacking. It is not sufficient to assume that 'Im urchristlichen Kontext hat das Wort aber noch tiefere Bedeutung'. Nor does it help to give a list of scattered evidence of parallels and of interpretative statements without arguing for the presence of genuine similarity.

serve at table, because they would then have had to appear in front of strangers. Under reduced conditions, this was presumably unavoidable. But the women did not themselves take part in the meal, although this could happen among the more aristocratic and well-off members of society.[111]

Meals in antiquity were subject to strict hierarchical regulation, both as regards places at table[112] and distribution of tasks. The one who waited at table was always the one with the lowest place in the household. Where house slaves were common, the role of waiter was more specific to slaves than specific to women.[113] But it is probable that by far the greatest number of families did not have house slaves,[114] and among Jews, especially in Palestine where it was not very common to have slaves,[115] the task probably fell to the women of the family. At the same time, Luke reflects a situation in which, at any rate, servants were not unusual: cf. 12.35ff. and 17.7ff. And Rhoda at Acts 12.13 is presumably a slave. Altogether, this was an area in which customs varied, because it represented an area of tension between tasks assigned according to gender and status and norms of propriety which implied segregation of the sexes. In later rabbinic material, the demands for propriety make strong advances, and women are forbidden to wait on any men other than their own husbands.[116] It is, however, difficult to say what praxis is presupposed by such exhortations. Perhaps they are better regarded as reactions and measures to exercise control over against a praxis which the rabbis considered as frivolous,[117] and which may have been subject especially to Roman influence.

[111] According to Thraede, 'Ärger', 41, this was quite common at symposia in Hellenistic and Roman circles.

[112] The exhortations in Lk 14.7ff. presuppose this with complete clarity.

[113] Schottroff, 'Maria Magdalena', 12. On the contempt for this service, cf. Beyer, 'διακονέω', 81ff.

[114] Cf. Verner, Household of God, 60f.

[115] Cf. Jeremias, Jerusalem, 110: 'We find most of the slaves in the city, and even here, except at court, their number is not large'; in more detail 345ff. On the discussion about slavery in Palestine, cf. Bartchy, First-Century Slavery, 31–34.

[116] Blank, 'Frauen', 14. But cf. the criticism by Schottroff/Stegemann against generalising about Judaism on the basis of individual rabbinic statements, 'Maria Magdalena', 10f. n. 26.

[117] It is no longer possible simply to assume that exhortations directly reflect the current ethos. Cf. Keck's pioneering article, 'Ethos of Early Christianity'.

Taken as a whole, therefore, it is uncertain whether it is correct to claim, as some have done, that when in the narrative about Peter's mother-in-law Jesus and others allow themselves to be waited on by a woman outside the closest family, or perhaps that a woman undertakes to wait on them, this represents a radical break with traditional norms of conduct.[118] It might just as well be the reflection of an entirely conventional situation with men and women in their usual places.[119] The narrative itself does not seem to suggest that the situation is extraordinary. It describes how Jesus enjoys much-appreciated hospitality in Simon's house, and how one of the women in the house, Peter's mother-in-law, waits on them or gives them food to eat as is right and fitting, as soon as the fever has left her thanks to the healing power of Jesus. Her service is a sign of health, the proof that she has become well. It is Jesus' act of healing which makes her service possible. She becomes capable of returning to her duties. The element of continuity in the service is emphasised by the imperfect form διηκόνει.

In 8.3, the healed women who follow Jesus are assigned a serving function in a similar manner – described in words which correspond to 4.39: διηκόνουν αὐτοῖς ἐκ τῶν ὑπαρχόντων αὐταῖς. Over against the Markan text in Mk 15.41, Luke has added a specification to διακονέω: the women serve them ἐκ τῶν ὑπαρχόντων αὐταῖς. Luke makes frequent use of ὑπάρχω and is the only author in the New Testament who writes τὰ ὑπάρχοντά τινι, that is the participle functioning as a substantive with the dative of the person (cf. also Lk 12.15 and Acts 4.32).[120] The addition alters the emphasis away from an actual meal situation and towards a more general sense of support and provision. This also makes good sense in the context supposed here, with the whole company wandering from place to place.

In the same way as in 4.39, a number of textual witnesses choose in 8.3 to read the singular αὐτῷ instead of the plural αὐτοῖς, so that the

---

[118] Blank, 'Frauen', 14; Schürmann, *Lukas*, 252. Witherington, *Women in the Ministry of Jesus*, 67, succeeds in contradicting himself when he claims on the one hand that this breaks with traditional role-patterns, while at the same time characterising the women's service as true to convention.

[119] Tannehill, *Narrative Unity*, 138, though there in connection with Lk 8.3.

[120] Jeremias, *Sprache*, 178.

women serve only Jesus and not the twelve as well. Once again, the variant can be explained technically as a harmonisation with a synoptic parallel, this time in Mk 15.41. In other words, it is to be considered as secondary. But at the same time, it sheds light on the change of meaning which Lk 8.2f. implies over against Mk 15.40f. on this point. In the Lukan version, the women who follow Jesus, serve – in the same way as Peter's mother-in-law – not only him (Jesus), but also them (the whole group of disciples). This is clearly an important point. When service is directed to Jesus alone in 10.40,[121] he rejects it as unnecessary. At the same time, the gospel portrays Jesus as surrounded by women's care from his birth to his grave – although the διακον-terminology itself is not applied. Mary wraps the new-born baby and lays him in a crib, 2.6.[122] And the Galilean women prepare fragrant oils and ointment, and run the risk of going to the grave with this, 23.55–24.1f.

If we take the passage as a whole, it can seem that when Luke changes αὐτῷ to αὐτοῖς and adds that element linking the women's service to their property, he is changing the strong sense of relationship to Jesus found in the description and terminology of discipleship in Mk 15.40f. The women are no longer seen as disciples, but are directed to a special function of care which is determined in material terms.[123] The parallel to Peter's mother-in-law is clear, and despite a certain expansion of meaning when compared to 4.39, διακονέω retains in 8.3 an important association with food and physical care. In 8.1–3, thus, we are given an apparently simple picture of Jesus accompanied by the twelve and by a group of women who use what they possess in order to provide for the men, who have forsaken everything (5.11) and no longer have possessions of their own. The women take care of the

---

[121] Gerhardsson, *Memory*, 239, does indeed hold that the (other) disciples too are present on this occasion, i.e. that ἡ καὶ παρακαθεσθεῖσα in 10.39 means that Mary *too* sat at Jesus' feet. It is doubtful whether καὶ may be interpreted in this way, cf. Jeremias, *Sprache*, 193.

[122] Friis Plum, *Tilslørede Frihed*, 64, 128 n. 72, claims that this is the only point in the birth narrative where a woman's experience is genuinely expressed.

[123] This is claimed by Schottroff, 'Maria Magdalena', 10, and Schüssler Fiorenza, *In Memory*, 50f. This means on their part, a critical evaluation of Luke and a preference for Mark's version.

material needs of the group. Whether they are on the road with Jesus or stay in the house which he/the company visits, they represent the basis of sustenance for Jesus and those who follow him. Luke's text is strikingly similar in its description of the wandering women who give support and the hospitable women who are stationary and have a household.[124] Irrespective of the situation, their activity is to be understood in terms of service: in three of the texts, διακονέω (4.39; 8.3) or διακονία (10.40) is used to express this.

The women's service often seems to be connected with a certain prosperity. As has been mentioned above, this is especially prominent in 8.2f. through the socio-economic localisation of Joanna. The expression ἐκ τῶν ὑπαρχόντων αὐταῖς also presupposes that the women have means at their own disposal, even if it does not necessarily imply that they are all equally well-off. Their contributions need not in each case have been great in quantity.[125] The forms of the names also indicate, as has been shown, that the women had their identity independently from any relationship to a man. This associates the group of women who follow Jesus in Galilee with the relatively well-off, independent women whom, as patronae accommodate the community and/or sustain it: Martha in Lk 10; Tabitha in Acts 9; Mary in Acts 12; Lydia in Acts 16; and also Priscilla in Acts 18.

Roman law at this period allowed women to inherit and to own and manage their own property. This was especially – some would say, exclusively – the case for women who were not *in potestate*, but were in one way or another *sui iuris*.[126] In practice, more women had means at

---

[124] In his analysis of the Jesus-movement, especially in 'Wanderradikalismus' and *Soziologie der Jesusbewegung*, Theissen has tried to understand the transmission and shaping of the tradition about Jesus in the interaction between itinerant charismatics and stationary sympathisers who supported the wandering prophets, but could not themselves live up to the ideal demands. It is, however, remarkable that Theissen never introduces the category of gender. When he tries to make amends for this with a chapter on women in *The Shadow of the Galilean*, what he writes is strangely romantic.

[125] Cf. Heine, *Frauen der frühen Christenheit*, 69: '... für die Gruppe nicht Reichtum und Besitz Bedeutung hat, sondern für einige Zeit leben zu können, bis das Eingebrachte aufgebraucht war'.

[126] Gardner, *Women*, 9f., 71ff. Schüssler Fiorenza, *In Memory*, 182, is more absolute. Cf. also Verner, *Household of God*, 39f.

their own disposal.[127] Even if the legislation in the Greek and Jewish contexts was stricter, a relaxation occurred in the Hellenistic period permitting women a certain right to own property.[128] The majority of women had their lives filled with and limited by domestic obligations and with little external activity, but there are also many examples in antiquity of professionally active women.[129] This was true, not only of slave women who had no choice but to work, or for small farms in the countryside which required the labour of the whole family. The women in question were not especially rich, nor particularly poor. Some worked in family businesses or workshops (cf. Priscilla, who operated a tent-making business together with Aquila, Acts 18.3). Otherwise, women tended to work in professions which were a natural continuation of their domestic duties, and were concerned with food, fabrics and clothes, health and comfort. This means that they were active in small-trade and in-service industries, and as doctors and midwives.[130] Some women were economically self-supporting. The archaeological material, despite all its limitation, indicates that they were proud of their work.[131] Some of the women not only contributed to the daily maintenance of the family, but were also able to lay by some reserves for themselves.

Women with means could function as financial benefactors for public and religious projects and for various kinds of groups with particular interests, and through their patronage they were able to acquire an influence which was otherwise formally denied them in public life.[132] This was also the case

[127] Gardner, *Women*, 17f., 69, 72.
[128] Witherington, *Women in the Ministry of Jesus*, 5f., gives evidence of this both from recent archaeological finds and from rabbinic sources. Verner, *Household of God*, 35f., discusses especially Hellenistic Egypt and also gives a very positive interpretation of Jewish legislation, 45.
[129] Kampen, *Image and Status*, has made a very interesting contribution on the basis of archaeological material from Ostia near Rome. Cf. also Meeks, *Urban Christians*, 24; Thraede, 'Ärger', 46f.; Portefaix, *Sisters Rejoice*, 24f.
[130] Kampen, *Image and Status*, 133f.; Portefaix, *Sisters Rejoice*, 24.
[131] Kampen, *Image and Status*, 131ff.
[132] Meeks, *Urban Christians*, 24f.; Hands, *Charities*, 54, mentions that public 'honorific patronages' were open to women when times were hard and there was a lack of willing male candidates. Also within Judaism, it was possible for rich women at least in Diaspora communities to attain the position of *Mater synagogarum*, cf. Brooten, *Women Leaders*; Thraede, 'Ärger', 92; Witherington, 'On the Road', 244f. It is a matter of discussion, what was contained in the title of honour in terms of power and practical functions. On this see further p. 99 n. 8.

for the earliest Christian communities, which included a considerable number of rich and highly placed women, and Luke gives, especially in Acts, a pertinent picture of such women who kept house for the community. The description of the women in 8.2f., however, cannot be explained simply against this background. Here various themes are combined in a condensed manner: the women's share in the social sacrifice involved in the movement around Jesus, the new healed life which Jesus has given them in serving the community, and the activity of the rich women as benefactors. The connecting element is a metaphorical use of kinship categories.

This Lukan conception implies ambiguously both the abandonment of women's traditional life and a reaffirmation of it. Like the men who follow Jesus, the women too have departed and set out on an itinerant life with Jesus. Mainly women who have received a new life (previously impure, sick and possessed women) through Jesus' intervention, they receive their new family in the group of disciples whether or not they actually give up their old family.

A key text in this connection is Lk 8.19–21 (par. Mk 3.31–5; Mt 12.46–50). Jesus, surrounded by his disciples (8.19) and by a crowd of people, rejects an approach by his mother and his brothers. In this special scene, Mary is not mentioned by name, as is the case elsewhere in the synoptic material.[133] The focus is not on her person but on her motherhood. Jesus challenges the claims of his biological family by transferring the categories of kinship to a new group: μήτηρ μου καὶ ἀδελφοί μου οὗτοί εἰσιν οἱ τὸν λόγον τοῦ θεοῦ ἀκούοντες καὶ ποιοῦντες. His mother and his brothers and sisters become those who live in the same obedience as he himself does. Yet compared with Mark and Matthew, Luke renders the statement of Jesus in a shortened version which is more inclusive of this biological family. The rhetorical question, τίς ἐστιν ἡ μήτηρ μου καὶ οἱ ἀδελφοί (μου); (Mk 3.33) is missing in Luke. Nor does he describe any gesture of election such as Jesus' look in Mark or in Matthew, the movement of Jesus' hand accompanying the utterance by which he confers this designation (cf. Mk 3.34) marking the group of disciples as his family in contrast to

---

[133] In John, on the other hand, the name Mary is never used, only the designation 'the mother of Jesus', cf. Seim, 'Roles of Women', 60–6.

his biological family. In the Lukan version neither the biological family nor the crowd nor any disciple is given any particular position. They are all included. This means that the proclamation of who is truly a member of Jesus' family has less the character of exclusion and election, and more generally becomes a statement of principle. The point is not primarily to exclude Jesus' mother and brothers and sisters in favour of the others who are present (the disciples), but rather to transform and transfer kinship categories on the basis of a new set of criteria. Thus Luke turns the abandoning of family relationships more in the direction of redefinition. Even the maternal claims which were essential to a woman's identity and status are revoked and replaced by discipleship as the new form of motherhood. But the option is kept open for his mother and his brothers and sisters too – to find their place in the new family – provided that, without any privileges and like the others, they fulfil the criterion of hearing God's word and doing it.[134] But the use of kinship categories in Lk 8.19–21 still retains a clearly critical function in relation to biological family and their demands. The new family does not merely surpass the old,[135] but replaces it.

The pericope in 8.19–21 lies within the proximate context of 8.1–3. Between these two texts, in 8.4–18, we find the parable of the sower and its exposition, with wisdom sayings and exhortations attached. In Mark, the parable of the sower follows the rejection of Jesus' original family, while the previous context takes up accusations against Jesus that he must be mad and possessed. According to Mark, Jesus' kin share the concern that he is 'confused' (3.21), and since they consider that he is not in a state to look after himself, they fulfil their obligations by going out to take responsibility for him. In comparison with this arrangement in Mark, the context is reversed in Luke so that the par-

---

[134] Robinson, 'Preaching', 133, 137 n. 20 and 21, who also points out that Luke has kept οὐδεὶς προφήτης δεκτός ἐστιν ἐν τῇ πατρίδι αὐτοῦ in 4.24 in the scene at Nazareth (4.16–30), but eliminates Mark's further embroidering of the scene, Mk 6.4: καὶ ἐν τοῖς συγγενεῦσιν αὐτοῦ καὶ ἐν τῇ οἰκίᾳ αὐτοῦ.

[135] Fitzmyer, Luke, 723, tones down the rejection by regarding the new family as transcending, not as replacing the original kinship group. Another Roman-Catholic exegete, Brown, Birth of Messiah, 371–8, even wishes to see 8.21 as expressing praise for the faith of the mother and the brethren. Cf. also Witherington, Women in the Ministry of Jesus, 16, 140f. n. 48.

able comes first. This also eliminates the negative considerations about madness which serves as the immediate occasion of the critical encounter with his mother and brothers and sisters in Mark – at the cost of having no concrete cause for the encounter in Lk 8.19ff. What errand Jesus' kin may have had at the outset in 8.19 is apparently of no interest. The dominant connecting link becomes instead the question about 'hearing the word' and the implications of this in people's lives.[136]

Lk 8.4–18 thus gives us the criteria for membership in the new family. The transfer of family terms also implies, however, that a new group is actually established. In the context this is taken care of by means of 8.1–3. Both 8.21 and 8.1–3 indicate that the group consisted both of women and of men. It does indeed appear that the Lukan text in 8.21 is not as gender-specific as that of Mark and Matthew in the listing of family terms. While they mention ἀδελφός μου καὶ ἀδελφὴ καὶ μήτηρ (Mk 3.35 par. Mt 12.50), Luke contents himself with two categories, μήτηρ μου καὶ ἀδελφοί μου (Lk 8.21). But there are many reasons for not interpreting this as an androcentric move rendering the sisters in God's family invisible.[137] The plural form ἀδελφοί, which is employed instead of the singular form used by the other evangelists, can be read inclusively as meaning 'siblings', that is as a plural common form for both ἀδελφός and ἀδελφή.[138] It is also possible that, as the representation of women was already taken care of by means of μήτηρ the point is to avoid a pleonasm, while at the same time creating a verbal parallel corresponding to the presentation of Jesus' biological family in 8.19 and 20, which mention precisely his mother and brothers/siblings. Moreover, the term 'mother' carries greater dignity than the term 'sister'.

The repeated μου in Lk 8.21 emphasises that the family terms do not primarily relate 'those who hear God's word and do it' to one

---

[136] Horn, *Glaube*, 236f. This is also a decisive argument against Dawsey's claim, 'Literary Unity', 15, that Luke here is only reproducing Markan material, and that the kinship terminology consequently cannot be considered to be significant.

[137] Tetlow, *Women and Ministry*, 137, claims that 'although Luke in this passage is attempting to omit the presence (of sisters) generally among the disciples, he cannot avoid affirming the presence of at least one woman, Mary'. She thus completely fails to appreciate the transfer of family terms.

[138] Cf. Hauglin, 'ἀδελφοί'.

another in a family relationship, but to Jesus. They become his mother and brothers (and sisters). Jesus establishes the new family as his family, at a critical distance from the ties and demands of his biological family. The family relationship which they gain in respect to one another is based on their adherence to him. By becoming his family, they are linked to one another by family ties. Possibly the fact that the family connection is established primarily in relation to Jesus and only indirectly among the believers themselves, explains why Luke prefers the term disciple in the gospel while Jesus is with them, but usually employs ἀδελφοί in Acts.[139]

The primary association to Jesus is also important because it opens the way to speak, not only of Jesus' family, but of God's family. In the parallel text in Matthew, this evangelist's preference for calling God the heavenly Father gives an explicit warrant for the constitution of the new family with Jesus' heavenly Father as the ultimate authority: ὅστις γὰρ ἂν ποιήσῃ τὸ θέλημα τοῦ πατρός μου τοῦ ἐν οὐρανοῖς αὐτός μου ἀδελφὸς καὶ ἀδελφὴ καὶ μήτηρ ἐστίν. This ultimate authority in the family is detached from the earthly context, so that no one in the new family can be assigned this dignity – it is reserved for God alone.[140] In Luke's version, if we narrow our view down to 8.21, this completion of the family is not equally obvious. But in the larger Lukan context, the infancy narratives already indicate this move. Naturally, the idea of the virginal birth is a point in itself here: in its Lukan version, Joseph is removed from the focus of the narrative. Jesus' distancing from his parents is also expressed unambiguously when, as a twelve-year-old in the temple, he emphasises that it is there, with his Father, that he is at home, rather than with them (Lk 2.41–51, especially 2.48f.). The parents cannot understand this, and the narrative

---

[139] Bovon, *Lukas*, 131, sketches a sociological model in which the various designations express various stages in the development of the 'sect': before the death of the founder, the sect is a circle of pupils/disciples, after his death, the disciples become brothers, and thereafter the sect develops to become 'Gemeinde'. He himself holds that Luke as a whole reflects the transition to the third stage.

Family terminology was customary in earliest Christianity, cf. Meeks, *Urban Christians*, 87. But the theological understanding of the transfer of such terms, i.e. the justification of the new relationship, is variable.

[140] In keeping with this is the fact that Joseph plays no role in this narrative.

69

closes with Jesus following them to Nazareth and being obedient to them, as is fitting for a good son. The theme of distancing has been thus introduced before it turns up anew in 8.19–21. God is Jesus' Father, and this has potential for creating conflict in the relationship to the original kinship group. When this original kinship is dismissed as irrelevant, in favour of obedience to God's word, the new, 'fictive' family of Jesus is created, with God as the Father.

It has been claimed that the lack of an earthly father in this 'fictive' family of disciples has the effect of de-patriarchalisation and means equality among the members of the family.[141] If no substitute for the father is to be found among the disciples, this implicitly denies the status and power of earthly fathers, and the patriarchal structures are removed in the messianic community. In other words, Jesus does not use 'God the Father' to justify and authorise a patriarchal order, but as a critical challenge to all earthly structures based on domination. No brother could demand 'the Father's' authority for himself, because this would be claiming a position reserved for God alone. Instead, the ideal of the disciple is determined by the ideal of the servant. The most humble in status according to the patriarchal system is exalted as a model, so that all claims to power and domination over others are challenged.

To what extent this image of an egalitarian fictive family is historically adequate needs further investigation, and it is also a question, whether it is reflected in the Lukan construction. So far it has become evident that the family of Jesus was constituted on other premises than the biological and conventional notion of kinship, and that it was possible to reject demands and obligations laid down in bio-social terms. But what obligations were implied in the patterns of interaction and rank in the new family? Even if there is no human replacement of the father, and the *patria potestas* is transferred to God alone, this does not automatically create equality between sisters and brothers. None of the family terms was neutral, or conveyed equality; each had its own con-

---

[141] This is an important point for Schüssler Fiorenza, *In Memory*, 140–54. It is, however, a weakness in her presentation that she never really makes it clear what she means by 'equality', nor does she discuss the relevance of this concept for the first century.

tents and connotations coloured by a patriarchal structure in which brothers were worth more than sisters, and where a mother was judged by her ability to give birth to sons (cf. Lk 1.27). What can certainly be said is that the family terms which are chosen (mother, brother, sister, perhaps 'brother and sister' instead, for example, of 'husband and wife') express desexualised relationships.[142] But the terms do not in themselves signify an equality in dignity. The fictive usage of such terms may just as well entail that the patriarchal structures of domination and subordination accompany them by a process of transference, and contribute to a patriarchal consolidation of the community of disciples. The Pastoral Letters bear witness to this.[143] The decisive difference between Luke and the patriarchal exhortations and regulations in the Pastorals may be due to the fact that the Pastorals do not reflect an ethos of abandonment which implies that the community of disciples is a replacement of the conventional family. Instead, the community is constructed on and reaffirms respectably ordered Christian households. In other words, it is important to examine further the distribution of tasks and functions within the family of God. And it is also necessary to see how the criterion of membershp in the new fictive family (ἀκούω καὶ ποιέω τὸν λόγον τοῦ θεοῦ) is dealt with in other gender-related contexts.

The function of waiting at table which women fulfil in the passages which we have examined thus far, has the immediate effect of confirming their conventional role. It can seem that the healing of the women giving them a new life, serves to reaffirm a traditional serving role in the family. The new life becomes a variant of the old life. The function assigned to them in the fictive family lies safely within the conventional

---

[142] Cf. p. 186f.

[143] Cf. Verner, *Household of God*. Also Schüssler Fiorenza, *In Memory*, 291, discusses the situation of the Pastoral Letters thus: 'The patriarchal order of the house, when applied to the order of the church, restricts the leadership of wealthy women and maintains the social exploitation of slave-women and men, even within the Christian household community'. In this situation, therefore, Schüssler Fiorenza no longer connects equality with an understanding of the community as fictive family/household, but shifts the community-model so that it is more like an association or club which meets in private houses. So it seems that Schüssler Fiorenza positively accepts the family model in an early phase, but rejects it as soon as it demonstrates its patriarchal potential. Her quest for equality is in this assessment and shift of models the decisive factor.

confinement of women's place and duties. Only the group for whom they are to exercise practical care, is widened and changed.[144] Fathers and husbands and sons and brothers are replaced by brothers in the faith. In the *familia Dei*, it is still the women's task to wait on the men, even if this takes place independently of marital obligation, and even if some of the 'sisters' happen to have stronger resources than most women. Whatever they have, they use αὐτοῖς.

From several of the texts which have been discussed so far, it is clear that the women's service included more than food. It is nevertheless typical of the Lukan use of διακον-terminology that the original connotation of the Greek word, 'to serve food', 'to wait at table', is constantly brought into play (cf. Lk 4.39; 10.40; 12.37; 17.8; 22.26f.).[145] As has been shown above, the frequency of διακον-words is high in Luke, and he is also continually concerned with meals and food.[146] Women are those preparing and providing the meals both in the narrative about Peter's mother-in-law and in the case of Martha (10.40).

Some scholars see this as an expression of the responsibility which women in the early church had for the common meal including the celebration of the eucharist, as a natural continuation of their traditional tasks in connection with meals.[147] Therefore when the Hellenist widows are overlooked, according to Acts 6.1 ἐν τῇ διακονίᾳ τῇ καθημερινῇ, this need not mean that they are not getting the daily ration to which the widows are entitled:[148] rather, it suggests that these

---

[144] Cf. Witherington, 'On the Road', 247, who makes a similar observation. But rather than speaking of a new male target-group for female service, he wraps it all up in imprecise and beautiful verbiage about a new intention.

[145] Jeremias, *Sprache*, 194.

[146] Via, 'Women', 48, 54: 'Including the διακονέω-passages in which the ordinary use of διακονέω occurs, there are 31 places in the gospel of Luke in which meal imagery occurs. Of this, a significant portion (approximately 40%, Lk 8.3; 10.40; 12.37; 17.8; 13.26; 22.30; 11.37; 14.1, 15; 15.2; 16.19; 22.15; 16.30) is redactional to Luke'. Cf. also Neyrey, *Passion*, 8f.

[147] Via, 'Women', 56f., and I understand Quesnell, 'Women', 59–79, in the same sense, even if his main point is that the female disciples must be assumed to share in the meal in Lk 22. Schüssler Fiorenza, *In Memory*, 164ff., argues in the form of a (historical?) reconstruction and limits it, on the basis of Acts 6.1, to the 'Hellenistic' women.

[148] As is supposed by the completely dominant interpretation of 6.1: The daily service is the community's practical provision for needy widows; cf. Jervell, 'Töchter Abrahams', 92; Haenchen, *Apg.*, 213ff.; Schneider, *Apg.*, 423f.

widows are passed over when it is their turn to preside at the daily meal.[149] Quite apart from the vested theological and political interests of this interpretation,[150] it associates the women's service exclusively with meals – even if it is extended to cover every possible task connected with a meal.[151] Nor is it clear what role is played by texts which give men the task of preparing or distributing food (9.13; 22.7ff.; Acts 6.1–6) other than a general (redactional) point of suppressing the mention of women.[152]

Even those who claim that the reference to meals is a characteristic of the Lukan employment of διακονέω/διακονία in the gospel, see 8.3 as an exception. But not even there can one speak of a kind of transferred or absolute significance; the addition ἐκ τῶν ὑπαρχόντων αὐταῖς ensures the term has practical value. The service is necessary for the sustenance of those who follow Jesus. The women's use of their

---

[149] Schüssler Fiorenza, *In Memory*, 165. In her opinion, it is not a question here of *poor* widows, and: 'serving at table (Acts 6:2; cf. Acts 16.34 also Lk 10.40; 12.37; 17.8) does not mean administration of funds but table service at a meal ... most likely the eucharistic table'. Elsewhere, 'Biblische Grundlegung', 36ff., she insists that διακονία and διακονέω should always be interpreted in the light of a broader usage, with a titular ring, for leadership functions. As mentioned in the introductory chapter, her feminist reconstruction involves sharp criticism of what she calls the Lukan rhetoric, which serves exclusively to conceal the original usage of the term and, in the case of 6.1, the original conflict.

[150] Note that these are Roman-Catholic exegetes who wish to give women access to the priestly administration of the sacraments. For Protestant scholars, it can be correspondingly important to associate women to preaching – or exclude them from this. It is, of course, no objection in itself to an exegetical result that it may serve as an argument in a theological debate – especially as traditional theological positions and church order are based on androcentric presuppositions. Feminist hermeneutics claim with confidence that its main goal and purpose is the liberation of women.

[151] Schüssler Fiorenza, *In Memory*, 165.

[152] The last point is, as has been said, Schüssler Fiorenza's solution. Luke contributes to the invisibility and silencing of women, 'Biblische Grundlegung', 58f., etc.

In an addendum, Via, 'Women', 60, says: 'While it is in the spirit of a meal as a discipleship for men to become involved in the preparation and service of the meal, it is not in the spirit of the metaphor for women to be excluded from it'. But this is what happens: 'The historical process which ultimately resulted in a symbolic meal known as the Eucharist, also resulted in the exclusive preparation and service of this "meal" by men'. In her opinion, however, Luke not only escapes this later development, but is opposed to it. It is therefore significant that she does not deal with Acts 6.1–6 in her article.

property is a contributory factor that permits the group around Jesus to be free of concern about what they shall eat or what they shall wear (Lk 12.22, 30–4. Cf. also the point that Tabitha, according to Acts 9.39, sewed clothes). The departure which the call to follow Jesus demands and the costs of discipleship are covered by the new community, the new family (Lk 14.26ff.; 18.28ff.). This is well in keeping with Luke's perspective on the family. The focus of interest is upon the family as an economic unit.[153] This is why most family-related activities are aimed at pooling resources and at the distribution of food, possessions and work. This distribution is the primary expression of the relationship between the members of the family.[154]

The women's service thus transcends the specific framework of the meal; it is a case of 'ausgeweitet wirtschaftliche Fürsorge',[155] while Luke still emphasises the practical and material character of the term by means of a preference for the verbal form διακονέω and additional designations. However, even scholars who agree on this point draw very dissimilar conclusions from it. For example, very different assessments have been given of the extent to which the women's service as described in Luke, represents a step forward or a step backward in relation to contemporary praxis; this depends, *inter alia*, on the background against which Luke is read. For those who presuppose a background in a strict Jewish patriarchal setting, the women's service in the community means that women have access to tasks *ad extra* from which they were traditionally excluded because the recipients are outside the family. The social provocation lies, not in what the women are doing, but in where and for whom they are doing it.[156] This leads on the one

---

[153] Moxnes, *Patrons*, 46. Cf. Lampe, 'Funktion der Familie', 536, on the family as a unit of production both in the cities and in the countryside.

[154] A good example of this is the parable about the father and the two brothers in Lk 15.11–34.

[155] (extended domestic care). Schürmann, *Lukas*, 447.

[156] Blank, 'Frauen', 14, 53f.; Marshall, *Luke*, 317; Schürmann, *Lukas*, 446f. But the way back to the historical Jesus is often covered too quickly, merging levels of traditions without differentiation. There is also a tendency to paint Judaism in darker hues so that Jesus and early Christianity can be seen in a more flattering light against this background. For the discussion of anti-Jewish tendencies in New Testament scholarship, cf. Brooten, 'Jüdinnen', 281ff.; Plaskow, 'Christian Feminism', 306ff.; Schüssler Fiorenza, 'Biblische Grundlegung', 19.

hand to an emphasis on the radical offence given by the presence and the tasks of the women who followed Jesus, while on the other hand it offers an edificatory and comforting confirmation of women's task as exclusively confined to charitable activity.[157] The gospel's 'setting' in Palestine makes such a Jewish background easy to suppose.

Others concentrate on the Lukan redactional level, and take as the background an image of early Christian communities and missionary activity in which women played an active role in proclamation, worship and leadership. Against this background, Luke's construction is seen as an attempt at limiting the activity of women to areas which were less socially provocative than proclamation and leadership. When modern interpreters use the text, to confirm an ecclesiastical praxis, this is therefore in keeping with the intention of the author. According to this version, Luke reduces the women to benefactors, subordinate to the spiritual authority and leadership of men.[158]

In both cases, there lies more or less implicit a distinction between a function of caring, especially appropriate for women to undertake, and a male function of proclamation and teaching, represented by Jesus and the twelve. Understood in this way, Lk 8.1–3 not only gives a positive description of the women's service, but also attests to a differentiation in service which is distributed according to gender.[159] But such a gender-determined differentiation becomes problematic when it is confronted with other passages in Luke-Acts. As we shall see, women are protected at other places from being assigned exclusively to a life spent waiting on others, and men are exhorted to undertake such tasks and are appointed to them.

[157] This is extremely clear in Schürmann, *Lukas*, 447: 'Alle in der "Gemeindehilfe" stehende Frauen bekommen hier nun ihre Einweisung: Sie sollen sich angenommen, aber auch in ihrem Dienst ermutigt wissen vom Herrn' (sic!).

[158] Jervell, 'Töchter Abrahams', 84–93; Tetlow, *Women and Ministry*, 103; Schüssler Fiorenza defends this view on Luke everywhere in her work. See also the introductory chapter, p. 1 n. 3 and p. 4 n. 15.

[159] Hengel, 'Maria Magdalena', 248, indicates explicitly that Luke here 'ähnlich wie in der Apg. 6, 2ff. eine paradigmatische Vorstufe des späteren Diakonamtes sichtbar werden lasse: Jesus und seine Jünger sollten durch diesen Dienst der Frauen freigemacht werden zur prophetischen Verkündigung'. Cf. also the objections to such a distribution of tasks between the 'disciples' and the women on p. 29ff.

In my opinion, the weakness with the interpretations outlined above is an insufficient account of the movement, the progress and the lines of transfer, that is to say the significant patterns emerging from the narrative sequence in Luke's story. They miss the alternations of roles in Luke's play and also the nuances. The same criticism holds true in the case of those who automatically see typical and almost titular disciple-terminology in the διακον-expressions employed in speaking of women.[160] Even if this claim primarily applies to Mark, and to Luke only with certain reservations, it is nevertheless – somewhat inconsistently – given a general validity for the early Christian period.[161] Some scholars also wish to assign functions of proclamation to the female disciples at 8.1–3.[162] On the basis of such an understanding, the women's service is neither a limitation due to a differentiation in service nor a possibility: it is quite simply the way in which their full status as disciples is expressed.

This interpretation does justice to the fact that the women, as persons who serve, relate closely to the ideal image of discipleship in the gospel. But conclusions still are reached too quickly, without evaluation of the whole concept of discipleship, and often with an attack (usually only implied) on a gender-specific differentiation of service: women are not specially to be assigned to a (subordinate) service of their own.

But as has been shown earlier, there is no way to get round the fact that women are portrayed in Luke, sometimes *expressis verbis*, as serving and providing for men who benefit from their service. If the status and significance of the women in God's family is to be seen in its full light, this part of the picture cannot be suppressed. The important thing is

---

[160] Cf. p. 88 n. 4. Kirchschläger, *Jesu exorzistisches Wirken*, 58 n. 11; Witherington, 'On the Road', 244, 247. A broader discussion in favour of the women as disciples in Luke, primarily with help of audience criticism, is found in Quesnell, 'Women', 67f.

[161] Schottroff, 'Maria Magdalena', 11f. Schüssler Fiorenza claims, without convincing evidence, that διακον-terms had very early on a titular meaning of leadership, 'Biblische Grundlegung', 36ff., but she sees in Luke's rhetoric of service a programmatic break with this apparently common early Christian usage. Luke is said to stand in contrast to Mark and especially John.

[162] Quesnell, 'Women', 68 – with further references p. 77f. n. 52. Witherington, 'On the Road', 247f.

not primarily to get the women immediately categorised and enrolled as disciples, but rather to investigate how the portrait of women in Luke-Acts has significance for the general picture and ideal of discipleship, reflecting back on the women themselves.[163]

III.4. '... with what they owned.'
The realisation of possessions and the sustenance of the community.

The notice in Lk 8.3 makes it clear that when the women serve the group around Jesus, this is ἐκ τῶν ὑπαρχόντων αὐταῖς. This information associates the presentation of the women in 8.2–3 to another important and all-pervasive motif in Luke. Both the epic and paraenetic material in the gospel and with especial emphasis in the first part of Acts, voices a demand/ideal of giving up possessions and realising property for the benefit of the community (cf. Lk 12.13–14; 14.33; 18.18–30; 19.1–10; Acts 4.35–7; 5.1–11). This is not an idealisation of poverty, but a model of radical redistribution.[164] Zacchaeus, for example, can content himself with giving away the half of his goods (Lk 19.8). Through the realisation of property, almsgiving and an organised distribution of means, the community is able to meet the basic and legitimate needs which everyone in God's family has for food and clothing and a place to sleep.[165] This is presented as conditions of the kingdom of God, and reflects the practical implementation of the divine reversal. God is the ultimate guarantor of the system,[166] compensating for the lack of human reciprocity in a last divine return.

---

[163] This, however, is not to reject the argument that women in Luke-Acts are to be considered as disciples, cf. p. 151ff.

[164] Countryman, *Rich Christian*, 84ff., 100f., 116f., 128f., sees the limitation to the gospel and the earliest chapters of Acts as due to the fact that Luke inherited the motif from a Palestinian tradition and does not himself defend it in any special way. Luke addresses primarily those who are better off and challenges them to generosity rather than poverty, i.e. he changes an earlier and more absolute demand of voluntary abandonment to a request for almsgiving and benefactions. A somewhat different perspective, but with a similar conclusion in, Moxnes, *Patrons*, 82, 119ff., and Larsen, *Menigheden uden sikkerhed*, 124f.

[165] On χρεία and χράομαι in Luke, cf. Moxnes, *Patrons*, 82ff., 72ff.

[166] Larsen, *Menigheden uden sikkerhed*, 122; Moxnes, *Patrons*, 187–90. In later patristic texts the further point is made that the intercessions of the poor are their effective return for the material gifts. Cf. further p. 244.

The widow by the treasure-chest in the temple (Lk 21.1–4), who makes available all that she had to maintain her life, is the most drastic example in the gospel.[167] Some scholars also interpret 8.3 in a paraenetic sense: rich women in the community are called by the example of the women who followed Jesus, to serve with their property.[168] The married couple Ananias and Sapphira (Acts 5.1–11) cast a harsh light on the same phenomenon through their negative example. The widow puts in what she has: she risks her life. The married couple try to safeguard themselves by holding something back for their own disposal: and their reward is death. Both wife and husband agree in keeping the money back, both attempt to lie, and both are punished for their lack of honesty and for their breach of loyalty.[169] And this is not simply an oversight that can be tidied up amicably: through their action, they have challenged the Spirit of the Lord. Even if Ananias is portrayed as the one who does the deed, Sapphira explicitly takes part, and she must receive her own terrible punishment. The suggestion that Sapphira was the more to blame, since she prevented her husband from using her money (perhaps her dowry) to fulfil his duties to the community,[170] is based on a hypothetical reconstruction of the situation that is more dependent on an interpretation of Jewish law than of the narrative itself. It has the character of guesswork that is interesting only because it is so rarefied. In terms of the account itself, Ananias and Sapphira are measured against the same demand, and both fail equally to meet the demand. The narrative about this married couple who told lies in financial matters, demonstrates with clarity the seriousness of the demand for loyalty to the community. No one forces them directly, but the pressure is obviously strong (cf. Acts 4.32–7). And when once

---

[167] Against Wright, 'Widow's Mite'. His article gives a good overview of various interpretations, and he himself proposes that the story is to be understood ironically as a lament and exemplification of Lk 20.47: '… it provides a further illustration of the ills of official devotion'. For fuller discussion of the pericope cf. p. 95 and p. 245f.

[168] Horn, *Glaube*, 117, with a list of references to other scholars, 321 n. 140.

[169] Countryman, *Rich Christian*, 79, is correct to say that the mortal sin which they have committed does not consist in having kept back some of the proceeds of the sale for themselves. Peter assures Ananias that he could have kept the ground, and that he himself had the right to dispose of the profit when the ground was sold. The betrayal lies in the dissimulation and lie. The couple make pretence of a solidarity which is not authentic.

[170] Derrett, 'Ananias', 225–32.

someone, be it woman or man, commits themselves to serve the community with what they possess, this must be done wholeheartedly and without falsehood. In positive terms, this means that the women in Lk 8.3, through their continuous realisation of property, implement the ideal that disciples, whether they possess much or little, shall renounce without reserve what belongs to them in order to meet the needs of the others, so that no one suffers from indigence.

The distance which the summary notice in 8.1–3 marks between the twelve and the women is determined by the special position which the twelve later receive in Luke as the apostolic college.[171] The distance between them and the women is therefore to be understood as the relationship between the (coming) leadership and the community. The women are the anticipated presence of the community in Jesus' life. Abraham's daughters are the core of the new Israel which is being restored.[172] This is also reflected in the fact that the twelve in 8.1–3 are still without any specific task, while the women already carry out in an exemplary fashion a function of fundamental significance and universal validity in God's family. In this connection, it is noteworthy that the description of the women in Lk 8.3 and the description of the community in Acts 4.32, have in common the special expression τὰ ὑπαρχόντα τινί.

In other words, the women who follow Jesus, live up in a prototypical manner to a demand that has more general validity for the people of God. At the same time, their support explains how Jesus and the twelve can live without cares. The women represent the community which supports leaders who have no property of their own. To the extent that one can speak of an ideal of poverty in Luke, this holds good in the strict sense only for the leaders of the community.[173] Their poverty, however, is possible thanks to others' generos-

---

[171] Cf. p. 161f.

[172] Cf. Lohfink's demonstration that the women enter surprisingly where the rest of the disciples is to be expected, 92 n. 22. This, however, does not mean that Jervell's classification of the women as 'Gemeinde' is appropriate as is shown above.

[173] In agreement with Degenhardt, *Lukas*, 215–20. He does not, however, balance this with a more comprehensive model of almsgiving or of redistribution, because he explains this tension primarily in terms of tradition history.

ity, while the ideal ensures that they do not misuse their position to enrich themselves, when they distribute the gifts to all the needy members of the community.[174]

In the Lukan context, therefore, as we have seen earlier, it is the plural form αὐτοῖς and not, as at Mk 15.41, the singular αὐτῷ that gives the appropriate meaning. This is also in keeping with the use of διακον-terminology in Luke. Διακον-words are directed in Luke mainly to other persons and not to God. This is very different from Paul's usage, when Paul for example describes himself and others as διάκονος θεοῦ/Χριστοῦ (2 Cor 6.4; 11.23).[175] Luke in fact never uses the substantive διάκονος, and the human person is named in the Old Testament terms δούλη/δοῦλος (κυρίου) giving expression to the relationship to God (cf. Lk 1.38, 48; 2.29; Acts 2.18; 4.29; (16.17)).

It is, however, true that the redactional combination in Lk 8.3 of the verb διακονέω and the renunciation of one's property is an exception. The realisation of property for the benefit of the community, the distribution of common goods and the bestowal of alms are usually described by means of other verbs – usually δίδωμι with derivative variants, and, from the recipient's point of view, λαμβάνω and its derivatives.[176] This linking of two fields of associations cannot be reduced to a question of redactional adjustments of Mk 15.41 by Luke. It is misleading to see in αὐτοῖς and ἐκ τῶν ὑπαρχόντων αὐταῖς a Lukan attempt to weaken the dimensions of discipleship present in the original and more absolute Markan form of expression; that is to consider the question in too great an isolation from other factors. The choice of words in 8.3 gives the summary notice an affinity to two central themes of discipleship in the gospel which are closely related, but which are

[174] Moxnes, *Patrons*, 168f., 174–8. Cf. also Johnson's demonstration, *Literary Function*, 174–83, that Judas is punished with death when his treachery takes the further form of greed and lust for property. The tense exchanges between charismatic and itinerant preachers without private property, and resident support groups, as mentioned in n. 123 above, is one aspect of this. But the pattern indicated by Luke's description of the relationship between groups of believers, the stationary leadership and the itinerant missionaries, is more variable and complicated.

[175] Paul also shows a certain preference for δοῦλος in such contexts, cf. Rom 1.1, Gal 1.10.

[176] Moxnes, *Patrons*, 81, 183f.

otherwise not combined at the level of the pericopae:[177] 'to serve' and the partial or total realisation of possessions in favour of the community and its needs.

III.5. *Women as models in service.*

We have already touched on the second of the two themes: how the women prototypically realise possessions in order to cover the needs of those who no longer have any means of their own. When this is characterised as 'serving', it constitutes a significant clue to the portrayal of women in Luke-Acts. At the same time, it links up with other texts which shed light on the importance and the paraenetic motivation of service. The service of women is generally referred to in the narrative, that is it occurs primarily in descriptive and not prescriptive sections of the text. But the repeated mention of the fact that women serve takes on a more fundamental significance through these other texts that teach and exhort. Moreover, it is exploited and included in a transposition of roles which also renders the description of women a wider address.

This transposition in Luke-Acts is manifest in the usage of διακον-terminology – that is in the shift of such terminology from the description of women, via paraenesis in parables, to the 'model' or 'mirror' held up for the guidance of the leadership of God's people. This is at the same time a movement from a concrete and direct employment to a transferred, metaphorical or rhetorical one.

Until Lk 12, διακονέω and διακονία are used only of women (4.39; 8.3; 10.40). From Lk 12 onwards, these terms are adopted in the instruction, especially in paraenesis directed to the twelve, or in any case to the disciples:[178] 12.35-8, (43-8); 17.7ff. The terminology is also transferred from the sphere of women to the sphere of men by means of imagery combining the aspect of the meal with a master and slave relationship. Here too we are dealing with material peculiar to Luke. The διακον-terms are still clearly associated with the meal, while

---

[177] It is true that the parable about the vigilant servant in Lk 12 comes as the immediate continuation of an instruction about the correct attitude to property.

[178] The wide address of 12.1 is further reduced in 12.22.

it is assumed that it is the obvious duty of the servant to wait on his master. The first narrative deals with servants who must be in constant readiness for their master's return. If they manage to stay awake, they will be greatly surprised when he comes, because the master then will reverse the roles: he will seat them at the table and wait on them, διακονήσει αὐτοῖς (12.37). The application of the narrative does not directly identify the disciples with the servants, but it exhorts them to behave like vigilant servants, καὶ ὑμεῖς ὅμοιοι ἀνθρώποις προσδεχομένοις. Thus the parabolic discourse in Lk 12 glides further into other variants of the motif of vigilance and the image of servant and master, and is concentrated from 12.42 onwards on the steward, οἰκονόμος, who has the responsibility of supervision, managing the other servants and caring for their well-being. Peter's question, which is inserted as a point of transition in 12.41, also shows clearly that the instruction concerns primarily the leadership and not everyone. The good steward takes care of the other servants as the master wishes, and gives them their food at the proper time. It is possible that the master's conduct and his reversal of roles in the first part of the parable still plays a role. In contrast, the perverse steward is brutal and indulges himself excessively with food and drink.

The motif of role-reversal is completely missing in Lk 17.7ff. It is rejected as improbable at 17.7. Here, the situation completely retains its realism. The servant who has worked outdoors all day long must also prepare food and wait on his master, διακόνει μοι, when he comes home weary in the evening. Nothing else is to be expected, not even a word of thanks. In this case too, the service of the slave is explicitly applied to the disciples (17.10). There is, however, a remarkable twist for the addressee: from identification with the master at the beginning, Τίς δὲ ἐξ ὑμῶν δοῦλον ἔχων ..., to the concluding identification with the servants. It is possible that there lies implicit in this a conversion from a position as master to a position as servant.[179] The disciples are moved to understand themselves in the role of unworthy servants who have only done their duty.

---

[179] Via, 'Women', 40, misses this point completely when she seeks a solution by distinguishing between the audience of the text and the disciples in the text. Methodologically, her position is very unclear.

The noun διάκονος is used nowhere in these parables – only οἰκονόμος, in the case of the servant in a more prominent position. This, as we have seen, can be explained by the reversal of the relationship, especially in 12.37, when the master takes on himself the task of waiting on the servants and so becomes ὁ διακῶν, the one who waits at table. In other words, διακον-terminology is linked for Luke to functions involving provision, and is not used in a titular fashion for particular persons. Tasks of service exist, as do persons who carry these out, but not 'deacons'.[180]

In connection with the scene of the Last Supper in Lk 22.24–30, sayings of Jesus which speak of a radical reversal of roles – or, more correctly, of a ranking of roles – are used paraenetically. These sayings constitute a central part of Jesus' farewell discourse in Luke, his testament to the twelve. Attempts to include women among those whom Luke supposes to have been present,[181] overlook the fact that 22.14 focusses the attention exclusively on Jesus and the twelve. The discourse is to be understood as Luke's programmatic speech for the apostolate. It is emphasised, with the twelve as addressees, that among them, to be a leader is to be like the one who serves. The motif of service involves a fundamental characterisation and correction of the apostolic college's royal authority of judgment over Israel. The treatment of this motif in 22.24–7 presupposes the normal structures of power in society. The world is ordered in such a way that some lord it over others, that some exercise authority and others do not, that one is waited upon ('lies at table', ἀνακείμενος) while another waits on him. In a way, this is the structure present in 4.38f. and 8.1–3: the women serve and the men are waited upon and cared for in virtue of their status as men and lords. The ranking implied by this distribution of roles is presumably taken for granted. For who is indeed the greater? The one who lies at table and eats, the one who is served – or the one who waits on him, the servant? Is it not the one who lies at table? Or is something else the case?

---

[180] On the discussion of Acts 6.1–6, see pp. 108–110.
[181] Quesnell, 'Women', 69ff., followed by Via, 'Women' 42ff. This is, of course, not a historical judgment on my part, but concerns the Lukan construction.

We find scattered thematic parallels to these verses in Luke both in Matthew and in Mark: Mk 9.35; 10.41ff.; Mt 20.24ff.; 23.11. But they lack the connection to the meal which is so strong in Luke. The motif of the Last Supper can perhaps be sensed in Mk 10.39ff. and Mt 20.22ff., but Mk 10.45 par. Mt 20.28 show that they understand Jesus' service more directly in terms of his death. The pair of contrasts in Mark and Matthew, μέγας, πρῶτος/διάκονος, δοῦλος and the passive and active forms of διακονέω, also link the saying of Jesus more closely to the social relationship of master and servant. This means that they relate διακονέω primarily to another field of imagery, in which it is natural to employ the term διάκονος. As we have seen, Luke restricts the διακον-terminology to meals and providing for others, even on occasions where the image of master and servant is dominant. Even in 22.27f., the primary allusion is to connotations of a meal. This is clear, not only because of the meal setting in Lk 22, but just as much because of the pair of contrasts in the statement itself. Precisely the juxtaposition of ἀνακείμενος/διακονῶν gives shape to Luke's use of the words in the context of the Last Supper. By means of ἀνακείμενος, διακονέω is given greater precision in its primary linguistic significance of waiting at table, in keeping with its employment earlier in the gospel, whether this has been a direct or a metaphorical use. The participal form ὁ διακονῶν (unlike Mark's and Matthew's διάκονος) can be explained formally as a parallelisation to ἀνακείμενος. But it is equally a further example of Luke's consistent avoidance of διάκονος. The text is not concerned with 'servants', but with those who serve, that is those who enter functions of serving which would not be expected for their status and place in society.

This becomes clear when Jesus describes himself in this way, ἐγὼ δὲ ἐν μέσῳ ὑμῶν εἰμι ὡς ὁ διακονῶν (22.27c). Within the pericope itself, this refers back, of course, to 22.17 and 19, where Jesus gives the disciples bread and wine and thereby offers them himself. But thereby Jesus has turned on its head the expected answer to οὐχὶ ὁ ἀνακείμενος; (22.27b). This gives the exhortation to the disciples in 22.26 a christological motivation. Among them, an inverted ranking is valid, in which the greatest is like the youngest, and the one who is leader is like the one who serves. In virtue of the antithesis between 22.25 and 22.26, a protest against the designation εὐεργέτης, is implied. Instead, ὁ διακονῶν is proposed as the honorific designation. The inversion of role-expectations in these verses does not, however, mean that the roles themselves are abolished,[182] nor does it imply a clear reversal. The leaders remain leaders, but new ideals for their leadership are established.[183] It is not that the servants are now to rule, but those who rule are to be ὡς ὁ διακονῶν. With a view to the new leadership of the people of God, the college of the twelve apostles, there takes place a corrective and paradoxical coupling of two traditionally antithetical roles, that of servant and that of ruler.

The authority of Jesus is bestowed on the ideal of a serving leadership both through his words and through his own example. He is himself the foremost model for such a paradoxical combination. But at the same time, this gives an exemplary significance to all those who according to the presentation in the gospel story, have fulfilled a serving function. What happens is not only that a role of waiting on others (i.e., functions proper to women and to slaves), by means of general social references, is applied almost *in abstracto* to leading men as a corrective characteristic of the manner in which their leadership is to be exercised. In a much more concrete way examples of service are presented within the gospel itself.[184] Linguistically, this is assured by the consistent use of verbal forms; the women serve, and the model is ὁ διακονῶν, the one who serves. We have also seen how the christological motivation in the case of the women is found implicitly in the experience of healing. It is Jesus' action on their behalf, his servant exercise of power, that makes them become serving persons who follow him.

[182] Moxnes, 'Meals', 163, misses the point when, like many others, he sees here an *abolition* of a hierarchical pattern of roles.

[183] Neyrey, *Passion*, 21, is correct to emphasise that while in Mark it is a question of who is to sit at the right hand of the Lord, Luke presupposes that the twelve are indeed leaders. 'The issue is not whether leadership should exist or how close the twelve are to be to Jesus; the question is rather how the leadership is to be exercised.'

[184] Gill, 'Women Ministers', 15, 19f., observes a similar move in Mark, but sees the women's exemplary service in contrast to 'the hierarchical form of ministry represented in the narrative by Peter, James, John and the Twelve which he (Mark) thinks reflects a distorted christology and a mistaken discipleship'. This is an expression of a contemporary conflict 'In a church with a power-oriented leadership, Mark portrays women, children and Gentiles and disabled people as model disciples and sets forth the sacrificial service of the women of his community as the paradigm for Christian ministry', 20.

Even if the women's service receives an exemplary role in a christologically-mediated paradigm of leadership, it still remains to be seen if this has any significance for women's place in the actual position of leadership. In the case of the women, service apparently does not require any extensive justification, and their seemingly conventional life in service receives a new dignity in the new context. At the same time, it is remarkable that when the service function becomes a vital trait in the role of ruler, a gender shift also takes place – from serving women to rulers who are to be like those who serve. The reversal of the dignity of the roles coincides with a masculinisation, and in Acts, the διακον-terminology is applied exclusively to men.

The instruction about leadership in Lk 22.24–30 is followed up in Acts when διακονία is employed primarily to speak of the apostles' task (1.17, 25; 6.4) and later to speak of Paul's activity (20.24; 21.19). The last-mentioned passages dealing with Paul are those in Acts that come closest to Paul's own use of διακονία when he characterises his apostolate in this way in his letters (Rom 11.13; 2 Cor 3.8f.; 4.1; 5.18; 6.3).[185] It is, of course, possible that the original connotation of meals still echoes in the Pauline usage: to preach is to offer God's word as the bread of life.[186] In the Lukan context this association is made much more evident than elsewhere in the New Testament. Service means to see that others receive what they need. And when the concept of διακονία is employed in Acts to speak of the apostolate and of missionary activity, this must be seen against the background established in the gospel – with the farewell discourse in Lk 22 as the programmatic viewpoint for Acts.

At the same time, the Lukan usage shows that διακον-terms have not solidified so as to become a fixed terminology (bearing a Pauline stamp).[187] This means that allusion is made in Acts to a spectrum of shades of meanings – echoing the gospel. The usage may sound Pauline, as in 1.17, 25; 6.4; 20.24; 21.19. In 11.29 and 12.25, it is used of the

---

[185] Haenchen, *Apg.*, 524, rejects the idea that this is due to the use of sources, and sees it as a stylistic instrument used by Luke to create a Pauline note.

[186] Beyer, 'διακονέω', 87.

[187] Cf. Schottroff, 'Maria Magdalena', 12 n. 28. This is also an argument against the view that διακονέω is almost a technical term for discipleship.

contribution which the community in Antioch makes for the relief of the brothers and sisters[188] in Judea, and of the commission which Barnabas and Saul have received to hand over the collection (cf. Paul's usage in Rom 15.32; 1 Cor 16.15, 2 Cor 8.3; 9.12, where the collection of funds for Jerusalem is called Paul's διακονία for Jerusalem or for the saints and their needs). But this is a usage which nevertheless fits well into Luke's understanding of διακονία. The community at Antioch is led by the Spirit to show the same solidarity with the community in Jerusalem that the earliest community in Jerusalem has practised internally.

A final passage in Acts (19.22) presupposes that Paul is accompanied by people who serve and that he can send two of them in a sovereign manner to Macedonia, ἀποστείλας δὲ εἰς τὴν Μακεδονίαν δύο τῶν διακονούντων αὐτῷ. The pattern resembles the one drawn in the gospel, of Jesus followed by women who serve, but in the case of Paul the 'assistants' are (also) men.[189] Paul's example shows how the ideal of service operates on various levels: on the one hand, Paul's activity is to be named as service, on the other hand, there are people on whose service he depends.

We have seen earlier how the redactional summary notice in Lk 8.1–3 emphasises typical traits in the Lukan presentation of women. And we have established that 8.1–3 provides a concentration of significant motifs which are central elsewhere in Luke (1) such as the instruction of the disciples, and later in the description of the life of the community (renunciation of property, realisation and redistribution of private means, the giving of alms), and (2) the understanding of leadership (aspect of service).

When the women are described as early as 8.1–3 as persons who already live this, they become thereby anticipatory examples both in relation to the people of God (where no one says that what one pos-

---

[188] The masculine plural ἀδελφοί is best understood here inclusively as 'siblings', and not exclusively as 'brothers'.

[189] The two who are sent to Macedonia and mentioned by name, are both male, Timothy and Erastus. The genitive construction δύο τῶν διακονούντων presupposes, however, that the group was larger. It also reveals an androcentric mind when the 'serving persons' in Acts 19.22 are understood and translated without further discussion as Paul's 'fellow workers', cf. Schneider, *Apg.*, II 274.

sesses is one's own) and in relation to the leaders of this people of God (whose authority is to manifest itself in service). The idealisation and the matching rhetoric of service do, however, legitimate a masculinisation and means in practice that the women who served are excluded from the actual positions of leadership.

III.6. *The acts of women as a corrective to the leadership.*

The exemplary role of the women in relation to the leadership of the people has also an aspect of critical correction. This is seen most clearly in the conflict with false leadership, with those who pretend to be what their acts betray. In Luke, these leaders are portrayed in literary terms as antitypes to Jesus and his disciples.[190] This means that the positive exemplary function of the women who follow Jesus *vis-à-vis* the twelve is turned in a negative manner against the Pharisees and other groups of leaders (the rich, the chief priests, the scribes and the non-priestly aristocracy). 'Do you see this woman?' βλέπεις ταύτην τὴν γυναῖκα; Jesus says to the Pharisee Simon in Lk 7.44.

Complex problems of tradition history are connected to the narrative in Lk 7.36–50.[191] In the present version, it is often felt to be so full of contradictions that it can best be interpreted by means of a tradition-historical construction which assigns the differing points to various layers of tradition. The tensions are usually identified as (1) the relationship between the narrative framework and the parable which is incorporated in 7.41–3, and (2) the relationship between Jesus' final words to the woman (7.48–50), which confer on her the forgiveness of sins and salvation, and 7.36–47 which indicate that she acts as she does because she has already been forgiven much.[192] A third problem is the

---

[190] Cf. Moxnes, *Patrons*, 98ff.

[191] Marshall, *Luke*, 305ff., gives a good overview of the various attempts at the reconstruction of earlier versions. Cf. also Raven's exposition in 'Setting', 282ff. A suggested feminist reconstruction can be found in Schüssler Fiorenza, *In Memory*, 128ff.

[192] Cf. for example, Marshall, *Luke*, 306, who like many others, postulates an earlier meeting (unknown to us) between Jesus and the woman, to explain this. Kilgallen, 'John the Baptist', 675ff., shows that this solution is absurd in literary terms, but his own suggestion is just as fantastic when he identifies an earlier act of pardon with John's baptism. Cf. also n. 27 above.

relationship to similar narratives in the other gospels: Mk 14.3–9 par. Mt 26.6–13 and Jn 12.1–8.

Our aim here, however, is not a historical reconstruction of a more original narrative, or perhaps of several more original narratives. Our interest is accordingly limited to particular aspects of Luke's narrative – especially those which may contribute to comparisons between women and Pharisees. The second of the points of tension mentioned above has some significance here, because it touches on the relationship between the christological motivation and a woman's action, that is Jesus' forgiveness of sin establishing community, and her service. There is no reason for excessive hair-splitting in the discussion about what comes first and what comes last. If ὅτι in 7.47 is not understood causally, but 'logically', the woman's love is to be interpreted also in this verse as an expression of forgiveness.[193] This would correspond to the pattern in the narratives of healing, in which Jesus' benefaction creates benefactors. However, this is not essential for the comparison with the Pharisee: what is vital is not whether her loving action acquires forgiveness for her, or is the result of forgiveness, but that her action is contrasted with the Pharisee's lack of corresponding expressions.

Both in Lk 7.36–50 and in the narrative in Mk 14.3–9 par. Mt 26.6–13, the anointing of Jesus at Bethany, the host on this occasion is named Simon.[194] But while the name is mentioned at the very beginning in Mark/Matthew, and he is called Simon the leper, he is a Pharisee in Luke's version, and the name is completely missing in the introduction itself (7.36). It comes up suddenly and casually when Jesus speaks to him in 7.40. For Luke, therefore, the most important piece of information is to name him as a Pharisee. He is clearly a respected man who has invited Jesus to such a grand meal that they lie at table (7.36). When the woman then enters the scene of the meal, she is named as ἁμαρτωλός (7.37). Thereby an extreme contrast is already

---

[193] Fitzmyer, *Luke*, 691f. On the discussion, cf. Tannehill's good summary, *Narrative Unity*, 117f.

[194] Cf. Schramm, *Markus-Stoff*, 43f. The most important feature shared by the two versions is that the woman brings the ointment in a costly alabaster jar.

established emphatically in the introductory presentation, and this sets its stamp on the whole plot of the story.[195]

In the case of Matthew's gospel, it has been claimed that 'female gender renders the exemplary behaviour of women as more of an achievement and heightens contrasts with male characters'.[196] This is true also of Luke, but with the significant difference that the gender aspect is reinforced by means of supplementary characteristics on both sides. As in this case, the woman is a prostitute, while the man is a Pharisee; in another case, the woman is a poor widow, while the men are rich (cf. Lk 21.1–4). And as far as the women are concerned, the characteristics are gender-specific in such a way that they neither weaken nor lighten the gender dimension, but heighten it and strengthen it.

It is customary to interpret ἁμαρτωλός in 7.37 to mean that the woman not only failed to fulfil the demands of the Pharisees, but was well-known as the local whore.[197] This description of the woman is a characteristic (and possibly redactional)[198] feature of the narrative in Luke, making it an illustration of the saying in 7.34 about Jesus as φίλος τελωνῶν καὶ ἁμαρτωλῶν.[199] At least in Palestine, the prostitutes were despised not only for reasons of sexual morality, but like the tax-collectors – also for religious and political reasons. Their intercourse with anyone able to pay, meant that they were potential traitors.[200] The general moral and social judgment of such women was very harsh.[201] Apart from the moral reaction, a decisive factor was the per-

---

[195] Tannehill, *Narrative Unity*, 116f., shows clearly how the contrast is an expression of 'significant plotting'. Cf. also Moloney, *Woman*, 58. Fitzmyer, *Luke*, 609f., does not see any contrast in the story between the action of the two persons nor any serious reproach of the Pharisee, but only a different measure of love and forgiveness which they both receive. His understanding is, however, based almost exclusively on the parable.

[196] Anderson, 'Matthew', 16, 21.

[197] For more detailed evidence and an exposition of the discussion, cf. Blank, 'Frauen', 45.

[198] Cf. Schüssler Fiorenza, *In Memory*, xiii, 128f.

[199] Ernst, *Lukas*, 254.

[200] Friis Plum, *Tilslørede Frihed*, 29f. Apart from this, she has a very positive (and in my opinion, problematic) understanding of the prostitutes as the personification of independent female sexuality. This was made available to men, but was not subordinated to their lordship.

[201] '... only an abnormal (sic!) woman could defy such social and moral forces' (which the condemnation represented), Epstein, *Sex Laws*, 162. His mode of expression also betrays his own moral indignation.

manent cultic impurity attached to prostitutes.[202] The narrative in Lk 7.36–50 plays on the expectations of propriety: Jesus had no choice but to reject the woman, and at the very least protect himself against being touched by her (7.39) – provided that he really had the prophetic clear-sightedness enabling him to perceive at once what kind of woman she was. But Jesus allows himself to be touched by her, and demonstrates his prophetic ability rather by letting his Pharisee host understand that he knows or has read his thoughts. Naturally, Jesus is well aware that the woman he has allowed to wait upon him, is ἁμαρτωλός. But instead of keeping her at a distance, he emphasises community with her and distance from the Pharisee.

While 7.47 is directed to the Pharisee, Jesus makes a response to the woman herself in the concluding words of the story (7.48–50). Jesus addresses her and indicates that she shares in the salvation. He has disposed of the Pharisee, and what was said about the woman in 7.47 is now repeated directly to her. She is not reduced to a matter of discussion between Jesus and Simon, and, in contrast to the situation at the beginning of the narrative,[203] the final balance of the narrative is established through a reversal of status between the sinful woman and Simon the Pharisee.

Jesus' concluding statement is linked both in form and in content to the miracle narratives. It marks the woman as an example of faith.[204] It is identical with the words of Jesus to the woman with haemorrhages in Lk 8.48: ἡ πίστις σου σέσωκέν σε· πορεύου εἰς εἰρήνην. In both cases, this statement applies, remarkably enough, to women who were regarded as impure and therefore as infectious. Both narratives begin by relating reactions to the fact that the women touch Jesus (cf. 7.39c and 8.44ff.). For both the women, the impurity had its source in

---

[202] Blank, 'Frauen', 45; Witherington, *Women in the Ministry of Jesus*, 163 n. 21 with rabbinic references.

[203] Tannehill, *Narrative Unity*, 116f. He classifies the narrative as a 'quest-story' in which the woman is the one who seeks and receives an answer, even if her quest is not defined in words.

[204] McCaughey, 'Paradigms of Faith', 181. But there is no clear justification in the texts for his interpretation according to which healing and salvation are two different stages, and the saving faith consists of gratitude, confession and praise.

the female body. The one was troubled by unstoppable haemorrhages, the other was a well-known prostitute. Probably it would go too far if we were to see 7.50 as a special formula of commission for women. But it is remarkable that the second and active element in the formula, πορεύου εἰς εἰρήνην, is employed only in these two female examples, whereas the first element, ἡ πίστις σέσωκέν σε, is found also in 17.19 (healing of a leprous Samaritan) and 18.42 (healing of a blind man).

With its stylistic similarity to the healing narratives and with its concluding emphasis on the woman's share in salvation, 7.36–50 prepares the way for the almost immediately following presentation in 8.1–3 of the women who follow Jesus. The link between these passages has indeed been rejected earlier as being due to a common source, but this does not mean that there can be no strong connecting links in the present text in terms of content.[205] Moreover, the narrative in 7.36–50 is one further confirmation of the close relationship between miracle, faith and service.

The connection between 7.36–50 and 8.1–3 relates also to the women's function: 'they are positioned (in 8.1–3) as loving and serving below the sinful woman, who likewise had become a loving person from the mercy she received'.[206] It is true that nowhere in the story is the caring action of the prostitute characterised by means of διακον-terminology. But it is clear that she offers what she has, κομίσασα ἀλάβαστρον μύρου, in an extravagant act of waiting upon Jesus. So she takes her place in the gospel's portrait gallery of women serving, summarised in 8.1–3 as those who served out of their own resources.

At the same time, her case is different, in two respects. First, her service is not aimed at satisfying the elementary need for sustenance, or for the necessities in life. Both in terms of the means used and in terms of how it is carried out, her service has the character of surplus. Second

---

[205] Cf. p. 29. Dillon, *Eye-Witnesses*, 241, goes so far as to claim, on the basis of the parallel to Mk 14.3–9, that 'the repentant woman serves to illustrate the connection between the healed and exorcised women who served Jesus in Galilee and the corps of Easter witnesses'.

[206] Schürmann, *Lukas*, 447.

– and possibly this may contribute to explain the first point – her service benefits Jesus alone, and Jesus then turns her act into a criticism against the host, Simon the Pharisee: the excessive action of the despised woman is held up in 7.44–5 as a critical corrective for him. Through the service of the prostitute, it becomes clear what the Pharisee has failed to do.

It is a question of much in relation to little measured in love and measured in deed. Luke therefore overlooks the (uncomfortable?) insertion in Mk 14.4–7 par. Mt 26.8–11 and Jn 12.4–8.[207] The discussion by the disciples about whether the woman has wasted on Jesus means that ought to have been given to the poor, serves in the other versions a superior christological motif which is not present in Luke in the same way. And even if the narrative in Luke does have a certain christological stamp (Jesus as the prophet with the authority to forgive sins), the main point in the woman's example is not a paraenetic exhortation to make an extra fuss over Jesus. The issue is rather that the prostitute acts in such a way that the Pharisee is put to shame. Since the Pharisee has invited Jesus to his home for a feast, the contrast between him and the prostitute cannot be a question of meeting basic needs, but concerns 'little', ὀλίγον, in relation to 'much', πολύ. In her own way, described in hyperbolic terms, the local whore demonstrates her greater love by lavishing on Jesus a service which Simon the Pharisee did not even think of taking upon himself.

The woman's action is further depicted primarily in emotional brushstrokes which dramatise and intensify both what is humble and what is shocking in her conduct.[208] Instead of anointing Jesus' head as in Mk 14.3, which would have been more normal, she anoints his feet,[209] after

---

[207] Cf. Horn, *Glaube*, 118f.

[208] Marshall, *Luke*, 308f., is an example of the temptations this may imply for interpreters in terms of excessive emotional/psychological empathy in suggesting solutions to exegetical problems: after a vivid description ('… she spontaneously broke out weeping … In her anxiety to make up for this mishap …'), he concludes 'The whole account makes sense when we assume that the woman's original intention (*viz.* to anoint Jesus' head) was interrupted by her overwhelming emotions'.

[209] According to Matthew/Mark, the woman anoints Jesus' head, according to Luke/John his feet. Cf. Schüssler Fiorenza, *In Memory*, xiii, on the difference that this makes. Ravens, 'Setting', 285f., is too subtle when he interprets the anointing of the feet, on the basis of Isaiah 52.7, as 'the beautifying preparation of Jesus' feet, for he is the one who will soon announce the good news of God's Kingship to Jerusalem'.

first washing them with her tears, drying them with her loosed prostitute's hair,[210] and finally kissing them. This description is a messy mixture of tears, foot-washing and oil. The anointing of Jesus is combined with the woman's washing of Jesus' feet, and this in turn is combined with her standing behind Jesus weeping. The meaning of this need not be sought in suppositions about the woman's mental state, but rather in the saying of Jesus which later in the narrative renders meaning to the woman's action in relation to the Pharisee.

This is why it is unimportant that the failures in providing service with which the Pharisee is reproached, go beyond what one could demand or indeed expect to be included by usual hospitality.[211] We do not know with certainty whether the Pharisee can be blamed for neglecting his obligations as a host. It is when his hospitality is seen in relation to the woman's lavish service that it appears defective and full of omissions. It is her entry and Jesus' way of dealing with this that provoke the crisis in the relationship between Jesus and the Pharisee. At the same time, it is clear that it would indeed have been the host's duty to see that some of the services mentioned were offered to the guest, but it would have been the servant's duty to carry them out. The woman therefore does not take on the host's role, nor does she take over the full function of the Pharisee in the text. Her actions lie within the area for which a host had responsibility, but partly as a servant's tasks. This means that by performing a serving task, she represents a corrective critique vis-à-vis his leading role as host.[212]

The difference between the two characters in terms of action also expresses a difference in terms of love. Her action shows that she loves much, while he implicitly reveals that he has little love. The criticism of

---

[210] The prostitute's loose and uncovered hair marked her off from the virtuous and proper woman, cf. Epstein, Sex Laws, 39ff.

[211] Schürmann, Lukas, 435f. A detailed account in Marshall, Luke, 311f. Dillon, Eye-Witnesses, 240f., explains the whole narrative as a 'gradual assimilation of traditions that made an original paradigm of repentance and forgiveness into an episode of the hospitality denied Jesus by the "righteous" and lavished on him by the disenfranchised'.

[212] In Jn 13, Jesus the Lord takes on himself the role that Mary played in Jn 12.1–7, by washing the disciples' feet, cf. Seim, 'Roles of Women', 72ff. It is also worth noting that one of the criteria established in 1 Tim 5.10 for a true widow is that she has washed the feet of the saints.

Simon on this point is linked to the criticism of the Pharisees elsewhere in the gospel. The Pharisees are repeatedly accused of lacking love (11.42) or of loving what they ought not to love (11.43; 16.13f.).[213] Thus the motif of love makes it even clearer that the woman's example in this story functions as a critical corrective of the Pharisee leadership – represented here by Simon.

The Pharisees are represented in this part of the gospel (where the setting is country districts and small towns outside Jerusalem) as the leaders of the people.[214] In Jerusalem, other groups appear and are dominant in positions of leadership: the rich, the chief priests, the scribes and the non-priestly aristocracy. On one occasion, a woman is set up against these too as a critical example: the poor widow in Lk 21.1–4.[215] As with 7.36–50, this narrative is terminologically anchored in a preceding saying of Jesus. The scribes are criticised in 20.47 because κατεσθίουσιν τὰς οἰκίας τῶν χηρῶν, and they are reproached for their false piety.[216] The poor widow, victim of their mismanagement, is presented immediately afterwards as the one who truly displays piety. Thus, the widow in 21.1–4 must be seen in a double contrast. By means of the context, she is contrasted with the hypocritical scribes, and within the narrative itself she is contrasted with the rich, who merely give out of their superabundance an amount that they themselves hardly notice. Luke omits Mark's ὁ ὄχλος βάλλει χαλκὸν εἰς τὸ γαζοφυλάκιον (Mk 12.41) and concentrates on the rich. Nor does he say, with Mark, that the rich give much. The widow gives the little she has, and thus realises all that she has to support her life. Her action must be seen in the light of the ideal of giving up one's property and even one's life in passages such as 12.22ff., and it possibly also reflects a special piety connected with widows.[217] But not even in this

---

[213] Moxnes, *Patrons*, 123f., 144.

[214] On this, cf. Moxnes, *Patrons*, 98–104.

[215] Even though I am aware of the problems of tradition-criticism, the possible cross-religious parallels to the story, and the question of whether the narrative was originally a parable, I do not see the need to enter those discussions. Cf. n. 167 above.

[216] On the interpretation of this verse, cf. p. 245f.

[217] This is a decisive argument against Wright's interpretation in 'Widow's Mite'. Cf. n. 167 above, and also p. 244–245f.

case does the main point lie in an isolated evaluation of her action, but in her act as related to the action of others, in the critical function she exercises in relation to a leadership which fails to do what it should. By means of her sacrificial act, the failures of the rich rulers are exposed in the same way as in 7.36–50.

Up to this point, we have documented how the women in Luke fulfil functions of διακονία and how these functions are made valid for men as well. The service, which in the case of women, despite their voluntary abandonment, primarily reaffirms conventional roles and functions, is mediated christologically and redefines the function of leadership exercised by men. This transference gives the women an exemplary significance – positively, in relation to the people of God and to its new leadership, and negatively in relation to the old leadership of the people, as Luke antitypically describes this. But the idealisation happens at the cost of the women's exclusion from actual positions of leadership.

It has been important that each passage should not be read in isolation, *ad locum*, but should be interpreted in the light of the more comprehensive treatment of motifs associated with women and gender. Thereby the transpositions within the role pattern have become visible. This is articulated by means of gender differentiation, and takes the form of a transposition from women to men. It is when the function of service becomes an essential feature in the role of ruler that the shift of gender also occurs. The converting of the values of the different roles coincides with a masculinisation.

Chapter Four

Remember How He Told You ...

IV. 1. *In the conflict between word and table.*

Women's serving functions are given an exemplary significance for the whole community and for its leadership. But women are not restricted to functions of caring for others; they are also established in roles traditionally reserved for men. As is shown by the narrative about Martha and Mary at Lk 10.38–42, they have a disciple's learning relationship to Jesus. Here, women are related to the Lord's word in a way that creates conflict over against the obligation to service, διακονία.

In the narrative of Martha and Mary the scene is set in a world of women; apart from Jesus, only women appear, the two sisters Martha and Mary. Unlike the story in Jn 11–12, the Lukan version betrays no knowledge of a brother, Lazarus,[1] nor is the group which accompanies Jesus on his journey mentioned as being present.[2] The two sisters are cast in roles which, without becoming caricatures, are almost stereotypes. This has encouraged strong traditions interpreting the two women as symbols of various attitudes, forms of life or theological principles – e.g., righteousness by works as against righteousness by faith, Judaism as against Christianity, the *vita activa* as against the *vita*

---

[1] But in John too, Lazarus is a less central person than his sisters. Some scholars have held that the two sisters are presented in a very similar way in Luke and in John, with a consistent set of qualities linked to each one of them: Martha is restlessly active and takes practical responsibility, while Mary is more mild and withdrawn. But the picture is considerably more complicated, especially as far as John is concerned: cf. Seim, 'Roles of Women', 70ff. Augsten, *Stellung des lukanischen Christus*, 17, holds that Lazarus' presence makes Jesus' conversation with the two sisters less offensive to propriety. For a more detailed comparison, cf. Brutschek, *Maria-Martha-Erzählung*, 147–50.

[2] Cf. p. 63 n. 121. Also Brutschek, *Maria-Martha-Erzählung*, 98, 227 n. 543, ably rejects all speculations about this.

contemplativa, etc.[3] Not only does this kind of interpretation brush aside any historical understanding; it is also blind to the gender perspective. Some interpreters, inspired by form criticism, go to an opposite extreme: according to them, the Sitz im Leben of the narrative is hospitality towards itinerant preachers. The story was intended to regulate the extent of work implied for the hosting house, especially the women of the house.[4]

The episode in Lk 10.38–42 is quite clearly presented as a narrative about hospitality. It is localised within the Lukan narrative of Jesus' journey, and the event takes place in the home of Martha, who has received Jesus. The majority of the MSS. have the reading that Martha received him εἰς τὴν οἰκίαν αὐτῆς or εἰς τὸν οἶκον αὐτῆς. It is an open question, which of these readings should be preferred. Probably, however, Nestle-Aland's textual choice of omitting both as the *lectio difficilior* is the original one, even if one can adduce good internal reasons in Luke in favour of τὸν οἶκον αὐτῆς.[5] In terms of content, however, there is little difference; at any rate, the narrative makes it clear that Martha receives him in her own home. The rather brief construction ὑπεδέξατο αὐτόν, can also be read as a positive counterpart to the Samaritans at 9.53 who οὐκ ἐδέξαντο αὐτόν.[6] As far as the name Martha is concerned, this text is probably the oldest evidence of this Aramaic female name, a feminine form of 'mar', that is, 'sovereign lady', 'ruling lady', 'lady'.[7] Thus the name helps to emphasise Martha's autonomous, well-off and dominant position. She is the hospitable hostess who welcomes the itinerant preacher and performs herself the practical tasks which the visit demands.

---

[3]   Cf. Blank, 'Frauen', 54; Brutschek, *Maria-Martha-Erzählung*, 1–4. A critical assessment in Schottroff, 'Frauen', 121; Schüssler Fiorenza, 'Biblische Grundlegung', 31.

[4]   Laland, 'Martha-Maria Perikope', 80ff., followed by Augsten, *Stellung des lukanischen Christus*, 21, and Dillon, *Eye-witnesses*, 239.

[5]   Brutschek, *Maria-Martha-Erzählung*, 18, prefers the long variant for such reasons 'internal to Luke'.

[6]   Blank, 'Frauen', 55, has seen the point, but not the argument. On δέχομαι with its derivatives as a term for hospitality in Luke, cf. Laland, 'Martha-Maria Perikope', 72f. Besides this, the question about the significance of the story about Martha and Mary within the present context is very problematic, cf. Wall, 'Martha and Mary', who gives an account of the existing suggestions and rejects them. He himself finds the solution in a presupposed Lukan use of Deuteronomy, cf. p. 1 n. 4.

[7]   Leipoldt, *Jesus*, 189.

Martha is therefore a good example of a patroness in comfortable circumstances. The stationary setting of the scene in Lk 10.38–42 is thus more typical than the itinerant setting in Lk 8.1–3 which, however, is likewise coloured by experiences of the support found in rich women's benefaction. Other New Testament texts too convey more or less directly that women took the roles of householders and patrons of the community.[8] But it is not clear what this patronage further involved. Beyond doubt, the women who were materially able to accommodate the community in their house had thereby also power and influence. But it is, as yet, uncertain whether status as patron/ess implied a formal directive authority. Some scholars insist that the patronesses performed functions of leadership in communities. It is even, as has been set out above, claimed that διακονέω and διακονία are technical terms for this leadership of house churches, and that the terminology is due to the fact that the responsibility for the community's eucharist and for the common meal was assigned to these householders as well as preaching.[9] But it is difficult to establish with certainty that the functions of a benefactor and the status of patron also involved an institutional position of leadership,[10] and there are no texts that clearly couple such functions specifically with the

---

[8]   *Inter alia* Rom 16.5; 1 Cor 16.9; Phm 2; Col 4.15. Rich women had the reputation at this period of being (all too) willing to open their houses and their purses to new and alien cults that spread from the east, cf. Schüssler Fiorenza, *In Memory*, 176. Many inscriptions and memorial tablets in honour of women mentioned by name are a testimony to this kind of female benefaction. Christianity competing for the favour of these women, thereby took its place within a more general pattern – and with considerable success. Sociologically, the attempt has been made to explain the rich women's adherence to Christianity as a way out of a 'status dissonance'. Roman and Hellenistic women had acquired wealth or at least a relative economic independence, without attaining a corresponding political, social or religious influence and power. The status which wealth gave was not normally sufficient to counter the lack of status and the social limitations adherent to their gender. They therefore sought new, alternative social contexts that could ease the dissonance – and they found such a context in the Christian group, cf. Schüssler Fiorenza, *In Memory*, 182. This has been discussed earlier, p. 64f., to shed light on women's possession of property.

[9]   Cf. p. 70f. and p. 73 n. 149.

[10]   Mortley, *Womanhood*, 46. Lampe, *Stadtrömischen Christen*, 316, points also to the noteworthy fact that the house churches were called after 'the householders' (cf. the later titulus churches in Rome), '... auch wenn ihre Stellung im inneren der Hausgemeinden von den Presbytern und Diakonen übertroffen worden sein mag'.

διακονία-terms or with responsibility for the meal. Phoebe was διάκονος and προστάτις in the community in Cenchreae, but we are not told whether she had a community in her house. Indeed, some texts seem to indicate the opposite: those providing the material means, were not the ones to direct the distribution of these. Distribution was entrusted to a leadership who themselves lacked personal possessions and was chosen either by virtue of a charismatic endowment or else through a more institutional election. This does not, of course, mean that female patrons could not have dominant positions, especially if they also had the community in their house. Nor does it mean that the communities did not have female leaders. The point is simply that there was not an obvious connection between the status of patron and active leadership, and that there is no terminological evidence that διακονία was especially associated with this kind of leadership. Thus, even if Martha is a householder exercising hospitality, she is not to be understood automatically, in a presupposed 'subtext', to have been the leader of a community.

The consistent use of ὁ κύριος throughout the whole of the passage – Ἰησοῦς is not used – characterises Jesus as the teacher and as the authoritative Lord of the community.[11] This gives the narrative a transparence in terms of time, but it does not give us an indisputable reason to transfer this narrative especially to the situation of a later community in which appeal was made to the authority of the risen Lord, without any concern for available tradition.[12] Attempts to read the narrative in Lk 10.38–42 on a reconstructed subtext presupposing that its special and primary aim on Luke's part was to contest Martha's role of diaconal leadership[13] contain a number of sharp insights, especially into the portrait of Mary. But they are based on assumptions of a universally-diffused technical use of the διακον-terms; and, as has been set out briefly above, these assumptions are problematic. Not the least argument against this suggestion is its isolation *vis-à-vis* the role that the διακον-terminology plays elsewhere in the Lukan construction. Martha

---

[11] Marshall, *Luke*, 285, 452.

[12] As Schüssler Fiorenza, 'Biblische Grundlegung', 36, does.

[13] This is the main concept of Schüssler Fiorenza in 'Biblische Grundlegung'. Cf. also Tetlow, *Women and Ministry*, 104f.

fits well into this picture, since the use of διακονέω and διακονία in 10.40 is in harmony with the use of these terms elsewhere in Luke.

In many ways, Martha is representative of the typical female figure in Luke-Acts. She is one of a number of relatively well-off and autonomous women who have their own house and place it at the disposition of others, whether the community or itinerant preachers: she may be compared with Tabitha in Acts 9.36ff., Mary the mother of John in Acts 12.12 and Lydia in Acts 16.15, 40, who actively compels Paul to be her guest. The parallel to Peter's mother-in-law in Lk 4.38f. and to the women who follow Jesus in 8.1–3 is also clear. Martha's conflict with Mary, therefore, sheds a critical light on the whole of this presentation of women.

In the narrative in Lk 10.38–42, Martha is cast in the typical practical role of caring for others, repeatedly characterised by διακον-terminology in 10.40, ἡ δὲ Μάρθα περιεσπᾶτο περὶ πολλὴν διακονίαν, and ἡ ἀδελφή μου μόνην με κατέλιπεν διακονεῖν. Martha and her diaconal activity are set in contrast to her sister Mary, who listens in silence at the feet of the Lord. Mary for her part is portrayed in the typical position of the pupil as she sits at the Lord's feet and listens to his word in 10.39 (cf. Acts 22.3; PAb 1.4). This description of a teacher-pupil relationship is an important feature of the text. The role of student in which Mary is placed, goes beyond the normal opportunities for women to hear the word in the context of worship. Moreover, the text alludes to terms which in rabbinic tradition are connected precisely to teaching institutions.[14] A thanksgiving in bBer IV 2b employs 'lot', 'part' in relation to a pupil at a place of teaching and about the obligation of rising early for the word of the Law. This rabbinic passage is especially interesting because a contrast helps to emphasise that it is the student's lot that is good and praiseworthy. The comparison, however, is chosen and presented in such a way that the preference for the study of the Law becomes obvious: the lot of the diligent student of the Law is contrasted with the lot of the idler. In Luke's narrative the different value of the two types of activity is not as easily

---

[14] On this, cf. Gerhardsson, *Memory*, 239ff. He does not, however, reflect at all on the extraordinary point that Lk 10.38–42 is speaking about women.

assessed. It is not a case of studies as opposed to useless and vain activity, but in relationship to a task which someone must undertake – indeed, a task which the gospel emphasises in other places as necessary and good.

In the gospel narrative, when compared to the rabbinic material, it is also striking that the student in this case is a woman. Within Judaism, the study of the Law was, as far as we know, at that period restricted to men. Women had neither the right nor the obligation to be taught. In rabbinic sources, this can be expressed in the strictest case as a prohibition against teaching them (bKid 29b). We know less about how it was practised, but the sources indicate that praxis and theory in this field very largely coincided. Naturally, this does not mean that there were no individual cases of learned and quick-witted Jewish women.[15] Women needed also to have a certain knowledge of the Law, in order to observe the prohibitions and the rules that affected them. This knowledge was transmitted from mother to daughter.[16] But mainly it was a woman's

---

[15] Swidler, *Biblical Affirmations*, 99–110, examines the two examples of women versed in the Law that are usually presented, Beruriah and the servant girl to rabbi Judah. He concludes that Beruriah is the exception that confirms the rule that women did not study Torah. In the case of the servant girl, the conclusion is more negative. She has picked up a little Hebrew and learnt some of the jargon, but 'for all her strength of character, she is not evidence that women studied Torah'. Goodblatt, 'Beruriah Traditions', 84f., emphasises that the unique element in the traditions about Beruriah is that they depict a woman whose learning demands further instruction, not merely elementary teaching. However, the evidence for this is to be found in narratives with a Babylonian Amorean origin. It appears that those who handed on the traditions in Babylon in the fourth and fifth centuries have developed the earlier biographical tradition about Beruriah by raising the standard of her education.

It is characteristic that both of the women named here have lived as daughter or as wife (Beruriah was the daughter of a well-known rabbi, and married to rabbi Meir) or servant girl in a rabbi's house: cf. Witherington, 'On the Road,' 244. See also Epstein, *Sex Laws*, 86f.; Goldfeld, 'Women as Sources', 257–71. As the background to this, it is important to emphasise that to be exempted from the study of the Law and the general observation of the Law was no advantage. The study of the Law was regarded as a privilege in Israel: cf. Goldfeld, 'Women as Sources', 257f.

Let me conclude by noting that I question whether the type of argument brought forward here ought *eo ipso* to be rejected as apologetically determined and comparatively anti-Jewish (cf. Schüssler Fiorenza, 'Biblische Grundlegung', 33). It is, however, important to make the reservation that an intensive investigation of Jewish sources from a feminist perspective may alter the picture and add significant nuances to it.

[16] Goldfeld, 'Women as Sources', 258: 'The three positive mitzvot that fell on women and that are generally considered to belong to the women's realm are niddah (the laws of

task in connection with studies of the Law to give support on the domestic side, so that her husband could devote himself to his studies as much as possible.[17] In the light of this, it is not only noteworthy that Mary is given the position of a student: it also gives a perspective on the conflict dealt with in the narrative, between domestic obligations and the supreme right to listen to the word of the Lord.

Martha plays the active role that drives the narrative forwards; seen in this regard, she is the protagonist of the story. Her activity is emphasised with vivid words, περιεσπᾶτο περὶ πολλὴν διακονίαν (10.40), and her own words are related in direct speech, when she rebukes her sister's lack of practical activity and reproaches Jesus for his lack of interest in the division of labour. She takes it for granted that priority belongs to the service she herself carries out, and she takes Jesus seriously to task because he does not see to it that Mary takes a part in the same service. The reproach uttered by Martha, thus shows a certain set of priorities about what ought to be a woman's primary occupation. It is not, however, accepted by the Lord, even although it is formulated in such a way that it expects acceptance: the rhetorical question with οὐ presupposes an affirmative answer. Martha's choice of words also refers continually back to herself: ἀδελφή μου, μόνην με, μοι.[18] This intensifies the contrast with Mary's concentration on Jesus' words. But at the same time, Martha's appeal to Jesus implies that the relationship between host(ess) and guest is altered, when even the hostess Martha operates with Jesus' word as the ultimate authority.

There are large text-critical problems about Jesus' answer in 10.41f.[19] In some MSS., the two first parts are completely lacking (it, sy), and codex D has a much reduced version (only θορυβάζῃ). These have in common the omission of ἑνὸς δέ ἐστιν χρεία (10.42a). It is

---

family purity), hallah (the separation of dough to prepare loaves of bread) and the lighting of the Sabbath candles. Centred on the family and the home, these mitzvot illustrate the different modes of experience that men and women participated in and for which they were educated.' Cf. also Epstein, *Sex Laws*, 84.

[17] Goldfeld, 'Women as Sources', 258.

[18] Brutschek, *Maria-Martha-Erzählung*, 43.

[19] On the documentation of these, cf. Brutschek, *Maria-Martha-Erzählung*, 5–12, who goes into great detail. Cf. also Laland, 'Martha-Maria Perikope', 74f.; Noack, *Rejseberetning*, 36f.; Witherington, *Women in the Ministry of Jesus*, 103.

obvious that these words represent the sensitive point as is demonstrated in the fact that the textual witnesses are divided among three quite distinct variants, two of which are very well attested: 1. 'Few things, little, are necessary' (p38, p3, sy pal). 2. 'Few things are necessary, or only one' (Nestle's text in earlier editions, and attested e.g. by Sinaiticus and Vaticanus). 3. 'One thing is necessary' (attested by the oldest papyri and the koiné group).

Among scholars, there is a wide variety in the choice of which variant is to be preferred, as well as in the assessment of which represents the *lectio difficilior*.[20] In this case, the connection between textual critical and exegetical considerations is extremely close, and the choice is influenced by the question of whether Martha's activity can be totally dismissed as devoid of value and unnecessary. For those who cannot bring themselves to sweep Martha aside completely, the variants with ὀλίγον are the most comfortable. They imply that something is said in Martha's favour; her mistake is simply that she bothers with much *more* than is necessary (cf. also πολλήν in 10.40 and περὶ πολλά in 10.41). A little, or only one thing, can suffice – perhaps this refers to the number of courses to be laid on the table.[21] Such an interpretation can in fact be said to be covered by all three variants, provided that 'the one thing necessary' in 10.42a is not identified with 'the good part' that Mary has chosen (10.42b).

When Jesus rejects Martha's implicit demand that her sister should help, this is done by means of a two-sided argumentation. It is said negatively, about Martha that she fusses (μεριμνάω) and bustles about

[20] Noack, *Rejseberetning*, 37, holds to the first variant as the only one that can explain the two others. But it can just as well be claimed that the various insertions with ὀλίγον are included to soften the contrast. Marshall, *Luke*, 453: 'The transcriptional evidence ... is in favor ... "few", but the intrinsic and external evidence for ... "one" is strong and a final decision is difficult'. Fitzmyer, *Luke*, I 894, lets the oldest witness, p. 75, be decisive – also because it gives the clearest contrast in terms of content. In the same way, Brutschek, *Maria-Martha-Erzählung*, 12, concludes that the shortest and sharpest version is the original.

[21] Laland, 'Martha-Maria Perikope', 74ff., retains the longest textual variant and advances the possibility of a gastronomic interpretation. He himself, rejects this in part, and wishes to understand only ὀλίγων δέ ἐστιν χρεία as referring to the meal: Jesus does not need so much, while ἤ ἑνός is not concerned with food. The one thing necessary is to do what Mary does, 'dem Worte des Herrn zu lauschen'.

(θορυβάζω) with many things. Positively it is said about Mary that she has chosen the good part, τὴν ἀγαθὴν μερίδα. The transition between the two descriptions of the women is mediated by the saying of Jesus about the one thing necessary. Jesus' reply to Martha does not concern her serving, but the way it is done, with fuss and agitation. It can thus be claimed that the fundamental antithesis is not between hearing and serving, but between hearing and agitated toil.[22] What truly causes the problem, is that Martha, in her agitated busyness with so many things, demands her sister's assistance. Because of her own need (cf. χρεία in 10.42) for help she disregards Mary's choice, and even tries to ensure that Jesus supports this intrusion of hers. So Martha represents the threat that Mary's part can be taken from her.

We should note that this is not portrayed as a conflict between men and women, but as a conflict between two sisters.[23] Is there a deliberate ambiguity in ἀδελφή, such as the women need not be two sisters by

[22] This is a justified and important point in Brutschek, *Maria-Martha-Erzählung*, 47. At the same time, she later weakens the point (143ff.) by claiming that Luke has a positive and a negative use of διακονία with reference to Lk 10.38–42 and Acts 6.1–6. This means that she fails to recognise the dynamics in the employment of διακον-terms in Luke.

The contrast between listening and being anxious has certain points of similarity with Paul's argument at 1 Cor 7.32–5, cf. the overview of the available secondary literature in Brutschek, *Maria-Martha-Erzählung*, 251 n. 764. She herself accepts a link with certain reservations, whether because Paul knew an earlier version of the narrative now found in Luke, or because the narrative itself is to be attributed to 'einem Mann der Paulusschule', 147. Cf. also Wimbush, *Paul*, 50f. However, the differences between the two texts are also very striking. Even if the use of μεριμνάω links them terminologically, Paul uses this word in a quite different way to Luke, where it is exclusively negative in its associations. Not least, the whole point in Paul is the difference between the married person and the unmarried, while this plays no role at all in the context in Luke. On the contrary, both sisters are portrayed as single women.

[23] Schüssler Fiorenza, 'Biblische Grundlegung', 35, 40, criticises this pattern for being an androcentric move by the author to put into action clichés about women. In order to tame Martha and reduce her to silence, the opposite ideal of the quiet and listening Mary is created: But Schüssler Fiorenza cannot avoid establishing quite sharp antitheses, and her problem with the conflict seems to be primarily that Martha, who has her sympathy, loses out.

For others, the gender aspect plays no part at all. Brutschek, *Maria-Martha-Erzählung*, 109, who does not add anything to what is commonly said about Jesus and women in Luke, claims that the motif of women plays a subordinate role in this narrative; it figures only in the female proper names which were in fact already present in the tradition.

blood, but two Christian women, one of whom (Martha) has taken the other (Mary) into her house – (cf. the widows in Tabitha's house in Acts 9.39ff.)? The antithesis between the two sisters is provoked by Jesus' presence. But he is not the first to articulate the difference in categories of conflict: Martha has this part. Jesus does indeed confirm the antithesis, but not in Martha's favour. Instead, he rebukes Martha's toil and agitation, and defends the 'student' Mary when she is summoned to the kitchen.

For women, the traditional διακονία-role was not controversial, but taken for granted, and this can be clearly seen in the formulation of Martha's protest. It is only when the διακονία function is put forward as an ideal for free men and for the leadership that it becomes necessary to give special and christologically founded reasons for this. In indirect proportion to this, a special defence from ὁ κύριος is required in order for women to take on the role of pupil and even to prefer this, when other and seemingly more urgent women's functions make a claim upon them, and the different functions come into conflict with each other. Indeed, the defence is made with such emphasis that the implicit challenge in the narrative about Martha and Mary is to choose with Mary and to enter a relationship with Jesus in which one listens to his word rather than being concerned about the table. The question however, is to what extent are we to understand the antithesis between Martha and Mary as absolute?

Mary has chosen 'the good part'. The positive adjective, ἀγαθή, can be used here in a comparative sense, that is to say it is a case of the *better* part.[24] This means that Martha's part too can be good, even if Mary's is better. However, the determined form of the expression can just as easily imply a contrasting comparison, in other words the good part as opposed to the bad part. Against the background of the positive portrayal of the διακονία role elsewhere in the gospel, however, it is difficult to accept that it should suddenly come here to represent the mistaken choice. Immediately before this passage, the story of the Good Samaritan has given an example of love for one's neighbour. It makes

---

[24] Marshall, *Luke*, 454.

little sense to see the discussion with Martha as a calling into question this example of unexpected compassion or as a counter-balance to it.[25] For as we have seen, Jesus' objection does not concern Martha's serving, but her unease and agitation. It is also important to establish priorities as the outcome relates to a situation of conflict, in which Martha makes demands on Mary. Thus, the priorities are not necessarily absolute: the rejection of Martha's utterance becomes unambiguous only when Jesus adds that Mary's good part is not to be taken from her. When there is a set priority among 'the parts', these cannot be played off against one another.

A comparative understanding makes it unnecessary to interpret 'the good part' in an intensified manner in terms of the kingdom of God.[26] If the expression ἡ ἀγαθὴ μερίς alludes to Jewish terminology and to an assessment of the study of the Law as obviously the best choice, then Mary's choice of τὴν ἀγαθὴν μερίδα simply iterates that she has chosen to concentrate on the word. This means that there is a harmony between the characterisation in 10.39 and the description in 10.42. This idea finds support in other sayings of Jesus about 'hearing the word', which are also directly related to women. Moreover, the preference for Mary indicates that the real and primary host is Jesus himself providing his word.[27] The deeper structure of the narrative is therefore similar to that which we found in 8.1–3 – the service of Jesus comes first.

[25] Horn, *Glaube*, 238. Against Seccombe, *Possessions*, 124, who claims this with support in Goulder, Flender, and Talbert. Cf. also Witherington, *Women in the Ministry of Jesus*, 100. He does, however, mention the important point that other narratives in Luke too emphasise the significance of 'the one thing', cf. 15.8; 16.18; and especially 18.19, 22. See also n. 6 above.

[26] Schottroff, 'Frauen', 123, has not seen that a comparative understanding makes it easier, rather than harder, to accept that Martha's part too can be good. She maintains an absolute use in which 'the good part' is to be understood eschatologically as a 'share in the kingdom of God', 133 n. 98. Similarly Blank, 'Frauen', 57, who adduces Lk 12.31: 'Das Streben nach der Gottesherrschaft hat gegenüber allen anderen Lebensfragen eine absolute Priorität. Man wird deshalb das "unum necessarium" am besten mit der Gottesherrschaft gleichsetzen'.

[27] Cf. Canker, *Luke*, 133; Witherington, *Women in the Ministry of Jesus*, 103. In the light of this Danker reads the answer of Jesus in such a way that it takes on a touch of humour: 'That is, an olive or two will suffice at present, for Mary has already had the "best course" (good portion) and it cannot be taken away from her. Jesus has already dispensed the banquet of life, for Mary has been treated to his word'.

Acts 6.1–6 touches on a conflict which is solved on the basis of the same preference and with a terminological echo of Lk 10.38–42.[28] But the priority is presented in Acts 6 as being beyond discussion. When Martha reproaches Jesus for his lack of concern that Mary leaves her to serve alone, μόνην με κατέλιπεν διακονεῖν (Lk 10.40), Jesus surprisingly gives a decision in favour of Mary. But for the twelve, it is taken for granted that God is displeased[29] if they abandon God's word to serve at table, ἡμᾶς καταλείψαντας τὸν λόγον τοῦ θεοῦ διακονεῖν τραπέζαις (Acts 6.2). In its present Lukan context, the story of Martha and Mary in Lk 10.38–42 represents the normative regulation, explicitly backed by Jesus' authority, which then is further applied in Acts 6.[30] But it also betrays the fact that the conflict of preferences takes on another and an opposite form when prominent men are involved. When Martha demands Mary's help, her indignation is quite reasonable by conventional standards, and it is surprising when Jesus' authority is engaged to allow Mary to remain where she is. In the case of the male apostles, it is presumedly impossible that God should will anything but that they should be allowed to employ all their time in prayer and the service of the word. Taken together the other way round, the two narratives demonstrate that the preference which the leading men can maintain without hesitation, is – surprisingly – valid for women as well; although this must be said with the reservation that we have not yet looked more closely at the relationship between 'the service of the word' and 'hearing the word of the Lord'. It is at any rate clear that – unlike the Pastoral Letters, which make a corresponding distinction – Luke is not interested in making a gender differentiation so that men take on responsibility for the word while women are engaged in charitable activity, as some have wished to claim about Lk 8.1–3. His interest is to set a priority, so that the one service is subordinated to the other.[31]

---

[28] Gerhardsson, *Memory*, 240f.; Schneider, *Apg.*, I 426 n. 48; Schüssler Fiorenza, 'Biblische Grundlegung', 37f.

[29] On this understanding of οὐκ ἀρεστόν ἐστιν, cf. Haenchen, *Apg.*, 215.

[30] Gerhardsson, *Memory*, 241. Hengel, 'Maria Magdalena', 248, sees the two passages more as parallel and in line with 8.3, as 'paradigmatische Vorstufen des späteren Diakonamtes'.

[31] Cf. Schüssler Fiorenza, *In Memory*, 165, 315.

The particular occasion causing the conflict in Acts 6.1, the fact that the widows of the Hellenists were overlooked in the daily service, ἐν τῇ διακονίᾳ τῇ καθημερινῇ is of limited significance in our present context. There is apparently a daily provision in the community, described more precisely in 6.2 as διακονεῖν τραπέζαις. Whether this was a matter of a daily meal or of a more general structure of support to the needy members of the community,[32] is also of less importance.

Commentators do not agree about whether the twelve are supposed to have been directly in charge of the daily service or not. Have they done so up to now, but are no longer able to carry it out satisfactorily, due to the growth of the community, without neglecting their primary duties?[33] This suggestion would accord best with the argumentation used to resolve the conflict, and it would agree with a reading of Lk 9.13–17 as a commission given to the apostles. Or have others been in charge of the service, with conflict as the result, so that a potential solution would be for the apostles to take over?[34] Although we should not attach too much importance to this alternative suggestion, note that it is supported by D's variant of 6.1, ἐν τῇ διακονίᾳ τῶν Ἑβραιῶν. In this case, the solution means that οἱ δώδεκα, as the principal leaders of the community, dismantle the established division of labour, and initiate the new order with οἱ ἑπτά.

In my opinion, this last alternative has most to be said on its behalf, and it is supported by more arguments than are usually noted. Acts 5.42 describes the apostles as occupied all day with teaching and proclamation, and the result of this is the growth of the community (6.1a). In the beginning of Acts, Luke ably avoids a mode of expression that would point unambiguously to the apostles as in charge of the distribution of the community's resources, or for that matter, in charge of any meal.[35] It is indeed true that money is laid at the apostles' feet (4.35,

---

[32]   In the first case, τράπεζα means a table for eating, and is used as a metonym for a meal. Διακονέω is thus to serve at a meal. In the other case, διακονέω is to be understood more generally of material support, and τράπεζα of a banker's table. On the various possibilities, cf. Tyson, 'Problem of Food', 78, 83f. Cf. also p. 234.

[33]   Cf. Moxnes, Patrons, 178; Roloff, Apostolat, 221.

[34]   Most commentaries, cf. Haenchen, Apg., 215; Schneider, Apg., I 423ff.

[35]   Moxnes' interpretation, Patrons, 177f., which is based on the premiss that Luke describes the apostles as 'responsible for the redistribution of possessions', and that Acts

37; 5.2), but we are not told that they also distribute this money. In 4.35, a passive expression is used: the money is distributed (διεδίδετο) to each one in accordance with need. In 2.42 it is apparently presupposed that the people who offer resources themselves distribute these. The same text, 2.42, 46, also indicates that all the believers together participate in the breaking of the bread, that is the eucharistic community meal: πάντες δὲ οἱ πιστεύοντες in 2.44.

Therefore, the twelve in Acts apparently do not carry out the service which, according to the gospel, is enjoined upon them, and which is reflected linguistically when the apostolate is called διακονία in Acts 1.17, 25. The narrative in Acts 6.1–6 thus sheds further light on how the apostolate is to be understood as service. When the twelve reject the service of table, διακονεῖν τραπέζαις, in 6.2, the reason given is the preference for the service of the word, ἡ διακονία τοῦ λόγου (6.4). Διακονία τοῦ λόγου is not a fixed term, but 'eine ad-hoc Bildung des Evangelisten',[36] shaped by the need to contrast with διακονεῖν τραπέζαις.[37] This is a further example of the relative freedom with which Luke could form the use of terms in a way that produces close connections internal to the larger text. The construction ἡ διακονία τοῦ λόγου serves to insist that the twelve, even if they reject διακονεῖν τραπέζαις are just as fully occupied with διακονία and thereby perform their leadership ὡς ὁ διακονῶν (cf. Lk 22.27).[38]

The whole body of disciples, τὸ πλῆθος τῶν μαθητῶν, is to look out seven men whom the apostles can institute for the task which they themselves have rejected. Acts 21.8 indicates that there existed a fixed tradition about the group of seven, including their names, similar to

6.1–6 implies that the apostles are 'removed from any suspicion of economic misgivings', has therefore insufficient support in the text.

[36] Schneider, *Apg.*, I 427, n. 52, in a quotation from Conzelmann.

[37] Roloff, *Apostolat*, 223 n. 196, who convincingly rejects the idea that this is a case of a rabbinic *terminus technicus*. The expression is therefore to be understood 'im Rahmen der sonstigen lukanischen Bedeutung von διακονία'.

[38] Roloff, *Apostolat*, 223: '... wir es hier mit dem gleichen gefüllten διακονία-Begriff zu tun haben, wie in Lk 22, 26f.; Apg. 1, 25 ...'. The fact that the aspect of the meal is eliminated poses a problem, nevertheless. This also shows how sayings of Jesus contribute to an increasing rhetoric of service in the presentation of ecclesiastic functions, cf. Lampe, 'Diakonia', 49, 57, for the patristic period, and for a modern feminist-theological reassessment, cf. Schüssler Fiorenza, 'Dienst', 303–13.

the tradition about the twelve. Luke does not employ the term διάκονος for any of the seven. Indeed, considering the frequency of διακονία-language in the pericope, it is actually striking that such terminology is nowhere directly applied to them. Διακονεῖν τραπέζαις in 6.2 is not repeated about the seven in 6.3, where instead we find the expression ἐπὶ τῆς χρείας ταύτης, which in this sense is uncommon in Luke-Acts. In the following story the seven do not appear in connection with διακονία τραπέζων either, but as preachers and leaders of communities.[39] While the description of their specific function in this way is kept rather vague, the emphasis in 6.3 is given to their qualifications, which clearly anticipate the description of Stephen in 6.8 and 10. In the chapters which immediately follow, he dislodges the twelve from their place as protagonists, and Acts 6.1–6 serves as an introduction to Stephen (and Philip) by means of the list of names of the seven.

The list of names of the seven was for Luke, part of the given tradition as was also the list of names of the twelve.[40] Both lists consisted exclusively of male names, and this fact has been built into the narrative in such a way that at the elections for leadership reported in Acts 1.15–26 and 6.1–6 gender is an explicit criterion for eligibility: only men can be elected, δεῖ οὖν τῶν συνελθόντων ἡμῖν ἀνδρῶν (1.21), and ἐπισκέψασθε δέ, ἀδελφοί, ἄνδρας, (6.3). The specification of the gender criterion implies, however, that the exclusive status of the men has to be explicitly stated; it is not automatically taken for granted. The presentation of women in the gospel story, has actually

---

[39] This happens primarily after the expulsion from Jerusalem, 8.1. Stephen's address in ch. 7 is a defence speech, inspired by the Spirit, before the council, cf. Lk 21.12–15. In 21.8 Philip is called εὐαγγελιστής a rare designation in the New Testament, cf. Eph 4.11; 2 Tim 4.5. Presumably the aim is to distinguish him from the apostle Philip, as it is clear that from very early on there was a problem in keeping these two distinct, cf. p. 210f.

Although the seven are not called deacons, Haenchen, *Apg.*, 216, holds that Luke's readers understood them thus. Contrary to this, Roloff, *Apostolat*, 219, emphasises correctly that the fact that the association is so obvious makes it all the more striking that Luke avoids the term. So Jervell, 'Töchter Abrahams', 88, is not convincing when he claims that Acts 6.1–6 is the Lukan emphasis on the fact that those who have *the diaconal function* are all men and that the service of women therefore does not represent this specific function. On the question of female deacons in the early Christian period, cf. Lohfink, 'Weibliche Diakone', 320–8.

[40] Cf. Schneider, *Apg.*, I 428, for further evidence.

launched them as natural candidates – not least for the task of which Acts 6.1–3 speaks. But the historical fact that the twelve and the seven were men (as is seen from the lists of names) means that the eligibility of women is disallowed, and leadership is defined as the business of men. The fact that the leadership is shaped after the Jewish pattern probably also plays a significant role. The twelve are portrayed as rulers with the power of judges over the people of the twelve tribes (Lk 22.30b).[41] The seven equal in number a Jewish community council or leadership group.[42]

In other words, women are excluded from a leadership which is mediated christologically and established in keeping with Jewish models – the new leadership in Israel. The leaders are to devote themselves to service. But the women who have served cannot become leaders. We have seen how this is reflected in the narrative by means of the transposition of the διακον-terminology. At the same time, passages like Lk 8.19–21, 11.27f. and 10.38–42 show that the relationship to the word is decisive for women's discipleship, and that this opens the way to new opportunities.

IV.2. – *to hear the word of the Lord . . .* .

Mary's role in Lk 10.38–42 is passive; she listens, learns, and is silent. While Martha is active and engages in dialogue, Mary is passive and taciturn.[43] But Mary's silent listening is not exceptional: at the outset, this is true of everyone. In relation to the word of Jesus, they find themselves in the position of a listener. First, one must listen and be taught. And when we are told of Mary that she

[41] Cf. the fact that the *circa* one hundred and twenty in Acts 1.15 correspond to the number who must be present in order to establish a local sanhedrin. On the further treatment of women and the apostolate, cf. p. 161ff.

[42] Schnackenburg, 'Lukas als Zeuge', 236ff. The seven were probably Diaspora Jews, cf. the discussion in Tyson, 'Problem of Food', 78f.

[43] This is a trait to which importance is seldom attached by the commentators. But cf. Tetlow, *Women and Ministry*, 104, and Schüssler Fiorenza, 'Biblische Grundlegung', 35, 37f., who makes this a main point in her feminist reconstruction with Martha as the heroine in opposition to Luke's construction with the silent and submissive Mary as the ideal. Cf. also Jervell's emphasis that the women in Luke constitute 'die hörende Gemeinde', 'Töchter Abrahams', 87.

listened to the word of the Lord, ἤκουεν τὸν λόγον αὐτοῦ, this is an allusion to a number of more general characteristics of discipleship elsewhere in the gospel. These are more detailed, and emphasise that the word is not only to be heard, but also to be taken care of and to be carried out: 6.46ff.; 8.15, 21; 11.28. Two of these passages are clearly related to women. In 11.28, the connection with 11.27 suggests that we should understand the logion with special reference to women, even if the form, μακάριοι οἱ ἀκούοντες τόν λόγον τοῦ θεοῦ καὶ φυλάσσοντες, is general. And in 8.21, the similar statement establishing the criterion for membership in the fictive family of Jesus, refers explicitly both to women and to men. Thus it is characteristic that Lk 11.27f. follows the controversy about Beelzebub, which in Mark precedes the conflict with the family at Mk 3.31–4.

It is also noteworthy that three of the passages mentioned here are related to conflicts in a corresponding manner and in matters that are close to the narrative about Martha and Mary. When the parable of the sowed seed is expounded, a contrast is made in 8.14–15 between those who have heard the word and take good care of it (ἀκούσαντες τόν λόγον κατέχουσιν) and those who have heard it but then are crushed by (*inter alia*) concerns about maintaining their life (ὑπὸ μεριμνῶν ... τοῦ βίου ... συμπνίγονται cf. μεριμνᾷς βίου ... περὶ πολλά in 10.41). In 8.21, the attempt of Jesus' family, here explicitly his mother and his brothers, to lay claim to him is rejected. Jesus answers by giving a new definition and a relocation of the family relation, by proclaiming that his mother and his brothers are those who hear God's word and do it. The family of those who hear God's word takes the place of the original family. Even the honorary rights of motherhood, which rendered meaning and status to a woman's life, fall away and are replaced by other relationships. But as we have seen, the Lukan version of this story does not necessarily exclude members of Jesus' own family from *familia Dei*. In keeping with this Acts 1.14 relates that Mary, Jesus' mother, and his brothers are with the Galilean group of disciples lodging in Jerusalem. But when Mary is included in the new family of Jesus, this means that she appears as a disciple and not primarily as the mother who gave birth to him. Mary is called in Acts 1.14 Μαρία ἡ μήτηρ τοῦ Ἰησοῦ in order to identify which Mary is being spoken of.[44]

This is thrown into very sharp relief by the episode, peculiar to Luke, recounted at 11.27–8.[45] A woman in the crowd cries out to Jesus: μακαρία ἡ κοιλία ἡ βαστάσασά σε καὶ μαστοὶ οὓς ἐθήλασας. This is a macarism expressed in Jewish phraseology,[46] and it is in fact a blessing of Jesus and not of Mary, that is it says that a son such as Jesus makes a woman worthy of praise. As a description of a woman the beatitude in all its poetic power represents a concentration on the maternal functions of the female body: womb and breasts.[47] Jesus reacts by subjecting this to a critical appraisal, when he corrects her (μενοῦν)[48] and replies that μακάριοι οἱ ἀκούοντες τὸν λόγον τοῦ θεοῦ καὶ φυλάσσοντες (11.28). Mary is blessed, not because she is Jesus' biological mother, but because she hears the word of God and keeps it.

This brings into play, in a positive way, previous remarks about Mary: not only her obedience – γένοιτό μοι κατὰ τὸ ῥῆμά σου (Lk 1.38) – but also two statements in the infancy narratives about Mary who treasures up the words in her heart and ponders on them, 2.19 (what the shepherds tell about the words of the angels) and 2.51 (Simeon's prophetic words). The form of expression in these passages indicates that Mary does not immediately understand what is said, but

[44] Despite the various Jameses who appear in the gospel and Acts, James is never called 'the brother of the Lord' in Acts 12.17; 15.13; 21.18, as he is in Gal 1.19.

[45] On the Lukan character of the pericope, cf. Zimmermann, 'Selig', 115f.; Horn, *Glaube*, 237. When Bemile, *Magnificat*, 233, agrees with Schürmann in arguing that it is Q material, this appears to be governed by the need to anchor mariological elements in the oldest tradition possible.

[46] An almost verbally-exact parallel is found in the rabbinic literature: GnR 98, 62d. Cf. also Ab 2, 8. Zimmermann, 'Selig', 116.

[47] Κοιλία means 'belly', i.e. my translation does not make the anachronistic presupposition that people knew at that time about the womb and its function. Jesus' words to the daughters of Jerusalem (Lk 23.27–30) represent a twisted negated form of a similar macarism. Even if these words too turn the evaluations upside-down in a similar way, it is not due to the relationship to the word or the dominant role of discipleship, but because the time of tribulation makes normal life impossible. For a further discussion of this text, cf. p. 206ff.

[48] Bemile, *Magnificat*, 234, and Zimmermann, 'Selig', 117, reject – mainly for mariological reasons – any implication of contrast in μενοῦν. As with the 'polite' interpretations of 8.19–21, he prefers to claim that the macarism is 'korrigiert und steigert' by Jesus, i.e. that it is transferred from Jesus to God. Cf. also Fitzmyer, *Luke*, 423.

takes good care of the words in such a way that she continues to work on the meaning.[49] There is also a certain correspondence to 8.15, where the heart is said to be the place in which words are held fast, and to Lydia in Acts 16.14 who has her heart opened to what Paul said. Other traits in the narratives of Jesus' infancy and birth in Luke emphasise likewise that Mary is to be understood as the exemplary disciple, a Christian prototype, ἡ δούλη κυρίου.[50] Even if full discipleship is not possible at this early preparatory stage in the gospel, Mary is a disciple *in nuce* through her listening obedience and her openness towards the future explanation and fulfilment. But Mary's obedience is not portrayed merely in passive terms: she expresses active acceptance and positive response (1.38), and further she proclaims God's wondrous acts with prophetic authority (1.46–55).[51]

In the infancy narrative, however, Mary's role is still determined by 'maternity'. Even if the categories of discipleship are brought into play in contexts that speak of the 'word' (ῥῆμα), the occasion for these is pregnancy and the preoccupations of a mother. But Mary's virginal pregnancy does already imply a certain ambivalence.[52] Accordingly, Joseph plays a minimal role in Luke's infancy narrative and it is significant that Jesus' alienation from his family begins by affecting Joseph in particular (cf. 2.48f.). This episode concludes with the emphatic statement that his parents did not understand at that point, the meaning of Jesus' words, but that his mother took good care of all

[49] Brown, ed., *Mary in NT*, 150f. At the same time, the claim that these words indicate that Mary is an eyewitness or a source for Luke's account of these events, is rejected. On the meaning of 'heart' in Luke, cf. Bovon, *Lukas*, 89f.

[50] Cf. Brown, ed., *Mary in NT*, 105–77; Fitzmyer, *Luke*, 341; Karris, *Luke*, 55; Moloney, *First among Faithful*, 34ff.; Räisänen, *Mutter Jesu*, 154. Apart from Jesus and John, Mary is the only character from the infancy narrative who reappears in the following story – and also in Acts. It is therefore misleading when Tetlow, *Women and Ministry*, 102f., claims that 'Luke did not make a connection between the role of women in the periods of Israel and Jesus and the period of the church'. Tetlow introduces also an unjustified distinction between 'Israel's faith' and 'Christian faith', thereby dismissing the faith of the women in the gospel as 'still the faith of Israel'.

[51] On the prophetic elements in the infancy narratives, cf. p. 175ff.

[52] Mary's virginity is discussed in greater detail in the subchapter VI 2. 'Virgin and mother'.

these words in her heart. Remarks such as these, open the way for Mary's continued, but changed role, determined by the word rather than by her rights as mother. Mary becomes a receiver rather than a giver.

The group of texts discussed above, have shown how women's maternal functions are redefined in contrasting terms which emphasise that the decisive factor for women as well as men, is to hear the word of God and take good care of it, to do it. This is 'the good part' which shall not be taken away from them. But at issue here is not merely that women are not to be reduced to the role of wife and mother but to exemplify a priority which might solve a practical problem and meet a spiritual need for women in early Christian communities.[53] In a patriarchal culture where marriage is woman's destiny and childbearing her social and theological legitimation, such a redefinition of a woman's role presents the option of an alternative ascetic life supported by a new 'fictive' family.

Before investigating this, however, Mary's passivity and silence in Luke 10.38–42 raises some further questions. Does the idealisation of Mary mean that a woman's relationship to the word is to be understood in terms of silence: women are to keep silent and not to speak, to listen but not to teach? Does Luke represent an implicit variant of the same ideal as is explicit in 1 Tim 2.11f., where it is repeatedly and emphatically stated that a woman shall let herself be taught in silence?

The passive formulation in 1 Tim 2.11, γυνὴ ἐν ἡσυχίᾳ μανθανέτω, is in 2.12 turned into an active prohibition of women's teaching. The author of the Letter does not permit a woman to teach or to have authority over a man in any other way.[54] She is to subordinate herself

---

[53] As Schottroff, 'Frauen', explains. Both she and Laland, 'Martha-Maria Perikope', 81f., see this as an attempt at solving a problem for women in the congregations who were left with 'double work', that is both house-keeping and religious attendance. Housewives too should primarily have the opportunity to listen to the preaching. Schottroff, 'Frauen', 124, also points out the different social conditions between women: 'In den Häusern der reichen Christen, – wie bei Lydia, wird man den Sklavinnen diese Doppelrolle zugestanden haben'. This is one aspect of the matter, but it is too reductionist as a full interpretation of the passage.

[54] The anarthrous form of ἀνήρ is used, i.e. it is not (only) a question of the husband, but of men in general. This makes the prohibition universal and absolute: no woman can rule over any man.

and to keep calm and silent. The reason given for this is woman's secondary role in the creation and her primary role in the fall. The outcome of the paraenesis is therefore the hope for woman that she can be saved by giving birth to children, provided that these remain in the faith, in love and holiness.[55]

It is possible that this prohibition of teaching, both as it is formulated and as at is seen against the more general background of the Pastoral Letters, is primarily concerned with women's authority over against men.[56] Things were different in relation to children and to other women, perhaps especially younger women (cf. the employment of καλοδιδάσκαλος about older women, perhaps about female presbyters, πρεσβύτιδες, in Tit 2.3).[57] This is in keeping with the segregation of baptismal instruction, for example, for which there is evidence later in the second century. For reasons of propriety, deaconesses (and/or perhaps the widows of the community) were given the task of carrying out missionary work among women and of attending to female candidates for baptism.[58] Traditional ideas of seemliness are also prominent in the Pastoral Letters. They permeate the whole of the paraenesis. The elder women ought to teach the younger ones to live in accord with the author's own ideals for a virtuous woman's life: to love one's husband and children, to be respectable, pure and irreproachable, a good mistress of her household and subordinate to her husband.

Even if there are similarities between Luke's portrait of women and that of the Pastoral Letters, the differences too are obvious.[59] In 1 Tim

---

[55] The abrupt transition from the singular in 2.15a to the plural in 2.15b is best explained by supposing that a τέκνα from τεκνογονία in 2.15a is tacitly understood as the subject in 2.15b: cf. Ulrichsen, 'Bemerkninger', 19–25.

[56] Schüssler Fiorenza, *In Memory*, 290, interprets this to mean that female presbyters and patronae ought not to be eligible as bishop/president with responsibility for teaching in the community/ies.

[57] Schüssler Fiorenza, *In Memory*, 290.

[58] Christiansen, 'Women and Baptism', 1–8; Davies, *Revolt of Widows*, 97ff.; Swidler, *Biblical Affirmations*, 313f.

[59] On the more general debate about the relationship between Luke and the Pastoral Letters, cf. Quinn, *Last Volume of Luke*, 63ff., and Wilson, *Luke and the Pastoral Epistles*, both of whom tend independently to take Luke as the probable author of the Letters – but neither of whom discusses the question of women. Cf. also my own further discussion of this in the section on widows.

2.11, it is not at all a matter of discussion that women are to receive teaching. The author wishes to limit what he sees as improper consequences of this. The warning is not about women's access to instruction, but that they are to receive it in silence and in (total) subordination. In Luke's gospel, however, to defend women's choice of the word as the good part, is a positive aim, even if this is done at the cost of those virtues in a woman's life which are valued so highly by the Pastoral Letters and expressed in the domestic duties and care for husband and children. In Luke the sexually-based functions are set aside in favour of a relationship to the word of God, and the women in Luke-Acts are noticeably independent. The decisive dissimilarity between the Pastoral Letters and Luke-Acts in these matters is to be found in a totally different attitude to marriage and the family.

Nevertheless, there are in Luke-Acts some limitations at work concerning women's exercise of the word that have a certain likeness to the restrictions of the Pastorals. This is all the more striking in view of the rest of the gospel's portrayal of women. Luke has explicitly given place to women alongside the twelve in the group of disciples who follow Jesus. He emphasises their inalienable membership in the core group of God's people, and gives the function they fulfil an exemplary significance. They are granted a place at the feet of the Lord, and this is defended against protest and competing demands. But women are portrayed primarily as recipients and beneficiaries of the word – even if they carry it out in their own lives according to the word of the Lord (6.46ff.). They are not entrusted with any commission to preach,[60] nor do they appear as public preachers and witnesses.

IV.3. *'Domestic' women.*

This does not mean that women are always silent in Luke. But certain conditions are drawn up to define the context in which they may speak. Very often, when women appear with the power of the word, the text closes frameworks around them socially and locally. As was the

[60] In other words, I reject the idea that Luke includes women among the seventy (two) in Lk 10.1 – unlike Quesnell, 'Women', 67f.

case with Martha and Mary, they appear within the house, οἶκος. In Mark's gospel too, perhaps more consistently than in Luke, women are linked to 'the house'.[61]

Οἶκος was both a social and a local determination, like οἰκία. The distinction between the terms was not rigid,[62] and Luke shows a certain preference for οἶκος instead of οἰκία.[63] The house was normally the determining point of reference for a woman's life. In antiquity the distance between the world of men and of women, the different spheres in which they lived, corresponded generally speaking to the relationship between a private and a public sphere.[64] This does not mean that each held sway over their own sphere. The man could move in both spheres, and thereby ensured the connection between them. He held sway over both: over the public sphere, since this was reserved for him, and over the private sphere, since he was the lord of the household. The public role of men was partly based on their role as lord of the household, because the family/household was regarded in antiquity as the core unit in society.[65] In keeping with the close connection between household and society, the organisation of society itself can be articulated in domestic categories: for example, the emperor could have himself portrayed as the *pater patriae* with the *potestas* which this implied –

---

[61] Cf. Munro, 'Women Disciples', 227, followed critically but constructively by Malbon first in 'Fallible Followers', 39f., and later in 'Τῇ Ὀικία Ἀυτοῦ', 285ff.; Gill, 'Women Ministers', 15, 17.

[62] Elliott, *Home for Homeless*, 188. Verner, *Household of God*, 8–9; Gnilka, 'Hausgemeinde', 229f., shows that Roman/Latin terminology and juridical terminology were different. *Familia* belongs to the Roman context, and is a legal concept for the sphere administered by the *pater familias* and the basis of his position and power. *Domus* was not so precisely defined juridically, and designated the family fellowship constituted by ties of blood. A Roman woman in a marriage *sine manus* (which was the most usual form of marriage in the New Testament period) belonged to her father's *familia*, and became *sui iuris* on his death, being her own one-member *familia*. '... whereas the adult son now became fully capable of independent legal action ... and acquired the powers of a pater familias, a woman had no familia, or, rather, she is both the source and the end of her own familia, since she had no potestas over her children', Gardner, *Women*, 11, 76f.

[63] Brutschek, *Maria-Martha-Erzählung*, 180 n. 70 and 71.

[64] Balch, *Let Wives*, 3ff.; Claek, 'Women at Corinth', 257f.; Love, 'Women's Roles', 50ff.

[65] Gardner, *Women*, 77; Elliott, *Home for Homeless*, 173f., 183f.; Verner, *Household of God*, 71–81.

a projection of the traditional *patria potestas*, but also in a certain rivalry to this.[66]

A woman's life was bound to the private sphere. Her place was in the home; she lived in a space defined primarily and ideally as being within the house. Here she could indeed, by delegation from her husband, exercise a certain authority over the training and the direction of the household. Her own education was usually 'domestic',[67] and the world in which women found their fulfilment was in the house and/or in the company of small children and other women. Women could be seen in public places, but their conduct was strictly regulated and there were narrow boundaries for what was seemly. The exception was a number of religious rituals and feasts which gave women the opportunity, not only to appear in public, but also to behave in ways that would have been unseemly in their daily life.[68] Whereas women in the more official religious cults, played a withdrawn domestic role,[69] the 'new religious movements' of an oriental type were more open for women and had a corresponding attraction for them.[70] There was often considerable suspicion about women's participation in such 'foreign' cults[71] – even though women had more freedom to take part in this sort of non-

---

[66] Elliott, *Home for Homeless*, 175–9. For example, an essential point in Augustus' marriage legislation was the transfer of responsibility in such matters from the *pater familias* to the *pater patriae*, cf. des Bouvrie, 'Augustus' Legislation', 95, 101f.

[67] Balch, *Let Wives*, 143ff., shows that even Stoic philosophers who defended the right of daughters to have the same opportunity as sons to study philosophy, gave the instruction to girls a practical, 'domestic' slant.

[68] Clark, 'Women at Corinth', 257f.; Jeremias, *Jerusalem*, 361f.; Kroeger, 'Evidence of Maenadism', 331–8; Portefaix, *Sisters Rejoice*, 48ff.

[69] Portefaix, *Sisters Rejoice*, 43–8.

[70] Especially the cult of Dionysus, the cult of Isis and of the Dea Mater had won adherents, cf. Kraemer, 'Ecstasy and Possession', and Heyob, *Cult of Isis*. Heyob's book also shows that the impression created of the cult of Isis as a cult for women is not convincingly proved by the material. Women were never a majority in the cult, even if great local variations existed, and even if the cultic participation by women was larger than in other contexts; *Cult of Isis*, 81–7.

[71] Clark, 'Women at Corinth', 259; Heyob, *Cult of Isis*, 115; Lane Fox, *Pagans*, 310f., who also makes the interesting observation that later church leaders, with their claims that women are an easy prey for heretical teachers, share precisely this stereotyped picture of women as victims to feelings, irrationality and charlatans.

120

traditional worship because of their lack of a public role and official assignments.[72]

Women could also be active (although not to the same degree as men) in societies or clubs, κοίνα in Greek or *collegia* in Latin.[73] Well-off households could also provide lodgings on a short-term or long-term basis for philosophers and preachers.[74] Such instances as these created an intermediary zone in which the public and the private converged.

It was only to a limited extent and/or in indirect ways that women were able to exercise functions within the public sphere. Even if inscriptions show that wealthy women might be assigned honourable titles, they had seldom any official and direct political role to play.[75] Nor, with few exceptions, did they carry out key religious functions which were not linked to the home or to the more closed societies or associations. In every important aspect, public life was a life by, with, and for, men.

This is, of course, to paint a picture with too few nuances. The details in the picture will have been different in a Jewish, a Hellenistic and a Roman setting. In keeping with oriental customs, Jewish societies were restrictive – with certain reservations in the cases of Asia Minor and Egypt.[76] Nor did Greek and Roman customs coincide. For exam-

---

[72] McNamara, *New Song*, 66. It is also a fact that in many cases of mixed marriage known to us, it is the wife who is a Christian. A Christian man with a pagan wife is an exceptional phenomenon, cf. Lane Fox, *Pagans*, 310. Rich women were in fact often the first Christians in their family, cf. Lampe, *Stadtrömische Christen*, 123.

[73] MacMullen, 'Women in Public', 211ff.; Meeks, *Urban Christians*, 234f.; Sordi, *Christians and Roman Empire*, 182f. Clubs consisting only of women are unknown. Cf. also p. 71 n. 143.

[74] Stowers, 'Social Status', 65ff. The host provided the audience and bestowed social legitimation.

[75] Cf. Cameron, 'Neither Male', 63; MacMullen, 'Women in Public', 212f. There were indeed many honorary functions which women could carry out – with corresponding titles. Usually, these were linked to donations of various kinds, cf. p. 65 n. 132. It is, however, typical that women are virtually never given functions that require them to speak in public. They can be seen but not heard, 'Women in Public', 215.

[76] Jeremias, *Jerusalem*, 359–63, even though his observations are dependent on later and perhaps more restrictive rabbinic material; cf. also Kuzmack, 'Aggadic Approaches', 249f. This picture is, however, confirmed by earlier Jewish writers as Philo and Josephus, cf. Dautzenberg, 'Stellung der Frau', 201; although it may be difficult to decide the actual situation addressed by, for example, Philo's exhortations and ideals. Cf. Friis Plum, *Tilslørede Frihed*, 17, 26. Brooten's picture, *Women Leaders*, is more nuanced. It is based primarily on inscriptions from Egypt and Asia Minor. Cf. also Johnson, 'Asia Minor', 98f.

ple, the Roman, Cornelius Nepos relates that much that was considered right in Rome, was shocking to the Greeks.[77] No Roman would have found it offensive to take his wife with him to a party, and at home the *mater familias* was the centre of the house's social life; in Greece, on the other hand, respectable women were almost never present at parties. For the most part, they kept to the innermost 'women's quarters' of the house, to which no man but the most closely related had access. The Greek women belonged to the house, and were to seek their honour in not being spoken of, whether negatively or positively. The point is 'the inviolability of the οἶκος'. Deviant conduct by women threatened the fundamental values of society, whereas a conformist conduct safeguarded these.[78]

Even Roman matrons spent the greatest part of their time in the house. They could not vote or hold public office, and it has been claimed that an essential reason why Roman women never fully attained equality with men was the persistent and deeply-rooted tradition that the house was exclusively the women's sphere.[79] The sources available indicate that women's rights and possibilities were best established and practised in Egypt and Asia Minor.[80] But marriage contracts from these regions show, nevertheless, that even if the male partner was strictly reminded about his obligations, and a greater limitation than previously is placed on his freedom to do whatever he wants, traditional restrictive ideals about subordination and confined movement continued to be prescribed for the wife.[81]

Variations also existed from place to place, between city and countryside, and between the different social strata.[82] In some places, women's freedom of movement was limited by the house, while in other places they moved more freely in the outside world. An important factor for most women was doubtless the extent to which the family

---

[77] Balsdon, *Roman Women*, 200; Verner, *Household of God*, 41.

[78] Andersen, 'Widows', 34f.

[79] Balsdon, *Roman Women*, 282.

[80] Witherington, *Women in the Earliest Churches*, 14f. This clearly had a 'contagious effect' also on, for example, Jewish groups in these areas – with corresponding attempts at restriction.

[81] Verner, *Household of God*, 38f., 43, 65f.

[82] Cameron, 'Neither male', 61f.; Thraede, 'Ärger', 42.

was dependent on their work outside the area that was strictly speaking domestic. Small trading activity and crafts in the cities, or a small family farm requiring hard work in the countryside, can have offered women an opportunity to live a more extrovert life – and to become even more exhausted.

The limited space in small houses, meant that the whole family would have had to live at very close quarters. The density of population in the towns was similar to that in today's slum areas, and much of life had to be lived for most people 'in the streets and squares'.[83] This, however, does not remove the distance between what was public and what was private, even if it meant that the private sphere was not an especially hidden life: the closer people live to one another, the more important it can be to establish and to preserve other types of distance than the purely physical.[84]

The openness may have been greater, especially among the upper social strata, in Hellenistic cities under Roman influence. Nevertheless, both literary and archaeological sources indicate that in south-eastern parts of Asia Minor and in Syria and Arabia, ideals of propriety dictated that women should be veiled when they moved in the public, external sphere.[85] Contradictions in the available source material for the eastern provinces also suggest that while women who were well-off had themselves portrayed without a veil and with fashionable hairstyles, ordinary women encountered the world outside the house more or less veiled.[86] We have already mentioned women who established an autonomous economic basis either through the affluence of their family or through their own business activity, and who made their mark in the public sphere through their donations and projects. The point therefore is not necessarily the absolute physical segregation and the delimitation of women's space, but the exclusive sig-

---

[83] Meeks, *Urban Christians*, 28f. Cf. Verner, *Household of God*, 57–9, for archaeological descriptions of the way people lived.

[84] Stowers, 'Social Status', 81f.

[85] Thompson, 'Hairstyles', 113.

[86] MacMullen, 'Women in Public', 217. It is, however, very interesting to note that the tension in the source material is usually due to the fact that pictorial representations do not agree with literary sources. Segal, *Edessa*, 38, who is dealing with later sources from the third century onwards, points out that even if women depicted in mosaics and reliefs are not veiled, this does not have to mean that they normally went unveiled. But on an expensive portrait, they ought to be recognisable!

nificance the family and home had as the sphere of life shaping their identity and determining their functions. The term 'house' often serves in the texts as a social or architectural expression of this.

It can be objected that the division between a private and a public sphere betrays an understanding of society which is androcentrically determined in its implicit proclamation of values. In an androcentric perspective the public sphere is regarded as the important and central sphere, while the private sphere is of less significance and interest: it does not influence history, except in an indirect way. It can therefore be argued that such a model is inappropriate from a feminist perspective, since it may easily serve to render women invisible and value women's social life as less essential. Instead of focussing centrally on women, it accepts that women are out of focus. This, however, indicates that it is the evaluation of the pattern that is being called into question, the values with which it has been charged, and not necessarily the pattern *per se*.

I consider the model to be serviceable as a frame of reference in this work, because it clearly plays a decisive role in the Lukan concept. It is generally true of the early church that, like many other forms of organised social life, it was a movement which itself lived in a field of tension between the private and the public spheres. While the division between the two spheres was maintained, it was also exploited. In an early phase, the house became the community centre, where social functions were carried out, as well as a common life, which otherwise tended to belong to the official sphere. The locus of the community was the private house, where small groups ('families'?) of Christians came together in the most appropriate room of the house, which the householder placed at their service. This means that special sacral rooms were not furnished in the earliest period; there were no architectural changes to the buildings, nor did the communities acquire a room 'set aside' for their meetings.[87] Apart from the outward-directed proclamation taking

---

[87] On the question about the early Christian house churches, cf. Finney, 'Early Christian Architecture'; Gnilka, 'Neutestamentliche Hausgemeinde', 229–42; Klauck, *Hausgemeinde*; Lampe 'Funktion der Familie', 538. Prof. Siri Sande of the Norwegian Institute in Rome has drawn my attention to Roman archaeological material indicating that the 'house churches' did not always meet in the *domus* itself, which tended to be small and have small rooms, but in structures such as storerooms beside the house itself or on the lower ground floor. These had more space and were perhaps more 'anonymous'.

place in public, in the temple and the synagogue, in streets and on lanes and squares, and before councils and authorities, the first communities developed in the shelter provided by the home. In other words: the community's focus moved into the world where women too had a place. Somewhat later, it was said ironically that Christians surreptitiously made their way into households through the women's chamber.[88] Despite the polemical thrust, this accusation shows that women played a central role in the early propagation of Christianity and that this represented a bridgehead into the households.

It was, however, not to be taken for granted that women could play an active role, even in that which took place in the house. Even if a woman's sphere was usually the house, this did not mean that the house represented a place of freedom for her. The place she had, was given to her in a household which was organised patriarchally and hierarchically. The order of the house was a structure of subordination exercising control and creating silence. In the dominant patriarchal structure, the man was also the lord of the house, and the women's 'room' was to be understood in a more specialised sense both with regard to the social organisation of the house and sometimes with regard to the lay-out: it was limited and sheltered in the innermost corner of the house, furthest from the entrance.[89] When the private and the public converged, as the outer world found a place in the house, this – in keeping with what we have seen was the case with the transposition of family categories – was not without ambivalence with regard to its implications for the role of women. On the one hand, it meant a potential for equality, because women, protected by the private sphere, were given new scope for their abilities within the community; on the other hand, the association with the order of the household could contribute to an intensification of the demands for subordination in the community, and thus provide a useful path to a reinforced patriarchal development of the household of God.

---

[88] Weiser, 'Rolle der Frau', 178, quotes Clement of Alexandria, Strom. III, 6, 53: διὰ τῶν γυναικῶν καὶ εἰς τὴν γυναικωνῖτιν ἀδιαβλήτως παρεισεδίατο ἡ τοῦ κυρίου διδασκαλία. Cf. also Gülzow, 'Soziale Gegebenheiten', 199f.

[89] Clark, 'Women at Corinth', 257.

We can see clearly in the Pastoral Letters how the church's association with the house contributed to the canonisation of a conventional
patriarchal household morality. This functioned in two ways. On the
one hand, traditional ideas of superior authority and of subordination
in a household were developed by means of the *Haustafeln* and applied
to Christian families or family-members.[90] This moral stereotyping and
accommodation must also be seen in connection with a strong official
emphasis on the traditional roles of woman/wife in the Roman empire
at that period. Obedient, dutiful wives bearing many children were an
expression of loyalty to the state. Domestic morality was not a private
matter.[91] As has been mentioned above, women were often the first
Christians in a household. Many paraenetic texts, especially in later
writings, are concerned with the possibilities these Christian wives had
of winning their husbands for the faith. They are exhorted first of all to
be exemplary wives who by means of a conventional obedient and
virtuous conduct, convince their husbands. On the other hand, the
community (God's family, God's household) adapted to the same patriarchal pattern. The original association of the community with the
household had the contributory effect of a patriarchalisation of the
community. The directive functions, which became more and more
institutionalised and placed in a hierarchical setting, were reserved for
well-respected men. In this way, the church prepared its house and was
ready for an irreproachable life in the public eye. Only modest conces-
sions were made to ensure a continued activity on the part of women in
the communities. Married women were for the most part assigned a
place in domestic subordination; unmarried women (virgins and widows), however, could be entrusted with special tasks in the community.
Women who chose a life outside marriage were an exception to the
norm within the patriarchal pattern. As we shall see, their number
rapidly increased and regulations were established to sustain them. The

---

[90] It is still an open question whether the *Haustafeln* represent a Christian variant of
an already-existing topos, or whether they are a Christian formalisation of general domestic ideals of the period. The contents were well-known and widespread, but the strict
double construction and the fixed terminological categories are found only here in this
generalised and codified form; cf. Witherington's exposition in *Women in the Earliest
Churches*, 42–60, with convincing criticism of Crouch and Balch on this point.
[91] On this and on what follows, cf. Balch, *Let Wives*, 74ff., 109.

tasks entrusted to them did not, however, break with the pattern: these were often of a diaconal character, and/or oriented to other women. The distance between the world of men and the world of women was marked by the fact that women were accepted as active in the women's world where men could not possibly appear with propriety.

In relation to this, in the architecture of the Lukan text, how is a place given to women? We have already seen how a group of women following Jesus together with the twelve is given a significant place. Women take on the traditionally male 'student's place', and they are defended against protests which demand they go back to the conventional female tasks, to the kitchen and to waiting at table. Women's gender-determined functions (as wife and mother) are rejected and redefined in contrasting phrases. The decisive point, both for women and for men, is whether they hear the word of God and do it. But women are primarily presented as hearers of the word. And the analysis of the usage of διακονία-terms in the Lukan narrative has shown, how the idealisation of the 'early' women at the same time serves to distance them. They are portrayed as shining examples – of repentance, of discipleship, of service. Indeed, they are exalted as prototypes of the virtues that are to be characteristic of the community's leadership. But the leadership positions are *de facto* reserved for men, and the women in Acts (as opposed to the gospel) seem to play a much more withdrawn role on a scene dominated by the leadership and missionary activity of (the great) men. This tension in the textual material is also structured redactionally and explained by means of the distance between the private and the public spheres.

In Luke, women do not receive any commission to preach, and, with a few exceptions, they do not appear as public witnesses and preachers. On most occasions when women speak up, the text draws the framework of the house or of the intimate sphere around them, and/or they appear primarily together with other women. As the miracle narratives imply, women can be found in most places, although many of these women were already socially exposed in one way or another. But when women carry out non-traditional functions, they are linked to the house, although they are not determined by domestic affairs or tied down by these.

While the angel Gabriel reveals himself to Zechariah in the temple, the meeting with Mary takes place in the house where she lives. Otherwise it is not possible to understand the statement that the angel is sent to Nazareth and εἰσελθὼν πρὸς αὐτήν (Lk 1.26–8). The outpouring of the Spirit on Elizabeth and Mary (Lk 1.40–56) takes place in Elizabeth's home, where the two women are together (cf. 1.40). Mary's song of praise is no public proclamation. In this connection, it is of less importance that the gospel narrative, as a text, oversteps the boundaries of the house by making the story public. This is the work of the male author or narrator. And he is careful not to let the women in the text step over the threshold.

The pair of parables about the shepherd with the sheep (Lk 15.4–7) and the woman with the coins (Lk 15.8–10) reflect the distance and difference between the world of men and that of women. Naturally, the fact that these stories are parables introduces another, fictional level, that is, the social world of the parable is not necessarily the same as in the contextual framework. Nevertheless, the example is striking and the gender complementarity in the structuring of the two stories emphasises the point all the more clearly. Both the man and the woman go in search of what they have lost. But in the woman's case, she seems certain that the coin must be lost in the house; characteristically enough, the radius of her action is limited by the walls of the house. Finally, when what was lost has been found again, both the man and the woman must share their joy. While the man, after his return home, calls together his friends and neighbours καὶ ἐλθὼν εἰς τὸν οἶκον συγκαλεῖ τοὺς φίλους καὶ τοὺς γείτονας (15.6), the woman, who never left home, goes to her female friends and neighbours (15.9), εὑροῦσα συγκαλεῖ τὰς φίλας καὶ γείτονας. In both cases, the celebration takes place at home: that is, the man moves in both spheres. But the celebration is located in a segregated man's world and woman's world. While the man rejoices with other men, the woman calls on other women and rejoices with them.

This gender-segregated pattern is not however unamibiguous throughout Luke-Acts. Priscilla joins Aquila in seeing to the further instruction of the gifted Apollos (Acts 18.24ff.), ἀκριβέστερον αὐτῷ ἐξέθεντο τὴν ὁδόν (18.26). Priscilla (the short form Prisca is also used) and Aquila are mentioned as often as six times in the New Testament (Acts 18.2f., 18, 29; Rom 16.3; 1 Cor 16.19; 2 Tim 4.19). Acts 18.2 informs us that they were a Jewish married couple whom Claudius' edict had banished from Rome. They made their living together as tent-makers, and Paul met them for the first time in Corinth and worked together with them in their workshop (Acts 18.3). The text in Acts gives a detailed presentation of Priscilla and Aquila. But they are not given any independent role as long as they are together with Paul: Paul is *the* missionary, and the others are reduced to persons who support him.[92] According to Luke, Priscilla and Aquila provide the material base for Paul's missionary activity in Corinth; they give him a place to live and work. In other words, Priscilla is one of Luke's rank of supportive and hospitable women, and her role is at least as important as her husband's. She is explicitly added in 18.2 in a way that almost causes a rupture in the grammatical structure.[93] Besides this, the plural forms which clearly include her are maintained consistently: *they* are tent-makers by profession, and Paul visits *them*, αὐτοῖς, and remains with *them*, παρ' αὐτοῖς.

In fact, Priscilla is mentioned first in most of the texts in which the couple are mentioned by name: Acts 18.18, 26; Rom 16.3, 2 Tim 4.19. The unusual prefixing of her name indicates that she was the more active and significant of the two.[94] When some textual witnesses, including D, transpose the order back to what is normal, this happens precisely in the case where her prominent position is most problematic: the instruction of Apollos. D's relocation of Priscilla to the second place in 18.26 is also in keeping with a pattern, shown earlier, of attaching women to their husbands.[95] Thus it is also significant that when Priscilla is mentioned last in 1 Cor 16.19, this happens in a letter that is concerned with the subordination of married women to their husbands.

[92] Cf. Haenchen, *Apg.*, 475. He maintains that Priscilla and Aquila were so important for the early Christian mission that there was no possibility of Luke overlooking them completely. See also p. 3f.

[93] Cf. Haenchen, *Apg.*, 473.

[94] For further evidence cf. Weiser, 'Rolle der Frau', 173f. Jervell, 'Töchter Abrahams', 90f., has no convincing arguments against such an understanding, and Priscilla is therefore one of the stumbling-blocks for his interpretation.

[95] Cf. p. 22, Witherington, 'Anti-Feminist Tendencies', 83, makes use of this and indicates, with support by Blass, 'Priscilla', 124–5, on the basis of John Chrysostom's text of Acts 18.26, that Aquila has been added at a secondary stage. Originally, Priscilla was mentioned alone.

In Acts 18, Luke relates that when Paul left Corinth and set out for Syria, Priscilla and Aquila were with him at the beginning – an indication that they in fact were missionaries as well. In a somewhat incomplete and abrupt manner, the story implies that they stayed on in Ephesus while Paul continued his journey (Acts 18.18ff.). 1 Cor 16.19 suggests that they kept house for a community in Ephesus, even if this is not a point in the Lukan story. For Luke, their stay in Ephesus serves (once again) to introduce a third person, in this case Apollos. As part of the congregation they listen to Apollos' brilliant preaching and take care of him. Even if προσελάβοντο αὐτὸν (18.26) strictly speaking can mean only that they drew him aside, it probably indicates that they took him to their home.[96] Their further instruction of Apollos[97] thus takes place in their home – and not in the synagogue.[98]

Priscilla's instruction of the rhetorically-gifted Apollos says something about her personal status. Her example also weakens the impression of segregation, and is one element which goes to suggest the view that social life in the community is not supposed to have operated with firm barriers between women and men. But even Priscilla is portrayed as listening in the synagogue and as active in instruction only at home; she is not granted any dispensation from the rule that women's activity belongs in the house.[99]

---

[96] Bauer, 'προσλαμβάνω', 1422; Schneider, *Apg.*, 216 n. 20.

[97] Ideas about the contents of this instruction remain too speculative to have a credible effect, cf. Witherington's attempt, *Women in the Earliest Churches*, 154, to show that it was a question of Christian baptismal praxis. The same is true of Schüssler Fiorenza's supposition, *In Memory*, 178, that Apollos' 'Sophia and Spirit theology might have been derived from her (Priscilla's) catechesis'.

[98] Brooten's use of this example, *Women Leaders*, 140, to provide evidence of women's teaching activity in the synagogue is thus misleading. When Witherington, *Women in the Earliest Churches*, 154, claims that 'this act takes place in semiprivacy' and that this positioning actually is of no importance, because nothing suggests that Luke is trying to avoid having Priscilla instruct Apollos 'in a worship context', this is a supposition determined more by his introductory categorisation of Priscilla as a 'teacher' than by a reading of Luke as a whole. This is moreover one further example of his methodological lack of distinction between the literary, rhetorical and the historical level in his interpretation of the text.

[99] As is indicated by Anderson, 'Mary's Difference', 200 n. 35.

On the day of Pentecost, the promise in Joel 3.1–5 is fulfilled when women as well as men are filled with the Spirit and speak prophetically (Acts 2.4ff.). Indeed, the participation of women in prophecy is of vital importance for the evidential force of the event.[100] But Acts 2.1–4 emphasises just as strongly that this happens in the house, and that when a great crowd of the people notice the phenomenon and rush together, it is Peter and the eleven who appear in public and address the crowd. In the same way as with Priscilla, the women remain in the shadow of the house even when they perform an important and decisive function.

There are, however, some exceptions to the rule. The aged widow Anna, daughter of Phanuel, who has almost made the temple her home, οὐκ ἀφίστατο τοῦ ἱεροῦ[101] praises God and speaks prophetically about the child to all who await the liberation of Jerusalem (Lk 2.36–8). This example is all the more noteworthy in that her activity not only takes place over a period of time (the imperfect ἐλάλει indicates that this happened repeatedly),[102] but also has the mark of a public proclamation – unlike Simeon's prophecy.[103] Simeon's prophetical acceptance takes place primarily in a dialogue with the parents/mother of the child, while that of Anna, related in less detail, is nevertheless, explicitly addressed πᾶσιν τοῖς προσδεχομένοις λύτρωσιν Ἰερουσαλήμ.

Luke structures the narrative about the woman with the continuous flow of blood in such a way that at the end, trembling and afraid, she must come forward and tell her story before all the people: she must say why she had touched Jesus and relate how she was cured instantly. In the earlier version in Mark, this is the only healing of a woman that takes place outside the house. In Luke, we have also the rescuing of the widow from her plight in 7.11–17 and the cure of the bent woman in

---

[100] On the event of Pentecost and the gender perspective of the quotation from Joel, see p. 164–172.

[101] This anticipates the description of those who believe in Jesus in Lk 24.53 and Acts 2.46.

[102] Cf. Fitzmyer, *Luke*, 431.

[103] Both Fitzmyer, *Luke*, 423, and Laurentin, *Truth of Christmas*, 205, use the expression that her function is 'to spread the word/the good news' (my italics).

13.10–17. In those cases, however, the women remain silent receivers, while Luke especially in the narrative about the woman with the flow of blood, unfolds the aspect of publicity.[104] At the close, the woman does not only speak to Jesus as in Mark (cf. εἶπεν αὐτῷ in Mk 5.33), but tells what has happened ἐνώπιον παντὸς τοῦ λαοῦ (Lk 8.47). There is also a difference in the reason given for her coming forward, emphasising the same point. In Mark, she is indeed urged by Jesus, but she comes forward because she realises what has happened to her. In Luke, she begins by denying, along with all the others that she knows she has touched him (18.45), but when Jesus insists that he knows, she is pressed forward because she understands that she cannot possibly remain hidden (18.47). This makes the woman appear, provoked by Jesus himself and against her own will, a public witness to Jesus' prophetic perspicacity and his power to work miracles.

Nevertheless, the woman has a much more modest role to play in Luke's version of the narrative, taken as a whole, than in Mark's. The description of her situation (8.43f.) is considerably shortened in relation to that in Mark, and the monologue of the woman (Mk 5.28) is omitted completely. What remains is a brief introductory presentation of a woman with a flow of blood who up to this point has not been able to find anyone who could help her, but who touches Jesus' cloak and is at once cured. The main point in the Lukan version is shifted in a christological direction.[105] It is a question primarily of Jesus' miraculous power and his prophetic knowledge. The testimony of the woman before all the people is necessary in order to confirm that Jesus was right when he repeatedly insisted to the crowd that someone had touched him, and refused to accept their denial and Peter's alternative explanation. Since Jesus' healing activity takes place in public, the same applies to the woman's testimony. This is a trait that is clearly reflected also in a later allusion to this narrative, in the apocryphal Acts of Pilate 7. There potential objections are expressed, even if they are not accepted. The woman, who here is called Berenice, relates her story briefly, but

---

[104] Cf. Busse, *Wunder*, 227f.; McCaughey, *Paradigms of Faith*, 182; Robbins, 'Woman', 511. Even Tetlow, *Women and Ministry*, 104, must reluctantly admit this.

[105] Robbins, 'Woman', 511ff., with the point of departure in Theissen's analysis, *Miracle Stories*, 135.

the opponents, who are Jews, counter with an appeal to the law that a woman cannot be a witness.[106] In Luke, there is no trace of such an opposition in the narrative itself, but such reflections and reservations have their effect in further dealing with the question of women's ability to bear witness.

In Luke-Acts, the public character of the proclamation is an important element. Jesus' activity and the preaching of the apostles and missionaries take place openly, not in secret. While this public life in Jerusalem has the temple as its centre, it is otherwise marked by a synagogue context, by various meetings with the official machinery of power, or simply by general characteristics such as δημοσίᾳ, 'in full public view'. It is emphasised, in the case of the earliest community in Jerusalem, not only that the apostles worked and preached in the temple area, but that parts of the common life of the community took place ἐν τῷ ἱερῷ, while other parts were located κατ' οἶκον. Correspondingly, Paul emphasises, in his address to the elders from Ephesus in Acts 20.20, the open character of his teaching activity and the growth of preaching. Not holding back anything that was for their good, he has taught δημοσίᾳ καὶ κατ' οἴκους, both in public 'out among the people' and from house to house. And in Acts' narratives about Paul and other missionaries a pattern is discernible: they begin by preaching in public places where people are gathered, awaken positive and negative reactions, and then follow up the positive reactions by taking up residence for a period in prominent and/or well-off local households. They appear as itinerant philosophers with considerable success among the mass of the people and with local support from some powerful men and many wealthy women.[107] Another programmatic statement similar to that in 20.20 is found in Acts 26.26, where Paul adduces, in his defence before king Agrippa, that none of these things can possibly have escaped the king's notice, for οὐ γάρ ἐστιν ἐν γωνίᾳ πεπραγμένον τοῦτο. This alludes to an expression that in the contemporary context articulated a philosophical ideal about participation in public life, and was used in defence of the activity of philosophers.

---

[106] Robbins, 'Woman', 511.
[107] Meeks, *Urban Christians*, 28.

This made it well-suited to counter accusations about clandestine and covert activity: the Christian community was open to suspicion on this count, especially because of its 'house meetings' and the potential subversive nature of the trouble they were said to cause domestically. Luke has Paul proclaim that Christians are not a threatening or secret society: everything has happened openly, so that those in power ought to be well-informed about it.[108] A comparison with the epistolary literature shows that this large-scale picture has elements that are clearly special to Luke. The letters bear witness to an activity that does not address quite such a grand public audience, but rather follows personal networks.[109] In other words, the aspect of publicity is a particular theme in Luke, and serves apologetic aims. Besides this, there is the point that both those in power and the people as a whole cannot excuse themselves from taking a stand on matters about which they are already informed.[110]

While the activity of women is associated with the house, the public preaching in Luke-Acts is to an overwhelming extent, the concern of men, and is directed towards men.[111] The speeches in Acts especially are dominated by forms of address in which ἄνδρες gives a gender determination to the following word, which might be ἀδελφοί, Ἰσραελῖται or something similar: 1.16; 2.14; 3.12; 7.1; 13.16; 14.15; 15.7, 13; 17.22, 30; 22.1; 23.1; 28.17.[112] Most of these speeches are addressed to Jews, and the occasion is always a public event, either for a great crowd of people in Jerusalem (2.14; 3.12; 22.1), for the Jewish leadership in Jerusalem (7.1; 23.1) or in Rome (28.17), or for a synagogue assembly in Antioch of Pisidia (13.16). Twice it is a pagan

---

[108] Cf. Malherbe, 'Not in a Corner', 202, 205f. Like Meeks, Malherbe is most concerned by the fact that Luke thereby gives an apologetic presentation of Christianity as a justifiable and good philosophy. Cf. also Stowers, 'Social Status', 61.

[109] Meeks, *Urban Christians*, 28.

[110] Cf. Jervell, *Luke*, 78: 'Everything happens in public, while all Israel watches, which in turn is a presupposition in Acts for the preaching of repentance to Israel'.

[111] Cf. Collins, 'Ministry of Women', 161; Jervell, 'Töchter Abrahams', 78; Schüssler Fiorenza, *In Memory*, 49f., 161, 167.

[112] Jervell, 'Töchter Abrahams', 84ff.; Zehnle, *Peter's Pentecost Discourse*, 26. MacMullen, 'Women in Public', 212, also points out that women were not normally included either in apparently inclusive expressions such as 'all citizens' or 'all the people'.

assembly: the crowd of people in Lystra (14.15) and the philosophers on the Areopagus (17.22, 30).

Naturally, this does not exclude the possibility that women are present and even among those who are converted by the public witness of the apostles and missionaries (5.14; 8.12; 17.4, 12, 34). In the course of the legal process against Paul, the local governor Felix and king Agrippa bring with them respectively Drusilla (Felix's wife) and Bernice (the king's sister). But the dialogue that occurs, takes place between the men – even if Drusilla's presence is justified because as a Jewess she has a special interest in the case and presumably also an understanding of it.[113] The possible presence of women does not, however, mean that even the male-oriented forms of address in Luke are to be read inclusively, as is sometimes claimed with the help of 'audience criticism'.[114] On the contrary, Luke emphasises, by means of the term ἀνήρ, an exclusive understanding of the masculine plural forms which otherwise could have been interpreted inclusively. Only the men are addressed in public contexts, which officially were all-male. This was the world of men. Even if physically women were present, for example at synagogue worship (cf. Priscilla in 18.26), they did not count in the quorum necessary for worship to take place.[115]

The use of exclusive forms of address in 1.16 and 15.7, 13 causes a greater problem. These are not public occasions but gatherings within the community; and it has been underlined repeatedly that the communities consisted of women as well as men, ἄνδρες τε καὶ γυναῖκες. These two passages, however, refer to quite special situations in which narrower groups within the community take on a particular function. In 15.6ff., only the community's leadership, consisting of the apostles and the elders (15.6), is assembled. In 15.22 it is indeed emphasised that the whole community agrees on the resolve to send two men(!) to Antioch together with Paul and Barnabas. But the preceding decision has been a matter for the apostles and the elders alone.

---

[113] Cf. Haenchen, *Apg.*, 588.

[114] Weiser, 'Rolle der Frau', 163, is a typical representative here. Cf. also Portefaix, *Sisters Rejoice*, 3 and 155.

[115] Cf. Leipoldt/Grundmann, *Umwelt*, 173f. It is, in other words, characteristic that the God-fearing women in Philippi did not have a synagogue, but only a place of prayer (Acts 16.13).

In 1.15ff., the group which elects a new apostle after Judas, assembles. Its number is given as about one hundred and twenty, and it is usual for interpreters to consider these one hundred and twenty to have been the whole of the community at this early stage. So the women too are presumed to be present, as indicated by Acts 1.14.[116] When Peter in his address includes only the men as indicated by the introductory ἄνδρες ἀδελφοί, this is explained as a reflection of the fact that only the men were considered capable of taking decisions. There are, however, good reasons to assume that Luke, already at the outset, makes the election of an apostle an exclusively male affair. The group of one hundred and twenty men corresponds to the minimum number for a Jewish sanhedrin constituency, to which only men could be counted.[117] Accordingly, the assembly is addressed in exclusively masculine forms, and only men are eligible to the ministry of apostle (1.21).[118] In other words, the one hundred and twenty in Acts 1.15ff. form an exclusive assembly for the election of an apostle, which fulfils the criteria for a Jewish sanhedrin constituency and consists only of men. It is therefore misleading to identify πάντες in Acts 2.1ff. with the one hundred and twenty from 1.15. The emphasised πάντες in 2.1 are rather to be understood as *all* in the community, both women and men, unlike the narrower male circle who elected the new apostle in 1.15ff.[119] The vital importance of Joel 3.1–5 for the line of argument in Peter's speech in Acts 2, makes the representation of women there essential.

This means that the various interpretations, especially of 1.15ff., which postulate that the women from 1.14 must be supposed present among the one hundred and twenty create new problems without actually solving any of the old ones. This is the case, irrespective of what conclusions the interpreters draw from this. They may (1) only men-

---

[116] Cf. Haenchen, *Apg.*, 124 n. 3, 131; Schneider, *Apg.*, I 215 n. 24, 247. More on this: cf. p. 164f.

[117] When Schneider, *Apg.*, I 216 n. 27, appeals to Conzelmann in rejecting such a link to Jewish models because women in Luke are counted as being among the one hundred and twenty, this is a circuitous self-confirmatory argument.

[118] Concerning the gender criterion for the apostolate, cf. p. 161.

[119] The text does not permit us to judge whether the πάντες in Acts 2.1 can be identified with the 'more than five hundred ἀδελφοί' whom Paul mentions at 1 Cor 15.5, as suggested by Schneider, *Apg.*, I 247; cf. Munck, *Acts*, 14.

tion it as a remark in passing;[120] (2) emphasise that the masculine plural form ἀδελφοί can also include women while ignoring the problem with ἄνδρες;[121] or (3) take advantage of this to claim that only the men are capable of making decisions,[122] so that the women present are represented by their husbands, with the consequence that even salvation is to be given to women only through men.[123] This last interpretation passes over the greatest part of the gospel's portrayal of women, and disallows the significance of 'Abraham's daughters' by restricting Abraham's children anew to his sons.

The reasonable conclusion is that Luke has not conceived of women as being present on the occasions mentioned here. This is not a statement about the historical basis or information involved, and it does not mean that Luke constructs communities where women are rendered completely invisible. But the male dominance of the lists of names won its way in the Lukan image of the earliest community, so that the apostolate and the leadership are presented as almost programmatically restricted to men. Women cannot become public witnesses in an Israel dominated by men who had no confidence in women.[124] For the most part, the men keep hold of the public sphere and decision-making while women's activity remains bounded by the home.

At the same time, it is clear that the community of faith develops increasingly within the home. It is a simplification to say that Luke distinguishes between the public missionary proclamation and the life of the community as it took place in homes.[125] The sending of the twelve in Lk 9.3ff. is orientated to the house, οἰκία (9.4). Luke has eliminated the Markan alternative of τόπος, so that οἰκία 'als alleinige Zielangabe des εἰσέρχεσθαι voll zur Geltung kommen lässt'.[126] Rather, an original division develops to become an ever stronger alternation and transfer from the temple, square and synagogue to the house. To

---

[120] Schneider, *Apg.*, I 215 n. 24.
[121] Quesnell, 'Women', 61; Weiser, 'Rolle der Frau', 163.
[122] Haenchen, *Apg.*, 124.
[123] Jervell, 'Töchter Abrahams', 85.
[124] Cf. p. 155f. and p. 161f.
[125] Klauck, *Hausgemeinde*, 7.
[126] Brutschek, *Maria-Martha-Erzählung*, 230. Cf. also n. 145 to this chapter.

some extent, this takes the form of Paul's seeking refuge in the house when the conflicts outside become critical, and he can no longer appear in the local synagogue. In other words, the house takes on the character of being a place of refuge and of sheltering/assembling the faithful. At the same time, it gives the preacher a platform by the increase of social status bestowed by the householder and a recognised role as a visiting philosopher.[127] This is the more pragmatic side of the matter. But the move from the public external sphere to the domestic sphere is evident from the very thrust of the Lukan narrative. In the gospel, the movement of the narrative is continuously towards the temple and the centre of Jewish power in Jerusalem. The gospel narrative begins in the temple (Lk 1.8ff.). *En route*, the infancy narratives lead to the temple (2.22, 41–51), and large parts of Jesus' activity are located on his long journey up to Jerusalem from Lk 9.51 onwards.[128] The gospel's orientation towards the temple is a positive one, and is connected with the observance of and obedience to the Law. The infant Jesus is brought to the Lord in the temple as the Law ordains for a firstborn male child (Lk 2.22f., 27, 39). In the temple, the child's significance for Israel is proclaimed (2.25–38), and the family goes on pilgrimage to Jerusalem and to the temple at Passover (2.43ff.). Later in the gospel, when Jesus' long journey to Jerusalem has reached its goal, he drastically cleanses the temple before he begins (or rather reopens, cf. 2.46f.) his teaching activity there (Lk 19.4ff.). After Jesus is arrested, the disciples flee, but they remain in Jerusalem, where the risen Jesus later appears to them. Finally, the closing statement of the gospel tells that the disciples are continually in the temple praising God (24.53).

In the first part of Acts located in Jerusalem, those who believe in Jesus remain faithful in their attendance at the temple. They gather in the temple (2.46); the apostles observe the times of prayer in the temple (3.2), where they heal and preach (3.2–4.2, cf. also 5.12ff., 25, 42). In some later passages, the temple plays a corresponding role in the narrative about Paul. According to one of the three versions of Paul's

---

[127] Cf. Stowers, 'Social Status', 65–8.
[128] Gasque, 'Fruitful Field', 121.

conversion, he receives his missionary commission (22.17–21) while he is praying in the temple. And when Paul visits Jerusalem for the last time, his opponents begin their rush against him while he is in the temple performing rituals of purification to show his fidelity to the Law (21.17–30). He can thus confidently claim that he has committed no crime either against the Law of the Jews, against the temple or against the Emperor (25.8). But these examples also show repeatedly that the temple is a place for confrontations and for conflicts both with the leaders and with the people, and that this – on the basis of a revelation given in the temple itself – implies a movement away from the temple and from Jerusalem (cf. especially 22.17ff.).[129] The course of the narrative in Acts changes the direction slowly, but definitively, away from Jerusalem and temple. In Acts 21.30, Paul is dragged out of the temple, and – as a demonstrative expression of the definitive rupture – the gates of the temple are shut behind him.[130] So the Jewish opposition is finally consolidated in the closed temple.

The movement away from the temple is at the same time a movement towards the house. The summary account of the Jerusalem community's life in 2.42–7 emphasises an alternation between temple and house (2.46) in which the common meal, naturally enough, is held in people's homes. A corresponding but less precisely defined alternation is expressed in 5.42. This is in keeping with the use of οἶκος elsewhere in the New Testament, which is clearly different from what we find in the LXX, where οἶκος (τοῦ θεοῦ, τοῦ κυρίου) is a customary term for the temple in Jerusalem. In the New Testament, the overwhelming majority of texts employ the term to speak of a dwelling or a household.[131] The use of οἰκ-terms in Luke-Acts is, however, no less complex

---

[129] Cf. O'Neill, *Theology of Acts*, 81: 'it seems that God himself is driving Christians out of the Temple, and showing that they cannot confine themselves to its limitations'.

[130] Tyson, 'Emerging Church', 135.

[131] Cf. Elliott, *Home for Homeless*, 184, 197. Elliott holds that this can be due either to a polemical criticism of the temple or to 'the appropriation of Israel's social identity and fulfilment of its history as the household with whom God has established a final covenantal and familial bond'. In my opinion, this is to regard the criticism of the temple on the one hand and the positive transposition and appropriation on the other as too exclusive alternatives. Naturally, the criticism of the temple is less relevant after its destruction, but it remains a basic structural point for the transposition.

than the attitude to the temple. In Stephen's discourse (Acts 7:2–53), which is a much discussed key text for the understanding of the temple, there is also a subtle and ironic word-play on a register of οἰκ-terminology.[132]

This speech is a critical reply to the false witnesses' claim that Stephen never ceased speaking κατὰ τοῦ τόπου τοῦ ἁγίου τούτου καὶ τοῦ νόμου (6.13). This is the same charge that is made against Paul later (21.28). The critical prophetic tradition within Israel's own history is brought forward to counter this claim. Those who now persecute Stephen are the children of those who killed the prophets, and thus they demonstrate a persistent opposition to the Holy Spirit (7.51ff.). Their accusation is turned back against themselves.[133] The prophets, with Moses as the most prominent example, mediate the promises and the Law, living words, in the struggle against rejection and opposition on the part of those who believe that God can be held fast in the work of human hands. Seen in this light, Solomon's temple is not worth anything more than the calf of idolatry in the wilderness (cf. 7.41 and 7.47f.). This brings us to a passage that is much discussed among exegetes. Which textual variant to 7.46 is the most credible? What is the relationship of 7.46 to 7.44–5 on the one hand and to 7.47 on the other? Is Solomon's temple a fulfilment of David's wish, or is it a betrayal of his wish – and if the latter, in what way? What is the relationship of this section to the rest of the speech, and how is it to be reconciled (or not) to Luke's theology of the temple at other places?

There is no agreement among the attempts at an answer, but there seems to be a certain consensus[134] that 7.44 marks a new section which says that the fathers had the tent of witness until David's days, that is before Solomon's temple. This tent was built according to a divinely revealed model, and they bore it with them when entering the promised land. David wishes thus to find a tent, σκήνωμα, for Jacob's God. Solomon realises this, but instead he builds for God a house, οἶκος. Most interpreters[135] prefer, with

---

[132] On this, cf. Elliott, *Home for Homeless*, 187.
[133] O'Neill, *Theology of Acts*, 79.
[134] Summarised in Wilckens, *Missionsreden*, 212.
[135] Including Wilckens himself.

support in a few manuscripts, to read τῷ θεῷ Ἰακωβ in 7.46 instead of τῷ οἴκῳ Ἰακωβ, and the relationship between 7.46 and 7.47 is defined as a tension between the σκήνωμα wanted by David in accord with earlier tradition, and the οἶκος which Solomon took upon himself to build and which is attacked by the criticism that the Most High does not dwell in houses (κατοικεῖ) built by human beings. Thus οἶκος is defined negatively and σκήνωμα positively. But it is not necessarily the temple in itself that is rejected, but may be only the idea that it is a house in which God dwells.[136] Those who wish to interpret the text in terms of a more radical criticism of the temple tend to resolve the tension in other places where Luke speaks differently and more positively about the temple, by distinguishing among the various sources at play – whether they see the Lukan preference in the more radically critical elements or in the more positive traits.[137] Usually, Stephen is felt to be more radical than Luke. Luke therefore endeavours to subdue the effect of the criticism by building it into a milder treatment of the temple elsewhere and by claiming that the assumed accusations against the temple were false.

An attempt at a harmonious resolution sees the argument in 7.44–7 in the light of the special adaptation of the promise to Abraham in 7.6–7 that afterwards they will be freed καὶ λατρεύσουσίν μοι ἐν τῷ τόπῳ τούτῳ.[138] The goal of the exodus is thus neither the adoration of God on Sinai nor the occupation of the land of Canaan as such, but the worship of God in the land which he had promised to Abraham and his descendants. This is the meaning of David's wish; he prays that the promise to Abraham may be fulfilled. Solomon's temple might appear to be the fulfilment but the quotation from Isa 66.1f. excludes this possibility. Implicitly presupposed passages such as Ps 131.11 and 2 Sam 7, help to indicate that the promise to Abraham and David's

---

[136] Cf. Schneider, *Apg.*, 467.

[137] Cf. Wilckens, *Missionsreden*, 213f. Wilckens' own solution is that this section of Stephen's discourse is an older text which Luke used, or else perhaps a later insertion.

[138] Dahl, 'Story of Abraham', 145f.

wish rather are fulfilled only by the worship carried out by the disciples who led by the Spirit are gathered in Jerusalem in Jesus' name, whether this takes place in the temple or in private homes. Thus τὴν σκηνήν Δαυὶδ τὴν πεπτωκυῖαν (Acts 15.16) is set up again and rebuilt. This attempt to harmonise does, however, reject the idea that a radical criticism of the temple is implied: the point is rather that worship in Jesus' name overtakes the temple in such a way that the promise is fulfilled. The more precise wording in 7.46–7 therefore plays no role in this interpretation; it is not even necessary to take a position on which textual variant should be preferred.

I find it difficult, however, to reject totally that element in the argument of Stephen's speech which is critical of the temple. The variation in the choice of words at 7.46–7 is noteworthy, and we have good reasons to begin by trying to find a meaning in the well-attested reading τῷ οἴκῳ Ἰακώβ, which also is the *lectio difficilior*, before one has recourse to the apparently more comfortable reading (in terms of its contents) τῷ θεῷ Ἰακώβ.[139] If one compares the two verses, one notices immediately a great number of differences. David prayed that he might find, while Solomon built. David wished to find a tent, while Solomon built a house. The tent was to be for Jacob's house, but Solomon's house was for God. Taken together, this makes Solomon's temple a mistake. The orientation to the people instead of to God is in harmony with the narrative about David as this runs in 2 Sam 7 and 1 Chr 17. Nathan's message about David's building plans is that God does not wish for a house: on the contrary, God will give the people a dwelling, and thus he will build David a house. During David's period, the people were able to settle down in peace. But it did not bind God

---

[139] The only argument in favour of τῷ θεῷ is that αὐτῷ in 7.47 otherwise comes somewhat abruptly. The text-critical considerations are convincingly set out and argued by Klijn, 'Stephen's Speech', 29f. His own interpretation is also interesting, but is influenced by his decision to neglect the difference between σκήνωμα and οἶκος on the basis of a reference back to Hebrew terms. He thinks historically rather than redactionally about the speech. Cf. also Storch, *Stephanusrede*, 96ff., who likewise argues for the most difficult reading and at the same time chooses to ignore the difference between σκήνωμα and οἶκος. Solomon's mistake was to build the temple for *God*, and not for *the house of Jacob*, i.e. the people. For the Most High does not dwell in houses made by human hands. Wilckens has given good reasons for rejecting this interpretation as untenable in relation to 7.44–5: *Missionsreden*, 213f. Cf. also Synge, 'Studies', 25.

to a place or a house. Solomon's temple was, further, an expression of Solomon's own activity; it was not 'given' as the tent of witness had been given, in agreement with God's revelation and commandment. The Law is understood in this speech through prophetic categories, and fidelity to the Law can involve criticism of the temple. While the antithesis between σκήνωμα and οἶκος is certainly not to be maintained absolutely, it is not without meaning. The critical employment of οἶκος in 7.47 prepares for the verb κατοικεῖ in 7.46, and both are governed by the vocabulary in the quotation from Isaiah at 7.49c. Solomon's house for God promoted the illusion that God could be made to dwell in a house. Besides this, of course, σκήνωμα for its part not only creates continuity with the tent of witness, but also means a correspondence to σκηνή in 15.16.

Altogether, Luke avoids characterising the existing temple positively as God's house. Lk 2.49 employs a formulation, ἐν τοῖς τοῦ πατρός μου, which can refer just as easily to persons and to occupation as to a locality.[140] Lk 19.46, Jesus' saying in connection with the cleansing of the temple, is somewhat more complicated. But when read with attention, it does not come out as a positive word about the existing temple. The temple is characterised on the contrary as a den of robbers, while God's house is to be a house of prayer. Later, those who believe in Jesus fulfil this by their presence in prayer in the temple, as did the prophetess Anna. But they also have 'houses of prayer' in other places than the temple, in 'the upper room' (Acts 1.14); 'in their own houses' (Acts 4.23f.); in Mary's house (Acts 12.13) – to mention the examples in Jerusalem. Those who believe in Jesus continue to fulfil the demands of the Law concerning the temple, but their worship is not bound to particular times and places.[141] It is emphasised that both men and women take part together in the private gatherings; here they do not need to follow the temple's gender-segregated organisation, which per-

[140] Cf. Weinert, 'Multiple Meaning', 19–22, who also emphasises that Luke here consciously avoids οἶκος but for other reasons than those which I adduce. His point is that Luke plays on an open meaning which unites the local, the functional and the personal in order to bring out 'the transforming power of the pilgrimage experience'. Fitzmyer, *Luke*, 443f., does indeed choose the traditional translation, 'in my Father's house', but with clear statements that the other possibilities cannot be rejected.

[141] Bagger Larsen, *Konflikten om sabbaten*, 4–16.

mitted women to enter only the women's forecourt. It is also noteworthy that the Holy Spirit comes over them like a rushing wind in the
house where they are all gathered – and not in the temple. And after
the first confrontation with the temple authorities, it is only when they
are once again among their own group in the house that they pray for a
renewed confirmation that the Holy Spirit is with them. Here too the
gender perspective plays a role, as is especially clear in the event of
Pentecost. The fact that both men and women are filled with the Spirit
and prophesy is decisive for the fulfilment of the quotation from Joel.
This cultic freedom in the Spirit is a potential which means that neither the exclusion from the temple nor even the destruction of the
temple has any damaging significance for them. The flexibility is covered better by 'tent' than by 'house'. The tent of witnesses followed the
people on their wanderings. Perhaps we can sense something of the
same preference for categories of movement in Luke's absolute employment of ἡ ὁδός (Acts 9.2; 19.9, 23; 22.4; 24.14, 22) as the expression
which the believers themselves prefer (cf. 24.14).

The critique of the temple in Stephen's speech can be maintained
within the Lukan composition due to its place in the narrative progress.
It is a misunderstanding to construct a unified and consistent systematic theology out of the various temple passages, irrespective of where
they occur in the narrative.[142] Stephen's speech establishes that the
remnant in Jerusalem who believe in Jesus, are to be understood as
David's tent that has been raised up again. At the same time, it fore-
shadows the exodus from the temple and from Jerusalem and indeed
itself becomes the occasion for the serious intensification of this movement outwards. After the narrative about Stephen, the temple disap-
pears more and more from the picture. When Philip in Acts 8 helps the
Ethiopian court official to understand the Scriptures, so that he accepts
baptism, the courtier is on his way *from* the temple. Even if the movement continues to oscillate back and forth, the move from Jerusalem
determines its direction (cf. the programme in Acts 1.8).

---

[142] Weinert, 'Meaning of Temple', 85f., emphasises 'Luke's dependence on narrative
progress to develop his thought', but is equally concerned to establish a unified 'view on
the temple' through the whole of Luke-Acts. In his version, this is primarily a positive
view. The temple itself is never the object of criticism, although it can be misused.

This corresponds with a transfer to the house; not only as an alternative to the temple and its lust for power, but also as an alternative to the social control exercised by the public sphere of the city.[143] A recent analysis of Acts' narrative of Paul's stay in Philippi (Acts 16.11–40) shows that the scene repeatedly shifts from the public sphere of the city to the more private sphere of the household.[144] The public place forms a point of departure, and the preaching of the Christian missionaries is successful both at the Jewish meeting-place (which is not a synagogue: 16.13f.), in the city (16.18f.), and in the prison (16.35f.). But the outcome of the activity is households that are converted and offer a base for the missionaries and for the community.[145] Of those named, Lydia and her household are primary and most significant.

The book of Acts closes in Rome, the centre of the imperial power, where Paul has rented private accommodation for himself while he waits for his case to be heard. He preaches and teaches in the house where he lives. Even if the terminology referring to the place is varied and possibly also unclear,[146] the picture drawn is nevertheless clear. Paul's activity is linked and limited to the place where he lives. This confinement, however, does not prevent him from continuing his work. Instead of his going out, the movement is turned towards his house, where he receives those who come to him. The house has become the only possible alternative.

[143] Elliott, *Home for Homeless*, 193f. Elliott goes too far, however, when, inspired by Mottu's analysis of Lk 18.9–14 (itself inspired by Sartre), he claims that Luke operates with an absolute contrast between household and temple, 'the bankrupt seat of Jewish power and piety', 193.

[144] Redalie, *Conversion*, 102–8. However, he does not reflect on the fact that the Jewish meeting-place is not a synagogue, but a place of prayer where women come together.

[145] Cf. Witherington, *Women in the Earliest Churches*, 148: 'Luke is at pains to show that the Gospel and its followers can exist within the confines of a place of Roman authority by creating its own space in "house".' Bovon, however, *Lukas*, 81, bases the argument on Redalie (see previous note) and does not see the house as a goal, but as a mediator: the city is won with the house as the base of operations. This emphasises at the same time the collective dimension both of conversion and of the church.

[146] Haenchen, *Apg.*, 649 n. 2, discusses Lake's suggestion that μίσθωμα in Acts 28.30 means 'at his own expense', but concludes that 'Gemeint ist auf alle Fälle nichts anderes als 28.16 mit καθ' ἑαυτόν und 28.23 mit ξενία'.

When women in the story appear in the house, they are therefore not on the periphery, but are in a central position in relation to the place where the community of faith has much of its life. This is also emphasised by the priority of 'non-domestic' functions as 'the better part'. At the same time, the public sphere retains its importance as the place of power. In the house, the women have a certain freedom and religious significance. But for most of the women, the house also represents their limitation: the men keep hold of the public world as a male world of power. In other words, a radical and positive use is made of the possibilities within the given framework of the patriarchal system, and boundaries are touched and perhaps stretched. But the patriarchal system itself is not threatened so that the more the communities orientate themselves to the world outside the house, the more women's activity will have to be restricted.[147]

It is therefore interesting to make a comparison with another New Testament writing, the gospel of John, which is rich in centrally-placed female figures.[148] Much of the theological vocabulary and the symbolic world of the gospel of John has a strongly androcentric stamp. At the same time, traces of a noticeably egalitarian reflection and praxis are evident. Women carry out some of the same functions as in Luke's writings, but in full public view and *vis-à-vis* both women and men. It is actually a consistent trait in John's gospel that women when meeting Jesus, cross the threshold of the house – indeed, they are quite directly summoned forth. As we shall also see from later sources, it seems as if the egalitarian potential is furthest developed, not when women break the role-boundaries in the shelter of a house community, but when they break out of the house and demonstratively enter the public space.

The Apocryphal Acts written two or three generations later are also highly relevant to the question of women's leeway in regard to a private and a public sphere. The narratives presuppose that a woman's tradi-

---

[147] In this connection, it is interesting that both Theodore of Mopsuestia and John Chrysostom consider the prohibition of teaching in 1 Tim 2.12 as a question about public order and therefore something that affects only public teaching activity, not whatever might take place privately. Cf. Gryson, *Ministry of Women*, 83, 85.

[148] On the discussion of this, with further references, cf. Seim, 'Roles of Women', 67–73.

tional 'proper place' is within the private world, in her father's or her husband's house. The man, on the other hand, moves freely in the external, public world. By remaining in the house, a woman will normally show her acceptance of the place given her. Leaving the house, means that she crosses boundaries and penetrates the man's domain. Thereby she arouses suspicion and hostility. The social and sexual exodus therefore takes on local expression.[149] An ascetic life within the boundary of the house is a borderline case, breaking open the house's presuppositions from within. This is expressed locally by the fact that the ascetic wives annoy their family by continually slipping out. It represents, however, a less problematic and provocative solution, because the surface structure is not broken up definitively.

The radical consequences of an ascetic choice become clearest in the majority of the cases where women break out. By defying the physical boundaries placed around women's space, they express their defiance of the social and sexual norms which culminate in patriarchal marriage. The Apocryphal Acts show that a woman's choice of an ascetic life meant a challenge to the very foundations of the gender-determined boundaries between the private and the public spheres. The ascetic women also enter the public world, by projecting themselves in functions that were unusual for women. A kind of ascetic 'transvestism' is the sporadic expression of the fact that they are actually taking up a man's life, living in the men's world.[150] This shows that even if the basic foundations are challenged, they are to some extent maintained in another level. But the idea of an ascetic life implies, taken to the logical consequences, that both spheres become relativised and disowned, as it is later expressed in a – subversive – withdrawal from the world.

IV. 4. *The women at the cross and grave.*

The ambiguous tension in the picture of women in Luke – between the possibilities that are opened up and the boundaries that are drawn at the same time – emerge clearly from the Lukan version of the narrative

---

[149] Burrus, *Chastity*, 110.
[150] Cf. further p. 221, also n. 111, 112 and p. 223 n. 115.

about the empty tomb in Lk 23.55–24.12. The women are a linkage between cross (23.39), burial (23.55f.) and resurrection (24.1–10); they form the continuity that confirms that it is the crucified and buried Jesus whose tomb is empty. They also represent the connection back to Galilee, the path that has been taken from Galilee onwards. Both these perspectives are essential to the Lukan narrative about Jesus' death and resurrection. They have their roots in the material common to the synoptics, but as they appear in Luke they have their own special form.

According to the Lukan narrative, the disciples do not flee, but remain in Jerusalem, and they are not directed to meet the risen Lord in Galilee, as is the case in Mark and Matthew. The Galilean perspective in Luke is primarily one of memory and retrospect, the connection backwards.[151] The point is that the group of disciples have preserved with him all the way from Galilee. This is emphasised several times in the case of the women. In Lk 23.49, the information that the women had followed him from Galilee, αἱ συνακολουθοῦσαι αὐτῷ ἀπὸ τῆς Γαλιλαίας, is the only reference from Mark about the group of women that Luke has kept in its original place in the crucifixion scene. The grammatical feminine also indicates that only the women have followed Jesus from Galilee, and not the whole group of οἱ γνωστοί.[152] In connection with the burial scene, the women are decribed once more as those who ἦσαν συνεληλυθυῖαι ἐκ τῆς Γαλιλαίας. A third reference to the time in Galilee in 24.6 makes its significance clear. The message to the women at the empty tomb mobilises and activates them by reminding them of what Jesus had told them while he was still in Galilee. Since the Galilean women were with him at that time, they can

---

[151] Dillon, *Eye-Witnesses*, 6: '... the artful twist which made the Galilee of Marcan promise become the Galilee of memory and retrospect'. Cf. also Ritt, 'Frauen', 126.

[152] It seems therefore somewhat imprecise for Tyson, 'Jewish Public', 583, to claim that 'The impression that is conveyed in these verses is that of a loyal but beleaguered group of Galileans, whose support of Jesus is totally ineffective when put up against the rejection of the crowd as a whole'. Since his chief point is that, 'the motif of diminishing support ... focusses attention on Jesus himself, who virtually meets his opponents alone, without human aid, and after apparent defeat and death overcomes them', he does not see the positive function that the group of women nevertheless fulfils. Danker, *Jesus*, 242, thinks that a distinction can be seen between the men, οἱ γνωστοί who stand at a distance, and the women. This, however, presupposes that καὶ is to be read only as a juxtaposition and not emphatically, as I propose (cf. p. 20).

remember and perceive the fulfilment, because they recognise the prediction. The repeated reference to the women following Jesus from Galilee corresponds to the threefold association of the passion predictions within the Easter narratives which is unique to Luke.[153]

The women from Galilee represent then, the link between the crucifixion scene and the narratives about the tomb; they ensure the continuity between the crucified Jesus and the risen Lord.[154] The women are primarily onlookers, both in the crucifixion scene and at the burial: they 'see' (cf. ὁρῶσαι in 23.49 and ἐθεάσαντο in 23.55). In the narrative about the tomb, however, they become those who carry the action forwards. But already at the burial, Luke assigns to the women a more active role than does Mark. By including the women's preparations for the anointing of Jesus' body already in the burial scene,[155] he connects the narrative about the burial and the narrative about the empty grave more closely to one another so that they become one single sequence. The temporal reference in 23.54, which Mark has at the introduction to the burial narrative, is placed in Luke immediately before the arrival/return of the women to the tomb. Thus it explains why the anointing of Jesus' body cannot be done at once, even if they do as much and as quickly as they can, without breaking the sabbath regulations. Faithful to the Law, the women observe the rest on the sabbath day. But even before sunrise[156] they return to the tomb with the fragrant oils they have already prepared on the burial day itself. The women's service continues, and they undertake what was women's work, attended to by no one else.[157]

---

[153] Perkins, *Resurrection*, 154. Cf. Dillon, *Eye-Witnesses*, 24.

[154] Ritt, 'Frauen', 130; Talbert, *Literary Patterns*, 113ff., who sees this as an expression of Luke's anti-docetic christology.

[155] Perkins, *Resurrection*, 152; Dillon, *Eye-Witnesses*, 12ff.

[156] Grass, *Ostergeschehen*, 35, points out that Luke, in relation to Mark, has moved the time forward to before sunrise: 'Da nach Lukas die Frauen ihre Spezerien schon am Begräbnistag bereitet haben, können sie noch früher zum Grabe eilen. Ihr frühest mögliches Kommen bezeugt die Grösse ihrer Liebe und Verehrung'. It is, however, characteristic that he interprets this primarily in emotional categories which serve to sentimentalise the women.

[157] Augsten, *Stellung des lukanischen Christus*, 27, points out that it is justifiable that the women in Luke should anoint Jesus' dead body, since this has not been done, either in anticipation (as at Mk 14.3ff. par. Mt) or by Joseph of Arimathea.

The thorough description of their preparations (23.56–24.1) ensures in literary terms, the element of surprise at the open and empty grave. At the same time, it is obvious that the women must go into the grave, if they are to carry out their intention. Luke has omitted the women's preoccupation with the heavy stone that must be rolled away: it does not represent any point of significance. The surprise and confusion are linked to the fact that they do not find Jesus' body, which they had come to anoint, inside the grave itself.[158] The situation which the women encounter makes the preparations which they have carried out futile, and renders their practical concern and service unnecessary. The situation finds them therefore unprepared, and makes them perplexed, καὶ ἐγένετο ἐν τῷ ἀπορεῖσθαι αὐτὰς περὶ τούτου (24.4). But the Galilean women's service brings them to the grave so that they become the first witnesses of the resurrection.

It has been suggested that the women's role in the structure of the grave narrative is temporary. They are merely transient bearers of the news of the resurrection. The message with which they are sent away is not for the women themselves, but for the disciples, the men. In relation to the content of the message, the women remain passive, without understanding, in fact, outsiders. The message is for the men, and the women are only 'errand girls'.[159]

Such an understanding is inadequate for Luke's version. It can indeed be claimed that the women in Luke too, run immediately to the male disciples with the news (24.10f.) But this is a spontaneous action on their part. In Luke, no commission is given to the women to go and tell the other disciples that he is risen (Mt 28.7) and/or to tell them to meet him in Galilee (Mk 16.7, par. Mt). Instead, they are reminded of how Jesus told *them*, ὡς ἐλάλησεν ὑμῖν,[160] that the Son of Man must be handed over to the hands of sinners, be crucified, and rise again on the third day (24.6–7). Thus the 'errand girl' commission which is central in the communication made in Mark's version is replaced in

---

[158] Dillon, *Eye-Witnesses*, 17, is therefore wrong to claim that Luke has reduced the tension in the narrative. On the focussing on Jesus' body, cf. Perkins, *Resurrection*, 158; Talbert, *Literary Patterns*, 113.

[159] Marin, 'Frauen am Grabe', 67–85; Fatum, 'Selvtoegt', 238f.

[160] Dillon's supposition, *Eye-Witnesses*, 38, that ὑμῖν focusses on 'the evangelist's own audience' rather than on the women, has no basis in the text.

Luke by a statement that focusses on the women's own role as disciples.[161] They are asked to remember what was said while he was still in Galilee, where they were together with him. As has been mentioned earlier, this explains the repeated characterisation of the women as those following Jesus from Galilee. It is necessary in order for this retrospective reminder to be meaningful. The summary notice in 8.1–3 is once more activated in the narrative, and the reference to the passion predictions imply that the women are counted among αἱ μαθηταί in 9.18ff. and 17.22ff.[162] Unique to Luke is also the use of the feminine form μαθήτρια which is found in Acts 9.36. As a common designation of both male and female disciples, however, the masculine plural form is the most obvious linguistic device.

The women's role in Luke's grave narrative is thus not one of substitution. On the contrary, the women are themselves the first addressees of the resurrection message in a way that confirms their discipleship and the instruction they have received as disciples. In this situation, it is not their diaconal resources that are needed. Relevant is their relationship to the word of the Lord: they have listened to his words. In these words they have the resources that now may help to overcome their confusion and anxiety. They are asked to remember, μνήσθητε, how he told them (24.6). And so the women remembered his words, ἐμνήσθησαν τῶν ῥημάτων αὐτοῦ (24.8).

The use of μιμνῃσκω/μιμνῃσκομαι combined with the word of the Lord in 24.6 and 24.8 has parallels in 22.61; Acts 11.16; 20.35; Mt 26.75; 27.63; Jn 2.(17), 22; 12.16; 15.20; 1 Clement 13.1; 46.7;

---

[161] Even the commentators who register this shift in Luke fail to see what difference it makes to the women's role in the narrative. A characteristic example is Perkins, who pays more attention than most scholars to the fact that Luke lacks 'the element of commissioning' so that 'The report of the women to Peter and the other disciples is presented as a spontaneous action rather than as a divine mandate', *Resurrection*, 157. But she does not develop this further, because at the same time, without giving more detailed reasons, she supposes that a commission to the women 'is implied in the angel's use of a kerygmatic formula'. Therefore she can also state that the women in Luke 'are clearly presented as fulfilling the mission given to them' just as in Mark, 152. Tetlow, *Women and Ministry*, 105, interprets – in keeping with her consistently negative treatment of Luke – the lack of a commission exclusively and without further qualification as 'critical of women'.

[162] Against Ernst, *Lukas*, 652; Grass, *Ostergeschehen*, 33; Schweizer, *Lukas*, 298. A positive defence is made by Dillon, *Eye-Witnesses*, 38, even if he later modifies this surprisingly, as mentioned in n. 160 above.

Polycarp to the Philippians 2.3. It may have been a traditional phrase to introduce words of Jesus.[163] But there are great differences among the various passages in terms of the way in which the 'remembrance' of the word of the Lord functions. In 1 Clement 13.1; 46.7; and in Polycarp the 'remembrance' serves in a relatively uncomplicated way as a paraenetic motivation.[164] The author's own exhortation is anchored in particular logia of Jesus which confirm it and are therefore called to mind for the community. This naturally involves an activation and actualisation of the community's treasured logia of Jesus, but it is primarily the author's own words that are given authority by means of relevant words from Jesus. In practice, therefore, to remember the words of Jesus will mean to follow the exhortation of the Letter. The call to remember the Lord's words has its effect on the readers in this way, while also confirming the authority of the author. It does not supply any key of interpretation that would open otherwise closed doors, nor does it give words and meaning to something that would be unfathomably confusing and difficult without the word of the Lord.

In Luke (with the exception of Acts 20.35), however, and in John to 'remember' the Lord's word has precisely such a key function. 'To recall/remember' seems to be a firmly established, perhaps indeed a technical term, a 'topos' that occurs in connection with later activation of prophetic predictions.[165] After his threefold denial of Jesus, the Lord's look makes Peter remember the word of the Lord that this would happen – despite Peter's own denial (Lk 22.31–4 par. Mt). He perceives what has happened and goes out and weeps bitterly (22.61–2 par. Mt). In Acts 11.16f., Peter relates that confronted by the surprising outpouring of the Spirit on Gentiles, he recalled the word of the Lord: 'John baptised with water, but you shall be baptised with the Holy Spirit' (cf. Acts 1.5). This meant that he could not possibly stand in God's way, and the Gentiles were baptised (10.7f.). In the same way, the women at the empty tomb are helped to make the transition from confusion to reassessment and new insight by means of the messengers'

---

163 Dahl, 'Anamnesis', 25; Haenchen, *Apg.* 300 n. 2.
164 Dahl, 'Anamnesis', 24f.
165 Berger, 'Materialien', 3, with reference to TestJob 13.5. Cf. also Witherington, *Women in the Earliest Churches*, 130f., and Perkins, *Resurrection*, 154.

exhortation to remember the word of the Lord, how Jesus himself had predicted, while still in Galilee, what they are now experiencing. In Luke, this overcomes the women's fear. In a striking difference from Mark and Matthew, nothing is said in Luke about any fear the women felt after having received the divine message. Thus dramatic events which the actors of the narrative themselves have not foreseen, are given their interpretation when the prophetic word of the Lord is remembered – and the story may proceed. It is, in other words, another special expression of the fundamental Lukan concept of promise-fulfilment.[166]

The Lukan use is also somewhat more specialised than the Johannine. In John, μιμνήσκομαι refers to earlier words and actions of Jesus as well as to scriptural evidence, (cf. especially Jn 2.17, (22c) and 12.17). In Luke it is exclusively linked to the instruction of Jesus entrusted to the disciples. His words are to be *remembered*, while the word of scripture is to be read, interpreted and expounded, opened up – *inter alia* in the light of words that Jesus spoke while he was still with them, and which are entrusted to their 'memory' (cf. the general references to the scripture in Lk 24.25ff., 32, 44f.).[167] Nor is there any reason to claim that to remember his words is a type of interpretative key referring especially to 'the post resurrection interpretation of Jesus' words' (cf. Jn 15.20 and Lk 22.61f.).[168]

The preservation and application of the Lord's words, the 'remembrance', is not a task reserved to the male apostles. The exhortation to the women at 24.6 to recall what he had told them, echoes various statements earlier in the gospel about hearing the word and taking care of it (λόγος (8.15, (21); 11.28; 10.39); cf. λόγοι (24.44) or ῥήματα

---

[166] Cf. Dahl, 'Story of Abraham', 151ff.; Johnson, *Literary Function*, 15–28.

[167] Gerhardsson, *Memory*, 226, 228ff., documents this double anchoring in Luke, but interprets it as a variation of 'the two-witness theme', and wishes to make it specific to the apostles, 229f. The women's role in 24.1–12 is discussed only in passing, and despite the title of the book, he is not interested in the 'memory' term in Lk 24.6 and 8.

[168] This is a quotation from Perkins, *Resurrection*, 154, who claims that 'remember' is used 'as a technical term for the post resurrection interpretation of Jesus' words in the light of Old Testament prophecies'. As the quotation also shows, she links the argument from scipture more closely to the term 'remember' than Luke warrants. What she claims is more appropriate in the case of John.

(2.51; cf. 24.6, 8)). Thus, when 24.8 says that the women remembered his word, this means that they have both heard the words and taken good care of them, in other words they have fulfilled the criterion granting membership in God's family and are included among the blessed.

The exhortation to the women to remember does not insinuate that they might have forgotten.[169] Certainly, the interpretation offered here does not imply that the word addressed to the women should be understood as a sharp reproach, like the accusation against the disciples on the road to Emmaus in 24.25f.;[170] which is heavy with negative undertones. These are totally absent in 24.5f. The introductory question, Τί ζητεῖτε τὸν ζῶντα μετὰ τῶν νεκρῶν; has a note of mild reproach; the women are seeking Jesus where he cannot be found. But the main emphasis lies on the positive proclamation of the resurrection, which explains to the women why the tomb is empty. In Luke, the women themselves have already established that Jesus' body is no longer there; this fact is not only made explicit (as in Mark) by the explanatory proclamation of the angels. The kerygmatic formula, οὐκ ἔστιν ὧδε, ἀλλὰ ἠγέρθη, is further strengthened by appealing to the women to recall Jesus' earlier prediction. The communication by the *angeli interpretes* in Lk 24.5f. does not carry less meaning than the joyful Easter message in the corresponding narrative in Mark.[171] Those who express such reservations, tend also to disallow that when the women do in fact remember Jesus' words, this implies understanding and faith on their part.[172] This very reserved position is closely related to a theological position claiming that only the christophanies can evoke faith. The empty tomb is nothing if not ambiguous.[173] But it is not easy to be

[169] Cf. Gerhardsson, *Memory*, 228 n. 3.

[170] As is claimed by Dillon, *Eye-Witnesses*, 18f.

[171] As Dillon, *Eye-Witnesses*, 18, suggests.

[172] Dillon, *Eye-Witnesses*, 18, 26, 28 is sharply opposed on this point by Perkins, *Resurrection*, 155, and Plevnik, 'Eyewitnesses', 90–8. Brown, *Apostasy*, 75, claims that the resurrection is not at all the object of faith in Luke's understanding of this word; faith relates to what the prophets said, Lk 24.25.

[173] This is a main point in Dillon's interpretation of Lk 24, and it is characteristic that he has recourse to German theological terminology and speaks of 'the transition from Ostererfahrung to Osterglaube', *Eye-Witnesses*, 18. Cf. also Guillaume, *Luc*, 50, and Lohfink, *Himmelfahrt Jesu*, 171f., 253f.

persuaded that even the positive confirming statement of the kerygmatic formula, together with the activation of the interpretative key in Jesus' word, is a 'cryptic designation' and an expression of the fact that 'the evangelist carefully keeps all the witnesses in the dark throughout the account', so that 'the tomb sequence ends with the cover of the passion mystery still intact'.[174] This is justified by pointing to the fact that the real meaning of the passion predictions was hidden from the disciples and was always misunderstood.[175] But this is not convincing as it overlooks the fact that it is precisely the fulfilment which contributes to give meaning to the promise,[176] as is also indicated by the sequence of statements in the angelic message. Since the exhortation to the women to remember what Jesus told them in Galilee serves to support the message of the resurrection, the explicit emphasis that the women ἐμνήσθησαν τῶν ῥημάτων αὐτοῦ must also imply that they truly accept what these words mean.[177] The specific use of μιμνήσκομαι as has been set out in detail above, indicates the same.

The women's service leads them to a tomb which they find to be empty, to a body that is no longer there – among the dead. In this situation, the women are reaffirmed as hearers of the word: they are the first to hear the message of the resurrection proclaimed, and this calls to their remembrance the word they once heard from Jesus. This makes them leave the tomb behind,[178] and they go forth and tell everything to the eleven and to all the others (24.9). As has been mentioned earlier, no commission is given to the women in Luke's version of the story. Their witness is due to their own spontaneous initiative as a continuation of what they themselves have heard and remembered.[179] The women appear as the first witnesses of the Lord Jesus' resurrection, and the

---

[174] Dillon, Eye-Witnesses, 26.

[175] Dillon, Eye-Witnesses, 26, 51f.

[176] Plevnik, 'EyeWitnesses', 93.

[177] Cf. Perkins, Resurrection, 155: 'To presume that the women have some inadequate faith or that the angels are not recalling the kerygma, dissolves the obvious links that Luke has established between this passage and the rest of the gospel'.

[178] But when Dillon, Eye-Witnesses, 28, speaks of a 'stigmatisation' of the grave, this must be called an exaggeration: cf. the fact that the women's words bring Peter to set out precisely for the tomb.

[179] Cf. O'Toole, Unity, 123.

narrative in Lk 24 says nothing about any hesitation or confusion or fear on their part as they make their way from the grave – unlike the narratives in Mark and Matthew.

The narrative itself guarantees for the reader that the women are trustworthy and credible witnesses and speak the truth. The integrity in their testimony is emphasised first by the statement that they told everything, πάντα.[180] The later repetition of what they said, included in the Emmaus narrative (24.22),[181] demonstrates afresh the reliability of the women. The women are also sufficiently numerous to satisfy the formal demand about the number of witnesses (cf. Dt 19.15). Lk 24.10 singles out three of the women by naming them,[182] and the list of names comes pointedly at the close, just as a protocol of testimony concludes by mentioning the names of the witnesses.[183] The imperfect from ἔλεγον in 24.10 can in fact be understood to mean that the women repeatedly told all that they had experienced.[184] Nevertheless, they are not believed. Their words seem to the apostles and the male disciples to be λῆρος, empty chatter (24.11a), and they disbelieve the women, ἠπίστουν αὐταῖς, (24.11b). The form of expression in 24.11b links the apostles' unbelief directly to the women, αὐταῖς.[185] This is in keeping with the fact that women were considered less credible (than men), and, as a rule, they were not accepted juridically as witnesses.[186]

---

[180] Perkins, *Resurrection*, 156.

[181] Such resumptive repetitions in direct speech of earlier narrative material are 'a familiar feature of this author's historiography', cf. Dillon, *Eye-Witnesses*, 108f.

[182] Hengel, 'Maria Magdalena', 245 n. 3: 'Das betonte ἔλεγον ταῦτα nach dem ἀπήγγειλαν ταῦτα in v. 9 ist ein deutliches Zeichen dieser Hervorhebung'. Against Marshall, *Luke*, 881, who without any detailed argument claims that 'the names are added rather as a second thought'.

[183] Hengel, 'Maria Magdalena', 245. Witherington's explanation, *Women in the Earlist Churches*, 131, that the list of names is placed at the conclusion because at this point the women are no longer the only witnesses to what has happened, and that place is thereby made for the eleven as 'primary recipients', is at best unclear. Moreover, in his own subsequent argument, he emphasises precisely the fact that the women's testimony is decisive for what has happened up to this point, and that the apostles can do no more than confirm this. On the linguistic problems in the verse, cf. Marshall, *Luke*, 887.

[184] Marshall, *Luke*, 888.

[185] Brown, *Apostasy*, 74.

[186] Cf. Hengel, 'Maria Magdalena', 252. Witherington, *Women in the Ministry of Jesus*, 135f. n. 88, undertakes a critical examination of the rabbinic material on the issue of the admissibility of women as witnesses, and brings considerable nuances to common

The positioning of the list of names at the close serves also to accentuate a contrast between the women and the men. This contrast is to be understood consistently, since Luke (as compared with Mark and Matthew) widens the group of women and men to include all. The whole group of women, ἡ Μαγδαληνὴ Μαρία καὶ Ἰωάννα καὶ Μαρία ἡ Ἰακώβου καὶ αἱ λοιπαὶ σὺν αὐταῖς (24.10), are set over against the whole group of men, τοῖς ἕνδεκα καὶ πᾶσιν τοῖς λοιποῖς (24.9).[187] All the women give a detailed (ταῦτα πάντα) testimony that all the men refuse to believe.

As a consequence of the narrative's own confirmation of the credibility of the women an ironic tension is created for the reader: the women are absolutely to be believed, and the men make a mistake when they do not believe them.[188] This slightly ironic contrast is maintained in the description of Peter's visit to the tomb in 24.12.[189] His reaction puts him in a positive light – but only in relation to the rest of the men and their total lack of belief. Over against the women, however, he comes in as a poor second. He sees nothing other than the wrappings and so goes to his home, wondering at what has happened. In other words, he establishes that Jesus' body is no longer there, just as the women had done, but no message is transmitted either to him or by him. His wondering, θαυμάζων τὸ γεγονός, corresponds best to the women's confusion, ἐν τῷ ἀπορεῖσθαι αὐτὰς περὶ τούτου (24.4). But while in the case of the women this is their initial reaction, which is later overcome, in Peter's case this is (for the present) the last word.[190]

---

and more absolute points of view. The point, however, remains standing for the most part that women alone could not bear witness to a matter unless their presentation was confirmed by male witnesses.

[187] Munro, 'Women Disciples', 237.

[188] Cf. Wilckens, *Auferstehung*, 49: 'Die Erzählung baut geradezu einen Kontrast zwischen der objektiven Feststellung für den Aspekt des Lesers und dem baren Unverständnis der damals beteiligten Jünger auf'. Cf. also O'Toole, *Unity*, 123, and Witherington, *Women in the Earliest Churches*, 133.

[189] On the text-critical foundation of this verse, cf. Bode, *First Easter Morning*, 68f.

[190] This is completely overlooked by Dillon, *Eye-Witnesses*, 66, when he makes use of this parallel to show that every meeting with the empty grave ends in a total lack of understanding *ex parte hominis*. Witherington, *Women in the Earliest Churches*, 132, who otherwise is clear about the contrasts in the two visits to the grave, also gets things wrong by making parallels without further qualification of Peter's wondering and the women's

It is possible, of course, that this is due to a combination of different traditions about the tomb (cf. the ingenious combination in Jn 20.1–18). It may also serve to prefigure the version given by the two disciples on their way to Emmaus (24.22ff.), which in its turn points directly to the christophany traditions. But I see no reason to hold that, at this stage in the narrative (24.9–12), a kind of Petrine primacy is promoted to replace the women's testimony. Of all the men, Peter comes nearest to the women, but the ironic distance is maintained none the less.[191]

At the same time, the apostolic men come out of the situation unscathed. The way in which the tomb narrative is followed up, shows to an extreme degree the mixed message in the Lukan portrayal of women. The gospel narrative gives prominence to the women's following of Jesus over a long period of time: it emphasises their faithful and fearless perseverance in service, their discipleship, their insight and their credibility. In the continuation, however, it is accepted out of hand that the women are inappropriate as witnesses of the resurrection. Account is taken even of reactions that are revealed to be prejudices.

Some interpreters reject the idea that the aspect of witness plays any part here. They connect the apostles' unbelief exclusively to the contents of the women's story, and the lack of faith is explained primarily as expressing the theological point that the empty tomb does not and cannot create belief in the risen Lord. It is irrelevant whether women are involved or not. The men's unbelief says nothing about their relationship to women, but only demonstrates the limited significance of the tomb narrative vis-à-vis the following christophanies. Faith can arise only in the direct encounter with the risen Lord himself.[192] Some traits

confusion. It should, however, be admitted that θαυμάζω has a somewhat more positive note in Luke than ἀπορέομαι, a kind of 'not yet, but …' quality, cf. Plevnik, 'Eyewitnesses', 92.

[191] Neirynck, 'John and the Synoptics', 173ff., also argues against the idea that Luke's redactional employment of traditions about Peter in 24.12 means that Peter alone is set in focus. He sets 24.12 positively in parallel to the women's visit to the grave, but he goes further than is warranted in identifying the pattern in the two accounts. Peter's visit thereby becomes a total verification of the women's account.

[192] Apart from those mentioned earlier, cf. Schottroff, 'Frauen', 110f.; 'Maria Magdalena', 13f., 25.

in the christophany narratives are invoked in support of this (cf. 24.24 and especially 24.34: ὄντως ἠγέρθη ὁ κύριος καὶ ὤφθη Σίμωνι – with an emphasis on ὄντως).[193]

This last phrase is also one of the primary pieces of evidence adduced by those who wish to see in Luke, an early trace of a conflict in the early church between groups who appealed to Mary Magdalene as their authority and other groups appealing to Peter.[194] The gender aspect takes on central importance, and in the predominant ecclesiastical tradition – to which it is assumed Luke belonged – the Peter-tradition emerges as the victor. Mary Magdalene could not be passed over completely in silence, but the risen Lord's revelation to Peter was the point where the church's faith was anchored.[195] For this reason, the traditions about the resurrection were adjusted by Luke in such a way that the women, with Mary Magdalene as the central figure, were not believed, and the tradition guaranteed by women runs out into the sand. The revelation to Peter also anticipates what the disciples on the way to Emmaus have to tell the others (24.33ff.), that is that the struggle for Peter's primacy affects all who could be said to have forestalled him, not only the women.[196]

It is indeed true that in Luke the risen Lord himself is supposed to have shown himself to Peter first – although this is not reported in a particular revelation narrative. But the narrative of the women at the empty tomb is not thereby deprived of its character as proclamation of the resurrection. This is why none of the interpretative models referred to above, does justice to the special character of the narrative in Luke, as a point of tension where the gospel's positive emphasis on women's participation encounters the confining and oppressing conditions de-

---

[193] Cf. Dillon, *Eye-Witnesses*, 65f.

[194] Schüssler Fiorenza in various studies, including: 'Beitrag der Frau', 71ff.; 'Word, Spirit and Power', 51–6; Pagels, Gnostic Gospels 64ff.; cf. also Hengel, 'Maria Magdalena', 247, 251f., 255.

[195] Brown, 'Roles of Women', 692; Schüssler Fiorenza, *In Memory*, 51.

[196] Plevnik, 'Eyewitnesses', 91, 100f., is thus consistent when he holds that the primary interest of the evangelist is to ensure an independent and direct basis for the apostolic testimony. The point is not to disallow the other and earlier witnesses, but to show that at the end the apostles themselves were also allowed to see. Besides this, 'the slowness of the disciples to accept, guarantees the asphaleia which it is the author's purpose to establish', 101.

termining the relationship between women and men. The women's experience is sufficient for them to appear as proclaimers, but when they attempt this, they are not believed, even by those who should have the ears of faith. It is the men's unbelieving reaction that creates the distance in the Lukan story between the women's early faith and witness, and the male disciples' late acceptance.[197] In the Emmaus narrative, the risen Lord reproaches them for being so dull of understanding and so slow to believe what even the prophets said (24.22–7), in other words, the preconditions necessary for faith ought to have been abundantly present. At the same time in the continuation of the narrative, it is accepted that women cannot be approved as witnesses in a man's world. We have seen how the Lukan missionary activity is characterised by men's proclamation and that explicit gender criteria exclude women from eligibility for positions of leadership.

In the resurrection narratives, Luke clearly emphasises that while the eleven constitute a unit on their own, they are always part of a larger group. This solidarity is more important than the establishment of the small exclusive group.[198] In Acts, the close interdependence of the whole group is still important, but the apostolic college emerges as its leadership and the front figures. The Lukan criteria for an apostle are listed in Acts 1.21–2 when a twelfth apostle is to be elected to take the place of Judas (1.15–26).[199] It is presupposed that more than the eleven fulfil these criteria, which require personal experience of the history of Jesus

---

[197] Munro, 'Women Disciples', 237, gives an exclusively historical explanation of this 'in terms of a female circle in which the conviction of Jesus existed before it was accepted by a reconstituted male following'.

[198] Plevnik, 'Eyewitnesses', 92.

[199] With a few exceptions (about Paul and Barnabas in Acts 14.4) Luke consistently employs the term 'apostle' as a privileged title reserved to the twelve. This is a peculiarly Lukan use of the term, and it has as one of its consequences that Paul, who himself ardently defended his apostleship, falls outside the privileged category; cf. Jervell, *Luke*, 75–112. This means that the use in Acts 14.4, 14 is not representative for Luke, cf. Maddox, *Purpose*, 70–6. Via, 'Women', 42 n. 18, attempts to use Acts 14.4, 14 to constitute a wider group of apostles, of whom 'the twelve' would be only a section, with the aim of showing that thus women too can be included in Luke's use of the term apostle even if there is no direct evidence of this. The attempt is not convincing, and she herself admits that it poses problems. The basic problem is that she wishes to use Luke's construction directly in favour of a feminist reconstruction, and does not distinguish well enough between the different hermeneutical levels.

from the early time in Galilee onwards[200] until the separation at the ascension. In the course of the gospel, the presence of women is emphasised, and in the narratives about the cross and the tomb they represented the followers of Jesus from Galilee. In other words, they ought to be obvious candidates. But an initial demand of maleness already excludes them from this possibility: δεῖ οὖν τῶν συνελθόντων ἡμῖν ἀνδρῶν, the candidates must be men.[201] The women from Galilee are ineligible; interest is concentrated on the Galilean men (cf. also Acts 1.11).

Luke knew, of course, from the lists of names that all the twelve were men.[202] When he restricts the title of apostle exclusively to them, it thereby becomes a male privilege. The reason for this lies, however, not only in the historically-given presupposition that the known names were all men's names; the Matthias who Luke tells us was elected in place of Judas is otherwise unknown. The criteria are related to the function that the apostle is to exercise. The twelve are selected to be witnesses to Jesus' resurrection (Lk 24.48 and Acts 1.8), and the one chosen will therefore *become* (γενέσθαι) a witness to the resurrection along with the eleven (1.22). This means that the twelve, the apostolic college, are primarily designated as witnesses to Jesus' resurrection, μάρτυρες τῆς ἀναστάσεως αὐτοῦ and this is something not shared automatically, in view of their role as eyewitnesses or something similar, by all who appear in the resurrection narratives: it is an exclusive function, the result of a selection and limited to the twelve.[203] They appear as witnesses after Jesus' resurrection and ascension as soon as the number twelve is completed anew after the election of Matthias. Their function is however limited to Israel, and is carried out in Jerusalem

---

[200] Robinson, *Way of the Lord*, 59, emphasises that it is the geographical point of departure which interests Luke, and not the temporal beginning. This is also one of the reasons why the women are already visible in the Galilean period, since 'as far as witnesses were concerned, Luke was interested in "from Galilee".'

[201] Cf. Schüssler Fiorenza, 'The Twelve', 119; 'Apostleship of Women', 138; 'Beitrag der Frau', 71. This element is often not mentioned at all by the commentators, cf. as examples both Haenchen and Schneider *ad loc.* Is this because it is taken for granted?

[202] Schüssler Fiorenza, 'Apostleship of Women', 138.

[203] Brox, *Zeuge*, 44f.; Roloff, *Apostolat*, 178, 196.

between Acts 2.1 and 8.25.[204] Then 'David's fallen tent' is raised up again through the great mass conversions of Jews both from Palestine and from the Diaspora (cf. 2.41; 4.4; 5.14, etc.). When the apostolate has thus fulfilled its task, its function of witnessing in Israel, one apostle can die (James at Acts 12.2) without any necessity to elect a new apostle in his place. After ch. 15 the twelve disappear completely from the picture, and there is never any mention of successors. The position of the twelve as witnesses to the resurrection and as eschatological rulers in Israel is a non-recurring phenomenon which neither can, nor should be, repeated. In the further narrative, Paul becomes the dominant figure with his proclamation δημοσίᾳ καὶ κατ' οἴκους.

When women in Acts are excluded from becoming apostles or from being leaders in other ways, this is a consequence of Luke's restricted and special concept of apostleship and acceptance of the public sphere as a man's world. So the public act of witness has to be carried out by men. This is nowhere justified in theological terms, and women are never explicitly adjured to keep silent or to be subordinate. What is demonstrated is a structure imposing silence. The narrative about the women on Easter morning shows this with considerable clarity. When the message fails to reach its destination, this is not due to the women, but because the men do not believe them. They refuse to be convinced, because their prejudices hinder them. But this does not shake the relationship of power, and the conclusion is therefore none the less a rejection of women's possibility to bear witness – despite the ironic distance to the presuppositions which make this rejection necessary. Even the two dazzling figures who proclaim the resurrection in the empty tomb (Lk 24.4) and later explain the ascension (Acts 1.10), are characterised in Luke as men, ἄνδρες, and the aspect of witness is emphasised by the fact that there are two of them.[205]

---

[204] On this and what follows, cf. Jervell, *Luke*, 89–96. Cf. also Plevnik, 'Eyewitnesses', 100f., and März, *Wort Gottes*, 45f., who emphasises that it is the collegium that bears witness.

[205] Cf. also Lk 9.30. Bode, *First Easter Morning*, 60, discusses the aspect of witness and the character of the two figures in relative detail, but misses the gender aspect and hints that when they are called men and not angels, this is meant to make the witnesses 'human'. Dillon, *Eye-Witnesses*, 25, contents himself with the remark that they are 'cryptically designated'. When he rejects a role for the witness aspect, this is, of course, because he does not wish to attach any evidential force at all to the traditions about the empty tomb.

When the revelation at the empty tomb in Luke does not communicate any other task to the women than to 'remember' the words of Jesus, this reveals the by now well-known ambivalence in the Lukan image of women. On the one side, the passage contains a divine statement that reaffirms the women's status as disciples: the message of the resurrection is addressed directly and completely to them, as a consequence of the place they had among those who followed Jesus. They are not to be understood as the apostles' 'errand girls'. On the other side, they do not recieve any explicit commission to preach. Even if μιμνήσκομαι is supposed to be an active process, they remain in the position of addressees and good listeners, not of mediators and proclaimers – at least not to men and/or in the public arena. Their own immediate attempt to break through the boundaries shows how stillborn this is. Men's lack of confidence in women makes it useless. The effect is that women are withdrawn from the public proclamation and activity as teachers, and the way is laid open for the men's assumption of power in Acts when public testimony to Jesus' resurrection is borne from Jerusalem to Rome.

Chapter Five

Prophesying Daughters

The spiritual excitement of the Pentecost is described in Acts 2. The risen Lord, exalted as Messiah at the right hand of God, pours out from heaven the Spirit on his followers like a tempestuous rain of fire.[1] Thus they are equipped for a prophetic proclamation that transcends their normal calculable capacity. The Jews, familiar with the scriptures, ought themselves to have the interpretative key enabling them to understand the events here taking place. The same Spirit of God who in ages past had made the promise in the sayings of the prophet, is now fulfilling this promise before their very ears and eyes. The words of the prophet Joel take on flesh and blood in the, as yet, small group which had followed Jesus from Galilee (Acts 1.14). The promise of the gift of the Spirit including and equipping people across the boundaries established by traditional patterns of authority, is thus realised. The Holy Spirit is poured out over all flesh expressing itself in the gift of prophecy, so that the young see visions just as much as the old have dreams, so that women speak prophetically just as well as men.

When the scene of Pentecost is set at the beginning of the chapter, it is underlined that *all*, πάντες, are present. They are *all* assembled, the

---

[1]   Against Fitzmyer and Lampe, Jervell, 'Sons of Prophets', 105, argues convincingly that Luke does not make the Spirit a substitute for the exalted Jesus in heaven. Apart from this, countless suggestions have been made of a parallelisation between the gospel and Acts concerning the introductory bestowal and activity of the Spirit. Hill, *New Testament Prophecy*, 95, holds that the event of Pentecost occupies a position in the structure of Acts that corresponds to Jesus' baptism in the gospel, cf. Acts 1.5. Others, Laurentin, *Truth of Christmas*, 61, 458; Madddox, *Purpose*, 141, point out that the activity of the Spirit in connection with Jesus' conception and birth introduces the gospel in the same way as the event of Pentecost introduces Acts. Laurentin calls the infancy narrative 'Proto-Pentecost'. According to Brown, *Birth of Messiah*, 466, the similarity between the infancy narrative and the first chapters of Acts is due to the fact that 'the Anawim of the infancy narratives are so close to the Jerusalem community of Acts'.

storm of the Spirit fills the *whole* house, the tongues of fire settle on each one of them, and they are *all* filled with the Holy Spirit and begin to speak as they are inflamed by the Spirit (Acts 2.1–4). But who are πάντες? Is this perhaps all the twelve apostles? Do they now appear, after the election of a new apostle, as an assembled *collegium*, with the focus concentrated exclusively on them? If so, πάντες in 2.1 would refer straight back to the last verse in ch. 1, where we are told that Matthias was enrolled from then as an apostle along with the eleven. We should then take the twelve, who appear in 2.14 with Peter as their spokesman, to be the totality of the assembly which was filled by the Spirit. When Peter in his speech draws attention (2.15, 16 and 33) to what is still happening, this would refer to the other eleven. Even if most commentators do not restrict the Pentecost assembly as rigorously as this, but at the least widen it to include the 'about a hundred and twenty' persons of 1.15,[2] this is not a point to which much importance is attached. It is the twelve who count as important, and the outpouring of the Spirit is considered to function primarily as a consolidation of the apostolic authority. Evidence can be adduced in support of this understanding, especially from the fact that the first part of Acts, on the whole, concentrates on the activity of the apostles. But, unwarranted by this particular text itself, it tends to draw attention away from the whole community of Spirit-filled women and men. Our 'popular image' of the scene at Pentecost consisting of the twelve, each with a tongue of fire on his head, has meant that many other persons in the picture have been screened off. The women in the company are, not surprisingly, among those who have been obscured by the shadow.

If πάντες refers to the whole community, then naturally the women are included in the group (in accordance with the list in 1.14) which, however, is not identical with the one hundred and twenty mentioned at 1.15. The frequent repetition and emphasis of πάντες in the beginning of ch. 2 may indicate that, this time, they are all present – both the group of men and the group of women, unlike the immediately preceding assembly which elected the apostle. It is possible too, that the emphasis on inclusiveness also hints that even persons likely to be

---

[2]   On this, see p. 136f.

excluded from participation, now play their part in the events. The emphatic πάντες also strengthens the correspondence with the quotation from Joel 3.1–5 introducing the substantial portion of Peter's discourse (Acts 2.17–25); cf. 2.17, ἐπὶ πᾶσαν σάρκα.[3] The implication is certainly that they are all gathered and the Spirit is poured out over them all, because, according to the prophet Joel, the Spirit is to be poured out in the last days over all flesh, young as well as old, woman as well as man. Peter's summary answer at Acts 2.38f. reflects the same inclusiveness. The promise of the Spirit's gift is given to them and to their children, τοῖς τέκνοις ὑμῶν, and to all who are far away. When the inclusive term τέκνα is used instead of the masculine υἱοί, this sounds like an echo of οἱ υἱοὶ ὑμῶν καὶ αἱ θυγατέρες ὑμῶν in 2.17.[4] For the promise by Joel to be fulfilled, women too must indeed prophesy. The setting of the scene and the word of scripture interpreting it must be in reasonable accord with one another. The point is well taken by John Chrysostom in his homily on this particular text: 'The Spirit is poured out over the one hundred and twenty (i.e. not only over the twelve), for Peter would not have quoted the prophet's testimony, "your sons and your daughters", without any reason.'[5]

When the twelve step forward from the rest of the group and stand on the stage apron, while Peter, on behalf of the college of apostles, expounds what is happening, he can therefore point to the ecstatic

---

[3]   Cf. Kraft, 'Altkirchliche Prophetie', 250f. Jervell, 'Sons of Prophets', 102f., argues against the idea that the 'quantitative' factor in the bestowal of the Spirit plays any important role at all in Luke. But he is too narrowly focussed on his polemics against the idea that the prophetic power of the Spirit is now to be available for all, unlike a more sporadic presence of the Spirit previously: cf. the list of references, 175 n. 141, to which we can also add Schelkle, *Geist und Braut*, 153. Jervell brings a double argument against this – though not with total consistency – on the one hand, Luke understands himself in the continuation of the earlier Jewish prophecy and activity of the Spirit, and certainly does not have a picture of a previous age lacking the spirit of prophecy. On the other hand, it is not the case in Luke that all are prophets. It is, however, difficult to get around the fact that the emphasis on the quantitative 'all' has a central significance in Acts 2, and that this is linked to an eschatological fulfilment with reference to Joel 3. How the relationship between this general outpouring of the Spirit and the special Spirit-filled persons and prophets who appear later, is to be understood, is another question which will be dealt with later on.

[4]   Cf. Zehnle, *Peter's Pentecost Discourse*, 34.

[5]   Cf. Quesnell, 'Women', 78 n. 56.

behaviour of the other men and women in the group, still continuing on the stage itself, 'in the house'. He continually directs the spotlight back towards them.[6] As Peter's speech explains, this general, non-discriminatory outpouring of the Spirit, which brings those who see it, to give loud voice to their amazement, expresses the fact that God's Spirit does not accommodate itself to the established structures of authority: God raised up the Jesus whom they killed, and made him Lord and Messiah. Now he pours out the Holy Spirit over contemptible Galileans and even over the women among them. And exactly this represents the fulfilment of the holy promises of scripture, while at the same time driving history onwards so that the given promises are also fulfilled.[7] In Luke, the act of fulfilment is portrayed as something at the same time substantially old and new, predicted and unpredictable. There is not only a correspondence, but also an effect of tension in the relationship between promise and fulfilment. Even for those who recognise the promise, the fulfilment does not necessarily carry self-explanatory and obvious conviction. Interpretative struggle and argument are needed to substantiate that a promise is truly fulfilled. This process involves elements of surprise and of overcoming opposition, the promise must be mobilised as the proof of a present occurrence.[8] Thus it is the combina-

---

[6]   Haenchen, *Apg.*, 131 n. 4; Quesnell, 'Women', 61. This division in Acts is also in keeping with Paul's demand in 1 Cor 14 that ecstatic speech should always be accompanied by interpretation. It is debatable how far Luke genuinely considered the prophetic activity to have been ecstatic. While prophecy and speaking in tongues converge in the description in Acts 2, other prophetic messages in his presentation are markedly 'rational' (cf. the examples in the infancy narratives and Agabus' prophecies in Acts) as in the same way Peter's discourse is an explanation of the activity at Pentecost. On the whole, therefore, the speaking in tongues at Pentecost is an accompanying phenomenon, cf. Jervell, 'Sons of Prophets', 112, while Dunn, *Jesus*, 174ff., maintains that the relationship between speaking in tongues and prophecy is one of the problems which Luke leaves unclarified.

[7]   On the close connection between the Holy Spirit and salvation history, cf. Bovon, *Lukas*, 58. Cf. also what has been mentioned above in association with the Abraham motif, p. 49.

[8]   Bock, *Proclamation*, 27–37, gives a good overview of the history of scholarship with regard to 'the Proof from Prophecy debate' as this affects the discussion of Lukan material. His own conclusion has certain similarities to mine, in emphasising that it is not a case of 'a defensive apologetics', but of 'proclamation'. In my view, however, he exaggerates the typological pattern in this.

tion of experience and the use of scripture that in Acts 2 legitimates the charismatic prophecy of women.

When the Spirit has intervened actively and overcome human objections and prejudices, it is not possible afterwards to negate the legitimacy of the event or phenomenon. 'The compulsion of the Spirit' serves to make sense theologically of a seeming abnormality by bearing witness to God's sovereign activity. 'If then God gave the same gift to them as he gave to us when we believed in the Lord Jesus Christ, who was I that I could withstand God?' is Peter's reply when he is reproached, after having allowed the uncircumcised Cornelius to be baptised, (Acts 10.44f.; 11.17). The meeting of the apostles in Acts 15 has in reality no other choice, unless they wish to prove themselves disobedient (cf. 15.8). The Spirit blows where it wills, but the Spirit's intentions are declared by means of the divine promises uttered by the ancient prophets (15.14ff.). In parallel to this, the women's share in the gift of the Spirit cannot be denied, even if the presentation in Acts is characterised by a certain obscurity. The prophesying daughters are themselves the guarantee that the eschatological outpouring of the Spirit has actually taken place, in keeping with the promise of Joel's prophecy.

On the basis of rabbinic sources, this period in Judaism has been characterised as a period 'without prophets'.[9] The valid prophets were the 'classical' prophetic texts. In the Hebrew scriptures four women were named as prophets: Miriam in Ex 15.20, Deborah in Jg 4.4, Huldah in 2 Kg 22.14, and Noadiah at Neh 6.14. The rabbinic tradition counted four others: Sarah, Hannah, Abigail and Esther, while keeping silent about Noadiah. Thus the Rabbis ended up with seven female prophets in all (bMeg 14a).[10] They were not, however, afraid to

Jervell, 'Sons of Prophets', 101f., also comes close when he emphasises that the prophetic act of pointing to fulfilment does not add anything really new in terms of substance, but has an indicative, identifying function. However, he does not sufficiently take into consideration that when this identification is not obvious and does not communicate clearly, a considerable interpretative effort is needed to make sense of it in terms of substance.

[9] Foerster, 'Heilige Geist', 117, 119. It has, however, become more and more clear that to employ later rabbinic texts as witnesses to the New Testament period requires a good deal of historical-critical care: cf. Alexander, 'Rabbinic Judaism', 237–46, and, of course, J. Neusner's work.

[10] Isaksson, *Marriage*, 159.

make critical comments about the activity of these women, and tried to reduce their significance. Deborah and Huldah were reproached for being too proud. It was also customary to build up a picture of men accompanying these women in such a way that the women's gift really only strengthened the significance of the men (bMeg 14a).[11]

With certain reservations, it seems that the idea of a lack of credible prophetical activity is in accord with Jewish sources from the New Testament period. The concept that prophecy had ceased, was admittedly not an affirmation of a principle but rather functioned as a criticism of contemporary prophets, who were thereby dismissed as false. The lack of prophetic spirit was also considered to be transitory, and the expectation of a future, or perhaps an eschatological, flowering of prophecy was always alive.[12] Referring to texts such as Isa 32.15; 34.16; Ezek 11.19; 36.26f.; 37.4–14; and Joel 3.1–5, contemporary Judaism maintained the anticipation of a time to come when the Spirit would be poured out anew and all *Israelites* would be prophets.[13] It is this eschatological expectation that gives the quotation from Joel in Peter's speech at Pentecost its argumentative value.

Within the New Testament, the use of Joel 3 in Acts 2 can be seen as a continuation of allusions to Joel 3.5a found in Paul. In Rom 10.13, and perhaps also in 1 Cor 1.2, Paul alludes to this half-verse, but without any reference whatever to the Spirit. In order to prove that for God there is no distinction between Jew and Greek, Paul adduces the quotation, 'everyone who calls on the name of the Lord shall be saved'. In the short Pauline version, Joel 3.5 is thereby changed from a

---

[11] Cf. Goldfeld, 'Women is Sources', 259ff.; Kuzmack, 'Aggadic Approaches', 250, 254.

[12] Leivestad, 'Dogma', 288–9, followed by Sandnes, *Paul*, 42–6. Apart from the examples given by Sandnes from Josephus, it should be mentioned that Dautzenberg, 'Stellung der Frau', 190f., maintains that when Job's daughters in the Testament of Job sing hymns in the language of the angels, this represents the most immediate parallel to the Christian glossolalia. He further links this to Philo's description of the Therapeutae and suggests that ecstatic and pneumatic experiences in Judaism could break up the traditional role division between men and women. However, the problem with this kind of evidence is the uncertainty about its representativeness.

[13] Cf. Leivestad, 'Dogma', 291; Foerster, 'Heilige Geist', 119. Joel 3.1–5, therefore, was understood in agreement with the Old Testament text as a promise made exclusively to Israel. Cf. also Dunn, *Baptism*, 46.

proof of Jewish exclusiveness to a proof of inclusiveness, and the text bears witness to the universality of salvation.

Acts 2.21 shows a similar abbreviation of Joel 3.5. Only the first half-verse καὶ ἔσται πᾶς ὃς ἂν ἐπικαλέσηται τὸ ὄνομα κυρίου σωθήσεται, is retained. But otherwise the whole quotation from Joel is carefully introduced in a manner that emphasises its eschatological significance. Unlike its use in Paul, we find an extensive quotation that also includes the preceding verses, Joel 3.1–4. [14] The expansion means that universalism is combined with the outpouring of the Spirit, while also implying the crossing of other socio-religious barriers. The Spirit overcomes the gulf between those who are near and those who are far off (cf. Peter's summary at 2.39), and also the gulf between woman and man and between slave and free, in other words, the antitheses which the baptismal formula at Gal 3.26–8 proclaim as having been overcome in Christ. [15] The addition of the personal pronoun μου in the statement about the slaves (2.18), [16] however, changes this from a social to a religious characteristic. The statement then applies to male and female servants *of the Lord*, and Luke further specifies, in another addition, καὶ προφητεύσουσιν that when the Spirit is given to them, they will speak

[14] Maddox, *Purpose*, 138, holds that 2.17–18 and 2.21 reproduce the parts of the quotation from Joel that are significant for Luke. What lies between these words is almost a filling, which Luke – true to his habit when he quotes – does not bother to omit. This understanding can also find support in the fact that Peter's summary in 2.38f. is concentrated on these points. Johnson, *Literary Function*, 45, however, maintains that Luke adjusts the text from Joel so that the whole quotation becomes important. By means of it, the gift of the Spirit is characterised as an eschatological gift; it is prophetic, and manifests itself in signs and the working of miracles. On Luke's redactional activity in the quotation, cf. also Zehnle, *Peter's Pentecost Discourse*, 28–34.

[15] Dautzenberg, 'Stellung der Frau', 192, sees the point of connection to Gal 3.28 in a pre-Lukan use of the quotation from Joel, and maintains, following Crüsemann: 'Gal 3.28 ist zwar noch ein Stück radikaler, ... aber ... in den bei Joel genannten Gegensatzpaaren doch bereits präformiert'. In Acts 2.18, Luke is said to have used the addition of μου to insert into the quotation a reduction of its interest to the relationship between Jews and proselytes, cf. also Lindars, *New Testament Apologetics*, 38. As will be shown in what follows, the significance of μου is to be understood differently. Dautzenberg draws excessively wide-ranging tradition-critical conclusions on the slender basis of Tit 3.6, Rom 10.13 and 1 Cor 1.2; and it is also difficult to grasp that the quotation in Luke, which is greatly expanded in comparison to Paul's use of the text, should have narrowed its interest to the relationship between Jew and proselyte.

[16] Haenchen, *Apg.*, 142; Schneider, *Apg.*, I 268, who also adds that it may possibly have been in the LXX text known to Luke.

prophetically. But the repeated gender-differentiated mode of expression in the quotation from Joel is fully retained in Luke's version. This means that when God in the last days pours out a share in his Spirit, this will take place – as they see it happen – without regard to age, and not least, without regard to gender. Only this common sharing in the gift of the Spirit can render the community eschatological legitimation. Because *all* who had followed Jesus, are present, both the group of women and the group of men, the text from Joel is really relevant.

The texts elsewhere in Acts that relate how large groups come to share in the gift of the Spirit, are based implicitly on the eschatological evidential force in the use of the quotation from Joel in Acts 2. But these later stories deal primarily with specific conflicts in which the gender perspective is less relevant. In the account in Acts 8.12–17 of how Peter and John go to Samaria to hand on the Holy Spirit to those who have already been baptised by Philip, it is said explicitly that this is true both of women and men (cf. 8.12). But here, attention is focussed on the relationship between baptism and the bestowal of the Spirit, and not least on Simon Magus and his attempt to buy for himself the miraculous power of the Spirit. In Acts 10.44–8, the Spirit comes over all who 'hear the world' in Cornelius' house, but in this case the all-consuming interest is in the fact that non-Jews thereby are given a status equal to Jews. Finally, in Acts 19.1–7, a group of male disciples of the Baptist (female disciples of the Baptist are never mentioned) is involved (19.2), and the point is to show that John's baptism cannot bestow the Spirit. The Spirit is given only through baptism in Jesus' name and the laying-on of the apostle's hands.

In association with Acts 2, it is interesting to note that Justin, in his Dialogue with the Jew Trypho, employs precisely the argument that Joel 3.1ff. is fulfilled among Christians because they have both men and women with gifts of the Spirit (Dial. 87.6–88.1); Καὶ πάλιν ἐν ἑτέρᾳ προφετείᾳ εἴρηται. Καὶ ἔσται μετὰ ταῦτα, ἐκχεῶ τὸ πνεῦμά μου ἐπὶ πᾶσαν σάρκα καὶ ἐπὶ τοὺς δούλους μου καὶ ἐπὶ τὰς δούλας μου, καὶ προφετεύσουσι. Καὶ παρ᾽ ἡμῖν ἔστιν ἰδεῖν καὶ θηλείας καὶ ἄρσενας, χαρίσματα ἀπὸ τοῦ πνεύματος τοῦ θεοῦ ἔχοντας. Justin's mode of expression is all the more interesting in that he combines Joel 3.1ff. and the terminology of creation from Gal 3.28, καὶ θηλείας καὶ ἄρσενας. Early in the third century further appeal is made to Joel 3.1ff. to demonstrate that the new prophetic revelations which the female martyrs Perpetua and Felicity had received, made the account of their deaths worthy to be employed in the church (Pass. Perpetuae 1).[17] The passage from Joel does not seem to have played any prominent role either in early Christian apologetics or in the internal debate.[18] Justin's Dialogue is the first patristic attestation of an apologetic use where the aspect of the Spirit is of importance. The existing examples seem, nevertheless, to indicate that Joel 3 was intimately associated with the prophetic activity of women.

Luke is acquainted with female 'prophets' outside Christian or Jewish circles. In Acts 16.16–24, there is an example of a woman exploited as a soothsayer – she herself is only a mouthpiece for the power that possesses her. At that period, women were often employed in mantic oracular activity in which the prophet herself was without any will or senses of her own, totally submitted to the divine inspiration and to interpretation by other authorities.[19] Nor was it unusual for women to be caught up in frantic possession by the Spirit.[20] Some even maintain that women were specially attracted by ecstatic religious movements, and see this as the release they found in what was otherwise a strictly regulated life.

The example in Acts 16, however, does not shed as much light on the relationship between mantic possession and the bestowal of the Holy Spirit as on the criteria implied by Luke to distinguish between true and false prophecy[21] – that is more specifically, the question about the Spirit as an item of commerce. The woman in Acts 16.16–19 refers is possessed by a soothsaying spirit, Python. The spirit is named, but

[17] Cf. Dautzenberg, 'Stellung der Frau', 192.

[18] Zehnle, *Peter's Pentecost Discourse*, 31f.

[19] Cf. Kraemer, 'Ecstasy', 55–80; Schüssler Fiorenza, *In Memory*, 296. One of the most celebrated was Pythia at the sanctuary of Apollo at Delphi. On the distinction between mantic and prophetic, cf. Kappelle, 'Prophets', 92: 'Whereas the inspired mantic is ecstatically possessed in such a way that God has taken away the understanding, a rational element is still intrinsic to prophets.'

[20] Cf. Bassler, 'Widows' Tale', 37; Schüssler Fiorenza, *In Memory*, 227; Kroeger, 'Inquiry', 331.

[21] It is not correct, therefore, to claim, as Dunn repeatedly does, *Jesus*, 175, 195, that Luke is not trying to clarify the question about false prophecy.

not the woman. She is a slave, and the word employed for slave is παιδίσκη and not δούλη. Her possession is a source of profit for the men who own her, οἱ κύριοι αὐτῆς. She is thus in every way under alien lordship. She annoys Paul and his companions by calling after them every day, and almost out of irritation Paul finally expels from her the soothsaying spirit. But this means that her owners lose a source of profit, and they react by persecuting Paul and Silas.

The account takes for granted that soothsaying prophets/prophetesses were to be found also outside the Christian communities (cf. also Bar-Jesus in Acts 13.6). Their activity is not an expression of the Holy Spirit; it is tiresome and false. In the case of Bar-Jesus this is obvious since he actively withstands those proclaiming the word of God. The female slave, however, is pestering them with nothing but the truth, with a cry that carries an echo of their own proclamation: οὗτοι οἱ ἄνθρωποι δοῦλοι τοῦ θεοῦ τοῦ ὑψίστου εἰσίν, οἵτινες καταγγέλλουσιν ὑμῖν ὁδὸν σωτηρίας (16.17b). Her cry has also a certain similarity to the demons' cry in the gospel (Lk 4.34, 41; 8.28), but the situation is different. In Acts 16, the spirit of soothsaying is not necessarily threatened initially and therefore it does not make any accusations either.[22] The cry of the spirit-possessed women is an affirmation rather than a challenge; she supports what the Christian preachers themselves are saying. In Acts, the Spirit is sovereign, and even after Pentecost, the communities have no rights of possession over the Spirit. It is outside their control, a gift that must be given them ever anew (cf. 4.31); and it can act independently of them (cf. 10.45ff., 16.6ff.).[23] How then is it possible to distinguish πνεῦμα πύθωνα from the Holy Spirit, when – as in this case – it even bears witness to the same truth?

Naturally, the criterion for distinguishing between true and false prophecy might be found positively in Paul's own possession of the Spirit. Negatively the certainty that her message is not from the Holy

---

[22] Cf. Haenchen, *Apg.*, 434. He goes so far as to say that it 'nur das wahre Wesen der fremden Prediger in einer für Heiden verständlichen Weise kundtut'.

[23] Perhaps also the strange story at Acts 19.13–20 where the word of the Lord meets with great success because a man possessed by an evil spirit has attacked and overpowered the exorcists who try to use the name of the Lord Jesus.

Spirit might be explained by the fact that her possession by Python was well known and took the physical form of a kind of ventriloquism, as Python in antiquity was associated with the stomach.[24] But the story itself does not voice any of these considerations, and they have a rather fanciful flavour. Nor does the aspect of gender play any explicit role. The suspicion of possession is not aroused especially because the slave in this case is a woman, nor is Paul's exorcism a fight against female prophets who are to be subjected to the spiritual authority of the male preacher. While the exorcism is presented as a liberation as far as the woman is concerned (cf. Paul's words in 16.18), the conflict becomes manifest in relation to those who exploited her condition and profited from it.

The incompatibility between material gain and the work of the Holy Spirit is repeatedly a criterion in Luke-Acts for the discernment between what is false and what is true prophecy. The Holy Spirit is not for sale, and will never promote personal enrichment. Simon Magus' attempt to buy the Spirit for himself (Acts 8.17–24) is rejected in the strongest terms. In financial matters, the demand of the Spirit is rather to give than to gain. The warning given in the Spirit by the prophet Agabus of the great catastrophe of famine, has as its result that the community in Antioch sends material help to the brothers and sisters in Judea (Acts 11.27–30). The married couple Ananias and Sapphira challenge the Spirit of the Lord when they lie about having kept back from the community money gained by the sale of their property (Acts 5.1–11). The Spirit serves not one's own interests, but those of the community.[25] This means that only a false spirit is a source of pecuniary profit.[26]

Both men and women who truly speak prophetically in the Spirit, are by the promise of Joel the servants of the Lord, the group whose

---

[24] Haenchen, *Apg.*, 434 n. 1.

[25] Even if Paul does not actually discuss money and material profit with regard to the activity of the Spirit, there is a point of similarity when he emphasises in 1 Cor 12–14 that the gifts of the Spirit are not to serve primarily one's own private edification, but are to be used in such a way that the whole community is built up.

[26] In Didache 11.3–12.5, the communities are given very concrete guidance about how to distinguish false prophets from true prophets by means of pragmatic and material criteria. False prophets seek to reap material gains from their activity. But the Spirit does not acknowledge any χριστέμπορος, any 'businessman in Christ'.

service he acknowledges. The Holy Spirit is given to 'those who obey him' (Acts 5.32). On the few occasions when Luke employs δοῦλος/δούλη to designate the relationship of human persons to God, it is always connected to the Spirit: Lk 1.38, 48; 2.29; Acts 2.18; 4.29 and 16.17(?).[27] The Spirit marks out God's total right of disposal over persons and history, as it is expressed through the series of directives given by the Spirit steering the course of events in Acts. But human beings are not puppets whose strings are pulled by the Spirit. They can choose to respond with obedience or disobedience, showing themselves to be servants of God or not. Sapphira is punished, like her husband Ananias, with sudden death for having challenged the Spirit of the Lord (cf. Acts 5.3, 9). Her outright lie is confronted by Peter's prophetic perception, so that the apostle thereby asserts his charismatically-based authority.[28]

Mary, on the other hand, is the very prototype of the Lord's servant in her obedience to the Spirit: Lk 1.38, Ἰδοὺ ἡ δούλη κυρίου. By God's creating Spirit Mary becomes pregnant, and she is also given prophetic power.[29] The angel's words to Mary in Lk 1.35 about the Spirit that is to come upon her, are strikingly similar to Jesus' words to the disciples in Lk 24.49 and especially in Acts 1.8. Probably this is a case of a conscious parallel.[30] The outbreak of the prophetic spirit is the

---

[27] While δοῦλος/δούλη is employed to designate the relationship to God, the disciples are to be like ὁ διακῶν for one another, cf. also pp. 59, 80, 83ff.

[28] Cf. Johnson, *Literary Function*, 206–11.

[29] Schürmann, *Lukas*, 70. McPolin, 'Holy Spirit', 120ff., emphasises the connection between the Spirit's expression in prophecy and the Spirit as 'power'. There is therefore *no* reason to make a sharp distinction between the Spirit as divine creative power in 1.35 and as prophetic Spirit in 1.41 and 67, as has been done by Tatum, 'Epoch of Israel', 187. Schüssler Fiorenza, *In Memory*, 338 n. 60, refers to an article by A. Grillmeier, 'Maria Prophetin', 295–312, which points out that the church fathers do not refer to Acts 2 (Mary must be presumed to have been present at Pentecost), but to the Magnificat when Mary is characterised as a prophet.

[30] Räisänen, *Mutter Jesu*, 101f. However, he, like many others (see n. 1 above), interprets this primarily as an expression of the parallelisation between Jesus' birth and the coming into being of the community. Cf. also Schürmann, *Lukas*, 52 n. 5. Both Räisänen and Schürmann reject, with good reason based on the Old Testament referential framework, the idea that the expression ἐπελεύσεται ἐπὶ σὲ and ἐπισκιάσει σοι contain sexual allusions.

premonitory sign that Mary's son is to be the promised Messiah and many of those prophesying are women. The women of Pentecost have their forerunners in Mary, Elizabeth and Anna. These three women seem to represent various forms and stages in a woman's life; – Mary is young and untouched, Elizabeth is married, but old and barren, Anna is an aged widow. The focus of interest is, of course, primarily the miraculous pregnancies of Mary and Elizabeth, but it is worth noting that not only the boy children whom they bear, but they themselves are filled with the Spirit. Their function is not merely to provide repositories for the, as yet, unborn Jesus and John. They have active roles as prophetic interpreters of what is happening to them (Lk 1.38–59).[31] Elizabeth's loud cry in the Spirit is not only an extended greeting, but an act of praise and confession and an interpretation of what she knows, with clear prophetic insight, to have happened to Mary even before she has met her. Elizabeth is the first to confess that Mary's child is Christ the Lord, and she speaks in the Spirit (cf. Paul's norm in 1 Cor 12.3). Mary's[32] song of praise (Lk 1.46–55) also fulfils a prophetic purpose.

When the child is born and is presented in the temple in accordance with the Law,[33] he is met by a male and a female prophet (Lk 2.22–38). They represent an apt example of the Lukan gender pairs, while at the same time the description of them is strikingly incongruent.[34] In the case of Anna, we are given detailed personal information about her, but hear all the less about the contents of her prophetic proclamation. In Simeon's case, the reverse is true. His discourse, inspired by the Spirit, is related in full. But he is characterised in relatively summary fashion as ὁ ἄνθρωπος – although with such attributes as δίκαιος καὶ

[31] Schürmann, Lukas, 67, 70. Laurentin, Truth of Christmas, 456, holds that the Lukan conception of the infancy narratives is 'a pneumatological reading' made by the charismatic Luke from Antioch which he claims was the most charismatic community in the early church.

[32] Some Latin textual variants have Elizabeth as the subject in 1.46. Since this reading can be defended as the lectio difficilior, it has given rise to a detailed discussion in the secondary literature. Carroll, Response, 43 n. 21, gives a good overview of the arguments that have been adduced, and concludes, like most commentators, that 'at least in Luke's story, Mary is the inspired speaker'.

[33] Jervell, 'Sons of Prophets', 116–21, gives evidence of the Lukan harmony between Spirit and Law.

[34] Cf. Laurentin, Truth of Christmas, 204f.

εὐλαβὴς προσδεχόμενος παράκλησιν τοῦ Ἰσραήλ. She is Anna, the daughter of Phanuel, of the tribe of Asher.[35] In other words, she is identified by means of her own tribal membership and apparently her husband, now long dead, has no relevance. Besides this, the term θυγάτηρ evokes associations with the quotation from Joel in Acts 2.17, where it is said that θυγατέρες ὑμῶν will prophesy. The same is true about the notice in Acts 21.6 about Philip's θυγατέρες.[36] So apart from Luke's general liking of gender pairs, Anna is placed here to complement Simeon because the outbreak of the Spirit in the messianic time is to be characterised by the fact that both men and women prophesy.

The prophetic activity in the infancy narrative shows that Luke apparently does not operate with the concept of a period 'without prophets'. But the question remains as to whether the prophets in Lk 1–3, primarily represent a continuation of earlier Jewish prophecy, or a preliminary/early expression of the eschatological breakthrough.[37] The

---

[35] Danker, *Jesus*, 36, who sees in the name Anna a contrast to the high priest Annas. Laurentin, *Truth of Christmas*, goes in for speculative subtlety in his symbolic interpretation of the names. For information about the tribe of Asher, cf. Brown, *Birth of Messiah*, 441f., and Fitzmyer, *Luke*, I 431.

[36] While this factor, to my knowledge, is not noticed in connection with Anna, it is mentioned in passing in connection with Philip's daughters by Tannehill, *Literary Unity*, 135. Cf. also Schille's negative variant, *Apg.*, 408: 'Die Töchter sind übrigens – trotz 2.17ff., die einzigen Frauen, denen Lukas in der Apostelgeschichte ein prophetisches Charisma quittiert'.

[37] I have consciously avoided the terms 'old' and 'new' age. Bovon, *Lukas*, 22, indicates, in a careful debate with Conzelmann, that there is only one big division of time in Luke: 'Mit dem Auftreten Jesu ist die Zeit des Heils angekommen', and with reference to Kränkl, 'Jesus', he sees the infancy narratives as a link 'zwischen den Zeiten'. This means that the prophets who appear prior to Jesus in the gospel – according to him, especially John the Baptist – are 'sowohl der letzte Prophet als auch der Eröffner der Heilszeit'. In his consistent attempt to interpret Luke as advocating an unbroken salvation-historical continuity, Jervell, 'Sons of Prophets', 102, calls the prophets in Lk 1–2 'the missing link' between what he calls 'classical prophecy' on the one hand, and the prophet Jesus and the Christian prophets on the other. What he says about their function, however, links them more closely to the latter; with them, the identification of Jesus as Messiah commences. This may be exemplified by the case of the prophet Anna. While Isaksson, *Marriage*, 16, and Maddox, *Purpose*, 141, primarily see the Lukan presentation of Anna as a reflection of a Christian ideal, Brown, *Birth of Messiah*, 468, and Müller-Bardorff, 'Exegese', 126ff., seek to define more closely dependence on Jewish sources. Brown underlines the similarity with Jewish Anawim-ideals, and maintains that even if the description of Anna

eschatological perspective is beyond doubt the dominant one: everything is oriented towards the birth of the Messiah as the inauguration of the messianic age to come.[38]

We find in Luke-Acts a certain tension between the more general outpouring of the Spirit and prophetic individuals, 'prophets', who come on stage on various occasions. It is not quite clear how the possession of the Spirit as a common characteristic of the Christian community is to be reconciled with the special prophetic gift that only some of the faithful possess on a more or less temporary basis.[39] Just as the general outpouring of the Spirit is for both women and men, both women and men are among the prophets in the more narrow sense. While the men are portrayed to some extent as itinerant (cf. the prophet Agabus in Acts 11.27f. and 21.10f.), the women appear to be stationary (cf. Anna's stable residence in the temple, Lk 2.38f., and Philip's daughters in Acts 21.9).

It is not a question in Luke of an exclusive prophetic office in which the prophet, whether stationary or itinerant, stands over against the community. The individual prophets mentioned by name, are rather seen as an instituted exemplification, on the one hand, of the fact that the Holy Spirit more generally has been poured out over the community;[40] and on the other hand, of the fact that the community does not have the Spirit at its own disposal and does not lead itself.[41] The association of the term 'daughter' from the Joel quotation in Acts 2.17 to the mention of Anna, daughter of Phanuel, and to Philip's daughters

is influenced by Christian ideals of widowhood, these probably originally stem from Jewish Anawim circles, Müller-Bardorff points to Judith, and sees in what he calls the 'ideal of God's widow' a radicalisation of already existing ideals in Jewish apocalyptic circles. More on Anna's relationship to other early Christian ideals of widowhood, p. 244f., below.

[38] Cf. Maddox, *Purpose*, 141: 'Luke's point is that the Spirit marks both Jesus' birth and his mission as fulfilling the hopes of the new age: after his ascension the same mark of fulfilled eschatology is shared by all who remain, or become, his disciples'.

[39] Dautzenberg, *Urchristliche Prophetie*, 214, distinguishes between 'pneumatics' (in principle all Christians) and 'prophets' who appear in 'historisch aufwertbaren Texten'. Dunn, *Jesus*, 170ff., makes this a question about regularity; 'the prophets' were active in a more stable manner. But at the same time he refers this tension, 175, to the list of the problems that Luke chooses not to clarify.

[40] Kraft, 'Altkirchliche Prophetie', 250.

[41] Jervell, 'Sons of Prophets', 115.

confirms that the special gift bestowed on them, is an exemplifying expression of the general possession of the Spirit.

Anna is very old, in her eighty-fourth or perhaps even her one hundred and fourth year,[42] and she has been a widow for the greatest part of her life. She has made the temple her home and she serves God with unceasing fasting and prayer.[43] While Simeon is led by the Spirit without being directly named as a prophet, Anna is explicitly called προφῆτις – the only woman in the New Testament to receive this name.[44] But none of her prophetic utterings is related in direct speech. The indirect report of her words, however, tells that she persistently (ἐλάλει in the imperfect) talked about him to all who awaited Israel's redemption. This implies that while Simeon's function was to identify this particular child as Israel's redeemer to his parents, Anna spread the message more widely.[45]

Anna's piety has a strong ascetic flavour. She demonstrates the Pauline claim in 1 Cor 7.32ff. about the unmarried woman who – unlike the married woman – can consecrate herself wholly to what belongs to God and thus may be holy in body and spirit. It was at the time not unusual for sexual abstinence and fasting to be regarded as an extremely favourable circumstance and a preparatory device for divine inspiration and prophetic activity, the so-called inspirational asceticism.[46] In some Jewish sources, for example, a thoroughgoing ascetic praxis was as-

[42] Brun, *Lukasevangeliet*, 92, maintains the biologically more plausible eight-four. But many read differently, e.g., Danker, *Jesus*, 36 and Schürmann, *Lukas*, 130. They allot her an age of one hundred and four years, eighty-four of these as a widow, with Judith as a model. Cf. also Elliott's detailed arguments for the same claim, 'Anna's Age', 100–2.

[43] Brown, *Birth of Messiah*, 466, sees in this description an 'eloquence vocalizing the ideas of the Anawim'. He points also more concretely to an institution that is clearly presupposed in 1 Sam 2.22, women who serve at the door of the sanctuary. The echo from 1 Sam 1–2 is also to be heard at many other points in the infancy narratives, cf. p. 198f. below.

[44] It is generally accepted that the Spirit in Luke is to be understood primarily as the prophetic Spirit, cf. Bovon, *Luc le Theologien*, 234. This means that when Anna is called προφῆτις in Lk 2.36, she is supposed to be filled by the Spirit even if the Spirit is not named explicitly. Likewise, those who express themselves in the Spirit are to be understood prophetically, even if the terminology of prophecy is not used, cf. Jervell, 'Sons of Prophets', 101f.

[45] Cf. p. 131.

[46] Cf. Lane Fox, *Pagans*, 396.

179

cribed to Moses, not only in preparing for his ascension of Sinai, but as a kind of constant readiness for revelation.[47] In the Greek context, Pythia, the woman over the cleft in the oracle at Delphi, had to be a chaste woman. Later Christian sources too, attest strong links between prophecy and asceticism. In the story of Thecla, we are told that it is to the chaste that God will speak (Acts of Paul and Thecla 5), as is confirmed by the narrative itself.[48] And in Montanism, the leading prophets obviously led a life of abstinence.

In Luke-Acts chastity is never explicitly stated as a prerequisite for revelations by the Spirit or the gift of prophecy. The passages in Acts where *all* are filled with the Spirit, (cf. 2.4; 4.3; 10.38), do not pay any attention to such concerns. It is, however, remarkable that out of the seven[49] concrete cases of prophesying women who are mentioned in Luke-Acts – Elizabeth, Mary, Anna and Philip's four daughters – six are said to be chaste. The only exception is Elizabeth, for good reason as will be shown later. So Mary's virginity should also be seen in the light of her prophetic capacity. As Anna is the old widow prophet, Mary is the young virgin prophet. Regarding the four daughters of Philip in Caesarea, the information in Acts 21.9 is very limited apart from the mention that they prophesied and were virgins, παρθένοι προφητεύουσαι. The present participal form προφητεύουσαι indicates that their prophetic activity was a constant and persisting phenomenon.[50] The combination παρθένοι προφητεύουσαι is linguistically significant, even if it is too far-reaching to read this as an allusion to an established order of 'virgin prophets'.[51] As has already been mentioned several times, the fact that these virgins are not identified by their own names, but are characterised as Philip's daughters, may function as an internal reference to Acts 2.17f. But this presentation serves

[47] Balch, 'Backgrounds', 360, and Vermes, *Jesus*, 9–102, on 'Prophetic Celibacy'.

[48] MacDonald, *Legend*, 58.

[49] Is this number fortuitous, or is it connected with the rabbis' seven female prophets in Israel? Jervell, 'Töchter Abrahams', 89, suggests that Luke, especially with regard to the female prophets of the community has the Old Testament models in view.

[50] Hill, *New Testament Prophecy*, 101.

[51] Witherington, *Women in the Earliest Churches*, 153. When he goes on to claim that they are leaders who exercise a prophetic office, it is unclear whether he is reasoning on a historical or on a Lukan basis.

to make the daughters add to the glory of their father and as evidence of his spiritual capacity as well.[52] This recalls the rabbinic tendency of letting women's gifts reinforce the significance of the men with whom they were associated.

Later information (Eusebius, Hist. Ecc. III 31.39) indicates that these sisters were well-known and enjoyed a high reputation both in their own time and also afterwards.[53] There is strong evidence that they were included in early Christian lists of prophets, and they were enlisted by the Montanists to support the activity of women within 'the new prophecy'.[54] Eusebius refers to two different sources; first he follows Polycrates of Ephesus who relates, in his letter to Victor of Rome (189–99), that two of Philip's daughters were laid to rest as aged virgins together with their father at Hierapolis, and like many others, he confuses this father with the apostle Philip. A third daughter 'who lived in the Holy Spirit' was buried at Ephesus, according to this source. Further, Eusebius draws on Caius' Dialogue against Proclus (from the beginning of the third century), which mentions that there were four prophetesses in Hierapolis who were Philip's daughters. In other words, the information we have is partly contradictory, despite Eusebius' attempts to harmonise it. Nevertheless, it unequivocally confirms the fame of the sisters, and it is interesting that Eusebius' sources agree that Philip and his daughters ended their lives in advanced age in Asia Minor, where charismatic activity was continuous and relatively hectic in the first few centuries.[55]

The mention of the four prophesying daughters in Acts 21.9 is further evidence that Luke does not pass over in silence women's prophetic gift, but remarkably little is related about their prophetic activity in terms of content. It becomes clear, however, that women continue to be active in prophecy in the communities. From this perspective, the day of Pentecost was no transitory puff of wind. But the women prophets

---

[52] Johnson, *Literary Function*, 53.

[53] The sisters are not mentioned in Eusebius either by name. They are first named in a manuscript of the Menaion from the fourteenth century, cf. Gryson, *Ministry of Women*, 128, who also gives a good overview and analysis of the patristic references.

[54] Cf. Tabbernee, *Opposition*, 527.

[55] Johnson, 'Asia Minor', 110; Kraft, 'Altchristliche Prophetie', 255.

are interesting only as exemplary phenomena. Philip's daughters are mentioned in passing and characterised as virgin prophets. For a moment, the light falls clearly on them and then they subside into the shadow of the prophet Agabus who comes on his wanderings from Judea.[56] It is possible that the summary mention of Philip's daughters and the preference given to Agabus are due to Luke's combination of dissimilar source material. The brief notice about Philip and his daughters is taken from the itinerary source and shows this source's special interest in those providing hospitality in various places. Thus the information about Philip's daughters may represent a type of catchword giving the cue to introduce the narrative about Agabus, which came from another source or context.[57]

A less traditional analysis[58] of the account in Acts 21 of Paul's stay in Caesarea however, bestows on the observations in 21.9 a more significant role in the pattern of interaction. According to this analysis, the information about Philip and his prophesying virgin daughters serves to maintain a certain (though unequal) local counterweight to the arrival of Paul's group, by emphasising that the local community has a prominent man in its midst and that the gift of prophecy also is fully developed among them. When Luke fails to include any dialogue between Paul and the Christians in Caesarea, this indicates a situation of blocked communication which is resolved only when Agabus comes in from outside. It is not necessary here to discuss in greater detail the psychological model of communication that underlies this method of analysis, nor the ramifications of its inferences and final conclusions.

---

[56] A similar but only partly preserved episode in the Acts of Paul and Thecla 10 can set the Lukan restriction in perspective: a prophetic spirit comes over a man and he makes it known that Paul must leave them – something that the community deeply laments. But a woman named Myrna is prophetically inspired, and reminds them of what great things Paul will be able to accomplish in the place he comes to (Rome). This calms the community.

[57] Cf. Haenchen, *Apg.*, 532, followed by Schneider, *Apg.*, II 351. Haenchen is correct to reject the moving descriptions given by some earlier commentators of the weeping virgins who beseech Paul to abandon the journey to Jerusalem. Tannehill's version, *Literary Unity*, 135: 'Apparently the narrator simply wanted to mention that there were female prophets in the early church', is not unusual. He also maintains that Luke positively wishes to mention them, whereas others maintain more critically that Luke could not avoid doing so. The result, however, is the same.

[58] Bovon, *Lukas*, 195–204.

The point in our context is simply this: Philip and his prophesying virgin daughters attest to the strength and significant resources which the community in Caesarea possessed. They are an expression of the community's capacity to be self-sustaining. The connection to a certain place indicates, as has been mentioned, that Philip's daughters are conceived as stationary and not itinerant prophets. The information elsewhere in Acts about Philip's previous movements implies that the daughters have accompanied their father – as Eusebius later narrates. In other words, Philip's four daughters are virgins who serve the community by their prophet activity in the place where they live with their father. In the Lukan context, they also bear witness to the fact that most prophesying women are chaste, and that exemplary Christian families accepted on a permanent basis an ascetic choice of life for their daughters.[59]

For Luke, the daughters' share in the gift of the Holy Spirit equipping them for prophetic activity is a significant feature of the eschatological fulfilment as promised by the prophet Joel. The eschatological age, in which the daughters too will prophesy, is in the process of breaking out. Accordingly the participation of women is particularly strong in the eschatological outbreaks of the Spirit's activity that introduce each of the two volumes. In the infancy narratives, set in a world of pregnancy and birth, the female figures prophetically interpret in the theological terms of salvation history, what they themselves experience.

In the gospel, after the infancy narratives, the Spirit is the privilege of Jesus alone. In Acts, the women from Galilee certainly have their share of the charismatic bestowal on the day of Pentecost. Later there are but few individual examples of female prophets, but they do exist and give evidence to the continued prophetic activity of women in the communities. As for the contents of their prophetic sayings, the text remains silent. In Luke-Acts, the prophesying daughters are mostly

---

[59] The mention of Philip's daughters thus provides very early evidence for a kind of 'family/house-monasticism', that is ascetic women who continued to live under the guardianship of the *pater familias* when he proved to be supportive, and that at any rate charismatically gifted girls in Christian families were not always given in marriage. Cf. Clark, 'Ascetic Renunciation', 244–50.

chaste women. Even the pregnant Mary combines chastity and the prophetic charism, and with the exception of Elizabeth – a figure drawn wholly in the Old Testament mode of the barren wife – all the named female prophets are virgins or widows.

Chapter Six

... They Neither Marry, Nor Do They Give Themselves in Marriage

In the preceding chapters, it has been shown repeatedly how marriage and childbirth, which was normally women's primary possibility in life and their legitimation, is dismissed as irrelevant in the community of Jesus as Luke describes it. As concrete expressions of this, we have met independent women among Jesus' followers who appear by virtue of their own story and identity. Women have charge of their own houses and their own resources, while household duties cannot be used to draw them away from devotion to the word of the Lord. Although some of the women travel around, and others are stationary, this does not make much difference with regard to their independent relationship to men. Most of the prophetically-active women lead a life of chastity either as virgins or as widows. Philip's four virginal daughters who prophesy also illustrate that daughters may remain unmarried in a prominent Christian family.

It is significant that the Anti-Marcionite prologue to Luke informs us that the author of the work himself ἀγύναιος, ἄτεκνος ... ἐκοιμήθη. Even if no independent historical value can be attributed to this information,[1] it does nevertheless capture a characteristic tendency in Luke's writings. This is a critical attitude which goes beyond the morality of radical abandonment which is attested elsewhere in the synoptic tradition, and it can be observed in otherwise dissimilar texts. Although many have noted this and have discussed significant passages in a rather unco-ordinated manner,[2] we lack not only a more comprehensive re-

[1]   A textcritical version of the full Greek text is to be found in Regul, Evangelienprologe, 16. Regul refutes the early dating by DeBruyne and Harnack, and concludes, p. 266, that the prologue to Luke (the only one in Greek) goes back to medio 4th century.

[2]   The explanations are also varied. Cf. Augsten, *Stellung des lukanischen Christus*, 36, 49, 103; Legrand, *Virginite*, 49; Leivestad, 'Pietisten', 194f.; Leipoldt, *Griechische*

flection on this subject in Luke-Acts, but also an interpretation of the
ascetic indications in the light of a gender perspective. In this context,
it is the latter which is more important; but in order to be able to look
at this, it is necessary to consider the relevant material in more general
terms.

VI.1. *Ascetic elements of the period.*

We have seen earlier how gender-determined family relationships in
Luke are neither maintained nor promoted, but are dismissed as irrelevant, being redefined as categories of discipleship, as a new criterion
for membership of the fictive family is established. The family terms
which are transferred to the new family of disciples express non-sexual
gender relationships, mother-child and possibly also sister-brother, rather
than wife-husband. Such a transferred use of family terms is frequently
attested in ascetic circles later on.[3] But the employment of non-sexual
terms does not of itself prove that the 'brothers', 'sisters' or 'mothers'
live a life of sexual abstinence. For even if the believers relate to one
another as brothers and sisters, they can still maintain a life of their
own with wives and husbands, who may or may not belong to the
group.[4] As an expression of an ascetic praxis, therefore, the use of

Philosophie, 35f., 111, who explains it by saying that Luke stands in a non-Jewish, Greek
context (and every ascetic tendency is due, in his opinion, to Greek influence);
Niederwimmer, *Askese*, 171f.; Schelkle, *Ehe*, 188f.; Schottroff, 'Frauen', 101, who is
followed by Heine, *Frauen*, 73, in giving Cynic influence as the reason; Seccombe,
Possessions, 11f., who is, however, more concerned with the ideal of poverty than with the
criticism of marriage; Horn, *Glaube*, 202, is ambivalent and does not wish to trace the
critical statements to a 'Skepsis des Evangelistens vor der Ehe', but to concrete and
particular experiences in the community that obligations in the family, especially those
arising from marriage, could hinder in discipleship. This is why Luke exhorts 'die familiären
Beziehungen einer Selbstprüfung zu unterwerfen'. Quesnell, 'Made Themselves Eunuchs',
344–6, followed with hesitation by Balch, 'Backgrounds', 353–7, maintains that Luke
here – unlike Matthew – basically preserves a tendency already present in the Q source.

[3]   Cf. Emmet, 'Female Ascetics', 509; Clark, *Jerome*, 54–5. They claim that the term
varies according to the age of the disciples in relation to one another.

[4]   The discussion concerning Paul's observation in 1 Cor 9.5 about what ἀδελφὴν
γυναῖκα means, is characterised by the following questions: does the apostle have with
him a wife who is also a Christian, i.e. a 'sister in the faith', or – although with less
probability – is the form of expression ascetically coloured, indicating a form of spiritual
marriage?

family categories must be linked to other expressions that have a more definitely ascetic content.

Nor is the refusal to marry, or a criticism of marriage, necessarily an expression of ascetic attitudes in itself. There are numerous examples in the New Testament period that an abstention from marriage is not motivated ascetically, but is connected with a libertine praxis and reasons of convenience, implying that one (that is, mainly men from the higher strata of society) should avoid the burdensome and confining obligations of marriage.[5] It is, of course, possible that an apologetic seeking to promote asceticism can take advantage of the fact that marriage and family life do not appear as a tempting alternative, and then make use of the literary modus of the tiresome worries of married life as a negative argument.[6] But the methodological point is that a critical attitude and a lack of interest in marriage do not necessarily imply an ascetic inclination. They must be supported by arguments, or stand together with other statements, which more generally defend a life of sexual chastity.

At the very outset, there is a difference between men and women on this question, since throughout antiquity men had more of a choice than women in questions concerning marriage. Technical details could vary, of course, but, relatively speaking, men's freedom was always greater than that of most women. This does not mean that girls of marriageable age simply had nothing to say on this matter, but one assumes that most of them, entering their first marriage at a very young age, were very largely

---

[5]   The fact that the refusal of marriage became so usual, especially in aristocratic circles, that Augustus sought to strengthen marriage and not least the production of legitimate heirs in a series of laws from 18 SC to 9 CE, is therefore not proof of sexual asceticism in the Roman context. Not even the Cynic philosophers were normally ascetics, even though they despised marriage. For this reason (among others), they scarcely offer a model for Luke's presentation, as Schottroff and Heine maintain (as mentioned in n. 2 above). For a more detailed presentation and references, cf. my discussion in 'Ascetic Autonomy', 126f.

[6]   This also happens in the sermons and discussions of the church fathers on this theme – cf. Rouselle, *Porneia*, 132–6, who also shows how both the rhetorical genre and the description of marriage change according to whether it is women (as is usual) or men who are being addressed. On the later patristic argument on this point, Rouselle holds that its strength lies in the fact that 'it takes a line of argument which was firmly established in male minds and changes the term slightly when applied to women so that the opposition prostitution or homosexuality versus marriage becomes marriage versus virginity', 136.

dependent on the decision made by others.[7] The decision to marry or to refrain from marriage, whether it be for libertine or ascetic motives, was to a large extent a choice for men, or parents on behalf of their children – or for women who had already been married once.[8] In addition, women (unlike men) were bound by extremely strict limits on sexual activity outside marriage.[9] Consequently, chastity was the only acceptable (if not the only practised) alternative for women, and even this was not without its problems. The positive Christian emphasis on a permanent ascetic choice in life for women as well as for men was exceptional at the time. For men, this excluded libertinism, and for women it meant an alternative to marriage at least the second time round.

It is impossible, in this work, to make a more complete general presentation and discussion of ascetic elements in the contemporary Jewish, Roman and Hellenistic context. Nor is it possible to answer the question of where the early Christian ascetics may have received their strongest influences. The secondary literature in this field is extensive[10] and far from unanimous in its judgment,[11] and the picture given in what follows, cannot be anything other than a sketch. Nevertheless, it may be useful to provide a sounding-board for the presentation of Luke's position by briefly outlining some characteristic features.

---

[7]   Cf. Rouselle, *Porneia*, 32; Verner, *Household of God*, 40.

[8]   Verner, *Household of God*, 40.

[9]   Cf. Rouselle, *Porneia*, 78–92, who concentrates mainly on Roman material. The particular rituals may have been various, but the moral picture in this area is dominated by common characteristics, and a double standard was widespread in all the relevant cultural regions. While women were expected to be virgins when they were first married, and then were submitted to a strict obligation of sexual fidelity in marriage, the man's sexual activity was limited only by the proviso that the woman with whom he had intercourse should not be too closely related to him, or belong to another man.

Cf. also my demonstration in 'Seksualitet og ekteskap' that Paul's apparently confusing use of shifting categories for women and men in 1 Cor 7 is logical and consistent in the light of these moral standards.

[10]   A selection can be mentioned: Balch, 'Backgrounds', 351–64; Bassler, 'Widows' Tale', 25–31; von Campenhausen, 'Askese im Urchristentum', 114–56; Fehrle, *Kultische Keuschheit*; Heussi, *Ursprung des Mönchtums*; Kretschmar, 'Frage nach dem Ursprung frühchristlicher Askese', 27–67; Lohse, *Askese und Mönchtum*; Peterson, 'Beobachtungen zu den Anfängen christlicher Askese', 209–20; Rouselle, *Porneia*; Strathmann, *Geschichte der frühchristlichen Askese*, 1 (further volumes never appeared).

[11]   Lane Fox, *Pagans*, 365, is probably too optimistic when he holds that a certain consensus is now emerging, and that it points in the direction of Jewish apocalyptic circles.

Within Judaism, Hellenism and Roman cults, chastity and other forms of continence were seen as furthering the charismatic dimension, and were frequently practised as a cultic prerequisite.[12] The divine sphere demanded purity. But in such cases, this was almost always a time-limited asceticism which served specific ends. The Isis cult, for example (which was one of Christianity's most important rivals), made severe demands for sexual abstinence, especially on the women who participated. For men, it is attested only in respect of the cult's male priests.[13] Although some statements by Tertullian appear to indicate the contrary, the Isis-cult did not involve an asceticism critical of marriage. It was only a temporary abstinence in order to be cultically pure on certain days.[14] In the Roman context, finally, the Vestal virgins, whose chastity guarded the state's holy hearth, still received a reimbursement designed to permit them to marry after the time of their service, which lasted for thirty years.[15]

Many Jews also practised temporary abstinence in connection with mourning, penance and prayer, and as a preparation for divine revelations (apocalyptic/prophetic asceticism, or so-called inspirational asceticism).[16] As has been mentioned earlier, it was not unusual to attribute to Moses a wide ascetic praxis, not only in connection with the revelation on Sinai, but as a kind of constant readiness to receive revelation.[17]

---

[12] Cf. Heussi, *Ursprung des Mönchtums*; Strathmann, *Geschichte*, 42, 206f., 212; Schüssler Fiorenza, *In Memory*, 226.

[13] Heyob, *Cult of Isis*, 119f.

[14] Heyob does not discuss this question as such, but she gives some examples, *Cult of Isis*, 123, which clearly show that criticism of marriage is not involved: Hellenistic novels portray Isis as the one who protects the lovers' honour when they are separated from each other, and girls are consecrated to Isis so that she may protect their virginity until they marry. Isis showed an immense capacity to adapt herself; she absorbed features of many local goddesses, and 'her capacity to meet the aspirations and needs of women was ... limitless' cf. Motley, *Womanhood*, 24. See also Portefaix, *Sisters Rejoice*, 116–26.

[15] Gardner, *Women*, 25. The principle is not affected by the fact that most of the Vestals did not make use of this right, but remained in service. It shows, however, that most preferred the status and importance they had as chaste Vestals to the status and the importance that they could attain even as rich matrons.

[16] Strathmann, *Geschichte*, 81. Fraade, 'Ascetical Aspects', wishes to draw the interpretation of Judaism in an ascetic direction by means of a wide and positive definition of asceticism.

[17] Balch, 'Backgrounds', 360.

Occasional practice of asceticism could serve individual goals: it could hasten forgiveness, lend strength to prayer, promote revelations. Asceticism can also be mentioned as a pious work alongside other pious works such as almsgiving, the study of the Law and continuous prayer.[18]

Recent research emphasises that ascetic ideals were a characteristic and central element in certain Jewish groups. Apart from some scattered evidence of individual anchorites, 'holy men in the desert',[19] we know of more collective attempts at an ascetic lifestyle within Judaism, the Therapeutae in Egypt[20] and presumably also the Essene community in Qumran.[21] It is difficult to estimate the ripple effect of this, and,

[18] Strathmann, *Geschichte*, 82.

[19] Cf. the hermit Bannus whom Josephus mentions (Jos. Vita 2). Lohse, *Askese und Mönchtum*, 111–12, compares Bannus and John the Baptist. Strathmann, however, *Geschichte*, 73, 81f., emphasises: 'Also es gibt in der Gemeinde *allerlei Asketisches*, aber so gut wi *keine Asketen*, und die religiöse Gesamtstimmung ist weit davon entfernt, asketisch zu sein', 82.

[20] This group is known only through Philo's report of them in *De vita contemplativa* 70, and some scholars are fundamentally sceptical about the historical value of the idealised description, cf. Fraade, 'Ascetical Aspects', 283. If Philo's description is to be trusted, it provides insight into a Jewish group outside Alexandria which combined ascetic and charismatic traits with a dedicated study of scripture. The community of the Therapeutae consisted of both men and women, and the women took part both in the study of the Law and in the sabbath worship and the great common meal every seventh week. Women and men, however, lived in strict separation; even when they came together to worship, a wall separated them from one another. The wall was so high that they could not see one another, but not so high that it made it impossible for the women to hear what the male(!) teachers and readers said to them all. At the meal, women and men lay each on their own side of the table. After the meal, the women participated in the singing of hymns with its emphatically ecstatic character. First the men and then the women formed a choir of their own (under the capable leadership of 'Moses' and 'Miriam') and sang antiphonally until they finally joined in a united choir. 'Thus they continue until dawn, drunk with the drunkenness in which there is no shame ...', cf. Schüssler Fiorenza, *In Memory*, 215f.; Lohse, *Askese und Mönchtum*, 95–101; Strathmann, *Geschichte*, 148–57; Swidler, *Biblical Affirmations*, 131ff.

[21] Qumran was presumably a monastic-like community for men who, through a life in sexual abstinence, cultivated their cultic purity and were in constant readiness for a holy war. Archaeological discoveries of the graves of women and children on the edges of the cemetery indicate, however, that some of those who lived there were families and/or slaves, and there has been much discussion as to whether marriage was accepted by the community or not. Perhaps the male recruits lived in marriage until a certain age (25 years?), when they could proceed into a 'pure life' after having fulfilled the traditional Jewish ideals about marriage and procreation. Perhaps there were several classes, with a core group of male celibates. If marriage was totally rejected, the graves of women and children can be explained by the hypothesis that the community kept servants or that

from this perspective, Philo's ambivalence on the matter is interesting. His dualistic anthropology made him open to ascetic arguments, and he clearly admired the frugal and pious life of the Therapeutae. But in other contexts, he vehemently advocated the conventional ideals of a patriarchal household.[22] It is probable that both the Qumran community and the Therapeutae functioned as esoteric groups living their own lives withdrawn and sheltered from the surrounding world, as an option for the few.[23] Permanent sexual asceticism never became a dominant element in mainstream Judaism, as is shown also by the later rabbinic tradition.[24] The command in Gen 1.29 to be fruitful and to fill the earth was interpreted as an obligation to marry (Jeb 6.6), and even before it was formulated in the categories of obligation, it already determined what was the norm in life.[25]

With the possible exception of the Therapeutae, it seems, further, that ascetic elements in Judaism were mainly concerned with men who cultivated their cultic purity and were in a state of constant holy readiness. For women, virginity had no positive value, except for very young unmarried girls. The loss of virginity before the proper time made them worthless, without any social future, so that a virgin daughter was protected for her prospective value as wife and mother. 'Maternity, not virginity was the highest vocation for women.'[26] It was also desirable

---

other groups in the population resorted there in troubled times. Cf. Augsten, *Stellung des lukanischen Christus*, 50ff.; Collins, *Crisis and Catharsis*, 129f.; Fraade, 'Ascetical Aspects', 268f.; Kodell, 'Celibacy Logion', 19f.; Leipoldt/Grundmann, *Umwelt des Urchristentums*, I 238; Lohse, *Askese und Mysterium*, 88–95; Meeks, 'Image of Androgyne', 178f.; Theissen. *Soziologie der Jesusbewegung*, 78.

[22] Cf. Fraade, 'Ascetical Aspects', 265f.; Lohse, *Askese und Mysterium*, 102–10; Meeks, 'Image of Androgyne', 176f.

[23] Schüssler Fiorenza, *In Memory*, 224; Theissen, *Soziologie der Jesusbewegung*, 36f., 38f.

[24] Even if Fraade, 'Ascetical Aspects', 271–6, tries to prove a tension between traditional ideals of marriage and family life and a demand that ascetic renunciation be made for the sake of the study of scripture both in rabbinic and pre-rabbinic Judaism.

[25] Daube, *Duty of Procreation*, wishes to demonstrate that procreation became an *obligation* in Judaism only at a later period. This, however, does not mean that the concern for procreation could not have played a decisive role in the argument that marriage was a regulation willed by God and valid for all. According to Meeks, 'Image of Androgyne' 177, this belief was 'widespread both in Judaism and in the Pagan moralists'.

[26] Callaway, *Sing, O Barren*, 102.

and normal that widows re-married if the opportunity offered itself at least twice.[27] Widows like Judith[28] seem to represent an exception. She was a female ideal figure in the pious imagination of the Maccabean period. After the death of her husband Manasseh, not only did she wear mourning for three and a half years, but she also remained a widow for the rest of her life and withstood all temptations and offers. Her life as a widow was marked by chastity and fasting (Jud 8.6). However, she is not an ascetic in the proper sense of the word, but the extreme monogamous wife who remains faithful to her one husband even after his death.[29]

For Romans, as for Jews, the family was the fundamental unit in society. There was no word for 'old maid', and bachelors were considered as failing to do their duty as citizens, with the result that their civil rights were reduced. Augustus' legislation concerning marriage (Lex Iulia, 18 SC, and Les Papia, 9 SC)[30] involved a restoration of the old Roman family ideals and aimed particularly at the legitimate reproduction of the Roman aristocracy to ensure the hierarchical power structure and the stability of the state. Characteristically enough, the laws were called *De maritandis ordinibus.* The essence of the laws was in harmony with ancient norms, but the drastically new element was that the responsibility and the supervision of this moral domain was transferred from the *pater familias* to the imperial power as *pater patriae.*[31]

The means warranted by the laws were: first, since men and women in the fertile period of life should be married as continuously as possible, the divorced of both sexes and widowers were to re-marry after one month. Widows were at first permitted to wait for one year, but after

[27] Stählin, 'χήρα', 431, holds that this was the usual practice, but that at the same time two marriages represented 'the moral boundary;' 'vor einer drei- oder gar viermaligen (Wiederheirat) wird freilich gewarnt.'

[28] Strathmann, *Geschichte*, 71f.

[29] The description of Judith has clear similarities to the Roman ideal of the *univira*. On this, cf. p. 235f.

[30] For a presentation of the major points in Augustus' legislation, cf. des Bouvrie, 'Augustus' Legislation', 93–113; McNamara, *Wives*, 583ff.; Pomeroy, *Goddesses*, 150–63.

[31] These points are especially emphasised by des Bouvrie, 'Augustus' Legislation'.

protests this interval was raised to three years. Only widows who were over 50 or 60 years of age – that is too old for bearing children – were allowed not to marry again. When considering the question of marriage in general and the more particular question of the age of widows (which also turns up in 1 Tim 5), it is important to bear in mind that the usual age of marriage for girls was between 12 and 15 years. Nor was it unusual for young girls to be given in marriage to older men – so that many became widows at a relatively young age.[32] Second, infidelity in marriage on the woman's part created uncertainty about the legitimacy of the children, and was the object of severe penal reactions. Third, childlessness entailed juridical and political disadvantages, while the opposite condition was rewarded. For example, free-born women with three children and freed women who had given birth to four children were declared to have authority *sui iuris*, that is they were set free from patriarchal guardianship. In this way, women could attain a relatively autonomous status – by giving birth to men's children. Augustus' restoration of the family was extended towards the end of the first century by the emperor Domitian. Even if it is probable that these laws were not observed strictly, they nevertheless bear witness to the cultural climate of the time as to what was held to be good social morality. Especially, there appears to be wide attestation of the point about autonomy gained by childbirth.[33] The legislation bears witness, therefore, to an ethos that linked the order of the family with the authority and well-being of the state, and that made a woman's rights and status dependent on her marriage and capacity for childbearing.

It is well-known that ascetic tendencies in the early church are attested in breadth and in detail especially from the third century onwards. For the period before this, the sources are more fragile and fragmentary, and it is not easy to follow the traces back to the earliest church.[34] But some texts can be adduced to show that strong and influential circles even at a very early stage promoted a life of sexual

---

[32] Castelli, 'Virginity', 61–88; Pomeroy, *Goddesses*, 68, 164, 169; and, especially for the Jewish situation, cf. Jeremias, *Jerusalem*, 365.

[33] Cf. Verner's assessment, *Household of God*, 40.

[34] Nor should we conceal the fact that this theme also opens the way to interpretations determined by confessional traditions.

abstinence, not simply as a time-limited means to an end, but as a permanent and ideal form of life. A central and early witness to this is 1 Corinthians. 1 Cor 7 especially indicates that ascetic ideals were powerful in a group characterised by charismatic enthusiasm. This resulted, not only in the refusal to marry and in sexual abstinence within marriage (something that later developed into the so-called 'spiritual' marriage), but even in the dissolution of marriage.[35] In this situation, Paul's standpoint was relatively moderate. In his reasoning he moves between a traditional Jewish-Pharisaic standpoint and sympathy with ascetic ideals. He gives low priority to marriage, but does not reject it. He even argues in favour of marriage allowing for the impact of passion and sexual desire. He recommends marriage to those who would have liked to live in abstinence, but were unable to control their burning desire. He indicates thereby that a life outside marriage does not allow for sexual activity. The whole thrust of Paul's argument is to avoid sexual libertinism and promiscuity by the regulation of marriage. In accordance with this, his admonitions to both husband and wife are focussed on their mutual sexual rights and obligations, and the wish of the one partner to practise abstinence should not force the other to seek satisfaction elsewhere. If both agreed, abstinence can be accepted for a short period, for example to prepare for prayer, 7.5 (cf. what has been said above about Jewish asceticism and prayer).

For Paul, it follows that married persons must accept that they are married, and come to terms with both the advantages and the disadvantages which marriage involves. He on his part considers that the disadvantages are great. Paul himself is unmarried, and he finds this preferable. Paul's outlook in 1 Cor 7 is an eschatological one, and he makes a strong case for the urgency, in the short time left for this world, in which to act adequately. In a situation where the remaining time for the world is considered to be short, where mission summons and the tribulations of the end-time are imminent, a life without marriage is to be preferred (7.28–31). In these verses, the escathological-

---

[35] On the discussion of 1 Cor 7, cf. my article 'Seksualitet og ekteskap', 1–20. Yarbrough's interpretation in *Not Like the Gentiles* is too much focussed on the problem of mixed marriages.

missiological perspective is combined with certain pragmatic reflections. He moves to the daily cares and worries of married life and on
the difference between married and unmarried persons as regards concerns and preoccupations with what belongs to God. According to him
the unmarried have a single-mindedness that the married cannot possibly have. The married man and woman are busy with pleasing their
marriage partner, while the unmarried person can have undivided concern for affairs of the Lord.[36] It is, however, noteworthy that in the case
of the unmarried women, this is further qualified by the subordinate
clause ἵνα ᾖ ἁγία καὶ τῷ σώματι καὶ τῷ πνεύματι (7.34).
Paul, accordingly, attributes to the unmarried woman a special possibility of being sanctified in body and spirit, thereby moving from a practical and pragmatic concern to an ideological, gender-determined argument. Especially in the case of women, chastity entails holiness.

Paul's statements in 1 Cor 7.28–31 have inspired an attempt to
harmonise the divergent and apparent inconsistency in his dealing
with the role of women in 1 Corinthians (especially 11.2–16 in relation to 14.33b–6).[37] On this understanding, Paul would distinguish
between 'holy', that is unmarried women (virgins, widows and the
legitimately divorced) and married women. The married women are

[36] Schüssler Fiorenza, *In Memory*, 226, observes ironically: 'One can only wonder
how Paul could have made such a theological point, when he had Prisca as a friend and
knew other missionary couples who were living examples that his theology was wrong.'
   Wimbush, *Paul*, 49–54, softens the Pauline position when he takes these verses
more as rhetorically descriptive, while the real argument is carried by the previous
verses. What Paul seeks to promote, in his opinion, is an 'inner detachment' that
relativises the ordered structures of this world, although this is not given expression by
physical withdrawal. The married woman is to live as if she was unmarried, and is
thereby able *in* marriage to concern herself undividedly with the things that belong to
the Lord. Wimbush's interpretation is fine as far as it goes, and it is correct to emphasise that Paul wishes for stability; it is best that all remain as they are. This is in accord
with Paul's sharp rejection of the dissolution of marriage for ascetic reasons. But
Wimbush overlooks the fact that, even if Paul advocates the least provocative practical
solution possible by means of 'inner detachment', a fundamental criticism of marriage
is still retained as revealed by the rhetorical description: those who are married ought
to live as if they were not. Theologically, and in principle, married Christians are left in
a disadvantageous position.
[37] Schüssler Fiorenza; *In Memory*, 229ff., 233, and also in 'Women in the Pre-
Pauline and Pauline Churches', 161.

admonished, according to 14.33b–36, to behave in the most passive and silent manner possible, and in keeping with Hellenistic-Jewish tradition[38] their subordination to their husbands is authorised. On the other hand, Paul would be willing to accept that holy, unmarried women empowered by the Spirit could participate in the worship service of the community. The pneumatic privilege of virginity would then mean that chastity became a prerequisite for female teachers and prophets.

It has, however, been objected correctly that this understanding of Paul does not sufficiently explain his vocabulary and argumentative thrust in 1 Cor 11.2–16. There, he speaks generically of women without further qualification, and the veil is justified because of the man's function as the head of the woman (11.3, cf. 7.9).[39] It cannot be said, therefore, that Paul was consistent in his treatment of this question. But there is no doubt that Paul, despite his reservations concerning the more radical asceticism in Corinth, gave expression, in 1 Cor 7, to an attitude critical of marriage implying a clearly ascetic strain, and he provided the community's unmarried men and women with good reasons to avoid marrying. He also gives, especially the unmarried women, an esteemed position in holiness *vis-à-vis* the married. But it is difficult to say whether Paul drew any consequences from this on the practical level, so that the unmarried women in the life of the community were given a greater freedom than the married.

Paul's reservations are indeed intended to maintain the conditions of marriage for Christian women and men who were already married. The married woman – although with smaller adjustments, and with somewhat greater rights *vis-à-vis* her husband[40] – was obliged to subordinate her life to the decisions of the patriarchal authority, and to live in fitting obedience, virtue and submission. But Paul's argument in 1 Cor 7 gave unmarried women of various kinds a warrant to remain as they

---

[38] Schüssler Fiorenza, *In Memory*, 229, makes a very close link with Hellenistic Judaism: "Paul probably derives his argument from Jewish-Hellenistic missionary tradition, which, as Josephus documents, has adopted the Greco-Roman exhortations for the subordination of wives as part of the "law"'.

[39] Dautzenberg, 'Stellung der Frau'. 193f.

[40] Cf. for example the unusual parallelism in the admonitions to husband and wife in the first part of 1 Cor 7.

were, contrary to society's custom and legislation. This meant that the tension created in many early Christian communities by women's active participation was channelled towards a counter-cultural lifestyle. In this way, Christianity offered a certain group of women an attractive opportunity for an alternative and more independent life in an age which, though admittedly with great ambivalence, had prepared the way on a theoretical level for a certain equality.[41] This can partly explain the relatively large number of women in the early Christian communities, many of them from the higher strata of society.[42] But on the basis of Pauline sources, less can be learned about how far an alternative ascetic lifestyle was feasible, and how ascetic women might have survived if they did not have private means. Paul gives an important but limited glimpse of very early ascetic tendencies in some Christian communities, and he partly justifies and develops these. Like Jesus, he himself exemplifies an ascetic choice of life.

If we look at the post-Pauline traditions, it is not surprising that they reflect this Pauline ambivalence about marriage and fall into two groups in the picture they draw of Paul in this regard. While the Pastoral Letters in Paul's name seek to enforce the traditional household ideals and reject ascetic tendencies by directing women to marriage and childbearing, the apocryphal Acts of Paul and Thecla paint an ascetic portrait of the apostle.[43] We hear of women who, captivated (their relations would say, seduced!) by the apostle's preaching, convert to Christianity, something that – to the horror of their families – first and foremost implies a life in permanent chastity. The main point of the apostolic preaching is ἐγκράτεια (cf., for example Acts of Paul and Thecla 5, when Paul enters the house of Onesiphorus: ἐγένετο χαρὰ μεγάλη, καὶ κλάσις γονάτων καὶ κλάσις ἄρτου καὶ λόγος θεοῦ περὶ ἐγκρατείας καὶ ἀναστάσεως).

This is a form of expression which seems tailor-made for the ascetic programme of the Acts of Paul and Thecla. But it can also be read as a

---

41 Bassler, 'Widows' Tale', 25–9; Swidler, 'Graeco-Roman Feminism', 41–51.

42 See n. 8 to ch. four above. Cf. also Harnack, *Mission*, 598.

43 McDonald, *Legend*, seeks to give tradition-historical documentation of this tension, and traces the oral traditions, on which he believes the Apocryphal Acts are based, back to the same circles which are critically addressed by the Pastoral Letters.

slogan-like combination from assorted older sources, among them Luke's account of the apostle. For the ascetic Paul is not unknown to Luke either: in Acts 24.24–5, Luke summarily relates that when Felix (and Drusilla) wish to hear περὶ τῆς εἰς Χριστὸν Ἰησοῦν πίστεως, Paul talks περὶ δικαιοσύνης καὶ ἐγκρατείας καὶ τοῦ κρίματος τοῦ μέλλοντος. Most interpreters attach little weight to the theological contents of this description, and consider it mainly as a polemical variant which, in the particular context, was well-designed to affect Felix and make him furious, because he by taking Drusilla as his wife had offended moral standards.[44] Her presence on this occasion makes this all the more clear. But the summary cannot be reduced to sheer opportunism. The use of δικαιωσύνη echoes Paulinisms, and the other terms mentioned are likewise not implausible in a portrait of Paul if we compare them to texts such as 1 Cor 7. But we must also ask whether Luke, in addition to portraying a credible Paul in confrontation with Felix and Drusilla, has also a vested interest in such an ascetic-sounding summary of the Christian position.

VI. 2. *Virgin and mother.*

At first sight, Luke does not give the impression of being determined by an ascetic attitude. On the contrary, the opening events appear immediately to confirm that pregnancy and birth represent the fulfilment of a woman's life. The miraculous pregnancies and births of the infancy narratives, where fertility and the birth of a male child are the results of divine intervention, are like an echo of traditional ideals. The case of Elizabeth and Zechariah is especially true to Jewish conventions. Despite their piety and their fidelity to the Law,[45] they have remained childless (1.6f.), and now they are so old that there is really no more

---

[44] Conzelmann, *Acts*, 201; Haenchen, *Apg.*, 588; Schneider, *Apg.*, II 352. They could mention (as, for example, does Haenchen) that justice, abstinence and the coming judgment 'sind Hauptthemen der nachapostolischen Verküdigung'. But apart from giving some reference (i.e. to Ethiopic Apocalypse of Peter 5) they do not develop this theme further in its potential significance for Luke.

[45] καὶ in the introduction to v. 7 is to be understood adversatively as 'nevertheless', cf. Brown, *Birth of Messiah*, 259.

hope. Inevitably, it is assumed that it was the woman who was infertile (1.7); and even if childlessness caused both of them sorrow, it was her shame and disgrace (cf. 1.12 and 25). For Zechariah, it has been his life's prayer to have a son (1.13); it is his prayer that is fulfilled in a wonderful way when the aged and barren Elizabeth is at last to bear him a son. The slant of this narrative is explicitly patriarchal from the very start: the divine message is addressed to Zechariah as the answer to his prayer, and the son who is promised, is described as his. God will overcome the hindrance that has stood in the way of Zechariah's wish, that is Elizabeth's barrenness and her advanced age.

The narrative alludes clearly to Old Testament models, and Elizabeth's pregnancy is to be seen within the connotational framework of a prominent series. In Israel's history, there were significant and well-known examples of barren women, in some cases advanced in years, who were given the grace of bearing a son so that their piety, or their husband's piety, in its perseverance and its fidelity, at last bore fruit in their lives. These stories reaffirm emphatically traditional ideals and goals for a woman's life, and they are composed in keeping with a relatively fixed pattern of literary conventions[46] (cf. Gen 18.1–15; Jdg 13.2–24; 2 Kg 4.8–17). A number of further narratives are intensified by an added motif of rivalry (cf. Gen 16.1–6; 21.1–21; 29.31–30.24; 1 Sam 1). The story of Sarah, viewed as a whole, shows to what an extent the two types can be mixed. When the infancy narratives in Luke allude especially to the story of Abraham and Sarah, but is also being coloured both by the story of Rachel and by that of Hannah,[47] this warns us not to isolate the various kinds of scenes or stories too strictly from one another in the examination of models. When the motif of

---

[46] Williams, 'Beautiful and Barren', 110, distinguishes between two 'typical scenes'. The first – which would be relevant for the infancy narratives – is called by him 'Promise to the barren wife', and operates with the following literary conventions: '1. The wife is barren; 2. messenger from God appears; 3. messenger promises a son; 4. the event is confirmed in spite of human doubt; 5. the promised son is born and given a significant name'. The other type 'The agon of the barren wife', derives its impetus from the motif of jealousy and rivalry between two women. As is shown in what follows, I take the distinction between the two types to be too sharply drawn.

[47] For concrete demonstration cf. Brown, *Birth of Messiah*, 268ff.; Drury, *Tradition and Design*, 56f.

rivalry is completely missing in the relationship between Elizabeth and Mary, this reflects that they are not rivals for the favour of one and the same man. Nor are their pregnancies victories for the women over against other, more fertile rivals. Elements that might involve mutual rivalry about importance and rank are settled harmoniously by means of Elizabeth's greeting to the much younger Mary in 1.42–5. The details of this comparison are less important for our immediate purpose; what matters is that Elizabeth (and Zechariah) are true to type and confirm that complete fulfilment and blessing of a woman's life could only come by giving birth in marriage – and best of all, by giving birth to a son. Barrenness was a disaster and a disgrace, and from this Elizabeth is freed when God hears Zechariah's prayer.

The story of Mary breaks with this pattern. Virginity is not included in the established variations of the literary convention, and there is a decisive difference between the infertility of a married woman and the protected virginal state of a young betrothed girl. Whereas childlessness in the first case means sorrow and shame and pregnancy removes this disgrace, the opposite is true of the virgin. What is more disgraceful than a premature pregnancy for one who ought to preserve her virginity until consummation in marriage? Not only does a virginal conception lack models in the tradition,[48] but it breaks up the very foundation of values for a conventional pattern which the narrative about Elizabeth rehearses.

At the same time, what happens to Elizabeth, coming first in the order of events, is to function as a confirmatory sign for Mary. Both Elizabeth's concealment of her pregnancy until Mary comes to her

---

[48] Brown, *Birth of Messiah*, 296ff.; Williams, 'Beautiful and Barren', 110, admittedly in certain opposition to Callaway, *Sing, O Barren*, 105f., who holds that ideas, already formed in the Jewish tradition, of Jerusalem as mother, created a precedence for associating fruitfulness with virginity and for the move from a physical conception to a spiritual one. She asserts therefore that 'The important point about the virginal conception is not that it is an altogether new and superior form of miraculous birth story, but on the contrary [?] that it brings together *all the traditions* developed around the barren matriarchs and Jerusalem as mother'. As the subsequent discussion will show, I hold that these Jerusalem traditions about spiritual birth play almost no part in Luke's portrayal of Mary's pregnancy. In any case, the non-metaphorical combination and invocation of a 'double story' as it happens in Luke's account about an actual and physical birth, would have to involve something new. Callaway also fails to discuss the social aspects.

(1.24f.)[49] and the angel's word to Mary herself when he tells her about it (1.36) indicate this. For the reader, this means that the well-known narrative pattern which is echoed in what happens to Elizabeth and Zechariah also functions as an interpretative key to understand the more unique circumstances surrounding the birth of Jesus.[50] But Mary's miraculous pregnancy is intended to surpass Elizabeth's – something that is expressed by Elizabeth herself (1.42–5). For Jesus is greater than John. This means that Luke truly presupposes a virginal conception, and not only a later impregnation by Joseph on which God's blessing would rest. Theories according to which Luke thinks of Mary as a virgin at the time of the annunciation, but that she then began to live together with Joseph, must be rejected.[51] Jesus was Joseph's 'putative' son (cf. the formulation at 3.23). As opposed to what was said to Zechariah, it is not the case that a long-desired son is to be born to Joseph. This does not, however, imply a notion of Mary as ἀειπαρθένος. Later on in the gospel, Luke introduces Jesus' brothers without hesitation.

The infancy narrative in Luke is focussed on Mary in a way that puts Joseph into the shade. This becomes clear both when compared with the parallel of Zechariah and Elizabeth,[52] and also when compared with the infancy narrative in Matthew's gospel, which gives more weight to Joseph's role. Zechariah's temporary dumbness gives Elizabeth a certain scope for action, and she is presented positively. But she still has her

---

[49] Brown, *Birth of Messiah*, 282, persuasively rejects all theological and not least all psychological speculations about the reasons why Elizabeth keeps herself apart from people, and argues that it is 'a literary device to prepare for the sign to be revealed to Mary in 1.36'. Daube, 'Shame Culture', 353, holds that it is also an expression of Luke's focus on shame and ridicule: 'shame avoids sight'. This, however, does not accord well with what Elizabeth says in 1.25: here she rejoices because her shame and disgrace have been removed by pregnancy.

[50] Cf. Callaway, *Sing, O Barren*, 101.

[51] Cf. Brown's frank discussion of this, *Birth of Messiah*, 301–8, where he rejects the most extreme theories on both sides. On the linguistic question, the term παρθένος, cf. Carmignac, 'Meaning of parthenos', 328f.

[52] Witherington, *Women in the Earliest Churches*, 138f., 143, makes too much of a parallel between the treatments of Joseph and Zechariah – with the gallant intention of giving Elizabeth all the more positive a prominence. On the question about Joseph's role, cf. also p. 69.

place in a pattern that is very largely conventional; she bears Zechariah his promised son, and it is he who praises God when the power of speech is regained after the birth. Only in her relationship to Mary does Elizabeth play an independent role. Mary's independence is much greater. She is the protagonist, while Joseph is almost to be considered an extra throughout the narrative. It is indeed true that ch. 2 presupposes that Mary lives in marriage with Joseph so that Jesus thereby is incorporated into David's descendants; but it is, for example, Mary who appears on behalf of both of them at 2.48ff. Nor does any other adult character from the infancy narrative appear in the following gospel story.

Elizabeth's praise of Mary is most of all a confirmation of the 'blessed motherhood' as the happiness in a woman's life.[53] And the more excellent the child proves to be, the greater the happiness. Elizabeth's beatitude reflects mainly the same values as the rest of Elizabeth's story; and she relates to Mary in the context of her own happiness. Nevertheless, there is an ambiguity in the choice of words and in the double cry of blessing in verses 42 and 45, an ambiguity that we have seen developed in all clarity later in the gospel, at Lk 11.27–8.[54] Mary is blessed among women because she believed that what was said to her by the Lord would happen. The words of Elizabeth already predict that Mary's relationship to the word is decisive. But this does not as yet stand in any tension with her task as mother; here, the contrary is true.

Both Mary's virginity and Elizabeth's barrenness and advanced age are obstacles that God overcomes. But it would still not be reasonable to maintain that Mary's virginity, in the same way as Elizabeth's infertility, should be understood as her weakness and humble position, ταπείνωσις, which God transforms into strength (cf. 1.48).[55] Rather,

[53] εὐλογημένη is not to be understood as a superlative, cf. Brown, *Birth of Messiah*, 333.

[54] Cf. Brown, *Birth of Messiah*, 343, who points out that while the woman in the crowd in 11.27f. must be corrected by Jesus, Elizabeth herself, who is filled by the Spirit, can supplement what she says.

[55] Thus Callaway, *Sing, O Barren*, 102ff., presupposes, with support in Legrand, *Virginite*, 117f. It is meaningless when Legrand asserts that Mary as a true Jewess does not see her own virginity as a quality, but as a form of unworthiness and humiliation. Can this be true of the Jewish girl who has not yet been together with her husband to be?!

a pregnancy in her situation would represent degradation and humiliation. Mary's ταπείνωσις must therefore be interpreted as a social category (cf. the manner in which it is developed in the Magnificat in 1.48–55). It is also significant that Mary is introduced at 1.27 without a set of respectable credentials corresponding to the detailed social and religious presentation of Zechariah and Elizabeth in 1.5–7.[56]

Nor is there any reason to speculate about the various grades of difficulty in the two miracles. Even if their situations, seen from the physical point of view, are not all that dissimilar, the social implications differ widely. Elizabeth has not only been barren: it is also clear that she is past the age of fertility. The miracle in her case is that, precisely when all natural hope is gone, she can become pregnant by Zechariah. At last they achieve complete fulfilment, ideologically and socially. Mary is of childbearing age, but she becomes pregnant outside all physical normality. This is in keeping with ideas that the divine can unite itself only with what is totally pure and virginal.[57] The corresponding attestation within Judaism in metaphorical and metaphysical examples, or when Philo postulates that the married but infertile Sarah must become a virgin again in order for Isaac to be conceived divinely, is far away from Mary's situation. Over against the metaphorical, symbolic usage, there is no talk in Mary's case of a spiritual birth, even if it is a birth from the Spirit. The child is real enough. In comparison with Philo's example of Sarah, it is certainly true that Mary is better placed since she is a virgin and does not need to 'become' one; but at the same time, Mary's virginal status implies, socially speaking, a situation in which a pregnancy provides neither happiness nor blessing, but an unseemly moral and legal offence.[58]

---

[56] Cf. Laurentin, *Truth of Christmas*, 15f., 144.

[57] Callaway, *Sing, O Barren*, 90, in connection with texts about Jerusalem, and 96ff., for Philo.

[58] This means that Callaway's models become less appropriate, and also excludes the possibility that Mary is to be understood as a representation of Zion's daughter or Jerusalem in the way many interpreters have considered, seeing a textual basis for this by reading the greeting χαῖρε as an allusion to Zeph 3.14–17. Cf. the critical summing-up by Brown, *Birth of Messiah*, 320–4, and Carroll, *Response*, 43 n. 22. Cf. also Callaway, *Sing, O Barren*, 106ff.

In Matthew's version of the story, the socially problematic element in the event is explicitly dealt with. In keeping with Matthew's focussing on Joseph, the social scandal is reflected as his problem (Mt 1.19). As a man faithful to the Law, he is obliged to divorce himself from Mary, and because he does not wish to put her to public shame, he is resolved to do this in secret (although it is not clear what that may have meant). But a special revelation to Joseph brings him to accept what has happened. Luke's Mary-oriented presentation is not preoccupied in the same way with the social offence. While Elizabeth speaks of her child-lessness as her disgrace among people, Mary's reaction is noticeably lacking in such considerations. Instead, she wonders how it may possibly happen – and when this is explained, she willingly makes herself available.[59] For Luke, it is decisively important that Jesus' birth is from God and is accomplished by the Spirit, and that Mary states her willing acceptance. In other words, we have another example here of the phenomenon that has been described earlier:[60] the Spirit acts in such a way that social boundaries, concepts of decency and appropriate objections are overcome. The 'compulsion by the Spirit' serves to deal theologically with the offence and the abnormality by bearing witness to God's sovereign action. Thus the interpretation in the Magnificat points out precisely how God's acts are characterised by his reversal of established power structures of estimation and status. The appropriate answer in such a situation of new evaluation created by the Spirit is obedience, as is shown by Mary in an exemplary fashion. On the whole, therefore, Mary's virginity is seen as a positive condition: instead of being a hindrance and a moral problem, it becomes an expression of election by grace.

This means that virginity is established in the initial phase of the gospel as a positive quality that is pleasing to God, with creative possi-

---

[59] Daube, *Rabbinic Judaism*, 33; 'Shame Culture', 363, is one of the few who have reflected on the aspect of shame in this context. He establishes a precedent in the story of Ruth and Boaz, which is interpreted in rabbinic reflections in such a way that what is apparently immoral, is presented as the highest morality. But this still does not explain the total lack of problematisation of this in Luke's text, nor does it provide any precedent for the point about Mary's virginity.

[60] Cf. p. 166f.

bilities for God's Spirit.[61] It also gives Mary independent significance and status. At the same time, it is primarily connected with Jesus' birth and does not lead to immediate ascetic conclusions – not even as a programme of life for Mary herself, since in marriage with Joseph she apparently gives birth to further children. As seen above, however, in connection with the transformation and transference of family terms later on in the narrative, Mary's role is converted prototypically from the conventional right of a mother to a motherhood that is constituted exclusively by the relationship to the word. Through the transference of Mary's maternal relationship from the physical family to the fictive family of God, the possibility of an alternative motherhood is opened up, and it is no longer limited to her, but is given to all women who hear God's word and do it. Jesus revokes and replaces the maternal honour and rights by introducing discipleship as the new form of motherhood.

The woman in the crowd at Lk 11.27 praises Jesus and his mother in words that recall Elizabeth's words in 1.42–5. Jesus' reaction when correcting this and emphasising that a mother's right and a mother's honour are replaced by the relationship to the word, represents a signal that procreation is no longer of vital significance. Jesus' words to the daughters of Jerusalem (Lk 23.27–30) include a negative form of a similar beatitude.[62] While the woman in the crowd (11.27) praises as blessed the womb that bore him and the breasts he sucked, Jesus prophesies in 23.29 that the daughters of Jerusalem – who are also women in the crowd (cf. 23.27: πολὺ πλῆθος τοῦ λαοῦ καὶ γυναικῶν (the genitive is governed by πλῆθος)) – will come to praise as blessed the barren, the wombs that never bore and the breasts that never gave suck.[63] Even if Jesus makes a reversal of established value in 23.28f. too,

---

[61] Many have proceeded from this to draw a trajectory to the resurrection, cf. Callaway, *Sing, O Barren*, 103; and Legrand's reference, *Virginité*, 114f., to πνεῦμα ζῳοποιοῦν. When God creates life in Mary's virginal womb, this is a prefiguration of the resurrection, which in Rom 1.4 is associated with the Spirit in words similar to those used of the virginal birth in Luke. This, however, is not convincing as Rom 1.3–4 separates Jesus' belonging to David's descendants through his birth, and his establishing as God's Son through the resurrection. When Luke associates 'virginity' and resurrection, as we shall see later, this happens via other routes.

[62] Cf. p. 114f., also p. 114 nn. 45 and 46.

[63] For a tradition-critical analysis of 23.27–31, cf. Giblin's support of Neyrey, *Destruction*, 95. In its present form, the composition is Lukan. In the Gospel of Thomas,

this is not determined positively by the relationship to the word or by the all-consuming dominance of discipleship, but by the fact that the turbulence and horror of the coming time of tribulation render normal life impossible. This is also expressed at Lk 21.23 in the form of a cry of woe over those who are with child and those who give suck when the days of vengeance come. The beatitude and the cry of woe are like obverse and reverse sides of the same thing: childlessness, and not fertility, is to be considered a blessing in the days to come. In this sharpened eschatological perspective, the conventions reflected in Elizabeth's story have no longer any validity.

Jerusalem's daughters and Jesus' words to them have been subjected to an extensive discussion.[64] Disagreement is concerned both with who these daughters are and/or whom they represent, and with whether Jesus' words are to be understood as words of judgment, of consolation or of warning. Various answers are given to the question of the women's identity. Some see them positively and concretely as faithful disciples of Jesus[65] or as women in Jerusalem who traditionally undertook certain functions at executions such as that of wailing women.[66] Others give them symbolic value and a negative function: in the light of Old Testament imagery, 'Jerusalem's daughters' are interpreted as a personification of 'the element of Israel, which continually rejected God's messenger', and perhaps more precisely as the personified Jerusalem in distinction from the people as a whole.[67] This would mean that the

---

log. 79, the two variants are linked together in such a way that the macarism of the barren serves as the justification of the preceding version of what corresponds to Lk 11.27f. The redefinition is therefore given both a positive and a negative justification. Both Fitzmyer, *Luke*, 1494, and Nagel, *Motivierung der Askese*, 26, maintain that the juxtaposition in the Gospel of Thomas clearly draws it in an ascetic direction; cf. Fitzmyer: 'In Luke the beatitude is uttered over barrenness or simply childlessness, but in the GTh it is over voluntary abandonment of conception'. This is to exaggerate the difference between the two versions.

[64] Cf. Neyrey, *Passion Account*, 109–21, and Giblin's discussion with him, *Destruction*, 95ff. Soards, *Passion*, 222–43, gives a good overview.

[65] Swidler, *Biblical Affirmations*, 277.

[66] Fitzmyer, *Luke*, 1495; Leipoldt, *Jesus*, 22.

[67] Neyrey, *Passion Account*, 110f. Fitzmyer, *Luke*, 1498, is, however, correct to emphasise that the connotations here clearly diverge from the expression 'daughter of Zion/Jerusalem' in the metaphorical usage of the Old Testament.

daughters of Jerusalem represent the part of Israel which denies Jesus. And when the Messiah they reject leaves the city on the way to his death, he utters a prophetic word of judgment on them which has significant traits in common with earlier words of judgment on Jerusalem in Lk 13.34–5 and 19.41–4.

This shows that there is a close relationship between the identification of the women and the understanding of what Jesus' words imply. The attempts at identifying the women more sympathetically, do not wholly do justice to the negative sting in Jesus' words; nor is the symbolic interpretation which sees it as a judgment satisfactory. It has been objected correctly that neither the people's nor the women's conduct in this scene is marked by rejection or dismissal.[68] Rather, they have sympathy with Jesus, and there is no verbal basis on which to oppose the crowd of the people and the women to each other.[69] It would also be an exception in the gospel for women to be presented negatively in this way. What happens is that Jesus, in the same way as in 11.27f., diverts the sympathy that is shown him, to a contrasting statement of a more fundamental character. This is not directly addressed to those to whom he is speaking, but has more general scope: note that the verb in 23.31 is in the third person plural, not in the second person. The women are to be understood as *victims* of the catastrophe and not as its cause, either concretely or symbolically. This is why they will have to weep over themselves and their children, while they will praise as blessed those whom they would otherwise lament – the barren and childless women.

From the perspective of this chapter, this is the substantial point. We have come to see how the relationship to the word of the Lord is constitutive for the family of Jesus and the community of the disciples, and transforms the obligations and relationships presupposed by the biological family. For women, this means that their reproductive functions cease, and the women who follow Jesus are portrayed precisely as women with an autonomous mobility; they do not seem to have been subordinated to family obligations. Seen in this light, the term 'daugh-

---

[68] Giblin, *Destruction*, 97ff., with criticism of Neyrey.
[69] Cf. p. 19f.

ters of Jerusalem' implies a contrast, not to the rest of the people, but to the 'women from Galilee' who also follow Jesus to the cross (cf. 23.49).[70] Unlike the 'women from Galilee', the 'daughters of Jerusalem' are bound by conditions of life that will intensify their suffering in the times of apocalyptic tribulation. And so, precisely in the time of distress in which they curse themselves, they will praise as blessed the childless (and ascetic) women – who 'follow Jesus'.

VI. 3. *The sons of the resurrection.*

Passages in the gospel like 23.27–30 provide a sounding-board within the whole of the literary construction for the formulation in Acts 24.25 about 'continence and the future judgment'. Other passages too express similar ideas. As part of a longer discourse in Lk 17.20–37, Jesus admonishes the disciples about the concerns or lack of concerns demanded by the 'days of the Son of Man'.[71] The instruction and the warning admonitions are backed by examples from history, and the lesson of the past serves to illuminate significant aspects of the future day of judgment: it happened suddenly and violently, and the catastrophe struck all who were not prepared so that only very few were rescued (Noah and Lot and their families).

The characteristic life-patterns of those who were destroyed in the catastrophes of judgment, are described in both cases, and this exemplification has caused a certain discomfort to the interpreters. In the example of Noah (17.26ff.), it is said about the mode of living of Noah's generation before their destruction that ἤσθιον, ἔπινον, ἐγάμουν, ἐγαμίζοντο up to the day when Noah entered the ark and the flood came and destroyed everything. Can eating, drinking and marrying be anything other than natural and normal expressions of life? Can people be reproached for seeking to preserve life? Is their fatal

---

[70] Both Hastings, *Prophet and Witness*, 41, n. 1, and Fitzmyer, *Luke*, 1521, see the link between the terms used of the two groups of women, but they draw no conclusions from this observation.

[71] Luke is based to some extent on Q material, but he has given it an active redactional treatment and has combined material from various sources. The remark about Lot's wife in 17.32 plays a key role in his redaction of the material, cf. Geiger, *Lukanischen Endzeitreden*, 118f., 142–9.

mistake not what they actually did, but the heedlessness they displayed by doing so?[72] Does the listing of ordinary activity serve in fact, only to emphasise that the catastrophe was unexpected and sudden? Or is, in this particular context, a critical and negative evaluation attached to an apparently reasonable and normal pattern of life?

To resolve such knotty problems, some have recourse to a distinction between the phenomenon 'in itself' as acceptable and good, and the use or misuse to which it is then subjected.[73] But it is in fact surprising that in the presentation of the conduct of Noah's generation nothing is said about their wickedness or lechery which is otherwise a well-known theme.[74] Mediating moral charactistics are totally lacking; nothing is said about heedlessness or about an exaggerated concern for food and drink, nothing about sin or misuse. Nor is anything said about the positive reasons why precisely Noah and his family should have been rescued. The information given limits itself to the fact that the catastrophe came while they were engaged in normal activities. While Noah was ready and could go into the ark, the others were not prepared. To this extent, therefore, it is correct to say that eating, drinking and contracting marriages are various kinds of irreproachable normalities in life. It is common to the whole set of activities – and also to those listed under the example of Lot – that they are activities that aim at preserving life and securing the future. Food and drink are normally necessary in order to live, while contracting marriage is primarily directed towards procreation and the legitimate future life of the human race. In other words: the usual physical strategy for survival is inadequate as eschatological readiness.[75]

---

[72] Fitzmyer, *Luke*, 1170; Quesnell, 'Made Themselves Eunuchs', 345.

[73] Typical here is Horn, *Glaube*, 201: 'Für Lukas aber sind die bürgerlichen Lebensformen *nicht an sich* böse, wohl aber ...' (my italics); Schelkle, 'Ehe und Ehelosigkeit', 189.

[74] Carroll, *Response*, 90. The sinfulness of the generation of the Flood had an almost proverbial character. Geiger, *Lukanischen Endzeitreden*, 95, holds this to be a decisive difference between this text in Luke and Jewish parallels which emphasise the necessity of God's judgment on the sinfulness of human beings.

[75] Carroll, *Response*, 90f., has recourse to a similar interpretation, but gives it a special twist by seeing the examples as an implicit instruction that one does not need to be directly evil in order to be judged. To be oriented towards the coming of the Son of Man is in direct contrast 'to the cares and affairs of this life'. Similarly Geiger, *Lukanischen*

In the following paraenesis (17.33), Luke has, characteristically enough, included the logion about winning life by renouncing it. Human beings themselves cannot make their life secure; on the contrary, it is the one who gives life up, who will win/preserve it (ζῳογονήσει).[76] Thus it did not benefit the rich farmer to lay up for himself ample goods for a future that he then was not able to enjoy (cf. Lk 12.13–21).

In contemporary Judaism and in later rabbinic sources, concepts can be traced that may help to cast light on this kind of ascetic rejection of normal activity in human life – spelled out precisely as eating, drinking and procreation in marriage. An example that has been adduced[77] is Philo's explanation in his commentary on Gen 8.18 (Quest. Gen II. 49): when men and women went separately into the ark, but came out of it by pairs, this is a subtle way of expressing that when they entered the ark, they observed sexual abstinence, but that they emerged ready to fill the earth anew. For Philo himself this further serves an allegorical anthropological interpretation of when it is right to keep the male and the female separate, and when the masculine can take possession of the feminine and beget virtue. Abstinence means that the male, τὸν ἡγεμόνα νοῦν, does not unite itself with the female sensual dimension, πρὸς

Endzeitreden, 95: '... verurteilt wird offensichtlich nur, dass diese Menschen darin völlig aufgehen'. In both cases, this is an idea that comes close to what Paul argues in 1 Cor 7.32–43: the one who is married, is divided between the Lord and the world, while the one who is unmarried, can be fully concerned about τὰ τοῦ κυρίου. And it is precisely at this point that Paul's distance *vis-à-vis* marriage transcends into a more direct criticism of marriage, even if he elsewhere tries to maintain a mediating position between the ascetic zealots and a traditional marriage praxis. Cf. p. 193f. and p. 195 n. 36.

One of Paul's key words in this context is μεριμνάω in a particularly neutral usage. Luke uses μεριμνάω in a few other passages, but – unlike Paul – he employs it with a clearly critical significance, cf. p. 105 n. 22. But μεριμνάω is not used in the paraenesis in Lk 17, even though some scholars in practice interpret the text as if it played a central role – whether we are told that Noah's generation showed their heedlessness by maintaining a normal life (while the admonition in other texts is directed to the fact that they are too much preoccupied with care!), or whether the interpretation is more in line with Paul's position. In other words, a too close comparison with Paul on this point does not get us any further – apart from offering evidence that an eschatological criticism of marriage, also governed by ideals of holiness in the case of women, was already prevalent in circles with which Luke may have been familiar.

[76] On the special Lukan variant of this logion of Jesus, cf. Geiger, *Lukanischen Endzeitreden*, 212–25.

[77] Cf. Balch, 'Backgrounds', 356.

αἴσθησιν. Applied to Noah, this means that his merit and that of his family was abstinence, which for Philo signifies that they did not yield to the senses (classified as female).[78] In other Jewish texts, the story about Adam and Eve is interpreted to show that eating, drinking and procreating belong to the 'animal' side of human beings. Adam and Eve did not have such physical needs in the primal condition in paradise; these arose after the fall.[79] This can also be expressed in the categories of life and death; the body Adam received at creation was a living body, and he was able to live from the 'food of angels' or from nothing at all. After the fall, Adam and Eve are dead, or perhaps mortal, and the body of death needs earthly food and drink; it also procreates – in order to overcome its mortality. This antithesis, however, is not to be understood as a description of an irrevocable development; it represents an anthropological tension in life at present. The human person lives continually with both predispositions and thereby with both possibilities: either to let oneself be controlled by one's bodily needs or to seek to overcome them; the latter means realising one's likeness with the image of God.[80] The idea of the human person as created in the image of God is, however, often transcribed in dogmatic terms by means of mediating concepts of similarity to the angels.[81] The likeness of the human person to the angels is not only determined relatively, as the positive counterpart to the 'animal' life controlled by needs: it can also be defined independently in epistemological and moral categories. Thus the human person possesses qualities that are characteristic of the angels, and is able to win eternal life, such as the life that the angels have, with the help of this qualitative similarity to them.[82] The material is strongly androcentric: likeness to the image of God is attributed only to Adam, while Eve is the weak one who easily lets herself be tempted and causes the fall.[83]

---

[78] On Philo's dualistic anthropology and his employment of gender categories, cf. Motley, *Womanhood*, 14–17

[79] *Vita Adam et Evae* 4. See further Troje, *AΔAM*, 31f.

[80] Cf. Jervell, *Imago Dei*, 86f.

[81] Jervell, *Imago Dei*, 89.

[82] Jervell, *Imago Dei*, 86f.

[83] Jervell, *Imago Dei*, 40f.

Spiritualising anthropological ideas like this presupposes notions of the eternal or heavenly life that cannot be said to have been general in the Judaism of that period. More common, both in apocalyptic and in rabbinic texts, were other and more concrete expectations. The heavenly life after the resurrection is conceived as a glorious and intensified version of what were regarded as blessings in this life: abundance of good food and drink and a great and untroubled fertility, so that women give birth every day and without painful labour. The spiritualised and ascetically orientated variants first appear in 4 Ezra and 2 Baruch,[84] and are also attested later in rabbinic material. In the latter texts, they are often employed to support a demand that the Law be observed,[85] in keeping with a definition of the human person's similarity to the angels as the possession of reason, the upright posture and the ability to speak Hebrew. It is, however, only a short step from this to a development of the tension between the 'animal' life, controlled by physical needs and the life like the angels, in such a way that an ascetic programme is initiated,[86] determined by the hope of overcoming death by cultivating the qualities similar to the angels and of attaining, like them, eternal life.

The point here is not to maintain generic connections between such ideas in Judaism and the Lukan position. This would require a thorough examination of the Jewish material and a more precise dating. The comparative juxtaposition of material would also have to be corroborated by establishing the historical probability of the connection. The aim of this outline description is therefore simply to show that Luke was not alone in finding support for an ascetic attitude in an anthropological and/or paraenetic employment of examples from the Old Testament. The comparison is, however, also positively supported by the fact that the concepts of the eternal life of the risen ones, as reflected in Luke, do not describe a painless accumulation of the physical goods of this life, but indicate an asexual existence like that of the angels.

This comes to expression in Jesus' dispute with the Sadducees about the resurrection (Lk 20.27–40). Here, the perspective of judgment is

---

[84] Stemberger, *Leib der Auferstehung*, 115f.
[85] Jervell, *Imago Dei*, 87.
[86] Stemberger, *Leib der Auferstehung*, 116; Troje, *AΔAM*, 32.

less dominant, and the attention is directed to the resurrection and the new life. The dialogue is concerned with marriage, death, offspring and the Sadducees try to trap Jesus and expose the belief in resurrection as absurd.[87] The narrative was known to Luke through its presence in Mark, but the first part of Jesus' answer (20.34–7a) is found in such a variant form in Luke that it has been suggested that the Lukan version must have been based on a separate tradition.[88] It is, however, customary to attribute the differences to a Lukan redaction of Mark's version, and this is presupposed in what follows.[89]

The institution of the Levirate was an extreme expression of a patriarchal regulation of marriage.[90] A woman/wife was something a man took and had, and she was instrumental to his need for progeny and an after-life. The institution of the Levirate was a provision to ensure posterity even for a man who died without leaving children of his own. This concern is reflected explicitly in the Sadducees' exposition of the problem in 20.28. But it is significant that the choice of vocabulary on precisely this point does not reproduce the Levirate regulation of Dt

[87] This can be understood in part to mean that they do not expect an answer to an absurd question – the only aim is to entangle Jesus in a trap. On the other hand, we know that at least later rabbinic tradition could engage precisely in this kind of casuistry. Cf. Schwankl, *Sadduzäerfrage*, 335f., who for this reason is unable to decide whether the question presented here is meaningful or not. In my opinion, it is *Jesus' answer* that proves the question to be absurd.

The picture painted by the passage of the Sadducees with their rejection of eschatological concepts of resurrection is also historically accurate. At the time of Jesus, they were 'old believers' from this point of view, cf. Schwankl, *Sadduzäerfrage*, 334ff. When the party ceased to exist after the year 70, or at any rate no longer had any power, while at the same time the Pharisees' belief in resurrection became dominant, the 'denial of the resurrection' became the essential characteristic of the concept or cliché 'Sadducee'. Thus it is typical that the Sadducees appear in the gospel tradition in this controversy about the resurrection. In the role of opponents, they belong to the 'Motivinventar der Auferstehungsthematik', Schwankl, *Sadduzäerfrage*, 337. This is also clear from Acts 4.1ff. and 23.6–8. In Acts 5.17 it is rather the Sadducees' character as priests that is brought into play, but – as 5.30ff. makes clear – the dispute here too concerns the apostles' testimony about the resurrection.

[88] Schramm, *Markus-stoff*, 170f.

[89] Cf. Schwankl's presentation and argument, *Sadduzäerfrage*, 445f.

[90] Not even the story of Tamar, who herself takes action to ensure that the obligations are met when the men of the family fail to do so (Gen 38.6–30), breaks with the patriarchal presuppositions; she only makes use of them with a certain shrewdness.

25.5ff., which is concerned that the man's name shall continue to live, but instead alludes to Judah's Levirate command to Onan in Gen 38.8, where the expression ἀνιστάναι σπέρμα is used. The ambiguity in the verb ἀνιστάναι which is also a term for resurrection, adds a polemical sting to their words, so that the Sadducees' position takes on a ring of an alternative concept of resurrection: a man's after-life is ensured by means of his offspring; that is immortality by posterity.[91]

All three synoptic versions of Jesus' answer reject the claim that the Levirate example represents a relevant objection to faith in future resurrection. Instead, the different nature of the resurrected life is emphasised, implying that the woman no longer belongs to any man. In Mark, followed by Matthew, Jesus refutes the Sadducees directly by accusing them of error in a second-person address. For, he says, when the dead rise up, they neither marry nor are given in marriage, but are like the angels in heaven. Further evidence for the resurrection is established by a reference to Ex 3.6, which is interpreted in the sense that Abraham, Isaac and Jacob cannot be definitively dead, since God is the God of the living and not of the dead. As far as marriage is concerned, it is clearly in this version a question of 'before' and 'after', that is of temporal categories and a temporal dichotomy. After the resurrection, when they have become like the angels, marriage has no further part to play.

Luke's version too confirms the combination of resurrection, likeness to the angels, and a state without marriage. But this is expressed in a manner that not unjustifiably made this biblical passage one of the favourite proof-texts of many later ascetics.[92] Luke omits the refutation directly addressed to the Sadducees, and the first part of Jesus' answer is considerably extended and given an antithetical form (20.34b and 35a). The emphasis is placed on the last and positive part of the antithesis, since 20.36 functions as an additional justification of 20.35. Compared to Mark, Jesus' answer in Luke has become a brief but independent

---

[91] van Eijk, 'Marriage', 213f., shows that this was not only the conservative Sadducee position, but was also important for Greeks like Plato and Aristotle, and is present in later patristic discussion. Cf. also the Athenian philosophers' reaction in Acts 17.18, 32 to Paul's speech about the resurrection.

[92] Brock, 'Early Syrian Asceticism', 5f.; van Eijk, 'Marriage', 212–35.

little treatise on the ethos of the resurrection and of immortality.[93] The antithesis is drawn up between οἱ υἱοὶ τοῦ αἰῶνος τούτου and οἱ καταξιωθέντες τοῦ αἰῶνος ἐκείνου τυχεῖν καὶ τῆς ἀναστάσεως τῆς ἐκ νεκρῶν. For the first group, it is characteristic that they γαμοῦσιν καὶ γαμίσκονται while the others οὔτε γαμοῦσιν οὔτε γαμίζονται.

The double set of terms for entering into marriage is the same as in 17.26, and this is all the more striking because the verb γαμίζομαι is very rare. Apart from the two texts mentioned here, it is found also in 1 Cor 7.36 and 38, but otherwise only once in extra-biblical Greek.[94] Remarkably enough, all the occurrences in the New Testament are found in contexts involving criticism of marriage, and it has been suggested that the phrase was 'a catchphrase which originated in ascetic Jewish circles older than Luke'.[95] The point here, however, is not the source of the term, but the fact that it seems to appear in this particular form of context. Like Noah's generation, which perished in the flood, it is characteristic of the 'sons' of this world that they γαμοῦσιν καὶ γαμίσκονται. The repeated parallel use of the verb also shows that it concerns both men (γαμοῦσιν) the women (γαμίσκονται). The forms reflect the unequal role of men and women in contracting marriage. But in the case of the women, it is not the customary passive form that is used here, although it is commonly interpreted and translated thus.[96] Rather, the rare middle form permits us to interpret the women as the subject:[97] it is they who let (or do not let) themselves to be taken in marriage. This means that the role of woman as mere object or instrument, as was implied in the Sadducees' question is brushed aside. They are the subject of a choice, even if the androcentric perspective continues to dominate indirectly the description of the act of matrimony.

---

[93]   Schwankl, *Sadduzäerfrage*, 464, 448: 'ein regelrecht kleiner Traktat mit Sachaussagen, die durchaus Einzelheiten mitteilen und präzisieren wollen'.

[94]   Balch, 'Backgrounds', 357; MacDonald, *No Male and Female*, 71. Balch wishes to suggest therefore that 'these passages in Luke (and perhaps originally in Q) were under discussion in Corinth'. Such a conjecture is sharply rejected by Niederwimmer, *Askese*, 81f.

[95]   Balch, 'Backgrounds', 357.

[96]   So most of the English translations, and also the latest Norwegian one.

[97]   Liddel and Scott, 337, refer to another Greek text witnessing to this, but choose, for reasons which are unclear, to understand it as passive in Mk 12.25.

Those who do not submit themselves to marrying, are those worthy to attain to the resurrection.

A vital question in interpreting Luke's variant is whether the Lukan instruction retains the temporal dichotomy of Mark's version. If this is the case, then the antithesis is to be understood exclusively in relation to a scheme of 'before' and 'after'.[98] This means that until the resurrection all human beings – including the disciples of Jesus – are to be counted as children of this world. It is only after the resurrection from the dead, when they can no longer die, that marriage is brought to an end. The large-scale alterations in Luke would accordingly, bring little that is new *vis-à-vis* Mark. The temporal dichotomy still dominates, and a negative qualification of marriage is avoided at least in this world. The Lukan redaction can therefore be explained primarily as a pedagogical strategy,[99] and the almost pleonastic compilation of various concepts and terms in 20.35–6 means only a Lukan adjustment of the position in Mark's text, mindful of Hellenistic readers using a number of different concepts that they understand more easily. So resurrection is recast as immortality.

Luke's text is, however, rather to be interpreted as a wide-ranging and detailed alteration of Mark's version that also involves an essential shift of meaning. The temporal categories are not abandoned and it is clear from the mode of expression in 20.35 that both 'that world' and the resurrection from the dead belong to the future. But the temporal scheme is developed in such a way that temporal categories are partially left behind. The antithetic layout expresses an actualisation of the contrast between what is present and what is to come in the already existing distinction between οἱ υἱοὶ τοῦ αἰῶνος τούτου and οἱ δὲ καταξιωθέντες τοῦ αἰῶνος ἐκείνου τυχεῖν καὶ τῆς ἀναστάσεως τῆς ἐκ νεκρῶν.[100] 'The children of this world' are thus to be seen as carrying with them a negative and demarcating characteristic and this is in keeping with the use of the phrase in Lk 16.8. It is set in opposition

---

[98] Cf. Schwankl. *Sadduzäerfrage*, 460; cf. also Gerstenberger/Schrage, *Frau und Mann*, 144, and Fitzmyer *ad loc.*

[99] Schwankl, *Sadduzäerfrage*, 451f.

[100] Cf. van Eijk, 'Marriage'; Nagel, *Motivierung der Askese*, 35f., and also Diderichsen, *Markianske skilsmisseperikope*, 53, with reference to Preisker, *Christentum und Ehe.*

to the positive counterpart, οἱ δὲ καταξιωθέντες τοῦ αἰῶνος ἐκείνου τυχεῖν καὶ τῆς ἀναστάσεως τῆς ἐκ νεκρῶν. This means that the aorist participal form καταξιωθέντες does not indicate a transfer to the last judgment so that all which follows in the present tense in 20.35b–6 should be attributed to the coming world. Both the elaborate expression καταξιωθέντες ... τυχεῖν and the neutral use of καταξιόω in Acts 5.21 indicate that a selection is already being made, and is to be recognised by ethical characteristics. Whether or not one enters upon marriage reveals to which group one belongs.[101]

This is not a simple form of realised eschatology; on the contrary, the justification for the criticism of marriage retains an orientation towards the eschatological future. But in Luke, the paraenetic interest colours the eschatological teaching in such a way that the attention is transferred from the future to the present and to how decisively important it is to live aright in anticipation of the eschaton. The time and hour of the eschaton, whether it be early or late, is of less importance in this perspective: the point is to be prepared through the proleptic assimilation to the life of the resurrection. This does not mean that the future is swallowed up by the present; on the contrary, it represents a way of keeping the expectation alive, warm and credible in a situation in which a postponement of the eschaton is already generally accepted.[102] Even if the paraenetic zeal is nourished by an eschatological expectation, it also inclines to compensate for the delay by means of a proleptic realisation in a life of sexual abstinence. The expression of eschatology in the present is the praxis of those who have been counted worthy to attain it one day. Their refraining from matrimony has a proleptic character; their abstinence is explained by their participation in the

---

[101] Witherington, *Women in the Ministry of Jesus*, 34, is correct to say that the verbs denote the act of marrying. Thus Luke cannot immediately be taken as witness to an ascetic demand that marriage be dissolved. In that respect, he represents a Pauline position. Witherington himself is, however, far too concerned to save marriage to see this, and he introduces several subtle arguments to show that it is not 'the state of marriage' that is under discussion.

[102] Carroll, *Response*, 166f., accepts Conzelmann's demonstration of 'Parusieverzögerung' in Luke. Unlike Conzelmann, however, he argues convincingly that Luke's adjustment does not contradict a strong expectation of the end of time, but helps to keep this alive in a time when the period of waiting was already a fact.

coming resurrection, which means that they can no longer die, but are like the angels and are called God's sons.

Such terminology and concepts like these play a significant role in later ascetic literature.[103] As well as the rejection of bodily needs mentioned already, the concept of likeness to the angels is often combined with the concept of the radiant glory, the divine δόξα distinctive of the risen ones; they shine brightly.[104] When Acts 6.15 says that all who were present in the council saw Stephen's face like the face of an angel, it is most probably such concepts that come into play. This example also shows that the likeness to the angels is not reserved to the coming aeon after the resurrection, but can be seen in 'those who are worthy' already in the present. In Stephen's case, it presumably also serves to mark him as a martyr. And when Stephen 'falls asleep',[105] the heavens have opened to receive him directly (Acts 7.55–60), and he beholds that δόξα of God which he himself reflects. It is further possible that a verse such as Lk 9.27 may have been retained because, instead of being read as an outdated statement about the early parousia, it serves as a statement about the immortality of those who are worthy of the resurrection. Even if they die, they do not perish (cf. Acts 13.37). The further argument in Lk 20.37–8 also confirms such an interpretation, especially in light of the Lukan addition in 20.38b, πάντες γὰρ αὐτῷ ζῶσιν, an allusion to 4 Macc 7.19, which implies concepts of immortality. In other words, even if the patriarchs 'died', they nevertheless live for God.[106]

The immediate context of Lk 20.35f. gives as the reason for this likeness to the angels, the quality that they cannot die. It may be adequate to say that immortality is a more essential characteristic of the heavenly life than asexuality,[107] but the text presupposes precisely an

---

[103] Cf. Frank, ΑΓΓΕΛΙΚΟΣ ΒΙΟΣ; Lane Fox, *Pagans*, 336–74.

[104] Cf. Stemberger, *Leib der Auferstehung*, 89.

[105] ἐκοιμήθη, v. 60 may have been preferred here for reasons other than merely euphemy.

[106] On this, cf. Fitzmyer, *Luke*, 1301f. Cf. also what is said in n. 74 to ch. Three above about the link between the historical and the eschatological Abraham.

[107] Witherington, *Women in the Ministry of Jesus*, 34f., denies that the text deals with asexuality at all. In his predisposition to take a positive attitude to marriage, he even adduces Luke as a witness to the idea that all existing marriages continue into eternity.

intimate connection between marriage and death. Since the need for marriage is considered to cease when the resurrection is promised, the reverse conclusion would be that it is death which makes marriage necessary, since the main purpose of marriage is procreation and thereby the possibility of gaining an after-life through one's own offspring.[108] This then refers back closely to the example of the Levirate and the understanding of marriage emphasised by the very regulation of the Levirate: marriage is instituted for the sake of man's procreation and in order to ensure his after-life and 'immortality' by means of children who legitimately bear his name. The fact that the manuscript D adds γεννῶνται καὶ γεννῶσιν in Lk 20.34 makes this clear on a secondary level. Since resurrection and personal immortality mean that procreation is no longer necessary in order to survive death, the patriarchal marriage as the legitimate framework for procreation is rendered superfluous for those who are found worthy to attain to the resurrection.[109] The criticism of marriage in Luke is not due to pragmatism, but is the expression of an eschatologically-determined ascetic reservation.

When participation in the future life is no longer dependent on procreation, with the result that the patriarchal intention in marriage can be abandoned, an end is set also to the man's fundamental need for the woman's assistance in procreating and perpetuating himself. Within an androcentric model, this actually means that the original reason and justification for the woman's existence *de facto* ceases to exist. Positively it promotes an ascetic liberation of the woman by providing an opportunity of life outside the confinement of patriarchal marriage. This dimension of liberation in early Christian asceticism has been seen in recent years by feminist scholars as a major explanation of why so many Christian women were attracted by an ascetic life-style, and also as an

---

[108] van Eijk, 'Marriage', 215: 'If we compare this text from the Gospel with the platonic-aristotelean view, it appears that the former reveals the reverse aspect of the other; whereas for Plato marriage (=procreation) means the overcoming of death and a way to immortality, in the Lukan text it is death that necessitates marriage and resurrection or (personal) immortality that makes it superfluous.' Cf. also Legrand, *Virginite*, 42: 'La procréation perd son sens qui était de réparer les ravages de la mort'.

[109] It is therefore interesting that when Paul in 1 Cor 7, despite all his reservations and ascetic preferences, argues that some should nevertheless marry, the aspect of procreation plays no role. His main concern is to avoid sexual promiscuity.

important aspect in Christianity's power to bring conviction to certain groups of women.[110] It gave them the possibility of a power and an

[110] The literature in this field has expanded greatly in the 1980s, and only a representative selection is mentioned here: Bassler, 'Widows' Tale', 23–41; Burrus, *Chastity*; Castelli, 'Virginity', 61–88; Clark, *Jerome*; 'Ascetic Renunciation', 240–57; Kraemer, 'Conversion', 298–307; McNamara, *New Song*; Ruether, 'Mothers of the Church', 71–98. Also Davies, *Revolt*; MacDonald, *Legend*.

Methodologically, it has been found fruitful to use evidence from the early patristic period to cast light on the New Testament material. Many of the best patristic examples are indeed too recent to have direct relevance to the New Testament period; the leap backward from the third and fourth centuries is too great. We come closer to the New Testament through the Apocryphal Acts of the Apostles, which should be dated in the second half of the second century and the first half of the third century. Their geographical origin probably lies in Asia Minor. Burrus, Davies and MacDonald, have made essential new contributions to the understanding of the Acts, cf. also the discussion in *Semeia* 38 (1986). It is a matter of debate whether the Acts are a purely literary product (Hellenistic popular novels) or are primarily based on older oral tradition. If the latter is the case, another problem is to document the history of the tradition and how the level of tradition relates to the level of redaction. For example, Schüssler Fiorenza, *In Memory*, 174f., in opposition to Davies and Burrus, takes the Acts in their present form to be products of male authors who were able to tolerate women as ascetics in persevering meditation and prayer, but not as itinerate missionaries. When they nevertheless happen to present women as preachers, this is wrapped up in a romantic disguise. Fiorenza's critique does not, however, exclude the possibility that the traditions about women on which these stories are based, had their origin in groups of women who took an active part in mission and had charismatic and encratite character. But it is not impossible that the core material in the Acts is based on oral tradition that goes back to the New Testament period and offers the reverse version of the debate which is also reflected in the Pastoral Letters. Cf. p. 197 and p. 197 n. 43.

In the Apocryphal Acts conversion to Christianity is synonymous with conversion to a life of chastity. Women especially are captivated by the apostles' preaching of ἐγκράτεια, so that the dramatic problems created by the choice of an encratite Christian life are given broad exemplification by means of women and are illuminated on the basis of women's experience. On the whole, women are presented positively and in solidarity, whereas men, even the apostolic heroes, often fail the women at crucial points. The Acts probably reflect a situation in which groups of ascetic women lived on the periphery of the regular community structure, but not wholly detached from it, cf. Davies, *Revolt of Widows*, 50, 87f., 100. The Acts provide a glimpse of a period of transition in the church, in which a charismatic leadership increasingly is being replaced by an institutionalised and centralised structure based on offices which were male prerogatives. In such a situation, the activity of women in the common life of the community is either forced to disappear, or is channelled into segregated 'communities' of women. The Acts also show, as do isolated references in Eusebius and polemic in Tertullian, that even in the late second century, women in Asia Minor exercised an activity in teaching and mediation of the tradition, and that traditions about ancient heroines (Eve, Miriam, Thecla, Ammia and the daughters of Philip) were used to legitimate female prophets and teachers in the church, cf. MacDonald, 'Virgins', 171; Ramsay, *Church in Roman Empire*, 375. The

authority from which they were otherwise excluded, and an opportunity to move outside the limiting constraints of the conventionally gender-determined roles as daughter, wife and mother. By withdrawing their sexuality from control by others and controlling it themselves, they also achieved a sort of control over their lives and property. Free from patriarchal dominance by either father or husband, free from risky pregnancies, free from painful and often life-threatening childbirth, free from the demands of constant caring, and even free from great economic worries, these women had a freedom that was usually reserved for the ἑταίραι, but furnished in their case with ecclesiastical and theological honour and respectability.

Freedom, however, had its price. Within an androcentric anthropology an ascetic liberation of women may imply that ascetic women no longer remain female. By means of asceticism, it is possible for them to escape their femaleness and develop maleness, which is superior to what is female.[111] Even if New Testament texts hardly give more than scattered and weak indications of this motif, the path is still prepared through an androcentric terminology,[112] as is expressed in Luke at 20.34ff.: the women are counted among the 'sons'. The fact that the term 'sons' apparently is meant to be inclusive also for women, is clear from the double use of the verb for entering upon marriage, explicitly referring both to women and to men. So the women who do not allow themselves to be married are to be counted among the 'sons' of the resurrection and of God. The terminology of 'sons' in this text, however, does not imply that these women achieve maleness in a special way and for this reason are named as 'sons'. For the term 'sons' is used in both parts of the antithesis, and the point of the statement is that

---

absolute majority of these were unmarried, celibate women, and (a point to which we shall return later), in many communities the order of widows provided them with physical sustenance and formal structural support, that is theological legitimation.

[111] For more detailed exposition and discussion of this, cf. my article, 'Ascetic Autonomy', 136f.

[112] Jewett, 'Sexual Liberation', 64ff., who, with the help of Meeks, 'Image of Androgyne' 193ff., wishes to interpret the androcentric terminology in Paul as liberating and androgynous rather than androcentric. He must, however, admit that we have at least in Galatians a discrepancy in the vocabulary – although he does assert that this 'was not yet felt'.

those who do not allow themselves to be married are 'God's sons' and 'sons of the resurrection' rather than 'sons of this world'. An androcentric preference for and use of masculine terms is thus partly taken for granted and partly not. This is, of course, a point in itself, but it cannot immediately be taken to prove that maleness is a special anthropological quality which women can achieve by means of ascetic praxis.

For the understanding of the term 'sons of God', the christological influence must be considered. It is not simply that Jesus' resurrection, to which credible witness is borne, gives support more generally to faith in the resurrection (cf. Acts 4.2 and 17.18). Jesus is also the prototypical Son of God, as is being repeatedly established in all the most important events in his life (Lk 1.35; 3.22; 9.35; 10.22; 22.70). Note also Acts 13.32, in which the relationship as Son and the raising-up in the resurrection are connected, although the link is not to be understood exclusively in the sense that Jesus is born as Son at the resurrection.[113] Here no exposition is needed as to the further implications of the use of the christological title. But reconsidering Lk 20.35f., it seems that the ethos attributed there proleptically to the angel-like sons of God, has its model precisely in the life that God's Son lived on earth.

Unlike John the Baptist, Jesus is presented without pronounced ascetic traits in the question of food and drink (cf. Lk 5.33f.; 7.33f.). But concerning the praxis of marriage and family life another picture emerges. Jesus leads a wandering life that is not anchored in a home and family of his own (Lk 9.57f.). It is presupposed that he has neither wife nor children, and that he himself prototypically fulfils the demand to abandon one's own life which he makes of others (Lk 5.11; 9.23–7, 57–62).[114] Non-sexual family relationships are transferred to the community of those who hear the word and do it; as we have seen, they are thereby established as Jesus' family. They become his mother, his sisters and brothers, and God – as Jesus' Father – becomes their Father too.

[113] When Schwankl, *Sadduzäerfrage*, 465, maintains this, it is due to blindness to the other attestations, and naturally also to the fact that he interprets the occurrence in 20.35f. in an exclusively future sense.

[114] On Jesus' significance both as ascetic initiator and later as an ascetic model, cf. Nagel, *Motivierung der Askese*, 5–19, Niederwimmer, *Askese*, 41.

Like Jesus, they are to be God's 'sons',[115] who neither marry nor allow themselves to be taken in marriage.

Luke has no parallel to the positive instruction about marriage and against divorce in Mk 10.1–12, although he does transmit, in isolation and presumably known to him in a Q version, the otherwise well-attested logion of Jesus about divorce and remarriage.[116] The location of the logion in Lk 16.18 represents a difficulty in terms of the contextual content. In the attempt to explain its location, most intepreters see it in some way as an exemplification of Luke's attitude to the Law, and its polemical value is considered to be stronger than the paraenetic value. So the logion demonstrates the continuing validity of the Law by means of a critical attack on the Pharisees who are accused – in contrast to the fidelity of Jesus and/or those who believe in Jesus – of not being faithful to the Law which they champion.[117]

None the less, it is interesting to note that the so-called 'divorce logion' in Luke has a quite distinct formulation when compared with the other variants. The wording indicates that the point is not to forbid divorce;[118] the negative judgment seems rather to be associated with remarriage.[119] The problem, however, is that a new marriage is called adultery (μοιχεύω), although nothing in Luke's text proves that the rejection of remarriage is due to the continued existence of the first marriage because divorce in principle is not accepted.[120] Such a line of

---

[115] It is clear from Paul in Gal 3.26–9 that the christological identification is a main source of the 'son' terminology, when this baptismal formula says that all baptised are 'God's sons' because in baptism they have 'clothed themselves with Christ'.

[116] Cf. Egelkraut, *Jesus' Mission*, 113; Fitzmyer, *Luke* 1120; Geiger, 'Stellung der geschiedenen Frau', 147f. When compared to the other variants, Luke's version is closest to Mt 5.32, even if it can also be said to possess elements that are closer to Mk 10.12. Egelkraut, *Jesus' Mission*, 114, holds that Luke reproduces the rule as it was known and practised in his own community, and that this explains the difficulties in finding clear source-critical explanations of the form.

[117] Egelkraut, *Jesus' Mission*, 120, and nearly the same in Moxnes, *Patrons*, 152; Schneider, 'Jesu Wort', 83.

[118] Thus both Fitzmyer, *Luke*, 1121, and Witherington, *Women in the Ministry of Jesus*, 28, assert.

[119] Catchpole, 'Synoptic Divorce Material', 239; Schaller, 'Sprüche über Ehescheidung', 29. If Niederwimmer, *Askese*, 20, is correct to say that καὶ γαμῶν ἑτέραν is a Lukan addition, this only becomes all the clearer. Fitzmyer, 'Matthean Divorce Texts', 201, however, attributes this clause to previous tradition.

[120] This is Catchpole's explanation, 'Synoptic Divorce Material', 239.

reasoning presupposes the argument in Mk 10.2–9 about marriage as an order of creation that cannot be dissolved by human beings – and precisely this context is excised in Luke.

Another possible interpretation, therefore, is that Lk 16.18 is not concerned with those who remarry after divorce, but excludes the possibility of remarriage by those disciples who have left their wives without necessarily divorcing them (cf. Lk 14.26 and 18.29). The same applies to new marriages with abandoned wives.[121] In such cases, Jewish Law too would count a new marriage as adultery, because the first marriage still exists formally despite the separation. In consequence, the logion is meaningful as evidence for the continued validity of the Law.

The intention in Luke, however, is not the positive protection of marriage. The point is not that the husbands ought to return to their wives again, nor is there any point in formally seeking to dissolve the marriage. The whole intention is to avoid the contraction of new marriages. This emphasises that the decision for God's kingdom is absolute and that one cannot fall back upon more comfortable solutions (by marrying a 'sister'?) once one has made an ascetic break with the past. It is hard to force one's way into God's kingdom (cf. Lk 16.16). It can also be worthwhile in this context to recall that the Lukan version of the transfer of family categories in 8.19–21 implies that even those family relationships that continue to exist, are redefined in the light of the new criterion of hearing God's word and doing it.

The wording of Lk 16.18 is totally male-oriented. The man is consistently the subject, the acting partner: it is he who leaves his wife and who also commits adultery if he marries anew or marries an abandoned woman. This masculine control is in accord with the dominant praxis

---

[121] Cf. Diderichsen, *Markianske skilsmisseperikope*, 52–87, refuted by Isaksson, *Marriage*, 94ff., and Fitzmyer, 'Matthean Divorce Texts', 212f. Their objections, however, are based on the misunderstanding that Diderichsen maintains that ἀπολύω is not a term for divorce; they produce evidence to show that this is indeed the case. But Diderichsen is clear in his assertion that ἀπολύω is *a less common* term for divorce and that Luke makes use of the fact that ἀπολύω can *also* mean abandon. When his main point further on, however, is that the wording protects the abandoned woman by insisting that she is still a wife, *Markianske skilsmisseperikope*, 71f., 79ff., this is well-meant, but utterly unrealistic. An abandoned wife would probably have an easier life if she was set free to remarry. Luke's concern is quite simply to avoid any new marriages whatsoever.

of marriage and divorce at least in the eastern regions of the Empire[122] (cf. also the use of the middle verb from γαμίζομαι for the female partner in 20.34f.). As we shall see, a similar male perspective dominates the texts about the costs of discipleship in 14.26 and 18.29. The interpretation of 16.18 suggested here is not, however, confirmed consistently by Luke's own vocabulary in the three passages. Neither 14.26 nor 18.29 uses ἀπολύω; 14.26 has μισέω and 18.29 ἀφίημι. Nevertheless, this interpretation should be left as an interesting option, especially because it also makes a good contextual connection to 16.16. The implication is that Luke, in keeping with Jewish law, would not have any great problems with accepting divorce; the critical and emphatic point is the question about a new marriage. This means that Luke has adjusted the 'divorce logion' so that it both clearly demonstrates fidelity to the Law and corresponds with the radical statements about a voluntary and ascetic abandonment elsewhere in the gospel.

We see also in several texts that describe or prescribe the conditions of discipleship, how Luke gives an ascetic emphasis to the common synoptic morality of voluntary abandonment. In the parable of the great banquet in Lk 14.16–24, the guests who are invited first give various apologies for not coming,[123] and recent marriage is one of these (14.20). Thus the very reason for the feast in Matthew – a wedding – is what prevents attendance in Luke.[124] While Matthew has a positive attitude to the image of the wedding, Luke's treatment is correspondingly negative. Matrimony is one of the activities that keeps people away from the feast in the kingdom of God. On this point, it should be noted once again that the perspective in this narrative is totally male-oriented; one of the men who were originally invited has taken a wife for himself and therefore cannot come. And the example of marriage

---

[122] Niederwimmer, *Askese*, 18. This does not exclude the possibility that women in particular cases could take the initiative for divorce, cf. Brooten, 'Scheidungsrecht'.

[123] In this context, the discussion of how far the reasons they give are normally acceptable apologies or not (cf. Ballard, 'Reasons for Refusing', 341–50) is less important.

[124] The version in the Gospel of Thomas, log. 64, is closest to Luke, but the corresponding excuse is not that of one's own marriage, but that one must arrange the banquet for the wedding of a friend. The rejection of 'the buyers and the merchants' is also intensified in GTh.

closes the list of the various acquisitions that can occupy a man, and that are emphatically given prominence in the formulation of the excuses: a field, a yoke of oxen and a wife. The apologies are symptoms of activity that also prevented the generation of Noah or Lot from recognising the time of their visitation (cf. also the use of ἀνήρ in 14.24). It is possible that there is a critical note to this; the specially chosen circle of men in the initial part of the story are later rejected, and instead the poor and the sick and finally 'anyone at all' are invited in such great numbers that there is no longer room for those first invited, even if they should change their mind. The context in the gospel has earlier made it clear that women were quite abundantly represented in the groups replacing the men preoccupied with possessions and anxious to get married.

The instruction about the costs of discipleship (Lk 14.25-7) reflects the reasons given in the parable for absence, reformulated as positive demands. The enumeration here, however, is less interested in fields and oxen, and concentrates on family relations: εἴ τις ἔρχεται πρός με καὶ οὐ μισεῖ τὸν πατέρα ἑαυτοῦ καὶ τὴν μητέρα καὶ τὴν γυναῖκα καὶ τα τέκνα καὶ τοὺς ἀδελφοὺς καὶ τὰς ἀδελφὰς ἔτι τὲ καὶ τὴν ψυχὴν ἑαυτοῦ, οὐ δύναται εἶναί μου μαθητής. A corresponding list is found in Lk 18.29, and there the same is repeated. *Vis-à-vis* his basic text in Mark (Mk 10.29), Luke omits ἀγρούς, but retains in a somewhat compressed form the household, brothers and sisters, parents and children. Besides this, Luke's version – as has already been mentioned in connection with the interpretation of 16.18 – has included an element both in 14.26f. and in 18.29, that is τὴν γυναῖκα, which is missing in all the synoptic parallels. It is not only the household, parents, brothers and sisters or children that are to be hated and given up, but also the wife. It is a matter of discussion whether Luke in this is faithful to Q,[125] or has himself been active in the redaction.[126] In any case, τὴν γυναῖκα is consistently and explicitly included in the present text of Luke – whether

[125] Balch, 'Backgrounds', 353; Quesnell, 'Made Themselves Eunuchs', 344.
[126] Augsten, *Stellung des lukanischen Christus*, 36; Horn, *Glaube*, 198ff.; Schelkle, 'Ehe und Ehelosigkeit', 189.

this is due to tradition retained for good reasons or not. The lists in Luke about the conditions of discipleship describe thus the break with the past, first and foremost as regards family relationships, and the explicit inclusion of the 'wife' involves an intensification towards asceticism. At the same time, the abandonment of sexual relationships may take on local expression in some cases.

Moreover, several of the same threads which are later woven together in 20.34ff., are found collected in 18.29f. The abandonment of one's family and spouse is realised already in the present, and it is done ἕνεκεν τῆς βασιλείας τοῦ θεοῦ, for the sake of the kingdom of God. This presumably indicates that only the kingdom of God is an acceptable justification for such a drastic action: other reasons are not good enough. All the synoptic variants have corresponding qualifying formulations, ἕνεκεν τοῦ ὀνοματός μου in Matthew and ἕνεκεν ἐμοῦ καὶ τοῦ εὐαγγελίου in Mark. But only Luke introduces, by means of βασιλεία τοῦ θεοῦ a marked eschatological dimension already in the justification for this pattern of action – and not only with regard to the reward to be gained (18.30). In the part of Jesus' saying which speaks of the reward, Luke follows Mark almost exactly, but with one essential exception. The compensation which is to be given in manifold measure to them in this age already, is not specifically named in correspondence to the list of all that they have given up. In keeping with the non-sexual family categories that characterise the family of God, Luke openly refuses to reward them directly with wives in plenty; sisters are not to compensate for the wives whom the men have abandoned. Instead, they are only given a more general promise of compensation already in this age.[127] In view of 20.35ff., however, it is essential that their voluntary abandonment should also be rewarded in the coming world with eternal life. Even if the formulation in Luke is identical here with that in Mark, it strengthens the link in the wider Lukan context between eternal life and a present life detached from family ties and obligations.

---

[127] This motif is already included in Peter's catch of fish, Lk 5.4–7. Peter leaves everything behind and follows the one who had demonstrated his miraculous power to provide. Following him, they will not suffer deprivation.

The passages in question serve to underline how very demanding it is to be a disciple of Jesus. The admonitions in 14.26, taken together with the masculine imagery used in the following pair of parables (which is not complimentary in gender terms) about adequate calculation, can indicate that the costs of discipleship represent a special problem for comfortably-established men. The negative form also suggests that a negative outcome is highly probable as also the context of 18.18–30 confirms. The ruler who did not follow Jesus' request because of his great wealth, forms a contrasting background to Peter's statement (with reference to himself) about those who have left everything and followed Jesus.[128] Jesus' answer, containing the list, is therefore primarily an answer to the men represented by Peter.

The position of men as acting subjects and women as passive objects in these last texts does not, therefore, imply that the ascetic following of Jesus is a male privilege, and that the list of costs is just another blatant example of Luke's extreme androcentricity.[129] Nor is it exclusively a matter of intensified demands made of an elite of male leaders. The question has already been raised in connection with the women who follow Jesus in Lk 8.1–3.[130] The fact that 'wife' is mentioned in these lists, but not 'husband', was then tentatively explained by the presumption that the majority of the women in the gospel from the outset were less integrated into family life than the men, who must be called more directly and emphatically to give up their established lives. Besides this, it was presumably the case within a patriarchal structure that primarily those women who had a choice were already independent to some extent – either because of sheer need with no one to take care of them, or because they were economically self-sufficient.[131] Luke's presentation of the women who follow Jesus alludes, as has already been shown, to this ambiguity of social exposure, vulnerability and sickness on the one

[128] So the narrative of the healing of Peter's mother-in-law precedes in Luke, the call of the disciples and Peter's act of abandonment.

[129] Schüssler Fiorenza, *In Memory*, 145f. Witherington, *Women in the Ministry of Jesus*, 150 n. 150, manages, however, to see in the addition of τὴν γυναῖκα 'Luke's interest in and concern for women' (sic!).

[130] Cf. pp. 37ff.

[131] To this extent, Schottroff's analysis identifies something essential, cf. my presentation and evaluation in 'Fattig og likestilt'.

hand and material resources on the other. And it is precisely the prominence which Luke gives to the Galilean women following Jesus, that makes it impossible to maintain that the male-dominated perspective in chs. 14 and 18 means that women are excluded from the ascetic discipleship and from discipleship's rewards. On the contrary, their discipleship and exemplary service form the alternative material basis also for the men who have given up everything to follow Jesus. In the fictive family of disciples, the contribution of the women is crucial to the sustenance of the group, and their involvement implies that sexually determined functions are disregarded. The dual emphasis on gender in the vocabulary of 20.34ff. is in accord with this; these women no longer allow themselves to be taken in marriage. The non-sexual family categories give expression to an ideal of chastity that is to be realised formally at least to the extent that marriage is no longer contracted.

VI.4. '... and she had lived as a widow since then'.

When Paul speaks about widows in 1 Cor 7.8, 39f., it is to urge them to remain unmarried – clearly because they form the group of women in the community left with a choice of their own and accordingly with the best possibility of realising the ascetic ideals. This is the only occasion on which Paul specifically mentions this group of women, whereas Luke-Acts indicates a large presence of widows when compared with other New Testament writings.[132] What role do these widows play, and have they any connection with the ascetic inclinations which the preceding discussion has demonstrated in Luke?

As with the rest of the material dealing with women, the largest part of the texts in which widows appear in Luke's writings, are found in the gospel and belong to the specifically Lukan material. Only two passages have synoptic parallels: the story of the widow's

---

[132] There are few other references to widows in the New Testament: 1 Cor 7.8: Jas 1.27; Rev 18.7 – and 1 Tim 5.3–16, which is the only text that can be said to measure up to Luke. There are synoptic parallels, as mentioned below, to a few of the passages in Luke. The concentration of material dealing with widows in Luke-Acts and 1 Timothy leads Freed, 'Judge and Widow', 44f., to assert somewhat categorically that they 'reflect a time later than Jesus'.

coin in 21.1–4 is common to Luke and Mark (Mk 12.41–4), but is not found in Matthew; the same is true of the previous saying in Lk 20.47 of widows as victims of the greed of the scribes, which has a parallel in Mk 12.40 but is attested only in doubtful variants of Mt 23.14.[133] The other four narratives and examples in which widows are explicitly mentioned are all unique to Luke: the prophetess Anna (2.36–8); the widow at Zarephath (4.25f.); the widow at Nain (7.11–17); the importunate widow (18.1–8). In Acts 6.1, the widows of the Hellenists are mentioned as a group in the community, and 'widows' appear also in the account of the raising of Tabitha (Acts 9.36–42). Some exegetes have supposed that Tabitha herself is a widow, and similar suggestions have been made about most of the other women who appear independently and 'without a husband' in Luke's narrative, for example Peter's mother-in-law (Lk 4.38f.); Martha (10.38–42); Lydia (Acts 16.14f.); Mary the mother of John (Acts 12.12).[134] But, with the exception of Anna the text itself does not apply the term widow to women whose names are mentioned.

The suggestions that these women who have their own households should be regarded as widows is all the more remarkable in that scholars, taken as a whole, seem to agree that Luke's interest in widows belongs 'to the larger chapter of his predilection for the oppressed and despised, especially for the poor and for women'.[135] What is then more fitting than 'poor women'? The widows are seen as significant expressions and well-chosen examples of a situation of extreme need, of persons without any prospects of fending for themselves.[136] They are primarily a social clientele in need of mercy and material care. It is true that special elements of an exemplary piety on the part of

---

[133] Stählin, 'χήρα', 437. While the high number of examples is striking in Luke, the same must be said about their lack in Matthew.

[134] Malinowski, 'Brave Women', 60; Pilgrim, *Wealth and Poverty*, 135; Portefaix, *Sisters Rejoice*, 159; Stählin, 'χήρα', 440; Swidler, *Biblical Affirmations*, 304f.; Thraede, *Ärger*, 96. Cf. also p. 38 on corresponding suggestions about the women in Lk 8.2f.

[135] Stählin, 'χήρα', 439.

[136] Haenchen, *Apg.*, 215, 286; Jervell, 'Töchter Abrahams', 92; Osiek, 'Widows as Altar', 159f.; O'Toole, *Unity*, 123, 126; Portefaix, *Sisters Rejoice*, 159f.; Tannehill, *Literary Unity*, 136; Tyson, 'Problem of Food', 80. Cf. also the contrast in Rev 18.7 between βασιλίσσα and χήρα.

widows are admitted to be present: in the case of Anna, it is the piety that predominates,[137] and exemplary significance is attributed to the widows also in Lk 18.1–8 and 21.1–4. These traits have not, however, been brought into play for the understanding of the widows in Acts 6.1 and 9.36ff. Indeed, taken as a whole, the various features in the Lukan narratives of widows are not brought into relation with one another. Thus, apart from sporadic suggestions that other apparently unmarried women in Luke can or must also have been widows – even if they are not so called – the widows have been treated as an isolated phenomenon without any apparent connection to the other women appearing in the story. It might be that they constitute an especially clear expression of the fact that women in general represent a socially vulnerable group in Luke-Acts.

On the one side, and with the greatest emphasis, it is claimed, accordingly, that widows in Luke are an extreme example of marginalised persons in need. On the other side, the suggestion is made almost *en passant* that the strong resourceful women in Luke-Acts must presumably be widows, since they appear with an independence that is so much taken for granted. The same unresolved tension as is found in the interpretation of the Lukan material is also present in the scholarly descriptions of the historical environment. At best, this is simply due to a lack of reflection on the fact that a widow's position was in reality ambivalent. Ideologically, to become a widow, especially in the case of a childless woman, was considered both in the Jewish and in the Roman-Hellenistic context as a misfortune. For many women, perhaps for most, this was also the case *de facto*. But at the same time, to be widowed meant greater freedom for a woman than she had ever had either as a young unmarried girl or as a wife. She received a more extensive right of self-determination; at least the right to be consulted in questions that concerned her own life.[138] As widows, women had a greater choice, something that is clearly presupposed, for example, in Paul's argument in 1 Cor 7.8, 39–40.

---

[137] This is admitted by Jervell, 'Töchter Abrahams', 92.
[138] Andersen, 'Widows', 41f.; Gardner, *Women*, 54ff.

Women were married early, and it is probable that they, in the case of their first marriage, had almost no voice in the matter.[139] Therefore the young girls themselves could hardly choose to remain unmarried; virginity was not an option. The early age of marriage and the frequent difference in age between the marriage partners meant that many women became widows at a relatively young age.[140] It was, however, customary at least for younger widows to marry again after a seemly period of mourning. This was in keeping with general views on morality, and the remarriage of widows within strict time-limits was laid down for example in Augustus' legislation.[141] Most women also had to have someone to support them out of pure necessity, and marriage was the normal and prescribed solution to this need of sustenance. As is often the case, freedom was primarily a freedom for those better off, who were able to take care of themselves and also capable of paying the ideological costs.[142]

The very term 'widow' reflects the exposed position of a widow. Etymologically, χήρα, means 'die herrenlos Gelassene', and apart from the narrower meaning of a 'wife who survives her husband', it can designate generally 'a woman who lives without a man'.[143] The equivalent term in Hebrew, 'almanah', is claimed to be derived from 'lm', 'to be dumb'.[144] A widow was without voice in society, she had no one to speak for her.[145] These linguistic explanations clearly express the fact that a woman without a man was also without status, without social

---

[139] Cf. p. 56 n. 98 and p. 187 above.

[140] Cf. Lane Fox, *Pagans*, 309. On demographic data concerning longevity etc., cf. Portefaix's overview, *Sisters Rejoice*, 10–13.

[141] Cf. p. 192 above.

[142] Throughout the Apocryphal Acts, we find that the women who actually break out of the home, come from the higher strata of society and are rich. While this is admittedly typical of the literary genre to which the Acts belong, it probably also reflects the social experience of women: '... only such women could be truly independent' – cf. Davies, *Revolt of Widows*, 114; see also Stählin, 'χήρα', 423. It is significant that Augustus' marriage legislation was directed primarily at the upper levels of society.

[143] Stählin, 'χήρα', 429f.

[144] Otwell, *Sarah Laughed*, 125. Friis Plum, *Tilslørede Frihed*, 27f. n. 9, maintains that 'almanah' is not only a woman whose husband is dead, but a widow with no sons to take care of her.

[145] Stählin, 'χήρα', 434, points out that a widow's need is often associated with legal quests. A widow had problems in asserting her rights and was an easy prey – cf. also the parable in Lk 18.1–8.

security, and without identity in societies pervaded by androcentric thinking and a patriarchal structure in which the identity of the individual was determined by the collective belonging.[146] The fundamental patriarchal evaluation of 'man's woman' meant that 'a woman lost in happiness and status through anything which diminished the closeness of her relationship with men'.[147] It is therefore characteristic that the masculine form χῆρος, 'widower', is a much newer term and is seldom used.[148]

Pending a new marriage, a widow who had sons could continue to live in their family, and in some cases, it was allowed for a woman who was abandoned or widowed, to return to her father's house.[149] As has been mentioned, the wealth of the family, inheritance and/or a woman's possibilities of personal income or possessions gave considerable reinforcement to her possibilities of taking care of herself. In the Jewish context, the exposed position of a widow is both reflected and counteracted by the continually repeated exhortations to protect widows and to give them their proper due. With the exception of some ancient oriental lists of 'virtues of great kings', such exhortations to a special protection of widows are unknown in antiquity.[150] The reason given for this concern was primarily theological: God is the helper of widows (and orphans), that is God takes the man's place in relation to them. The obedience of God's people to God's will is therefore to become manifest also in their special care for widows. In the Deuteronomistic legislation this is crystallised in several regulations about widows, for example Dt 14.29; 16.11, 14; 24.17–21, regulations which at the time of Jesus were fulfilled through a system of organised care for the poor

---

[146] Otwell, *Sarah Laughed*, 125f., 131f. Strangers, widows and orphaned children are often mentioned together, because all three are groups 'for whom no family provided identity'. And 'all three lacked participation in an Israelite family that could provide economic and legal security'. Cf. also Gowan, 'Wealth and Poverty', 344.

[147] Lightman/Zeisel, 'Univira', 27.

[148] Stählin, 'χήρα', 429f.

[149] Fensham, 'Widow', 136.

[150] Cf. Stählin, 'χήρα', 435. In the Old Testament, similar exhortations are addressed to all the members of God's people, and not especially to the rulers. Cf. also Sand, 'Witwenstand', 188f.

especially including widows.[151] This instituted provision took two forms, one on a daily basis and the other on a weekly one. The daily service was for the benefit of 'travelling people' and consisted of food that was collected by those in charge of the distribution. The weekly service took care of the residential poor, and it is unclear whether it consisted of food and clothes, or whether they received money to spend on daily meals through the week. The description of the twofold regulation is based on rabbinic sources, and it is not certain whether it also applies to the New Testament period.[152]

If 'the daily service' which is mentioned in Acts 6.1, was a similar provision for the poor in the earliest community,[153] it does not correspond to either of the two forms named. For in this case, it seems that the daily distribution is addressed to those who were taken care of on a weekly basis in the Jewish system. But even if the service described in Acts 6.1 differs from any known Jewish model, it is generally accepted, on the basis of this evidence, that the Christian community relatively early on, established (or was obliged to establish) a system of care for the poor similar to that of the Jews, aimed particularly at poor widows. This probably meant that poor persons who belonged to the group of those believing in Jesus did not (or could not any longer) benefit from the public Jewish care.[154]

The evidence thus seems to indicate that widows in antiquity were socially exposed persons and often, though not always, without decent means of sustenance. This is clearly reflected in the very term 'widow', and in practice it was difficult for most women to manage on their own, both materially and socially, without a male point of reference. It is also clear that the early Christian communities adopted the Jewish

---

[151] On the organisation of this provision for the poor, cf. Jeremias, *Jerusalem*, 131f.; Haenchen, *Apg.*, 215. Similar regulations existed in Rome, but they usually favoured men, cf. Pomeroy, *Goddesses*, 202f.

[152] Even Jeremias, *Jerusalem*, 131, who generally has great confidence in the historicity of these sources has reservations here.

[153] Cf. p. 72 and p. 72 n. 148.

[154] Freed, 'Judge and Widow', 44; Haenchen, *Apg.*, 215. This need not, however, presuppose 'eine längere Entwicklung und Entfremdung' as Haenchen maintains. For objections and an alternative interpretation of Acts 6.1, cf. Schüssler Fiorenza, *In Memory*, 165.

attitude and developed their own care for widows, as an important part of their provision for the poor.[155] In relation to the Greco-Roman environment, this was something special, but not necessarily controversial.

More problematic *vis-à-vis* the demands made by contemporary society were the specific reasons that the church developed for its support of widows and for honouring them. The large number of widows in Christian communities at a time with an otherwise marked shortage of women in the population,[156] must be accounted for by particular circumstances. What presumably happened was that the widows' material needs for support and the cultic community's obligation to take care of them merged with ascetic ideals and a restrictive praxis of remarriage to an ideal of widowhood. This meant that the term 'widow' took on a note of honour. Christianity contributed, at least within its own ranks, to an increase in the number of women who avoided remarrying and remained widows. Ideologically, the contribution came from Christianity's ascetic reservations especially against second marriages, and practically from an organised support system which meant that not even material need forced widows to marry again. A life as a widow was not only desirable; it was also rendered feasible.

Judaism also was acquainted with a piety for which widows served as models. Judith has already been mentioned,[157] a paradigmatic example who has lent features to the description of Anna in Lk 2.36–8. Judith, however, is not primarily an ascetic, but the extremely monogamous wife who remains faithful to her deceased husband until her own death. In the Roman context as well, we find a traditional idealisation of the *univira*, that is of the woman who remained faithful to one husband

---

[155] This could take on considerable dimensions. According to Eusebius, bishop Cornelius (ca. 250) writes that 'The Roman community supports 1500 widows and needy persons'. On the statistics of Cornelius, cf. Lampe, *Stadtrömischen Christen*, 116; Harnack, *Mission*, 184f. Care for widows also plays a role in Hermas, cf. Lampe, *Stadtrömischen Christen*, 71f.

[156] Cf. Pomeroy, *Goddesses*, 68f., 164, 227ff. The number of women in Christian communities was relatively large, and it is possible that they were even in the majority in some communities, cf. Gülzow, 'Soziale Gegebenheiten', 200.

[157] Cf. p. 191f. above.

for the whole of her life.[158] The Christian reservation against remarriage has often been seen in the light of this Roman *univira* tradition.[159] But it has been shown that much of the Roman material which attests factual cases consists of epitaphs raised by surviving husbands to wives who died young.[160] The term *univira* is, however, an example of how continuity and traditionalism could be enshrined linguistically when (or even if) social usage underwent great changes.[161] The term itself retained its original meaning of a woman married only once and also an elitist taste of 'the good old Rome'. The pre- and non-Christian usage of the term was either prescriptive and related to institutional and ritual activities for women whose husbands were alive (i.e., women who had not been married to any other husband than the one they now had), or else descriptive as a form of social approbation and used of women who predeceased their husbands (as in the epitaphs mentioned above). The prescriptive usage was restricted exclusively to the social elite. The descriptive usage was gradually democratised and spread to all levels of society, while retaining its suggestion of something noble. In other words, it conferred a certain social prestige. *Univira* became more and more detached from the prescriptive usage and the connection with the cult, and functioned as an archaising descriptive expression of social approval. This detachment from its pagan cultic roots, made it possible for the Christians to adopt the term, but their use of it is characteristically unique in the sense that they applied it to widows. This is a reflection of the new social phenomenon whereby the condition of widows in the Christian communities represented the ideal life for a woman. The widow was an *univira* and had fulfilled the conventional expectations of a woman's life, while at the same time she could realise the ascetic ideals and lead a life consecrated to God. As we

---

[158] Pomeroy, *Goddesses*, 161; Stählin, 'χήρα', 431. Pomeroy maintains that the custom is 'strictly Roman ... without counterpart in Greece'. She does not touch on Jewish examples.

[159] Lightman/Zeisel, 'Univira', 19.

[160] Pomeroy, *Goddesses*, 161. McNamara, 'Wives and Widows', 586, notes: 'The *univira* was more a symbol of luck than morality'. Lane Fox, *Pagans*, 344, reduces the term to mean only 'fidelity within marriage'. He does not, however, make sufficient distinctions within the quantity of material.

[161] On this and what follows, cf. Lightman/Zeisel, 'Univira'.

shall see later, it is therefore typical that the Pastoral Letters adopt the term *univira*.

Alongside Luke-Acts, only the First Letter to Timothy among the New Testament writings pays a more general attention to widows. Exegetes are broadly in agreement that 1 Tim 5.3–16 regulates an order of widows in the communities. It is more debatable whether the author is instituting a new order here, or is intervening critically in an order already well-established, while trying to diminish the importance of it by reducing the 'body of widows' with the help of both economic and doctrinal arguments. According to the common conjecture of most commentators, the author of 1 Tim 5.3–16 initiated a new order to settle the problems of widows in the communities. But this understanding is no longer quite so well-accepted. Recent contributions view this passage in the light of the treatment of women elsewhere in the Pastorals. They understand the regulations about widows as an attempt to curb an egalitarian and ascetic enthusiasm which was very attractive to many women, who therefore had themselves enrolled as widows.[162] The widows were subject to special restrictions, but these were different from the restrictions usually laid upon women's lives. 1 Tim 5 indicates indirectly that the decisive issue was the enrolled women's obligation to a life of chastity. It is therefore possible that the order of widows may have served as a means of support for other women as well, who for various reasons had been deprived of social security in the family or who had deliberately chosen a life free from marital bonds. They were all sheltered by the provisions made for the widows and may, as they entered the order, have gained the name of widow.[163] It is still likely

---

[162] Bassler, 'Widows' Tale, 31–41; McDonald, *Legend,* 73ff.; Müller-Bardoff, 'Exegese', 113–33. Possible reasons for this attraction are already mentioned in the previous sub-chapter, p. 219f.

[163] Ignatius' Letter to the community in Smyrna (ca. 107) contains an early and often quoted testimony to the fact that the order of widows included other categories of unmarried women. This reference shows not only that the order of widows apparently flourished, but also that women whom he calls 'virgins', were named among the widows: Ἀσπάζουαι ... καὶ τὰς παρθένους τὰς λεγομένας χήρας' ... (Ign. Smyrn. 13.1). This seems to have been an eastern praxis. Tertullian, De Virg. vel. 9, mentions with distaste examples he knows of Asian bishops who have enrolled young virgins among the widows.

It is interesting that the term 'widow' seems to be dominant until the middle of the

that most of the women involved, even the young ones, were real widows or, divorced women. But they were all able to remain unmarried thanks to this sustaining regulation by the community.

The difficulties with the transitions and the coherence in the pericope 1 Tim 3.5–16 are due to the fact that the author seeks, through two different types of argument, to limit an already-existing order, which throughout the text is presupposed to be familiar to the reader. To the author of 1 Tim 5, the many widows represent too heavy a burden financially, as well as a theological threat. He opposes their ascetic fervour, accuses them of lacking faithfulness and maintains that their weakness encourages easy access by heretics who advocated a similar ascetic lifestyle. There is also the fear expressed that the surrounding society will react negatively to such a lack of conformity to the domesticity expected of women.

The author of 1 Timothy wishes therefore primarily to decimate the group. This is done by launching the category of the 'genuine', 'true' widow, thus defining proper widowhood. The true widow is over sixty years of age, and so totally lacking in resources of her own that she can look for help only to the community. Limiting criteria are developed in order to reshape the existing regulations for widows into an indirect confirmation of contemporary social norms for a woman's life. Young 'widows' are directed to (re)marry (1 Tim 5.11–15).[164] This means that they are provided for, while at the same time an element of unrest is brought under control. Young widows are discouraged from entering upon obligations to celibacy that they are unable to keep which might lead them to 'act against Christ'. This mode of expression is possibly an early trace of the understanding of a widow's vow of chastity in terms of a betrothal to Christ or an irrevocable vow of marriage made to the heavenly bridegroom. She is the bride of Christ, and this means that to marry 'another' man is infidelity to Christ: she is then to be counted as

---

fourth century, when the title of 'virgin', which earlier occurred more sporadically, suddenly begins to appear frequently in the sources, cf. LaPorte, *Role of Women*, 103. Can this be connected with the fact that, in the period after Constantine, the social protection supplied by the term 'widow', was no longer needed?

[164] There is no compelling indication, linguistically, in 5.14 that it is a question of *re*-marriage.

a 'fallen woman'.[165] Next, children and grandchildren are told to take care of their mothers, so that the women do not become a burden on the community (5.4). The same is true for 'the believing woman who has widows (living with her)' (15.16). This is, in fact, evidence that some kind of 'women's house', that is household communities consisting of women, existed already as early as this. The verse is best explained as speaking of Christian women who have received other unmarried women, 'widows', into their houses. It is clear that the community has given support to such households. But now the female patrons (who were presumably relatively well-off) are urged to care for the widows at their own expense, so that the community can use its resources for those who have no one upon whom they can fall back, the 'true' widows. The one who is finally accepted as a true widow of the community, apart from being over sixty years of age and with no other possibility of maintaining herself, must also have been the wife of one husband only (cf. what was said above about the ideal of the *univira*), and she must have cared for children and shown willingness to serve and virtue in other ways (5.9f.).

The outcome of the Pastorals' intervention does at least ensure that some fundamental and controversial elements in the regulations for widows are maintained: the demand that the widows observe permanent sexual abstinence and the freedom which this gave them from a patriarchal family structure and family obligations. But the criteria which are then introduced as the author's own contribution to the regulations, reinforce precisely the domestic pattern of life, based on marriage, from which the widows were exempt. The ascetic ideal is presented as valid only for women no longer fit for childbearing, and who are old enough to be excused from the public pressure of remarriage. For most other women the conventional expectations of marriage and maternity is confirmed theologically, cf. 1 Tim 2.9–13. The old widows are in fact presented as outstanding examples of women who have

---

[165] Niederwimmer, *Askese*, 58–63, has shown how the image of Jesus as bridegroom has an ascetic flavour already in the gospel material. In later sources, the motif of the ascetic woman's marriage vow to the heavenly bridegroom is much elaborated. Cf., for example Davies, *Revolt of Widows*, 84ff. The stereotype of the 'loose widow' is thus picked up, cf. Stählin, 'χήρα', n. 131.

previously fulfilled their conjugal duties. The task of the older women is also to teach the young women to love husband and children, to live a decent and pure life, to be good housewives and subordinate to their husbands (Tit 2.3ff.). Thus the author comes to terms with two potentially conflicting ideals: 'a potentially objectionable office has been tamed, for even though the behavior of the widows may continue to deviate from society's expectations, the office now extols and rewards the expected virtues'.[166]

The convincing force of this analysis is not only that it unites otherwise disparate elements within the pericope itself (5.3–16). But the treatment of widows and the treatment of women elsewhere in the Pastoral Letters becomes logical and consistent. The Pastoral Letters are strongly in favour of marriage and emphasise the subordinate and domestic role of women to the extent that childbirth and the successful raising of children is made a prerequisite for women's salvation (1 Tim 2.3–16). The life and salvation of women are tied to their procreative function. Ideologically, therefore, the regulation for widows is adjusted to fit such ideals. From the author's side, the problem of the order of widows is tackled by strengthening the hierarchical structure of the community and by emphasising traditional values of subordination, especially for women.

In 1 Timothy, in other words, Paul is used against Paul. The Pauline exhortations in 1 Cor 7 to give preference, where possible, to a celibate life are brushed aside in Paul's name and reserved as an alternative only for elderly widows, as was permitted also by Roman legislation. In principle, the community's responsibility for widows was accepted. This was a responsibility deriving from ancient Jewish custom, which it would have been impossible to abandon completely. But if the author of the letter had his way – something that is, however, not so certain – the responsibility would be limited to only the truly needy and elderly widows who had no other possibility of support. Implicitly (although subject to ideological suspicion) a celibate option remained even for younger widows, if they were able to maintain themselves or found someone within or outside their family who was willing to support them.

---

[166] Bassler, 'Widows' Tale', 38.

In a way, the Pastoral Letters' attempt at a restrictive regulation represented a reactivation of the order's original character as the Christian communities adopted it from Judaism. But this implies that the order already had a history during which its character had undergone changes in many places, as far as its original aim was concerned. In the case of Luke, this also makes it impossible to assert (as many scholars do) that as 1 Tim 5 is the earliest evidence of an attempt to establish a regulated order of widows, Luke's description of widows cannot be influenced by this at all.[167] On the contrary, it is probable that both the daily service in Acts 6.1 and the widows in Tabitha's house in Acts 9 reflect an established order of widows in Luke-Acts.

Luke shares the presupposition, inspired by Judaism and common among Christians, that the religious community has the duty of providing for widows. The Jewish connection comes into play as the concern for widows in Luke-Acts and is strongly coloured by the idea of fulfilling the Law.[168] The care for widows is further motivated by two specifically Lukan resurrection stories both involving the situation of widows. Jesus raises up the widow's son in Lk 7.11–17, out of consideration for her, since he feels compassion for her.[169] By giving her the son back (cf. the expression καὶ ἔδωκεν αὐτὸν τῇ μητρὶ αὐτοῦ in 7.15) he also returns to her social security and sources of sustenance. In the second story, Acts 9.36–41, Peter raises up Tabitha after the (other) widows have shown him with tears, examples of Tabitha's charitable activity. Her resurrection makes it possible for her to continue her care for the widows in the community at Joppa. When the community subsequently is called in to witness her return to life, the widows are

---

[167] As a typical example, Haenchen, *Apg.*, 215f. A certain exception must be made for scholars whose primary interest lies in the institution of widows in the early church and who seek traces of this in the New Testament. Naturally, they latch on to 1 Tim 5.3–16 in particular, but they can also refer summarily to the Hellenistic widows in Acts 6.1 and more sporadically to the widows in Tabitha's house in Acts 9.39 and 41 as well. Stählin, 'χήρα', 440, also maintains that Acts 9.41 shows that the widows even then already formed an order of their own.

[168] Jervell, 'Töchter Abrahams', 92; Stählin, 'χήρα', 440.

[169] Cf. p. 40 above.

mentioned specifically and they appear to constitute a group of their own.[170] It may be that these narratives represent a faint link with the concern, known from 1 Tim 5, that the family should take care of its own widows. The same holds true of the believing women (in this case Tabitha) providing shelter for widows in their houses. Luke's narrative portrayal is, however, neither a prescription nor a regulation; rather, a miraculous act creates the continued possibility for maintenance. In both cases the widows' source of sustenance is revived; the benefit of the healing is benefaction.

Both narratives are, however, fashioned in such a way that the 'widows' appear as persons in need of help, and inviting compassion. They remain recipients, entrusted to the good will of the son or to Tabitha's care. This applies also to the example from Israel's history adduced by Jesus in Lk 4.25f., in the programmatic introduction to his ministry at Nazareth, when he wishes to demonstrate that no prophet is well-received in his home town. Elijah was sent to the widow in Zarephath in the time of famine. The point, however, is not primarily that she was helped unlike other people in Zarephath, but that the widow in Zarephath in Sidon was helped unlike the many widows in Israel.

The widow of Nain, like the widows in the other gospel texts, is categorised and her situation is defined by means of the term 'widow'. But she appears on the scene as an individual person. In Acts, however, the term is always used in the plural and functions more directly as the designation of a group. Both in 6.1 and in 9.39, 41, αἱ χῆραι appear as a fixed and well-known group in the community, familiar both to the author and to the readers. It is, therefore, characteristic that precisely Acts 6.1 and 9.36–42 give the impression of an organised service for the group of widows, either in the form of a daily distribution of food or by means of a benefactor, a better-off sister in the community

---

[170] It is tempting to consider the juxtaposition of οἱ ἅγιοι and αἱ χῆραι in the light of later usage especially in the Syrian area (cf. Brock, 'Early Syrian Asceticism', 11; Kretschmar, 'Ursprung', 40) and so speculate about a group of male ascetics, called holy men, and a group of female ascetics, called widows, who constitute elite groups within the community. This would explain why the two groups are set in parallel to one another. But it probably fails because οἱ ἅγιοι elsewhere, in Acts 9.13, 32 and 26.10, more generally denotes all the believers.

who took care of them and/or carried out charitable work together with them. This also shows that there is no abrupt transition from an organised provision for widows to an 'order of widows'.[171] The instituted order of widows was based on the regulation of care for them and on the fact that widows normally needed protection. This was, of course, also valid for women who chose to remain widows for ascetic reasons. The point is that the provisions offered by the community meant the possibility of a real choice. When morality no longer ordained that a new marriage was to be preferred, economic necessity did not compel this. But it is characteristic that the Lukan text does *not* say of Tabitha herself that she was a widow; she is called μαθήτρια (9.36) and is an active benefactor.[172] This may mean that a distinction is made so that the term χήρα primarily maintains its character of social exposure and is reserved for the 'needy' widows. Other prominent and well-off women, whose civil status is the same, are designated in other ways. The ambivalent combination of needy vulnerability and resources of sustenance characteristic of the description of women in Luke-Acts, may thus in the case of the widows, be traced terminologically.

The element of steadfast strength is nevertheless noticeable even in the cases where the designation 'widow' occurs.[173] Most of the narratives about widows in the gospel express the exposed, vulnerable position of the widow combined with an emphasis on the strength and piety that gives an exemplary character to her act. The parable in Lk 18.1–8 plays on a well-known theme: the widow who struggles for her rights over against a corrupt legal system.[174] In this case, she finally succeeds surprisingly – even in the face of an unrighteous judge thanks solely to her wearisome and persevering importunity. The Lukan intro-

---

[171] Remarks in many commentaries on Acts make here an excessively firm distinction, cf. Conzelmann, *Acts*, 44; Haenchen, *Apg.*, 286; Schneider, *Apg.*, II 52 n. 47: 'Die Witwen sind hier nicht als Stand, *sondern* als besonders bedürftige Gemeindemitglieder vorgestellt' (my italics).

[172] There is no basis whatever in the text for the assertion that she is thereby presented as a deaconess, and to give her a position parallel to the seven, as does Witherington, *Women in the Earliest Churches*, 150f., 155.

[173] Cf. Selvidge, *Daughters*, 109, who maintains that the widows in Luke 'seem to be able to take care of themselves'. As has been shown, the picture is more varied than this.

[174] Cf. n. 145 above.

duction to the parable[175] underlines its purpose: to voice convincingly the importance of an unwearying perseverance in prayer.

It is a matter of discussion, to what extent the widow alone is the protagonist, or whether the point is to prepare an inference *a minore ad maius* by means of the interplay between her and the unrighteous judge.[176] In the first case, the widow is to be understood in a more directly exemplary fashion, but even the other variant interpretation does not necessarily exclude the possibility that she functions as a model.[177] She is presented as a prominent example of persistent prayer, and those who hear the parable are to learn a positive lesson from her victory. Moreover, the example of Anna in Lk 2.36–8 is significant and it is not by chance that the figure of a widow illustrates unceasing and steadfast prayer: she too is said 'never to leave the temple, serving God with fasting and prayer night and day'. This gives expression to the single woman's possibility of single-mindedness, of living completely for God, without any interference from other obligations. This is also in agreement with 1 Tim 5.5 which almost descriptively affirms that 'she who is truly a widow and is all alone, has set her hope on God and continues in supplications and prayers night and day'. It is possible, therefore, that Luke's examples too are based on the idea that the

---

[175] Lk 18.1 is redactional, unlike 18.7–8, cf. Fitzmyer, *Luke*, 1176f. There has been much discussion about the limitation of the parable proper and the relationship between the original parable and the framework of interpretative remarks. But this discussion is scarcely relevant in this context.

[176] While Freed, 'Judge and Widow', 51, holds that the unrighteous judge 'serves only as a foil to emphasize the persistence of the widow, the main character of the story', commentators like Fitzmyer, *Luke*, 1177, with support in Marshall, *Luke*, 671, wish to defend the following interpretation, especially on the basis of 18.6: 'If a dishonest judge would yield to the persistence and prayer of a widow, how much more would the upright God and Father of all!' This interpretation concluding *a minore ad maius*, seems reasonable.

[177] When Fitzmyer, *Luke*, 1177, continues: 'If the helpless widow's persistent prayer accomplishes so much with a dishonest judge, how much more will the persistent prayer of Christian disciples!', this is not well-founded. While the first inference (see previous note) is reasonable on the basis of 18.6, this is not equally true of the second inference. Even if an inference *a minore ad maius* is to be drawn from the unworthy judge to the much greater, that is God, this does not necessarily imply a similar inference from the widow to the disciples, cf. the difference from, e.g. Lk 16.8bf.

desperately exposed position of widows renders a certain fervour to their prayers.[178]

Following a saying in Lk 20.47 about widows as victims of the scribes' greed, another example of a widow occurs in the narrative about the widow's mite in Lk 21.1–4. Here too, the apparently weak person acts with the full strength of faith, and in Jesus' evaluation, she who normally is considered as a victim, is the one to show strength. If the two actions of which the scribes are accused in 20.47, οἳ κατεσθίουσιν τὰς οἰκίας τῶν χηρῶν καὶ προφάσει μακρὰ προσεύχονται, are connected with each other,[179] then 20.47b is more than merely an accusation of hypocrisy, and the scribes are condemned because they extort from widows under the pretext of performing long (and well-paid) prayers for them. In the Lukan context, where widows are portrayed in other passages precisely as models in persevering prayer, the accusation thus assumes a strong note of irony.

The widow who places the whole of her livelihood at the disposal of the temple treasury has already been mentioned more than once, and her action has been interpreted as exemplary.[180] This interpretation differs from recent attempts to see the thrust of the story not as a praise of the widow, but as a complaint and accusation against those who have led her astray by false pretensions of piety.[181] According to their interpretation, Jesus first attacks the scribes in 20.47 for their economic encroachments upon widows, while the narrative in 21.1–4 is a condemnation of the temple authorities, who also deprive a widow of her

---

[178] Patristic sources also attribute special effectiveness to the prayer of widows (and sometimes also of the poor). This makes their prayer the recompense they give for support, in the form of an appeal directed to God, the ultimate benefactor. Cf. Country-man, *Rich Christian*, 111f.; Lampe, 'Diakonia', 53.

[179] Cf. Stählin, 'χήρα', 437. Nineham too, according to Fitzmyer, *Luke*, 1381, has suggested this.

[180] Cf. pp. 78, 95 and 78 n. 167. This interpretation presupposes that the temple institutions are positively accepted as the centre of the religious community at this stage of Luke's narrative, cf. the discussion on this in IV.3. 'Domestic Women'.

[181] Wright, 'Widow's Mites', who is supported by Fitzmyer, *Luke*, 1320f. Their interpretation is, of course, easier to handle, morally speaking; most interpreters find it objectionable that it should be an ideal for a poor widow to offer the last thing she has. Wright/Fitzmyer are correct to criticise the many interpreters who talk of the widow's attitude or feelings without any basis in the text.

living – although admittedly in a more subtle way: 'She has been taught and encouraged by religious leaders to do as she does ...' The widow is thereby denied any responsibility of her own, so that her whole identity is that of victim. Quite apart from the fact that this interpretation has not caught the irony in 20.47, it has accordingly no place for the contrast between the rich and the widow which Luke draws with considerably greater sharpness than Mark.[182] This is also the reason why Luke in this case especially emphasises that the widow was poor, χήρα πενιχρά.[183] In contrasting comparison with the rich who, seen from the perspective of a quantity, give more than her but relatively speaking actually offer less, the widow acts in an exemplary manner. By making such a radical act of abandonment, she exposes their lack of self-sacrificing generosity. She is a contrast also to the snobbish greed of the scribes against which Jesus warns in the previous saying. As has been indicated earlier, the main point lies not in an isolated evaluation of what the widow actually does, but in the critical contrast created by her action to the omissions of the rich, the rulers and the so-called pious. The fact that the widow is poor increases the contrast and gives her example all the greater strength. At the same time, her action of abandonment shows that she courageously and drastically trusts in God alone. Without a man to support her and without property, she lives a life with a radical eschatological orientation.

In both these cases, therefore, the widows, in a situation in which they apparently have few resources, act in such a way that they acquire exemplary significance. They are not portrayed primarily as recipients (as is the case with the widows in the miracle stories). Rather, they appear to develop features from the portrait of Anna (Lk 2.36–8). The brief presentation of Anna is an especially intense and concentrated introduction of an ideal widow – with roots in Jewish types of piety such as exemplified by Judith, and representative of the widows in the

---

[182] Cf. Marshall, *Luke*, 750f., and also p. 95.

[183] It is not possible to make very much of the distinction between χήρα πτωχὴ in Mark and χήρα πενιχρά in Luke, since Luke immediately afterwards calls her πτωχή. Neither is it possible to agree with Schüssler Fiorenza, *In Memory*, 165, that this means that other widows, like those in Acts 6.1, were better off.

Christian community in a way that apparently harmonises well with the criteria of the true widow set out in 1 Tim 5.[184]

The similarity between Anna and 'the true widow' in 1 Tim 5.3–16 is, however, much more limited than is commonly supposed, covering only some (though certainly essential) elements in the life of a pious widow, especially her persevering prayer. But Anna's function, as she appears in Luke's narrative, is primarily that of prophetic proclamation, and all the information issued about her serves as background and justification for this.[185] Not even Anna's advanced age represents anything other than a superficial correspondence: for even if she now is a very old widow, she has been a widow for most of her life, presumably from the age of twenty, after an early marriage that lasted seven years. In other words, the ideal is not the old and irreproachable widow as such, but a woman who, despite becoming a widow while young, nevertheless refrained from remarrying and remained a widow throughout a long life consecrated to God. Anna is identified by means of her own, not her deceased husband's, family and tribe. No independent importance attaches to the fact that she was once married and thus has fulfilled the conventional expectations of a woman's life, nor is it significant whether she has given birth to children. The point is the short duration of the marriage in comparison to the long period of widowhood. 'She lived with a husband' only for seven years, so that her life, seen as a whole, has been 'without a husband', characterised first by her virginity (cf. the explicit mention of her παρθενία in 2.36) and then by her widowhood. Anna is thus first and foremost an ascetic figure,[186] and she implicitly represents a model even for young women. Luke gives us no occasion to suppose that young women were obliged to marry so that they could be kept within bounds, and as a whole there is no trace in Luke of the criteria for the recognition of the true widows as we know them from 1 Tim 5.3–16. As we have seen, hospitality, care for

---

[184] Cf. n. 37 to ch. five.

[185] When Müller-Bardoff, 'Exegese', 124, sees Anna as an ideal example of the widows in 1 Tim 5 because 'Das Gebet erscheint ... als ihre eigentliche und entscheidende Aufgabe', this is not in keeping with Luke's use of the figure of Anna.

[186] Cf. Brenner, *Israelite Woman*, 64, who maintains that this is what makes her different from the Old Testament prophets.

those in need and even a kind of foot-washing are specified for women in Luke-Acts as praiseworthy and exemplary actions, but no special significance is attached to these as personal qualifications.

In other words, there is in Luke-Acts a considerable distance from the confining treatment of widows in the Pastoral Letters. This is due to differences in attitude that have important effects on the general portrayal of women and gender-related patterns. While the Pastorals primarily recommend marriage and see the bearing and raising of children as a way to salvation for women, so that even the ideal for widows is adjusted on the basis of this, Luke represents, to a large extent, the opposite stand. The Lukan ideal is a woman who has lived without a husband for the greatest part of her life, the virgin who makes herself available for God's Spirit, independent women who give support to the community, and women who allow their lives to be governed by their relationship to the word at the cost of their domestic obligations and as a replacement of their function in marriage. Luke's narrative does not support the admonitions of 1 Tim 5, but is rather an expression of the soil out of which grew the attitudes and the praxis that caused problems for the author of the letter.

The very term 'widow' has kept a traditional connotation in the Lukan usage, designating primarily 'a bereaved woman', whether the widows appear singly or in a group. There is no problem in understanding the order of widows as one in which the widows are portrayed as recipients of help, but at the same time this lends emphasis to the widows as a special group in the community. None of the texts concerning widows has a conclusion provoking compassion, even when a situation exciting compassion is their starting-point. We are told that the widows do in fact receive help, and the solution offered is never a new marriage. Many narratives also describe how widows transcend the role of victims and recipients, and realise in an exemplary manner, the life of faith.

So Luke voices ascetic preferences – and this also where women are concerned. The term 'widow' may be restricted to the poor and pious, but the ascetic ideal is applied more generally and has a vital theological significance as the proleptic sign of the resurrection to come.

Chapter Seven

Concluding Summary: The Double Message

The journey which we have taken through the Lukan story has shown that it is a preposterous simplification to ask whether Luke's writings are friendly or hostile to women. Luke's version of the life of Jesus and of the first believers cannot be reduced either to a feminist treasure chamber or to a chamber of horrors for women's theology. It contains elements that bring joy to 'dignity studies' and other elements that give support to 'misery studies'. It comes as no surprise that various scholars have found material in Luke that permits them to make assertions in both directions, as the introduction to this work shows. The tension in Luke's narrative has indeed shown itself to be its ambivalent evidence both of strong traditions about women on the one hand, and of the social and ideological controls that brought women to silence and promoted male dominance in positions of leadership on the other.

By means of a narrative sequence that gives rare insight into how and why structures enforcing silence are imposed, the tensions between seemingly opposite voices are dealt with. But by means of the narrative strategy this happens in a way that does not deny women dignity; they are brought to silence and at the same time they continue to be given the right to speak. Their voice is still to be heard. So it is not without irony that the picture is finally presented; the women are indeed good enough and well-qualified, but the men suspect and reject them. The male consolidation of power occurs against a background to which the men have shown weakness and failure rather than strength. The Lukan construction contains a double, mixed message.

A community of women and men.

The examination of the Lukan 'gender pairs' shows how a complementary parallelising of discourse and narrative material, especially in the gospel, corresponds to a repeated and explicit gender specification in many group descriptions both in the gospel and in Acts. The double message in the parallel examples of women and men functions as an epic rejoinder to the repetitive information that those who follow Jesus in the gospel story, the communities in Acts and also audience groups, consist of men as well as women.

The women are on a few occasions representative of the greater group, and taken as a whole, the gender-specified duality especially gives visibility to the women. However, their becoming visible also entails a certain distance and segregation between the sexes. Women and men belong to the same community, which is characterised by the fact that they are united in essential rituals and live together in mutual material dependence. At the same time, men and women form groups of their own, and when individual persons are given prominence on some occasions, Luke often notes that they represent a larger group – either of women or of men. Mostly, this is not a case of constant groups, but of a fixed pattern. We have here a social system which is not individually, but collectively focussed. The individual finds identity in her or his belonging to a family or group; it is a community-based identity. The community, however, has inherent gender-dividing organisational patterns. A woman belongs to the larger community of faith primarily among the women, a man primarily among the men. This means that the whole community ('all') consists of the group of men as well as the group of women. There is no clear hierarchical order between the two groups. Even if the community of faith is regarded as a fictive kinship relationship, the new family of Jesus, it is not addressed according to the subordinating pattern of patriarchal household codes. And in the example of narrative pairs, sometimes the example of the man comes first, and sometimes the example of the woman, and it can also happen that the group of women can represent the totality. So the women are not an appendage to the men, but constitute a group of their own.

Unexpected heirs.

Early on in the gospel, while 'he is still in Galilee', a group of women is established which follows Jesus together with the twelve. The summary description given of the women shows us a group that combines in an exceptional manner social insecurity and exclusion with autonomous energy and resources. The movement from social marginalisation and impurity to social integration and purity is given expression in the claim that they had all been healed by Jesus. Their social marginalisation as women is intensified at the outset by impurity and sickness. The healings articulate the fact that they are 'Abraham's daughters', and emphasise their share in the blessing and the promise of liberation and salvation that belongs to Abraham's progeny. They are not the pious Abraham-like heroes/heroines of faith whom we know from contemporary Jewish texts, but women who, bearing the burden of impurity, are excluded from respectable society. Together with similar sons, they are the children of Abraham whom God raises up 'from stones' to take the place of those who have impenitently taken for granted their own rights as children, and they form the nucleus of the reconstructed people of God. In the Lukan employment of the Abraham terminology, applied to particular women and men, there is a social expansion, going beyond all limits, and a legitimation that creates conflicts *vis-à-vis* the established religious leadership.

From serving women to the service of the lords.

In the process of healing, women are characterised, more than men, as passive partners, as persons who receive without any antecedent prayer or recommendation on their part. Jesus brings about a change in their lives by crossing boundaries created by concepts of impurity and by social marginalisation. There is therefore, implicit in the motif of healing, a christological motivation to service. The benefaction of Jesus finds a response in the women's subsequent benefactory activity as they follow him. This activity is not directed at Jesus alone, but benefits the whole community. The women who serve with what they possess, provide basic sustenance for Jesus and for those who follow him. Thereby, prototypically, they fulfil the demand that is later applied more universally to the people of God: they share what they have, in order to meet the needs of those who no longer have anything of their own.

251

It is typical of Luke's use of διακον-terms that the root-meaning of the word, that is, waiting on someone or service at table, is continually activated in the text. When we are told that the women serve, this can sound like a cliché confirming that a role of waiting on others is constantly theirs, even if those on whom they wait, are now no longer the men in their physical family, but the brethren in the fictive kinship community in the flock of disciples. It is also clear that, in the case of the women, service needs no particular justification; it is only when the role of servant is presented as an ideal for free men and for the leadership, that it needs a specific warrant. It is possible to discern in Luke's terminology a transfer of διακον-terms from being a narrative element found exclusively in the description of women, via paraenesis in parables, to a 'mirror for rulers' for the leaders of the people of God. For this Jesus himself serves as the model. At the same time this is a transfer from a concrete and direct use to metaphorical or rhetorical use. At important places in the early part of Acts, therefore, it is a rhetorical point that, no matter what task the leading men undertake, it is to be called 'service'.

It is not a question of a reversal, implying that the servants are now to rule. What takes place is a corrective and paradoxical yoking together of two traditionally opposite roles; the role of woman/servant and the role of ruler. The leaders are to enter into functions of service which would not normally be indicated by their status. It seems to be taken for granted by Luke that the leaders are men; and precisely Luke's positive and vigorous presentation of the women from Galilee in the gospel narrative makes it necessary to give a particular justification for the fact that they cannot have positions of leadership in the early communities. This is why an explicit criterion of gender is introduced in Acts to exclude women from the possibility of being elected to the service of leadership, whether of the word or of the table. Both a new apostle and the seven – who, according to the list of names given, were all men – had to be elected from among the men. The women who *de facto* served in the narrative are not considered eligible for the service of leadership.

It is admittedly true that the christological mediation bestows a new significance and dignity on the role of service which women carried out, and means that the women's service acquires exemplary value for the leadership function of the men. The model function of the women in this context is expressed, not only positively in relation to the new leadership of the people of God, whose authority is to find expression in service. It is expressed also critically in conflictual juxtapositions with those who claim leadership, but who are rich and false. However, while the women and their role are idealised in this way, they are excluded from actual positions of leadership. The reversal, not of roles, but of role values, coincides with and justifies a masculinisation – from serving women to lords who are to be 'as one who serves'.

The word creates a family.

Early on in the gospel all have a listening role *vis-à-vis* the word of the Lord; they are in a learning situation in which Jesus' proclamation dominates. The serving women from Galilee function as tradition-bearing figures ensuring continuity in the narrative up to the close of the gospel. They are custodians of the word, and they put into action what they have heard when this is demanded of them at the empty tomb. Early in the narrative, in contrasting terms, the biological gender-determined membership of a family and family obligations, which the women have, is rejected as irrelevant, in favour of hearing God's word and doing it. On the basis of this criterion, family categories both for women and for men, are transferred to the community of the followers of Jesus. Those who hear God's word and do it, become Jesus' family, the new family of God, and even those biological family relationships that do continue to exist, are integrated in the fictive family and are subordinated to it. Devotion to the word is given priority even where this may lead to conflict with the preoccupations of domestic provision, hospitality and service.

Silent women and talking men?

There is a limit to the activity which the women may carry out in connection with the word. Masculinisation not only occurs through the transfer of the service terms, but is also reflected in the relationship of men and women to the word. Women are never given any commission to preach, and due to their sex, they cannot be chosen to become witnesses of Jesus' resurrection, even if they otherwise satisfy all the criteria of eligibility: in the gospel narrative, emphasis is laid on the fact that the women accompany Jesus on his long journeyings, their faithful and fearless perseverance is underlined, as is their relationship as disciples, their knowledge of the Lord's word as well as their insight into it, and also their credibility. But in the further unfolding of the story, they are not accepted as appropriate witnesses when Jesus' resurrection is to be publicly proclaimed from Jerusalem to Rome.

In the concluding phase of the gospel, it becomes clear how certain factors come into play in silencing women. Luke's special version of the story of the empty tomb forms a lynch pin between the gospel's emphasis on women on the one hand, and Acts' reduction of women to invisibility in favour of the activity of the leading men on the other. By the use of ironic devices, the women become simultaneously recognised and rejected. The women come to the tomb in order to continue their service. But they discover that the body of Jesus is no longer there, and encounter the proclamation of the resurrection in a manner that confirms their role as disciples and activates their relationship to the word of the Lord. At the close of this passage, the assembled group of female disciples stands over against the assembled group of men. And it is the unbelieving reactions of all the men, and their difficulties in believing the women, that creates the gulf in the progress of the resurrection stories between the women's early faith and witness, and the male disciples' late acceptance – an acceptance so late that they are subsequently upbraided by the risen Jesus for their obstinacy. As in the case of the function of service, there is no direct transfer from women to men; here too, a christological link is necessary to bring about renewal and legitimation. In order to believe, the men must see the risen Lord himself.

Here we find an ironic distance between the narrative and the conclusions which Luke conveys. The narrative itself has established in detail that the women fully deserve credit. When the message fails to get across the first time, this is because of the unjustifiable disbelief of the men. But the conclusion is, all the same, that the persuading force of the women as witnesses is to be discounted. As witnesses, they possess credibility, but they are unable to convince – even to convince those who ought to have been the most readily prepared to believe. The

effect is that women are prevented from taking part in public proclamation and teaching, and the path is laid for the dominance of powerful leading men in Acts.

The same development, leading to the structures of silence, can be
seen in the more charismatic activity of women. At the beginning of
the gospel, in the context of pregnancy and birth, women play a more
prominent role than men in relation to the Spirit's activity that heralds
the birth of the Messiah and the eschatological in-breaking. The use of
Joel 3.1–5 as the key to the interpretation of the miracle of Pentecost,
in which the women from Galilee also share, is clearly designed to
emphasise that women's prophecy is a decisive characteristic of the in-
breaking activity of the Spirit that is to take place 'in the last days'.
Nevertheless, the women prophets in Acts are few in number, and their
message not reported.

Public men and domestic women.

The silence imposed on women is connected with the public character
of the proclamation in Luke, in societies where and at a time when the
distance between the world of men and the world of women very
largely coincided with the difference between a public sphere and a
private sphere. Women's lives were determined by the domestic rou-
tines and responsibilities, and even well-off and aristocratic women
were seldom direct participants in a public context. The men were
active in both spheres, though without having full and free access to the
'women's room'. The point is not necessarily to maintain that there
was a system of extreme physical separation, but to emphasise the
significance which family and home had as the life sphere determining
women's identity and function. In the texts, this is often expressed in
terms of locality as 'the house'. Acts' emphatic use of masculine forms
of address in discourses held by men reflects the situation that the
public world was reckoned to be exclusively the world of men. This
does not exclude the possibility that women might be present, but they
did not count. In other words, we have here a reality where the segregation of the sexes is ideologically undergirded and maintained.

Women's activity in Luke-Acts is most often linked to the house,
which also functions as a place where women gather. But the house

255

also increasingly becomes the place where the whole community comes together, although this does not weaken the significance of the public realm as the context of power. A gradual transfer from 'temple and market-place' to the house becomes apparent as the story unfolds. The women's identification with the house therefore does not imply a peripheral location, but, on the contrary, corresponds to a more and more central place in the life of the community. This is underlined by the fact that, even in domestic contexts, they are primarily asked to carry out 'non-domestic' functions, choosing 'the better part'. Even if the women are subordinated to the governing division between the public and the private, and consequently to the established masculine order of leadership, there is no demand, nor any narrative adjustment, to indicate that the women are to subordinate themselves more generally, or more directly, to (all) men. The independent integrity of the group of women is respected.

Angelic ascetics.

The ascetic tendency in Luke may help to explain the independent integrity of the women's group. Ascetic ideals liberated women from traditional role expectations in marriage and family. They thereby also limited the patriarchalising effect of the family model when this was transferred to the community in the house, and contributed to the special combination of inclusiveness and segregation between groups of men and groups of women within their community.

The analysis of the women's names already shows that none of the women finds her identity as a person in her relationship to a man, and women in general appear with their autonomy taken for granted, something that has led many scholars to speculate that they must have been widows. Mary's virginity is not necessarily exemplary, but it implies that in the initial phase of the gospel, virginity is established as a positive quality with creative possibilities for God's Spirit. Accordingly women's gift of prophecy is most often presented as a charismatic privilege of virginity; the women prophets are often either widows or virgins. A life without the obligations of marriage, or determined by sexual and bodily functions, is also adapted more generally as a permanent alternative for the women following Jesus. The transfer of Mary's relation as mother from the biological family to the fictive family of Jesus opens the possibility of an alternative motherhood for all the women who, like her, 'hear God's word and do it'. The opportunity for women to make a permanent choice of an ascetic life within the Christian communities is relatively unique in this period.

Chastity is also introduced for apocalyptic reasons. It is linked to ideas of the coming times of tribulation, which make a normal life an impossible burden. These times are so hard that women with children are to praise as blessed the childless women whom they would otherwise bewail. Unlike the 'women from Galilee', the 'daughters of Jerusalem' with their children are bound by conditions of life that will intensify their suffering. Since marriage is the legitimate framework for procreation, the ideal, therefore, is that while waiting for the catastrophe, one should not enter into marriage. Equally important is the positive reason, that those who neither marry nor let themselves be taken in marriage anticipate the angelic life of the resurrection.

Moreover, the abandonment and break with family relationships belongs more than anything else to the costs of discipleship. Even where the break does not take on a geographic expression, the family relationships that continue to exist are preferably to be arranged ascetically, and new marriages are to be avoided.

In terms of the patriarchal understanding of marriage presupposed by Luke, death necessitates marriage because marriage serves first and foremost a man's legitimate desire for procreation and thereby his 'immortality' through his progeny. This involves not only the subordination of the woman in marriage, but also implies that her *raison d'être* is to assist with a man's fundamental need to procreate and perpetuate himself. When ascetic ideals cause this orientation to be rejected, the woman is set free from her instrumental purpose in marriage. This provides one explanation for the attraction which a life in chastity obviously had for many women in the early Christian period. It offered them an opportunity to move outside the limiting constraints of the conventional gender-determined roles of daughter, wife and mother. By withdrawing their sexuality from control by others and by controlling it themselves, they gained the possibility of exercising a power and an authority from which they were otherwise excluded. They won a sort of control over their own life and property. Free from patriarchal

257

dominance in marriage, free from risky pregnancies and painful and life-threatening childbirths, these women had a freedom that was usually reserved for the hetairai, but one furnished with theological honour and respectability.

There is no clear trace in Luke of the idea that the ascetic life for women is a way of becoming male, as is the case in later sources. The androcentric phrasing in some of the ascetic passages in Luke reflects rather more pragmatically the reality that matrimony and marriage were normally men's initiative and responsibility. The attention is therefore focussed on those who have the greatest opportunity for choice, and who also have most to lose in giving up everything and therefore need to be urged. But this does not mean that ascetic discipleship is a male privilege or an intensified demand made of a male leadership elite.

The material in Luke dealing with widows is greater than in any other author in the New Testament. Even if the term χήρα itself in Luke has kept mainly traditional connotations of devastation, poverty and vulnerability, the interest in widows is not narrowly determined by motifs of care and compassion. The widows appear to form a special and respected group always portrayed in a positive light, and they transcend the roles of victims and receivers, and act in such a way that they become prominent examples of faith and piety. The portrait of an ideal widow in Luke also has a strongly ascetic profile: for most of her long life, she has lived without a husband. The widows were that group of women who, in formal terms, were free to choose for themselves in the matter of marriage. Many would, however, have difficulties providing for themselves, and the regulations for the care of widows which we glimpse in Luke, mean that even a poor widow could have real choice. If it was desirable to have a life without new marriage, this was also to be feasible.

It is characteristic that Luke employs a picture of Paul as an ascetic preacher. Not only does he preserve Paul's ascetic preference, but he also intensifies it to some extent. This tendency has its roots in the radical requirement of discipleship in the Jesus traditions and contains elements that may point forward to the later and much more direct ascetic preaching in the Apocryphal Acts. Nor is it without reason that later, Luke becomes a favourite gospel in the early Syrian church, in which asceticism is demanded of all who are accepted for baptism, and where 'to hear God's word' plays a prominent role in the liturgical tradition.

As for Luke's closeness to the Pastoral Letters, something that has often been asserted, the differences have been shown to be significant. The Pastorals are strongly in favour of marriage and emphasise the subordinate and domestic role of women to the extent that childbirth and the successful raising of children is made a prerequisite for woman's salvation. The image of the ideal widow and the regulations for the order of widows are adjusted accordingly. Luke, however, is fundamentally critical of marriage and encourages an attitude and a praxis that the author of the Pastoral Letters writing a little later, finds to be posing problems. The same is true of the Lukan defence of women's right to occupy themselves with the Lord's word even if this happens at the cost of all the elements in a woman's life that the author of the Pastoral Letters esteems so highly: a well-run household, hospitality and devoted, self-sacrificing care for husband and children.

The double message.

Luke draws up quite strict boundaries for women's activity in relation to the Jewish and the Greco-Roman public world. In this way, he is in accord with the apologetic considerations that also colour the epistles in questions dealing with women. But he transmits a double message. In his narrative he manages the extraordinary feat of preserving strong traditions about women and attributing a positive function to them, while at the same time harbouring an ironic dimension that reveals the reasons for the masculine preferences in Acts' presentation of the organisation of the Christian group, of the public missionary activity and legal defence before the authorities.

The masculinisation which dominates Acts, however, does not cover the whole of Luke's story cloaking women in silence and invisibility. Rather, the many possibilities opened up by the first phase of the narrative are narrowed down by the subsequent course of the narrative as it seeks a particular solution of leadership and public activity. By means of the narrative sequence and of the positioning of the gospel as a 'first volume', the traditions from Jesus' life, that is the life and voice of Jesus, lack the strong historical transparency of Mark and Matthew.

259

They are located in the past and given the character of remembrance. The same is true of the examples of women and the stories about them.

But this does not bring them to silence. What was, is not to be forgotten. Nor does it represent only a romantic and idealised version of what is irrevocably a story of the past. On the contrary, Luke's own employment of the motif of 'memory' shows that it is precisely in the remembrance of this past story that the key to critical insight and to a new evaluation and a new understanding is to be found. Remembrance unmasks critically and it also creatively opens up people's eyes so that by remembering, they can see and believe. Thus, the exemplary value and the critically correcting potential in the gospel's series of narratives retain their power for the present.

The double message nurtures a dangerous remembrance.

Bibliography

1. Sources.

ed. R. Kittel, *Biblia Hebraica*, Stuttgart 1937, 1968.

ed. H. B. Swete, *Septuaginta I–III*, 4th edition, Cambridge 1909.

ed. A. Rahlfs, *Septuaginta I–II*, Stuttgart 1935.

eds K. Aland, M. Black, C. M. Martini, B. M. Metzger, A. Wikgren, *Novum Testamentum Graece*, Stuttgart 1979.

ed. K. Aland, *Synopsis Quattuor Evangeliorum*, Stuttgart 1964.

Philo I–X, and Suppl. I–II, The Loeb Classical Library, London 1929, 1971.

ed. I. Epstein, *The Babylonian Talmud*, London 1961.

ed. R. H. Charles, *The Apocrypha and Pseudepigrapha of the Old Testament in English*, Oxford 1913.

Kautzsch, *Die Apokryphen und Pseudepigraphen des Alten Testaments*, Hildesheim 1972.

R. Riessler, *Altjüdisches Schrifttum ausserhalb der Bibel*, Freiburg/Heidelberg 1928.

E. Lohse, *Die Texte aus Qumran*, Darmstadt 1971.

E. Hennecke/W. Schneemelcher, *Neutestamentliche Apokryphen I–II*, Tübingen 1959–64.

ed. R. A. Lipsius/M. Bonnet, *Acta Apostolorum Apocrypha I–II*, Darmstadt 1959.

Apostolic Fathers I–II, The Loeb Classical Library, 1913, 1965.

ed. E. J. Goodspeed, *Die ältesten Apologeten*. Texte mit kürzen Einleitungen, Göttingen 1914.

ed. J. Regul, *Die antimarcionitischen Evangelienprologe*, Vetus Latina 6, Freiburg 1969.

ed. J. A. Robinson, *Passio S. Perpetuae*, Cambridge 1891.

2. Works of reference.

Aland, K., *Vollständige Konkordanz zum Griechischen Neuen Testament I–II*, Berlin/New York 1983.

Bauer, W., *Griechisch-deutsches Wörterbuch zu den Schriften des Neuen Testaments und der übrigen urchristlichen Literatur*, Berlin 1958.

Blass, F./Debrunner, A./Rehkopt, F., *Grammatik des neutestamentlichen Griechisch*, 16th edition, Göttingen 1984.

Gesenius, W., *Hebräisches und Aramäisches Handwörterbuch über das Alte Testament*, ed. F. Buhl, Berlin/Göttingen/Heidelberg 1915, 1962.

Hatch, E./Redpath, H. A., *A Concordance to the Septuagint and the other Greek Versions of the Old Testament I–II* + Supplement, Oxford 1897.

Lampe, G. W. H., ed., *A Patristic Greek Lexicon*, Oxford 1961.

Liddel, H. G./Scott, R., *A Greek-English Lexicon*, Oxford 1958.

Moule, C. F. D., *An Idiom Book of New Testament Greek*, 2nd edition, Cambridge 1971.

Moulton, W. F./Geden, A. S., *A Concordance to the Greek Testament*, Edinburgh 1897, 1957.

3. Secondary Literature.

Achtemeier, P. J., 'The Lukan Perspective on the Miracles of Jesus: A Preliminary Sketch', *Perspectives on Luke-Acts*, ed. C. H. Talbert, 1978, 153–67.

Alexander, P. S., 'Rabbinic Judaism and the New Testament', *ZNW* 74 (1983) 237–46.

Andersen, Ø., 'The Widows, the City and Thucydides (11.45.2)', *Symbolae Osloensis* LXII (1987) 33–50.

Anderson, J. C., 'Matthew: Gender and Reading', *Semeia* 28 (1983), 3–27.

——, 'Mary's Difference: Gender and Patriarchy in the Birth Narratives', *The Journal of Religion* 67 (1987), 183–202.

Augsten, M., *Die Stellung des lukanischen Christus zur Frau und zur Ehe* (Diss.), Erlangen 1970.

Baird, W., 'Abraham in the New Testament. Tradition and New Identity', *Interpretation* XLII (1988) 367–79.

Balch, D. L., 'Backgrounds of I Cor. VII: Sayings of the Lord in Q; Moses as an Ascetic θεῖος ἀνήρ in II Cor III', *NTS* 18 (1971–2) 351–64.

——, *Let Wives Be Submissive. The Domestic Code in 1 Peter*, SBL Mon. Ser. 26, Chico 1981.

Ballard, P. H., 'Reasons for Refusing the Great Supper', *JTS* 23, 341–50.

Balsdon, J. P. V. D., *Roman Women. Their History and Habits*, London 1962.

Bartchy, S. S., *First-Century Slavery and the Interpretation of 1 Corinthians 7.21*, SBL Diss. Ser. 11, Missoula 1973.

Bassler, J., 'The Widows' Tale: A French Look at 1 Tim 5.3–16', *JBL* 103 (1984) 23–41.

Bemile, P., *The Magnificat within the Context and Framework of Lukan Theology: An Exegetical Study of Lk 1.46–55*, Regensburger Studien zur Theologie 34, Frankfurt am Main/New York 1986.

Berger, K., 'Materialien zur Form und Überlieferungsgeschichte neutestamentlicher Gleichnisse', *NovT* XV (1973) 1–37.

Bernhard, T. Sr, 'Women's Ministry in the Church: A Lukan Perspective', *St Luke's Journal of Theology* 29 (1986) 261–63.

Beyer, H. W., art. διακονέω, διακονία, διάκονος. *Theologisches Wörterbuch zum Neuen Testament* II, Stuttgart 1935, 81–93.

Blank, J., 'Frauen in den Jesusüberlieferungen', *Die Frau im Urchristentum*, eds G. Dautzenberg/H. Merklein/K. Müller, Quaestiones Disputatae 95, Freiburg 1983, 9–91.

Blass, F. W., 'Priscilla und Aquila', *TSK* 74 (1901) 124–25.

Bock, D. L., *Proclamation from Prophecy and Pattern*, JSNT Suppl. Ser. 12, Sheffield 1987.

Bode, E. L., *The First Easter Morning: The Gospel Accounts of the Women's Visit to the Tomb of Jesus*, AnBiblica 45, Rome 1970.

des Bouvrie, S., 'Augustus' Legislation on Morals – which Morals and what Aims?' *Symbolae Osloenses* LIX (1984) 93–113.

Bovon, F., *Luc le Theologien. Vingt-cing ans de recherches (1950–1975)*, Paris/Neuchatel 1978.

——, *Lukas in neuer Sicht. Gesammelte Aufsätze*, Biblisch-theologische Studien 8, Neukirchen/Vlyin 1985.

——, 'Le Privilege Pascal de Marie Magdalene', *NTS* 30 (1984) 50–62.

Brenner, A., *The Israelite Woman: Social Role and Literary Type in Biblical Narrative*, JSOT Suppl. Ser. 21, Sheffield 1985.

Brock, S. P., 'Early Syrian Asceticism', *Numen* XX (1973) 1–19.

——/Ashbrook Harvey, S., *Holy Women of the Syrian Orient*, Berkeley/ Los Angeles/London 1987.

Brodie, Th. L., 'Luke 7.36–50 as an Internalization of 2 Kings 4. 1–37: A Study in Luke's Use of Rhetorical Imitation', *Biblica* 64 (1983) 457–85.

Brooten, B. J., 'Jüdinnen zur Zeit Jesu. Ein Plädoyer für Differenzierung', *TheolQuart* 161 (1981) 281–85.

——, *Women Leaders in the Ancient Synagogue. Inscriptional Evidence and Background Issues*, Brown Judaic Studies 3, Chico 1983.

——, 'Zur Debatte über das Scheidungsrecht der jüdischen Frau' *EvTh* 43 (1983) 466–78.

Brown, R. E., *The Gospel According to John I*, The Anchor Bible 29, New York 1970.

——, *The Birth of the Messiah: A Commentary on the Infancy Narratives in Matthew and in Luke*, New York 1979.

——, 'Roles of Women in the Fourth Gospel', *TS* 36 (1967) 688–99.

——/Donfried, K. P./Fitzmyer, J. A./Reumann, J. eds., *Mary in the New Testament. A Collaborative Assessment by Protestant and Roman Catholic Scholars*, Philadelphia 1978.

Brown, S., *Apostasy and Perseverence in the Theology of Luke*, AnBiblica 36, Rome 1969.

Brox, N., *Zeuge und Märtyrer*, Munich 1961.

Brun, L., *Lukasevangeliet*, Oslo 1933.

Brutschek, J., *Die Maria-Martha-Erzählung. Eine redaktionskritische Untersuchung zu Lk 10.38–42*, Bonner Biblische Beiträge 64, Frankfurt A.M./Bonn 1986.

Burrus, V., 'Chastity as Autonomy: Women in the Stories of the Apocryphal Acts', *Semeia* 38 (1986) 101–17.

——, *Chastity as Autonomy: Women in the Stories of the Apocryphal Acts*, Studies in Women and Religion 23, New York 1987.

Busse, U., *Die Wunder des Propheten Jesu. Die Rezeption, Komposition und Interpretation der Wundertradition im Evangelium des Lukas*, Forschung zur Bibel 24, Stuttgart 1977.

Callaway, M., *Sing, O Barren One: A Study in Comparative Midrash*, SBL Diss. Ser. 91, Atlanta 1986.

Cameron, A., 'Neither Male nor Female', *Greece and Rome* 27 (1980) 60–8.

Campenhausen, H. von, 'Die Askese im Urchristentum', *Traditionen und Leben*, Tübingen 1960, 114–56.

Carmignac, J., 'The meaning of *parthenos* in Luke 1.27 – a reply to C. H. Dodd', *The Bible Translator* 28C (1977) 327–30.

Carroll, J. T., *Response to the End of History. Eschatology and Situation in Luke-Acts*, SBL Diss. Ser. 92, Atlanta 1988.

Cassidy, R. J., *Society and Politics in the Acts of the Apostles*, New York 1987.

——/Sharper, P. J., *Political Issues in Luke-Acts*, Maryknoll, New York 1983.

Castelli, E., 'Virginity and Its Meaning for Women's Sexuality in Early Christianity', *Journal of Feminist Studies in Religion* 2 (1986) 61–88.

Catchpole, D. R., 'The Synoptic Divorce Material as a Traditio-Historical Problem', *Bulletin of the John Rylands Library* 57 (1974–5) 92–127.

——, 'The Fearful Silence of the Women at the Tomb: A Study in Marcan Theology', *Journal of Theology of South Africa* 18 (1977) 3–10.

Christiansen, E. Juhl, 'Women and Baptism', *StTh* 35 (1981) 1–8.

Clark, E. A., *Jerome, Chrysostom and Friends. Essays and Translations*, Studies in Women and Religion 2, New York/Toronto 1979.

——, 'Ascetic Renunciation and Feminine Advancement: A Paradox of Late Ancient Christianity', *Anglican Theological Review* 63 (1981) 240–57.

Clark, G., 'Women at Corinth', *Theology* 85 (1982) 256–62.

Collins, A. Y., 'The Ministry of Women in the Apostolic Generation', *Women Priests. A Catholic Commentary on the Vatican Declaration*, eds, A. and L. Swidler, New York 1977, 159–66.

——, *Crisis and Catharsis. The Power of the Apocalypse*, Philadelphia 1984.

Conzelmann, H., *Die Mitte der Zeit. Studien zur Theologie des Lukas*, Beiträge zur historischen Theologie 17, Tübingen 1954.

——, *Acts of the Apostles*, Hermeneia, Philadelphia 1987.

Countryman, L. W., *The Rich Christian in the Church of the Early Empire: Contradictions and Accommodations*, Text and Studies in Religion 7, New York/Toronto 1980.

Cranfield, C. E. B., 'Diakonia in the New Testament', *Service in Christ. Essays Presented to Karl Barth on his 80th Birthday*, eds J. I. McCord and T. H. L. Parker, London 1966, 38–48.

Dahl, N. A., 'Anamnesis. Memory and Commemoration in Early Christianity', *Jesus in the Memory of the Early Church*, Minneapolis 1976, 11–29.

——, 'The Story of Abraham in Luke-Acts', *Studies in Luke-Acts*, eds L. E. Keck and J. L. Martyn, Philadelphia 1980, 139–58.

Danker, F. W., *Jesus and the New Age. According to St Luke. A Commentary on the Third Gospel*, St Louis 1972.

——, *Luke*, Proclamation Commentaries, Philadelphia 1976.

——, *Benefactor: Epigraphic Study of a Graeco-Roman and New Testament Semantic Field*, St Louis 1982.

Daube, D., *The Duty of Procreation*, Theologia Biblica 10, Edinburgh 1977.

——, *The New Testament and Rabbinic Judaism*, London 1984.

——, 'Shame Culture in Luke', *Paul and Paulinism. Essays in Honor of C. K. Barrett*, eds. M. Hooker and C. H. Wilson, London 1982, 355–72.

Dautzenberg, G., *Urchristliche Prophetie*, BWANT 104, Stuttgart 1975.

——, 'Zur Stellung der Frau in den paulinischen Gemeinden', *Die Frau im Urchristentum*, eds. G. Dautzenberg/H. Merklein/K. Müller, Quaestiones Disputatae 95, Freiburg 1983, 182–234.

——/Merklein, H. Müller, K., eds, *Die Frau im Urchristentum*, Quaestiones Disputatae 95, Freiburg 1983.

Davies, S. L., The Revolt of the Widows. The Social World of the Apocryphal Acts, London/Amsterdam 1980.

Dawsey, J. M., 'The Literary Unity of Luke-Acts: Questions of Style – A Task for Literary Critics', *NTS* 35 (1989) 48–66.

Degenhardt, H. -J., *Lukas – Evangelist der Armen. Besitz und Besitzversicht in den lukanischen Schriften. Eine traditions-und redaktionsgeschichtliche Untersuchung*, Stuttgart 1965.

Derrett, J. D. M., 'Ananias, Sapphira, and the Right of Property', *Downside Review* 89 (1971) 225–32, repr. *Studies in the NT*, Leiden 1977, 193–200.

Diderichsen, B. K., *Den markianske skilsmisseperikope. Dens genesis og historiske placering*, København 1962.

Dillon, R. J., *From Eye-Witness to Ministers of the Word. Tradition and Composition in Luke* 24, AnBiblica 82, Rome 1978.

Drury, J., *Tradition and Design in Luke's Gospel. A Study in Early Christian Historiography*, London 1976.

Dunn, J. D. G., *Baptism in the Holy Spirit. A Re-Examination of the New Testament Teaching on the Gift of the Spirit in Relation to Pentecostalism Today*, Studies in Biblical Theology sec. ser. 15, London 1970.

——, *Jesus and the Spirit. A Study of the Religious and Charismatic Experience of Jesus and the First Christians as Reflected in the New Testament*, London 1975.

Egelkraut, H. L., *Jesus' mission to Jerusalem. A redaction critical study of the Travel Narrative in the Gospel of Luke 9.51–19.48*, Frankfurt/ Bern 1976.

van Eijk, T. H. C., 'Marriage and Virginity, Death and Immortality', *Epektasis. Mélanges patristiques offerts au Cardinal Jean Danielou*, Paris 1972, 209–35.

Elliott, J. H., *A Home for the Homeless: A Sociological Exegesis of 1 Peter. Its Situation and Strategy*, London 1982.

Elliott, J. K., 'Anna's Age (Luke 2.36–37)', *NovT* XXX (1988) 100–2.

Emmett, A. M., 'Female Ascetics in the Greek Papyri', *Jahrbuch der österreichischen Byzantinistik* 32 (1982) II 507–15.

Epstein, L. M., *Sex Laws and Customs in Judaism*, New York 1948.

Ernst, J., *Das Evangelium nach Lukas*, RNT 3, Regensburg 1977.

Fatum, L., Selvtœgt og seksualbegrœnsning. Noget om de bibelske kvindemodeller og deres appelvœrdi', *Fønix* 3 (1979) 238–58.

Fehrle, E., *Die kultische Keuschheit im Altertum*, Religionsgeschtl. Versuche und Vorarbeiten 6, Giessen 1910.

Fensham, F. C., 'Widow, Orphan and the Poor in Ancient Near East Legal and Wisdom Literature', *Journal for Near East Studies* 21 (1962) 129–39.

Finney, P. C., 'Early Christian Architecture: The Beginnings. (A Review Article)', *Harvard Theological Review* 81 (1988) 319–39.

Fiorenza, E. Schüssler, 'The Twelve'. *Women Priests. A Catholic Commentary on the Vatican Declaration*, eds L. and A. Swidler, New York 1977, 114–22.

——, 'The Apostleship of Women in Early Christianity', *Women Priests. A Catholic Commentary on the Vatican Declaration*, eds L. and A. Swidler, New York 1977, 135–40.

——, 'Women in the Pre-Pauline and Pauline Churches', *Union Seminary Quarterly Review* 33 (1978) 153–66.

——, 'Word, Spirit and Power: Women in Early Christian Communities', *Women of Spirit. Female Leadership in the Jewish and Christian Traditions*, eds R. Ruether and E. McLaughlin, New York 1979, 29–70.

——, 'Der Beitrag der Frau zur urchristlichen Bewegung. Kritische Überlegungen zur Rekonstruktion urchristlicher Geschichte', *Traditionen der Befreiung. Sozialgeschichtliche Bibelauslegungen*, eds. W. Schottroff and W. Stegemann, Band 2, Frauen in der Bibel, Munich 1980, 60–90.

——, *In Memory of Her. A Feminist Theological Reconstruction of Christian Origins*, New York 1983.

——, *Bread, Not Stone: The Challenge of Feminist Biblical Interpretation*, Boston 1984.

——, 'Der Dienst an den Tischen. Eine kritische feministisch-theologische Überlegung zum Thema Diakonie', *Concilium* 24 (1988) 306–13.

——, 'Biblische Grundlegung', *Feministische Theologie. Perspektiven zur Orientierung*, ed. M. Kassel, Stuttgart 1988, 13–44.

Fitzmyer, J. A., *The Gospel According to Luke I–II*, The Anchor Bible 28/28a, New York 1981–5.

——, 'The Matthean Divorce Texts and some Palestinian Evidence', *TheolStud* 37 (1976) 197–226.

Flender, H., *Heil und Geschichte in der Theologie des Lukas*, BEvTh 41, Munich 1968.

Foerster, W., 'Der Heilige Geist im Spätjudentum', NTS 7 (1961–62) 117–134.

Fraade, S. D., 'Ascetical Aspects of Ancient Judaism', *Jewish Spirituality* I, ed. A. Green, 1986, 253–88.

Frank, S., ΑΓΓΕΛΙΚΟΣ ΒΙΟΣ. *Begriffsanalytische und Begriffsgeschichtliche Untersuchung zum 'engelgleichen Leben' im frühen Mönchtum*, Beiträge zur Geschichte des alten Mönchtums und des Benediktinerordens 26, Münster 1964.

Freed, E. D., 'The Parables of the Judge and the Widow (Luke 18.1–8)', *NTS* 33 (1987) 38–60.

Gardner, J. F., *Women in Roman Law and Society*, London/Sydney 1986.

Gasque, W. W., 'A Fruitful Field. Recent Study of the Acts of the Apostles', *Interpretation* XLII (1988) 117–31.

Gaventa, B. R., 'Toward a Theology of Acts. Reading and Rereading', *Interpretation* XLII (1988) 146–57.

Geiger, R., *Die Lukanischen Endzeitreden. Studien zur Eschatologie des Lukas-Evangeliums*, Bern/Frankfurt A.M. 1973.

——, 'Die Stellung der geschiedenen Frau in der Umwelt des Neuen Testaments', *Die Frau im Urchristentum*, eds G. Dautzenberg/H. Merklein/K. Müller, Quaestiones Disputatae 95, Freiburg 1983, 134–57.

Gerhardsson, B., *Memory and Manuscript. Oral Tradition and Written Transmission in Rabbinic Judaism and Early Christianity*, Uppsala 1961.

Gerstenberger, E. S./Schrage, W., *Frau und Mann*, Stuttgart 1980.

Giblin, C. H., *The Destruction of Jerusalem According to Luke's Gospel*, AnBiblica 107, Rome 1985.

Gill, A., 'Women Ministers in the Gospel of Mark', *Australian Biblical Review* XXXV (1987), 14–21.

Gnilka, J., 'Die neutestamentliche Hausgemeinde', *Freude am Gottsdienst*, ed. J. Schreiner, Stuttgart 1983, 229–42.

Goldfeld, A., 'Women as Sources of Torah in the Rabbinic Tradition', *The Jewish Woman*, ed. E. Koltun, New York 1976, 257–71.

Goodblatt, D., 'The Beruriah Traditions', *Journal of Jewish Studies*, 26 (1975), 68–85.

Gowan, D. E., 'Wealth and Poverty in the Old Testament: The Case of the Widow, the Orphan and the Sojourner', *Interpretation* XLI (1987) 341–53.

Grass, H., *Ostergeschehen und Osterberichte*, Göttingen 1964.

Grillmeyer, A., 'Maria Prophetin: Eine Studie zur patristischen Mariologie', *Revue des Études Augustiniennes* 11 (1956) 295–312.

Grundmann, W., *Das Evangelium nach Lukas*, Theologischer Handkommentar zum Neuen Testament III, Berlin 1981.

Gryson, R., *The Ministry of Women in the Early Church*, Collegeville 1976.

Gülzow, H., 'Soziale Gegebenheiten der altkirchlichen Mission', *Kirchengeschichte als Missionsgeschichte I: Die Alte Kirche*, ed. H. Frohnes and U. W. Knarr, Munich 1974, 189–226.

Guillaume, J. -M., *Luc Interprète des Anciennes Traditions sur la Résurrection de Jésus*, Paris 1979.

Haenchen, E., *Die Apostelgeschichte*, Göttingen 1968.

Hallbäck, G., *Strukturalisme og eksegese*, København 1983.

Hamm, M. D., 'The Freeing of the Bent Woman and the Restoration of Israel: Luke 13.10–17 as Narrative Theology', *JSNT* 31 (1987) 23–44.

Hands, A. R., *Charities and Social Aid in Greece and Rome*, London 1968.

von Harnack, A., *Die Mission und Ausbreitung des Christentums in den ersten drei Jahrhunderten*, 4th edition, Wiesbaden 1924.

Hastings, A., *Prophet and Witness in Jerusalem. A Study of the Teaching of St Luke*, Baltimore 1958.

Hauglin, A., *Begrepet ἀδελφοί i NT*, unpubl. manuscript, Oslo 1976; abridged version.

——, 'Brødre eller søstre? Om oversettelsen av adelfos/adelfoi i NT', *Ung Teologi* 1 (1977) 1–17.

Heine, S., *Frauen der frühen Christenheit: Zur historischen Kritik einer feministischen Theologie*, Göttingen 1986.

Heister, M. -S., *Frauen in der biblischen Glaubensgeschichte*, Göttingen 1984.

Hengel, M., 'Maria Magdalena und die Frauen als Zeugen', *Abraham unser Vater*, F. S. Otto Michel, Leiden/Köln 1963, 243–56.

Hennessey, L. R., '*Diakonia* and *Diakonoi* in the Pre-Nicene Church', *Diakonia. Studies in Honor of Robert T. Meyer*, eds T. Halton and J. P. Williman, Washington 1986, 60–86.

Heussi, K., *Der Ursprung des Mönchtums*, Tübingen 1936.

Heyob, S. K., *The Cult of Isis among Women in the Graeco-Roman World*, Études Préliminaires aux Religions 51, Leiden 1975.

Hill, D., *New Testament Prophecy*, London 1979.

Horn, F. W., *Glaube und Handeln in der Theologie des Lukas*, Göttinger theol. Arbeiten 26, Göttingen 1983.

Ingerbrigsten, B., 'Kjønn og ulikhet. Et forsøk på begrepsavklaring', *Tidsskrift for samfunnsforskning* 28 (1987) 391–6.

Irvin, D., 'The Ministry of Women in the Early Church: The Archaeological Evidence', *Duke Divinity Review* 45 (1980) 76–86.

Isaksson, A., *Marriage and Ministry in the New Temple. A Study with Special Reference to Mt. 19.3–12 and 1 Cor 11.3–16*, Lund 1965.

Jeremias, J., 'Zöllner und Sünder', *ZNW* 30 (1931) 293–300.

——, *Jerusalem in the Time of Jesus. An Investigation into Economic and Social Conditions during the New Testament Period*, 3rd edition, London 1976.

——, *Die Sprache des Lukasevangeliums. Redaktion und Tradition im Nicht-Markusstoff des dritten Evangeliums*, Göttingen 1980.

Jervell, J., *Imago Dei. Gen. 1.26f im Spätjudentum, in der Gnosis und in den paulinischen Briefen*, FRLANT 76, Göttingen 1960.

——, *Luke and the People of God. A New Look at Luke-Acts*, Minneapolis 1972.

——, 'Die Töchter Abrahams. Die Frau in der Apostelgeschichte', *Glaube und Gerechtigkeit. Rafael Gyllenberg in memoriam*, Vammala 1983, 77–93.

——, English version: 'The Daughters of Abraham: Women in Acts', *The Unknown Paul. Essays on Luke-Acts and Early Christian History*, Minneapolis 1984, 146–157.

——, 'Sons of the Prophets: The Holy Spirit in the Acts of the Apostles', *The Unknown Paul. Essays on Luke-Acts and Early Christian History*, Mineappolis 1984, 96–121.

Jewett, R., 'The Sexual Liberation of the Apostle Paul', *JAAR Suppl.* (1979) 55–87.

Johnson, L. T., *The Literary Function of Possessions in Luke-Acts*, SBL Diss. Ser. 39, Missoula 1977.

——, 'On Finding the Lukan Community. A Cautious Cautionary Essay', *SBL Sem. Pap.* (1979) 87–100.

Johnson, S. E., 'Asia Minor and Early Christianity', *Christianity, Judaism and other Greco-Roman Cults. Studies for Morton Smith at Sixty*, ed. J. Neusner, Leiden 1975: 2:77–145.

Käser, W., 'Exegetische und theologische Erwägungen zur Seligpreisung der Kinderlosen Lc 23.29b', *ZNW* 54 (1963) 240–54.

Kaestli, J. -D., 'Response', (V. Burrus) *Semeia* 38 (1986) 119–31.

Kampen, N., *Image and Status: Roman Working Women in Ostia*, Berlin 1981.

Kappelle, R. P. van de, 'Prophets and Mantics', *Pagan and Christian Anxiety. A Response to E. R. Dodds*, eds. R. C. Smith and J. Lounibos, Lanham 1984, 87–111.

Kariamadam, P., *The Zacchaeus-Story (Lk 19.1–20): A Redaction-Critical Investigation*, Pontifical Institute Publications 42, Alwaye 1985.

Karriss, R. J., *Luke: Artist and Theologian. Luke's Passion Account as Literature*, New York 1985.

Kassel, M., ed., *Feministische Theologie. Perspektiven zur Orientierung*, Stuttgart 1988.

Keck, L. E., 'On the Ethos of Early Christians', *JAAR* 42 (1974) 435–52.

——,/Martyn, J. L., eds, *Studies in Luke-Acts*, Philadelphia 1980.

Kilgallen, J. J., 'John the Baptist, the Sinful Woman and the Pharisee', *JBL* 104 (1985) 675–79.

Kirchschläger, W., *Jesu exorzistisches Wirken aus der Sicht des Lukas. Ein Beitrag zur Lukanischen Redaktion*, Osterreichische Biblische Studien, Wien 1981.

Klauck, H. -J., *Hausgemeinde und Hauskirche im frühen Christentum*, Stuttgarter BibelStudien 103, Stuttgart 1981.

Klijn, A. F. J., 'Stephen's Speech – Acts VII.2–53', *NTS* 4 (1957–8) 25–31.

Kodell, J., 'The Celibacy Logion in Matthew 19.12', *BThB* 8 (1978) 19–23.

Koltun, E., ed., *The Jewish Woman*, New York 1976.

Kopas, J., 'Jesus and Women: Luke's Gospel', *TheolToday* 43 (1986) 192–202.

Kraemer, R. S., 'Ecstasy and Possession: The Attraction of Women to the Cult of Dionysus', *Harvard Theological Review* 75 (1979) 55–80.

——, 'The Conversion of Women to Ascetic Forms of Christianity', *Signs* 6 (1980) 298–307.

——, 'A New Inscription from Malta and the Question of Women Elders in the Diaspora Jewish Communities', *Harvard Theological Review* 78 (1985) 431–8.

Kraft, H., 'Die altkirchliche Prophetie und die Entstehung des Montanismus', *ThZ* XI (1955) 249–71.

Kretschmar, G., 'Ein Beitrag zur Frage nach dem Ursprung frühchristlicher Askese', *ZThK* 61 (1964) 27–67.

Kroeger, C. and R., 'An Inquiry into Evidence of Maenadism in the Corinthian Congregation', *SBL Sem. Papers* (1978) 331–8.

Kuzmack, L., 'Aggadic Approaches to Biblical Women', *The Jewish Woman* ed. E. Koltun, New York 1976, 248–55.

Laland, E., 'Die Martha-Maria Perikope Lukas 10, 38–42. Ihre kerygmatische Aktualität für das Leben der Kirche' *StTh* 13 (1959) 70-85.

Lampe, G. H. W., 'Diakonia in the Early Church', *Service in Christ. Essays Presented to Karl Barth on his 80th Birthday*, eds J. I. McCord and T. H. L. Parker, London 1966, 49–64.

Lampe, P., 'Zur gesellschaftlichen und kirchlichen Funktion der "Familie" in neutestamentlicher Zeit. Streiflichter', *Reformatio* 31 (1982) 533–42.

——, *Die stadtrömischen Christen in den ersten beiden Jahrhunderten* WUNT 2, Reihe 18, Tübingen 1987.

Lane Fox, R., *Pagans and Christians in the Mediterranean World from the Second Century SC to the Conversion of Constantine*, 2nd edition, London 1988.

LaPorte, J., *The Role of Women in the Early Church*, Studies in Women and Religion 7, New York 1982.

Larsen, B. B., *Konflikten om sabbaten. En undersøgelse af sabbaten i Lukasevangeliet med utblik til Acta*, unpubl. Ms., 1988.

Larsen, B. B. and J., *Menigheden uden sikkerhed. Sociale og økonomiske aspekter i Matthæeusevangeliet og Lukasevangeliet. Et bidrag til urkristendommens sociologi*, Aarhus 1976.

Laurentin, R., *The Truth of Christmas. Beyond the Myths. The Gospels of the Infancy of Christ*, Petersham 1986.

Legrand, L., *La Virginité dans la Bible*, Lectio Divina 39, Paris 1964.

Leipoldt, J., *Jesus und die Frauen. Bilder aus der Sittengeschichte der alten Welt*, Leipzig 1921.

——, *Griechische Philosophie und frühchristliche Askese*, Berichte über Verhandlungen der Sächsischen Akademie 106, Berlin 1961.

——/Grundmann, W., *Umwelt des Urchristentums I: Darstellung des neutestamentlichen Zeitalters*, Berlin 1971.

Leitmann, M./Zeisel, W., 'Univira: An Example of Continuity and Change in Roman Society', *Church History* 46 (1977) 19–33.

Leivestad, R., 'Pietisten blant evangelistene', *NTT* 55 (1954) 185–200.

——, 'Das Dogma von der prophetenlosen Zeit', *NTS* 19, (1972–3) 288–99.

Lindars, B., *New Testament Apologetics*, London 1961.

Lohfink, G., *Die Sammlung Israels. Eine Untersuchung zur lukanischen Ekklesiologie*, SANT XXXIX, Munich 1975.

——, 'Weibliche Diakone im Neuen Testament', *Diakonia* II (1980) 385–400.

Lohse, B., *Askese und Mönchtum in der alten Kirche*, Munich 1969.

Love, S. L., 'Women's Roles in Certain Second Testament Passages: A Macrosociological View', *BThB* 17 (1987) 50–9.

MacDonald, D. R., 'Virgins, Widows, and Paul in Second Century Asia Minor', *SBL Sem. Papers* (1979) 169–84.

——, *The Legend and the Apostle: The Battle for Paul in Story and Canon*, Philadelphia 1983.

——, *There is no Male and Female: The Fate of a Dominical Saying in Paul and Gnosticism*, Harvard Dissertations in Religion 20, Philadelphia 1987.

MacMullen, R., 'Women in Public in the Roman Empire', *Historia (Baden-Baden)* 29 (1980) 208–18.

McCaughey, J. D., 'Paradigms of Faith in the Gospel of St Luke', *Irish Theological Quarterly* 45 (1978) 177–84.

McEachern, V. C., 'Dual Witness and Sabbath Motif in Luke', *Canadian Journal of Theology* 12 (1966) 267–80.

McNamara, J., 'Wives and Widows in Early Christian Thought', *International Journal of Women's Studies* 2 (1979) 575–92.

——, *A New Song: Celibate Women in the First Three Christian Centuries*, Women and History 6/7, New York 1983.

McPolin, J., 'Holy Spirit in Luke and John', *Irish Theological Quarterly* 45 (1978) 117–31.

Maddox, R., *The Purpose of Luke Acts*, FRLANT 126, Göttingen 1982.

Malbon, E. S., 'Fallible Followers: Women and Men in the Gospel of Mark', *Semeia* 28 (1983) 29–48.

——, 'Τῇ 'Οικίᾳ 'Αυτοῦ': Mark 2.15 in Context', *NTS* 31 (1985) 282–92.

Malherbe, A. J., 'Not in a Corner: Early Christian Apologetics in Acts 26.26', *The Second Century* 5 (1985–6) 193–210.

Malinowski, F. X., 'The Brave Women of Philippi', *BThB* 15 (1985) 60–4.

Marin, L., 'Die Frauen am Grabe. Versuch einer Strukturanalyse an einem Text des Evangeliums', *Erzählende Semiotik nach Berichten der Bibel*, eds. C. Chabrol and L. Martin, Munich 1973, 67–85.

Marshall, H. I., *The Gospel of Luke. A Commentary on the Greek Text*, The New International Greek Testament Commentary, Exeter/Grand Rapids 1978.

Mary in the New Testament. A Collaborative Assessment by Protestant and Roman Catholic Scholars, eds. R. E. Brown/K. P. Donfried/J. A. Fitzmyer/J. Reumann, Philadelphia 1978.

März, C. -P., *Das Wort Gottes bei Lukas. Die lukanische Worttheologie als Frage an die neuere Lukasforschung*, Erfurter Theologische Schriften 11, Leipzig 1974.

Meeks, W. A., 'The Image of the Androgyne: Some Uses of a Symbol in Earliest Christianity', *History of Religion* 13 (1974) 165–208.

——, *The First Urban Christians. The Social World of the Apostle Paul*, Yale 1983.

Miller, R. J., 'Elijah, John, and Jesus in the Gospel of Luke', *NTS* 34 (1988) 611–22.

Moloney, F. J., *Woman: First among the Faithful. A New Testament Study*, London 1985.

Morgenthaler, R., *Die lukanische Geschichtsschreibung als Zeugnis. Gestalt und Gehalt der Kunst des Lukas, I–II*, ATANT 14, Zürich 1949.

Mortley, R., *Womanhood. The Feminine in Ancient Hellenism, Gnosticism, Christianity and Islam*, Sydney 1981.

Mottu, H., 'The Pharisee and the Tax Collector: Sartian Notions as Applied to the Reading of Scripture', *Union Seminary Quarterly Review* 29 (1974) 195–213.

Moxnes, H., *Theology in Conflict. Studies in Paul's Understanding of God in Romans*, SNT LIII, Leiden 1980.

——, *Patrons and Puritans. The Function of Economic Exchange in the Relationship between the Pharisees and the People in Luke's Gospel*, Unpubl. Ms., Oslo 1983.

——, The Economy of the Kingdom. Social Conflict and Economic Relations in Luke's Gospel, Philadelphia 1988.

——, 'Meals and the New Community in Luke', *SEÅ* 51–52 (1986–8) 158–67.

Muhlack, G., *Die Parallelen von Lukas-Evangelium und Apostelgeschichte*, Theologie und Wirklichkeit 8, Frankfurt A.M. 1979.

Müller-Bardoff, J., 'Zur Exegese von 1. Timotheus 5, 3–16', *Gott und die Götter: Festgabe für Erich Fascher zum 60. Geburtstag*, Berlin 1958, 113–33.

Munck, J., *The Acts of the Apostles*, The Anchor Bible, New York 1967.

Munro, W., 'Women Disciples in Mark?' *CBQ* 44 (1982) 225–41.

Nagel, P., *Die Motivierung der Askese in der alten Kirche und der Ursprung des Mönchtums*, Texte und Untersuchungen zur Geschichte der altchristlichen Literatur 95, Berlin 1966.

Navone, J., *Themes of St Luke*, Rome 1970.

Neirynck, F., 'John and the Synoptics. The Empty Tomb Stories'. *NTS* 30 (1984) 161–87.

Neyrey, J., *The Passion According to Luke. A Redaction Study of Luke's Soteriology*, New York/Toronto 1985.

Niederwimmer, K., *Askese und Mysterium. Über Ehe, Ehescheidung und Eheverzicht in den Anfängen des christlichen Glaubens*, FRLANT 113, Göttingen 1975.

Noack, B., *Lukasevangeliets Rejseberetning*, København 1977.

Nunnally-Cox, J., *Foremothers. Women of the Bible*, New York 1981.

Nuttall, G. F., *The Moment of Recognition: Luke as Story-Teller*, Ethel M. Wood Lecture, London 1978.

O'Neill, J. C., *The Theology of Acts in its Historical Setting*, 2nd edition, London 1970.

Osiek, C., 'The Widow as Altar: The Rise and Fall of a Symbol', *The Second Century* 3 (1983) 159–69.

O'Toole, R. F., *The Unity of Luke's Theology. An Analysis of Luke-Acts*, Good News Studies 9, Wilmington 1984.

Otwell, J. H., *And Sarah Laughed. The Status of Woman in the Old Testament*, Philadelphia 1977.

Pagels, E., *The Gnostic Gospels*, New York 1989 (1. ed. 1979).

Pape, D., *God & Women. A Fresh Look at what the New Testament says about Woman*, London 1976.

Parvey, C. F., 'The Theology and Leadership of Women in the New Testament', *Religion and Sexism*, ed. R. R. Ruether, New York 1964, 117–49.

Perkins, P., *Resurrection: New Testament Witness and Contemporary Reflection*, London 1984/85.

——, 'Marriage in the New Testament and Its World', *Commitment to Partnership*, ed. W. Roberts, Manwah 1987, 5–30.

Peterson, E., 'Einige Beobachtungen zu den Anfängen der christlichen Askese', *Frühkirche, Judentum und Gnosis, Studien und Untersuchungen*, Rome/Freiburg/Wien 1959, 209–20.

Pilgrim, W. E., *Good News to the Poor: Wealth and Poverty in Luke-Acts*, Minneapolis 1981.

Plaskow, J., 'Christian Feminism and Anti-Judaism', *Cross Currents* 28 (1978) 306–9.

Plevnik, J., 'The Eyewitnesses of the Risen Jesus in Luke 24', *CBQ* 49 (1987) 90–103.

Plum, K. Friis, *Den tilslørede frihed. Kvindehistorie og kvindehistorier i Det nye Testamente*, København 1984.

——, 'Kvindehermeneutik og bibelsk eksegese eller "Hvor gik den blødende kvinde hen, da hun ble frelst?"' *DTT* 50 (1987) 19–41.

Pomeroy, S. B., *Goddesses, Whores, Wives and Slaves. Women in Classical Antiquity*, New York 1975.

Portefaix, L., *Sisters Rejoice. Paul's Letter to the Philippians and Luke-Acts as Received by First-Century Philippian Women*, Coniectanea Biblica, New Testament Ser. 20, Uppsala 1988.

Praeder, S. M., 'Jesus-Paul, Peter-Paul and Jesus-Peter. Parallelisms in Luke-Acts: A History of Reader Response', *SBL Sem. Pap.* 23 (1984) 23–39.

Preisker, H., Christentum und Ehe in den ersten drei Jahrhunderten, Neue Studien zur Geschichte der Theologie und Kirche 23, Berlin 1927.

Quesnell, Q., 'Made Themselves Eunuchs for the Kingdom of Heaven (Mt 19.12)', *CBQ* 30 (1968) 344–6.

——, 'The Women at Luke's Supper', *Political Issues in Luke-Acts*, eds. R. J. Cassidy and P. J. Sharper, New York 1983, 59–79.

Quinn, J. D., 'The Last Volume of Luke: The Relation of Luke-Acts to the Pastoral Epistles', *Perspectives on Luke-Acts*, ed. C. H. Talbert, Danville 1978, 62–75.

Radl, W., *Paulus und Jesus im lukanischen Doppelwerk. Untersuchungen zu Parallelmotiven im Lukasevangelium und der Apostelgeschichte*, Bern/ Frankfurt A.M. 1975.

Räisänen, H., *Die Mutter Jesu im Neuen Testament*, AASF B 158, Helsinki 1969.

Ramsay, M., *The Church in the Roman Empire before AD 170*, New York 1893.

Ravens, D. A. S., 'The Setting of Luke's Account of the Anointing: Luke 7.2–8.3', *NTS* 34 (1988) 282–92.

Redalie, Y., 'Conversion or Liberation? Notes on Acts 16.11–40', *The Bible and Liberation: Political and Social Hermeneutics*, eds. A. C. Wire and N. Gottwald, Berkeley 1976, 102–8.

Reiling, J./Swellengrebel, J. L., *A Translator's Handbook on the Gospel of Luke*, Leiden 1971.

Richardson, P., 'From Apostles to Virgins: Romans 16 and the Roles of Women in the Early Church', *Toronto Journal of Theology* 2 (1986) 232–61.

Ringe, S. H., *Jesus, Liberation and the Biblical Jubilee. Images for Ethics and Christology*, Philadelphia 1985.

Ritt, H., 'Die Frauen und die Osterbotschaft', *Die Frau im Urchristentum*, eds. G. Dautzenberg/H. Merklein/K. Müller, Quaestiones Disputatae 95, Freiburg 1983, 117–33.

Robbins, V. K., 'The Woman who Touched Jesus' Garment: Socio-Rhetorical Analysis of the Synoptic Account', *NTS* 33 (1987) 502–15.

Robinson, W. C., *The Way of the Lord. A Study of History and Eschatology in the Gospel of Luke*, Basel 1962.

——, 'On Preaching the Word of God (Luke 8.4–21)', *Studies in Luke-Acts*, eds. L. E. Keck and J. L. Martyn, Philadelphia 1980, 131–8.

Roloff, J., *Apostolat-Verkündigung-Kirche. Ursprung, Inhalt und Funktion des kirchlichen Apostelamtes nach Paulus, Lukas und den Pastoralbriefen*, Gütersloh 1965.

Rordorf, W., 'Marriage in the New Testament and the Early Church', *JEH* 20 (1969) 193–210.

Rouselle, A., *Porneia. On Desire and the Body in Antiquity*, Oxford/ New York 1988.

Ruether, R. R., ed., *Religion and Sexism*, New York 1964.

——, 'Mothers of the Church: Ascetic Women in the Late Patristic Age', *Women of Spirit: Female Leadership in the Jewish and Christian Traditions*, eds. R. R. Ruether and E. McLaughlin, New York 1979, 71–98.

——/McLaughlin, E., eds., *Women of Spirit: Female Leadership in the Jewish and Christian Traditions*, New York 1979.

Sand, A., 'Witwenstand und Ämterstrukturen in den urchristlichen Gemeinden', *Bibel und Leben* 12 (1971) 186–97.

Sandnes, K. O., *'Paul – One of the Prophets?' A Contribution to the Apostle's Self-Understanding*, Diss., Stavanger 1988.

Schaller, B., 'Die Sprüche über Ehescheidung und Wiederheirat in der synoptischen Überlieferung', *Der Ruf Jesu und die Antwort der Gemeinde*, F.S. J. Jeremias, ed. E. Lohse; Göttingen 1970, 226–46.

Schelkle, K. H., 'Ehe und Ehelosigkeit im Neuen Testament', *Beiträge zur Auslegung und Auslegungsgeschichte des Neuen Testaments*, Düsseldorf 1966, 183–98.

——, *Der Geist und die Braut. Frauen in der Bibel*, Düsseldorf 1977.

Schille, G., *Die Apostelgeschichte des Lukas*, Theologischer Handkommentar zum Neuen Testament, Berlin 1983.

Schnackenburg, R., 'Lukas als Zeuge verschiedener Gemeindestrukturen', *Bibel und Leben* 12 (1971) 232–47.

Schneider, G., 'Jesu Wort über die Ehescheidung in der Überlieferung des Neuen Testaments', *Trier Theologische Zeitung* (1971) 70–87.

——, *Die Apostelgeschichte I–II*, Herders Theologischer Kommentar zum Neuen Testament V, Freiburg 1980.

Schneider, S. M., 'Women in the Fourth Gospel and the Role of Women in the Contemporary Church', *BThB* 12 (1982) 34–45.

Schottroff, L., 'Frauen in der Nachfolge Jesu in neutestamentlicher Zeit', *Traditionen der Befreiung. Sozialgeschichtliche Bibelauslegungen*, Band 2: Frauen in der Bibel, eds W. Schottroff und W. Stegemann, Munich 1980, 91–133.

——, 'Maria Magdalena und die Frauen am Grabe Jesu', *EvTh* 42 (1982) 3–25.

Schottroff, W./Stegemann, W., eds, *Traditionen der Befreiung. Sozialgeschichtliche Bibelauslegungen*, Band 2: Frauen in der Bibel, Munich 1980.

Schramm, T., *Der Markus-stoff bei Lukas. Eine literarkritische und redaktionsgeschichtliche Untersuchung*, SNTS Mon. Ser. 14, Cambridge 1971.

Schürmann, H., 'Die Dubletten im Lukasevangelium. Ein Beitrag zur Verdeutlichung des lukanischen Redaktionsverfahrens', *Traditionsgeschichtliche Untersuchungen zu den synoptischen Evangelien*, Düsseldorf 1968, 272–8.

——, 'Die Dublettenvermeidungen im Lukasevangelium. Ein Beitrag zur Verdeutlichung des lukanischen Traditionsverfahrens', *Traditionsgeschichtliche Untersuchungen zu den synoptischen Evangelien*, Düsseldorf 1968, 279–89.

——, *Das Lukasevangelium I*, Herders Theologischer Kommentar zum Neuen Testament III, 2nd edition, Freiburg 1982.

Schwankl, O., *Die Sadduzäerfrage (Mk 12, 18–27 parr). Eine exegetisch-theologische Studie zur Auferstehungserwartung*, Bonner biblische Beiträge 66, Frankfurt A.M. 1987.

Schweizer, E., 'Scheidungsrecht der jüdischen Frau? Weibliche Jünger Jesu?' *EvTh* 42 (1982) 294–300.

Scott, J. W., 'Gender: A Useful Category of Historical Analysis', *The American Historical Review* 91 (1986) 1053–75.

Seccombe, D. P., *Possessions and the Poor in Luke-Acts*, SNTU 6, Linz 1982.

Segal, J. B., *Edessa: The Blessed City*, Oxford 1970.

Seim, T. Karlsen, 'Seksualitet og ekteskap, skilsmisse og gjengifte i 1 Kor. 7', *NTT* 81 (1980) 1–20.

——, 'Fattig og likestilt, bedrestilt og underordnet, rik og selvstendig. Urkristendommens kvinner i Luise Schottroffs fremstilling', *Intern Debatt* 3/4 (1983) 26–34.

——, 'Gudsrikets overraskelse. Parablene om et sennespsfrø og en surdeig', *NTT* 84 (1983) 1–17.

——, 'Når sløret fjernes ... Kvinneblikk på bibeltekster', *Riv ned gjerdene*, F. S. Jacob Jervell, eds. R. Berg/I. Lønning/H. Moxnes, Oslo 1985, 85-95.

——, 'Roles of Women in the Gospel of John', *Aspects on the Johannine Literature*, Coniectanea Biblica, New Testament Ser. 18, eds. L. Hartmann and B. Olsson, Uppsala 1987, 56–73.

——, 'I asketisk frihet? Urkirkens enker i nytt lys. Glimt fra en forskningssituasjon', *NTT* 89 (1988) 27–45.

——, 'Ascetic Autonomy? New Perspectives on Single Women in the Early Church', *StTh* 43 (1989) 125–40.

Selvidge, M. J., *Daughters of Jerusalem*, Scottdale 1987.

Soards, M. L., *The Passion according to Luke. The Special Material of Luke 22*, JSNT Suppl. Ser. 14, Sheffield 1987.

Sordi, M., *The Christians and the Roman Empire*, 1987.

Stählin, G., art. 'χήρα'. *Theologisches Wörterbuch zum Neuen Testament* IX, Stuttgart 1973, 428–54.

Stagg, E. and F., *Women in the World of Jesus*, Philadelphia 1978.

Stemberger, G., *Der Leib der Auferstehung. Studien zur Anthropologie und Eschatologie des palästinensischen Judentums im neutestamentlichen Zeitalter (ca. 170 v. Chr. – 100 n. Chr.)*, AnBiblica 56, Rome 1972.

Storch, R., Die Stephanusrede, unpubl. diss., Göttingen 1967.

Stowers, S. K., 'Social Status, Public Speaking and Private Teaching: The Circumstances of Paul's Preaching Activity', *NovT* XXVI (1984) 59–82.

Strathmann, H., *Geschichte der frühchristlichen Askese bis zur Entstehung des Mönchtums in religionsgeschichtlichen Zusammenhängen. I Band: Die Askese in der Umgebung des werdenden Christentums*, Leipzig 1914.

Swartley, W. M., 'Politics and Peace (Eirene) in Luke's Gospel', *Political Issues in Luke-Acts*, eds. R. J. Cassidy and P. J. Sharper, New York 1983, 18–37.

Swidler, L., 'Greco-Roman Feminism and the Reception of the Gospel', *Traditio-Krisis-Renovatio aus theologischer Sicht. Festschrift für W. Zeller*, eds. Jasperts and Mohr, Marburg 1976, 41–52.

——, *Biblical Affirmations of Women*, Philadelphia 1979.

Swidler, L./Swidler, A., eds., *Women Priests. A Catholic Commentary on the Vatican Declaration*, New York 1977.

Synge, F. C., 'Studies in Texts: Acts 7, 46', *Theology* 55 (1952) 25–26.

Tabbernee, W., *The Opposition to Montanism from Chruch and State. A Study of the History and Theology of the Montanist Movement as Shwon by the Writings and Legislation of the Orthodox Opponents of Montanism*, Diss., Melbourne 1978.

Talbert, C. H., *Literary Patterns, Theological Themes and the Genre of Luke-Acts*, SBL Mon. Ser. 20, Missoula 1974.

——, *Reading Luke. A Literary and Theological Commentary on the Third Gospel*, New York 1986.

——, ed., *Perspectives on Luke-Acts*, Danville 1978.

Tannehill, R. C., *The Narrative Unity of Luke-Acts. A Literary Interpretation*, Volume 1: *The Gospel according to Luke*, Philadelphia 1986.

Tatum, W. B., 'The Epoch of Israel: Luke I–II and the Theological Plan of Luke-Acts', *NTS* 13 (1966–7), 184–95.

Tetlow, E. M., *Women and Ministry in the New Testament: Called to Serve*, Lanham/New York/London 1980.

Theissen, G., 'Wanderradikalismus. Literatursoziologische Aspekte der Überlieferung von Worten Jesu im Urchristentum', *ZThK* 70 (1973) 245–71.

——, 'Legitimation und Lebensunterhalt: Ein Beitrag zur Soziologie urchristlicher Missionare', *NTS* 21 (1974–5) 192–221.

——, *Soziologie der Jesusbewegung*, Munich 1977.

——, *The Miracle Stories of the Early Christian Tradition*, Edinburgh 1983.

——, *The Shadow of the Galilean. The Quest of the Historical Jesus in Narrative Form*, London 1987.

Thompson, C. L., 'Hairstyles; Head-coverings, and St Paul. Portraits from Roman Corinth', *Bibl Archaeologist* 51 (1988) 99–114.

Thraede, K., 'Ärger mit der Freiheit: Die Bedeutung von Frauen in Theorie und Praxis der alten Kirche', *Freunde in Christus werden … Die Beziehung von Mann und Frau als Frage an Theologie und Kirche*, eds. G. Scharffenorth and K. Thraede, Gellhausen 1977, 31–182.

Tolbert, M. A., 'Defining the Problem: The Bible and Feminist Hermeneutics', *Semeia* 28 (1983) 113–26.

Troje, L., *AΔAM und ZΩH. Eine Szene der altchristlichen Kunst in ihrem religionsgeschichtlichen Zusammenhange*, Sitzungsberichte der Heidelberger Akademie der Wissenschaften, Philosophisch-historische Klasse 17 (1916).

Tyson, J. B., 'The Problem of Food in Acts: A Study of Literary Patterns with Particular Reference to Acts 6.1–7', *SBL Sem. Pap. I* (1979) 69–85.

——, 'The Jewish Public in Luke-Acts', *NTS* 30 (1984) 574–83.

——, 'The Emerging Church and the Problem of Authority in Acts', *Interpretation* XLII (1988) 132–45.

Ulrichsen, J. H., 'Noen Bemerkninger til 1. Tim. 2.15', *NTT* 84 (1983) 19–25.

Vermes, G., *Jesus the Jew*, London 1973.

Via, J. E., 'Women, the Discipleship of Service and the Early Christian Ritual Meal in the Gospel of Luke', *St Luke's Journal of Theology* 29 (1985) 37–60.

Verner, D., *The Household of God. The Social World of the Pastoral Epistles*, SBL Diss. Ser. 71, Chico 1983.

Vogels, W., 'A Semiotic Study of Luke 7.1–17', *EgT* 14 (1983) 273–92.

Wall, R. W., 'Martha and Mary (Luke 10.38–42) in the Context of a Christian Deuteronomy', *JSNT* 35 (1989) 19–35.

Ward, B., *Harlots of the Desert: A Study of Repentance in Early Monastic Sources*, London 1987.

Weinert, F. D., 'The Meaning of the Temple in Luke-Acts', *BThB* 11 (1981) 85–9.

——, 'The Multiple Meanings of Luke 2.49 and their Significance', *BThB* 13 (1983) 19–22.

Weiser, A., 'Die Rolle der Frau in der urchristlichen Mission', *Die Frau im Urchristentum*, eds. G. Dautzenberg/H. Merklein/K. Müller, Quaestiones Disputatae 95, Freiburg 1983, 158–81.

Wilckens, U., *Die Missionsreden der Apostelgeschichte. Form- und traditionsgeschichtliche Untersuchungen*, WMANT 5, 3rd edition, Neukirchen 1974.

——, *Auferstehung. Das biblische Auferstehungszeugnis historisch untersucht und erklärt*, Berlin 1974.

Williams, J. G., 'The Beautiful and the Barren: Conventions in Biblical Type-Scenes', *JSOT* 17 (1980) 107–19.

Wilson, S. G., *Luke and the Pastoral Epistles*, London 1979.

Wimbush, V. L., *Paul the Worldly Ascetic: Response to the World and Self-Understanding according to 1 Corinthians 7*, Macon 1987.

Witherington, B., 'On the Road with Mary Magdalene, Joanna, Susanna and Other Disciples – Luke 8.1–3', *ZNW* 70 (1979) 243–8.

——, 'The Anti-Feminist Tendencies of the "Western" Text in Acts', *JBL* 103 (1984) 82–4.

——, *Women in the Ministry of Jesus: A Study of Jesus' Attitudes to Women and Their Roles as Reflected in His Earthly Life*, SNTS Mon. Ser. 51, New York/Cambridge 1984.

——, *Women in the Earliest Churches*, SNTS Mon. Ser. 59, Cambridge 1988.

Wright, A. G., 'The Widow's Mites: Praise or Lament? – A Matter of Context', *CBQ* 44 (1982) 256–65.

Yarbrough, O. L., *Not Like the Gentiles: Marriage Rules in the Letters of Paul,* SBL Diss. Ser. 80, Atlanta 1985.

Zehnle, R. F., *Peter's Pentecost Discourse. Tradition and Lukan Reinterpretation in Peter's Speeches in Acts 2 and 3*, SBL Mon. Ser. 15, Nashville/New York 1971.

Zimmermann, H., 'Selig, die das Wort Gottes hören und es bewahren. Eine exegetische Studie zu Lk 11, 27f.' , *Catholica* 29 (1975) 114–19.

Index of Biblical References

Index of Names